MORNING WITHOUT NOON

Morning Without Noon

Memoirs

SALVADOR DE MADARIAGA

SAXON HOUSE

ISBN 0 347 00014 2
LC No. 73-10625

Photoset and Printed in Malta by St Paul's Press Ltd

CONTENTS

Prologue

Part I

World Civil Servant

Part II

Academic Interlude

Part III

On Stage For the Tragedy

LIST OF ILLUSTRATIONS

Salvador de Madariaga (in Peru in 1934).

Joseph Avenol in 1934.

Albert Thomas.

Quiñones de León.

Madariaga with Louis Barthou, French Foreign Minister, in September 1934, while Madariaga was Ambassador to Paris.

Jean Monnet (1921) in his office at the League.

Harold Butler in about 1921.

Lord Robert Cecil in 1923.

Allen Dulles after the War in 1945.

Madariaga in Paris with the Rumanian Titulesco and Anthony Eden setting out in 1935, for a session of the Committee of Thirteen.

Sir Eric Drummond in 1926. A Dutch member of the Secretariat, Pelt, is opening the door of the taxi.

The 87th Session of the Council of the League (May 1935) presided by Maxim Litvinov, Madariaga is fifth from the left at the Council table.

The 91st Session of the Council of the League (March 19, 1936) at St James's Palace. Madariaga is at the far left.

A session of the Committee of Thirteen. The Rumanian delegate Petrescu-Commène is seated at Madariaga's right. At the far end of the table are Paul Brown and the Spanish delegate Palacios (with beard). On the left is the Japanese delegate Sato, behind him (white-haired) Lange. In front, facing the camera is the American Burton. Carton de Wiant is on Madariaga's left.

PROLOGUE

THIS book is not of the kind I choose of my own free will to write. It owes its existence to the gentle but steady pressure of my friends for many years. Which may help to explain why I was over eighty when I began to consider it. Why such a stubborn passive resistance? Mostly, I think, a matter of inner shape. One is inwardly made a certain way. My way is not prone to look back, but to look ahead. If I happen to miss the present it is sure to be the future that has lured me, not the past. This kind of inner shape is what we call *predisposition*.

I remember having read somewhere that Freud thought all autobiographies to be but lies. If such is the fact, I mean that Freud did say so, it may count as yet another case of that over-statement of which the Viennese magician seems to have been fond; for autobiographies need not be lies. What they nearly always are is inaccurate. But an inaccuracy only becomes a lie when it is deliberate; while most of the inaccuracies in a life written by the man who has lived it come from other causes than the intent to deceive the reader. Two of them seem to me more important than the rest.

The first is the mere fact that events are told by their protagonist. A first-hand observer, no doubt; but also, inevitably, a biased observer. This cause of inaccuracy is very hard to gauge; and its effect on the story may vary in a thousand ways, depending on the variegated gifts and shortcomings of the protagonist turned witness. A mere effect of distance and perspective may induce the writer to emphasise his share in the events that occur around him. I know of a child who, shown the moon in the sky for him to admire, so full and lovely it was, coolly reacted: 'I know. I put it there.' It is my hope that in the pages that follow the reader may not be tempted to remember that child.

More subtly, the author of his own 'Life and Miracles' may be tempted to justify every act and present every event in such a way as to emphasise his own intellect, morality and wisdom. This can be done without necessarily falling to the level of the liar. The mere dropping of a word may do wonders. In many cases, the trick is played at levels below the conscious eyesight of the author. I confess that this seems to me perhaps one of the most dangerous obstacles a writer of memoirs may find on his way to truth. To forestall any possible failure on my part in this respect, I have gone out of my way to tell episodes in which, in my own eyes, I was wrong.

There is, however, another cause of inaccuracy, far more insidious and harder to deal with. It is customary to describe the human memory as a kind of file or repository of past events, and the development of the computer has but strengthened this error. But the fundamental feature about memory is that it is alive. (This, by the way, condemns in advance any and every attempt at equating the memory of man with the 'memory' of a computer.) The life in it prevents human memory from remaining fixed and fossilised in the self. It moves on, ferments, grows and decays simultaneously; it changes and adapts itself to everything that is happening in the life that it is supposed to record. So that if, suddenly, the person concerned is confronted with a document of the day in which the event happened, he may find that the actual happening differs perhaps dramatically from what the memory of it had become in him. This actually was my experience, for instance, when I discovered a letter I had sent to my wife which altered my memory of the events of the Barcelona conference with which this book begins.

All, however, is not negative in this art of writing one's own life. I hold for instance, that the tendency to present ourselves as better than we are can be controlled, indeed mastered, with relative ease. Thus, there is a rule, by no means hard to apply, which will help in keeping the author true to his objectivity: *in the absence of clear and unmistakable circumstances that may otherwise guide you, take it always as likely that at least half of the responsibility for any trouble involving you is on your own shoulders.*

I believe this simple rule will make the author of memoirs avoid many errors of judgement. I also believe it is reasonable. Human beings rotating together in the huge cauldron of the world are bound to collide now and then; and it is puerile to imagine that it will be *always* and *only* the other fellow who is to blame for the collision. Once this is admitted, the responsibility is on both sides, and as a matter of probability, a fifty-fifty rule is sure to be the least unfair way of sharing it.

There is a second empirical law which is bound to be salutary for the writer of memoirs. It might be put in this way: the events of all kinds that occur in a man's life are for the most part of such marvellous complexity that no human being can be sure of dealing adequately with them. The most we can hope is that in the handling of them we prove less incapable than we might have been. The idea that I have been so clever, wise, prudent, bold, supple and inflexible, that I have come out on top in the matter of *This versus That*, is untenable. I did my very poor best and I got away with it. But why? Because the other fellow did even worse. Thus, let us hold fast to this conclusion. *In life there are no victories: only defeats of the adversary.*

Put it in other words. *Let us always hope that our adversaries are stupider than we are.* This is no disparagement of any man's ability. It is a wise estimate of the puzzles of life. They are nearly always above our capacity to handle them. Our pride in man's intellect comes from our victories over nature through science; but even the most recalcitrant of scientific problems are child's play compared to the management of a grocer's shop. Man and men are the trouble. And the acuteness, shrewdness, patience, objectivity, cunning, frankness, courage, gentleness and God knows how many more gifts required to triumph in our daily life are far too many for any one man to possess them all.

I don't believe a single general ever won a single battle. It was the other fellow who lost it. This is the golden rule. When one has mastered it, vanity itself becomes vain.

One step more and we are at the end of our path. Read any page of any history of any period. Remove the trappings borrowed from time and space. They are all the same. Human beings are struggling to solve their problems. Strange that after several thousands of years we should not have been able to find their solutions. Could it be that our problems outlive us; and if so, could it be that we are not capable of solving them, or, worse and better, that we are not meant to solve them?

The outward features of the problems of men's lives change, but the core of the problems remains the same: how to adjust the actions and interactions of beings who are both interdependent and absolutely independent of each other. My suggestion is that *our problems are not here for us to solve them but for them to solve us.* And I do not mind owning that I have written this book in order to try to solve myself.

Part I
World Civil Servant

CHAPTER I

TO GENEVA VIA BARCELONA

THAT sunny day of August (1921), Geneva was at her best. It was still a city, not yet a garage; and the light from the blue sky brightened and freshened the scene and made it as new as if it had just come out of the hands of the Creator. Then the Lake. What an enchantment! After so many doubts, struggles, frustrations, shadows and dead ends, to come to such a Paradise, where, between its two heavens, one above and one below, I found air and light, security and an intelligent, creative task, what more could a healthy man desire at thirty-five?

A place where one went to one's job in a pleasant public motor-boat for a few pence and the pence themselves were silvery; where the office itself was flooded with light and brightened with the coming and going of intelligent men and young women, every one of them, it seemed to me, animated with a new spirit and a new hope. No more wars. We were to organise things so that conflicts were all settled round the table. Who could doubt that we should succeed when the Lake reflected that immaculate sky and there was no shadow to be seen anywhere?

The time would come (and it was surprisingly near) when I would say farewell to my Geneva days as an international civil servant; and when, singing the praises of water in our landscape, I would say to my friends gathered round me for a good-bye dinner, 'among the ups and downs of the hard agitated land, water keeps a quiet steady horizontal, and among the variegated colours of natural land and of the shapes strewn on it or hewn out of it by men, water reflects the blue serenity of heaven above.' It was no longer the identification of heaven and earth of the first day; seven fruitful years of experience had brought in their bitter-sweet harvest.

That night I had been invited to dinner by Pierre Comert. He was my chief, the head of the Information Section of the League Secretariat. As I now see it, it was he who had bulldozed me into the Secretariat by inventing a job in his own section for a man with a scientific training, and a ready pen and tongue in three languages. Since the technical as distinct from the 'political' activities of the League were supposed to be more especially directed by Jean Monnet, the Deputy Secretary General, the French for whom I was one of them owing to my education

3

in Paris, had opened the way for me. I was transmogrified into some sort of a 'technical' journalist.

It had all begun at Barcelona. The war over, I found myself out of a job. I was not a man easy to place within the established institutions, for my abilities and my diplomas did not tally. I was a man of letters endowed with an uncommon mastery of Spanish, French and English; but professionally, a mining engineer though lacking the slightest interest in that honourable and lucrative profession. I was in the doldrums in Madrid, just managing to keep my family – then still in London – by odds and ends of work, when I read that a League of Nations Transit Conference was to meet in Barcelona. One of my uncles was a Member of Parliament. He introduced me to the Undersecretary of State in charge of Public Works and Railways. I got a cold reception for as a Madrid School of Mines old boy, he could hardly feel any sympathy for a Paris School of Mines man. Still, he granted me a post in the Delegation. I declined it. It was not good enough. I was not think-ing of the money but of the rank. My uncle intervened again, and the stiff official yielded. Thus it was that I became the Spanish Delegation to the Barcelona Transit Conference in the spring of 1921.

Yes. The Spanish Delegation. For there were lots of names, func-tions – and salaries – in that delegation, but only one man that could be seen and heard. At most two. My only companion was José Gallostra, the Spanish F.O. man, so far as I could see mostly in charge of the sherry and titbits. He was a young secretary with eyes like cart-wheels, tall, elegant and so fond of women that he was always busy in or rather out of a Conference in the wings of which the fair sex was so well represented.

On one of the earliest days at 8.30 in the evening, I wrote to C.H.M.A.

What a day! The sittings of the Conference begin at 11. I have been appointed Secretary to the Spanish Delegation. From 11 till 1, I was at my seat hearing and taking notes to send a wire to *The Times*. At 1.30, lunch with Ortuño, the head of the Delegation. At 2.30, translation into Spanish of Ortuño's speech (who had written it in French). At 4, a new sitting and a preparation of a second wire to *The Times*. Follow the sitting till 7.30 – cross over and dictate a wire at top speed–motor to the Telegraph Office–and here I am at last, having one minute to write to you.

It is, however, worth while, even though listening to 11 speeches in the afternoon with its [sic] 11 translations be really intolerable. But some of the men in the show are really interesting and I believe we shall be good friends.

We are going to have sittings daily. And I who had brought some work to do here! Of course, when we begin to do the actual technical work, it may be less tiring for the journalist side of me, as the public are less interested and there will be less to wire. Do watch *The Times* and keep account of what they publish in the way of wires from Barcelona as it will be the basis of my account for this month.

As straight a witness as one could wish from the past, was this letter to me when I discovered it, for in it I found the kind of English I could write when allowing myself a fair measure of carelessness and haste; I found evidence of my having worked as the *Times* correspondent for the conference, which I had so completely forgotten that even now, reminded as I am by that letter, I do not recollect the facts at all; and last, but not least, I found that Ortuño had been present at the opening ceremony and that he had prepared a speech in French. This is important as will soon appear in more detail. He certainly left the Conference at once for he never took part in a single working sitting.

I had at last found my element. I was not long in discovering that the driving force, the initiative, the intellect, the common sense, the brilliance, and yet the wisdom, the modesty, the ability to work in the dusk of the discreet offices, to shun the limelight – all these virtues were incarnated in the Secretariat. And in Barcelona, more especially in the Secretary General of the Conference. Robert Haas was a French Jew. An ugly man, he had one of the keenest brains and one of the finest hearts I have known.

During that Conference I learnt a good deal about the League and how it worked. Unknown to us, we were all learning. The delegates brought their instructions: each had to pull the common rug as hard as he could in the direction of his fatherland's interests as understood by the 'inkpot-in-chief' of the particular department at home, and he had to put his case so that everybody should consider him, or his country, as a regular St. Martin for generosity and self-denial.

The past master of this technique was the British Delegate, Sir Hubert Llewellyn Smith. He was the very image of the British civil servant, one of the outstanding types of humanity Europe has produced; responsible, active, concrete, ever on the spot, no waster of words or of time; and so able to put his case that you – as a Swede or a Brazilian – should think your country would be saved from sheer ruin by British generosity and abnegation.

Thanks mostly (I realised and duly noted) to Robert Haas and to the superb skill with which he handled the Conference, two permanent treaties were passed which eventually became part of the *de facto* constitution of Europe, a Convention on Freedom of Transit and a Convention on International Waterways. That they perished in the general conflagration of 1939–44 in no way diminishes these two achievements of the Barcelona Conference.

About half way through the Conference, Don Guillermo Brockman arrived. Despite his German or British name, he was an Andalusian who, owing to his rank, Chief Roads-and-Bridges Engineer, was the number two man in the delegation next to the ex-cabinet minister who was supposed to lead it. Brockman found that the Conference was used to my rising to speak whenever I thought my country's interests were at stake; but he was not converted. He never said a word, having no faith whatever in what was being done, and so, from the day he came, our delegation was dumb. He, a man of sixty or so, pale and wan, open-mouthed for lack of skin on his cheeks to allow his mouth to be shut, but by no means lacking in brains, was determined not to speak unless he absolutely had to.

'You wait,' said Gallostra. 'He will make at least half a dozen speeches to-day. I've arranged for a round of Tío Pepe before lunch.' He did deliver them. And when the Brazilian ambassador sat down after a speech he had had carefully prepared in Spanish, Brockman, sherry glass in hand, assured him he was delighted to find how easy it was for a Spaniard to understand Portuguese.

My exploits as Spanish Delegate on my own had conquered for me the sympathy, indeed the confidence of the President, Gabriel Hanotaux, an elder statesman of the French Third Republic, who had been Foreign Secretary in his forties and was now in his eighties. We often chatted of all kinds of things, for his was a mind open to wide interests, and he was a good historian, a member of the French Academy. One day, towards the end of the Conference, we were all whisked to Madrid to be received by the Royal Family.

It was a dignified occasion which I remember mostly because Queen Victoria Eugenia, wearing a cloth-of-gold dress and a diamond necklace, looked the part of a Queen more beautifully than I have ever seen it done anywhere in life or on the stage, screen or canvas; and because that night I committed the most blatant and least conspicuous gaffe of my diplomatic life. Both the Spanish Protocol and the League Secretariat had asked me to place the delegations. The rule was that there would be two alphabetic orders: the first for those nations that belonged to the Council; the second for the rest. I only forgot one detail: that the Spanish Delegation should have been included in the first group within the head of the long serpent. No one noticed it.

In my capacity as improvised and unofficial Protocol Officer, I followed down the line the royal and official group composed of the King, the Queen, the Queen Mother and the Duke of Lerma, resplendent in his ministerial uniform as Foreign Secretary, to whom I prompted the name and nationalities of every Delegation. When we stopped before the Yugoslav Delegation, the Queen Mother addressed its head, an Admiral, in a short, sharp rebuke in German, which I did not hear clearly enough to report with confidence. The rumour ran up and down the serpent, that Her Majesty, unable to control her Austrian emotions, had reproached the Admiral for having 'betrayed his country'.

After the presentation, there was a general conversation during which I found myself *tête à tête* with the imposing, tall, handsome Duke of Lerma. He congratulated me on my 'brilliant activity as Spanish delegate in Barcelona'. I had no time to admire the efficiency of his information service nor the generosity of my co-delegates, for he volunteered to add: 'Monsieur Hanotaux has told me all and he is very enthusiastic about it.' Happy the nation, thought I, whose Foreign Secretary can afford to be informed on her own affairs by a French President.

In a post scriptum of a letter to C.H.M.A. I find this:

> Last night, grand dinner at the Ritz. Host, the Italian Minister of Public Works. After dinner, Hanotaux had a talk with me about the speeches which he and Ortuño (my chief delegate) will pronounce on the closing day. 'I will quote Cervantes in my speech,' said Hanotaux. – 'I am glad to hear it', said I–'for *I* will quote Anatole France in Señor Ortuño's.' He smiled. He knows the world.

It was my first and perhaps my most successful prank in this tricky world I was beginning to tread in a mood as careful as it was carefree. By then, I was familiar with the mind of Hanotaux. He was very proud of being a member of the Académie Française, and actually *lived* the style of that illustrious lighthouse officially in charge of '*le rayonnement de la France*'. Knowing that I should have to write Ortuño's speech, I had set to work and had been gradually led to draft it in the form, style, phrasing and even mannerism of a speech delivered by a veteran Academician receiving a new colleague 'under the dome'. It was almost a pastiche. But this fact was bound to remain unperceived by every one of the three hundred guests in that wonderful Gothic room of *La Lonja* in Barcelona except Hanotaux himself and at most a couple of his aides and one or two of my French friends in the Secretariat.

So the great evening came and the great moment too, and I, at the lower end of the vast hall, among the youngsters, began to hear my own words, coming from the high table over yards of glass and crockery, not badly pronounced but out of melody, my phrases wrongly weighted, my points blunted, my periods lame. Still, there was the whole speech and I could see the broad smile on the nut-cracker mouth and sharp eyes of Hanotaux. The speeches were over. We flocked out slowly; and I suddenly felt a hand grasping my elbow, while a voice – Hanotaux's own – whispered in my ear: 'Your speech has been utterly spoilt.'

When we left Barcelona, it had been arranged by Comert and Haas that I was to enter the Secretariat in August of that same year.

CHAPTER II

I JOIN THE SECRETARIAT

NO women. Black jacket; Comert had said. His wife was in fact
that very night presenting him with a baby. I found there about a
dozen men drawn from different departments, all French *normaliens*
save Montenach a *fribourgeois*, diplomat, elegant, keen, a Catholic and
indistinguishable from a Frenchman. Was not I a kind of Frenchman
also? Well, well. Time would show. And it did not make us wait long.

How it began, I don't know. Suddenly I realised we were in the thick
of a discussion, a match, a Marathon: Shakespeare versus Racine; and
it soon dawned upon me that I was in a minority of one for Shakespeare
against about ten or twelve keen, alert, quick-minded Frenchmen (plus
the frenchified Swiss) all for Racine. 'How can you even dream of comparing them? The essence of all tragedy as of all comedy is the man-
woman relationship and Shakespeare knew nothing about women and
did not like them.' This was the stock argument I had to meet. In vain
did I point out that there was the dark lady of the Sonnets and that some
of these sonnets were pretty eloquent of Shakespeare's ability to deal
with a woman; in vain that, no matter his queer ways, he had created
a host of unforgettable women – my Gallic new friends evoked their
beloved feminine figures out of Racine's gallery, and asked – as they
thought triumphantly: 'Where in Shakespeare is there an Andro-
maque?'

I was beginning to feel that the game had lasted long enough and
could in any case lead nowhere; but how could I kill it? I bethought
myself of the possibility of at least widening its scope by getting rid
of those women on both sides, and in so doing, unexpectedly I achieved
my chief purpose with wonderful ease. 'Now, friends, only one word:
If Shakespeare had created no other character than Mercutio, he would
be worth ten Racines.' That did the trick. No one knew who Mercutio
was, so one of them, after a silence, asked: 'What time is the meeting
to-morrow?'

That literary evening, on top of my political-technical experience
in Barcelona, clinched my conviction that the Secretariat of the League
of Nations was bound to be a human group of the very best quality.
It owed its being mostly to two men: Eric Drummond and Jean Monnet.

9

And it would have been difficult to find two men more different, or more true to type as a Briton and a Frenchman.

Drummond's abilities and qualities were less his own (for as an individual, he was 'one of the heap' as we say in Spain) than those of an upper class Englishman, indeed so English that he was even a Scot. But a Scot who had deliberately blunted his edges so as the better to pass for an Englishman. So determined was he in this that he even managed to look stupid very convincingly as only true Englishmen, no matter how clever they are, can look. Herein lurks one of the secrets of this much maligned branch of *Homo Sapiens*; for the Englishman is ready to sacrifice his vanity to the job in hand, and will not mind seeming to be stupid when in fact he is being so clever that he can fold up his cleverness so as to show the rough and dull side to the foreigner. This is then one of the many cases in which the English put ethical and utilitarian values above individual and aesthetical satisfactions.

Drummond was a master at this game; but I was not taken in. In fact, it was my experience of this man, who could so cleverly hide his shrewdness, that led me to classify the League protagonists into four classes: the stupid who look stupid; the clever who look clever; the stupid who look clever; and the clever who look stupid. These last, of course, are the most dangerous of all; and there is a story of that brilliant and brilliant-looking diplomat, Talleyrand, confiding to one of his colleagues, who was dumb and looked it: '*Ah Monsieur, ce que je ferais avec une tête comme la vôtre!*'

This is a longing Drummond need not have felt; for he had a way of going into obscuration when he began looking at you open-mouthed and sleepy-eyed which made you feel like seeking for a sixpenny bit in your pocket and offering it to that poor beggar of wit, and yet you kept suspecting that *le plus roublard des deux n'est pas celui qu'on pense.* Drummond was endowed with every one of the solid virtues of the British civil service. In his actual, concrete work, he was excellent, his judgement sure, his temper even, his patience inexhaustible, his courtesy unfailing. He was a superb draftsman, aye, and that was to be for a good part at the core of my troubles with him.

Drummond was one of the four men to whom the world owes the birth of a world civil service. Not that the elements had not sprung up here and there in such organisations as the Berne Postal Union; but the two creations of the Treaty of Versailles, the League and the International Labour Office, widened the scope of these first sketches of a world government still to come and bestowed a universal importance on the world civil service.

The second man I have in mind was Harold Butler, who nearly became the first and was the second Director General of the I.L.O. He was a typical British don, a competent economist, a perfect gentleman, an impeccable example by himself of that excellent British civil service to which the world civil service owes so much. He was also, perhaps inevitably, more a class type than an individual person, by which I mean that (as was the case with Drummond) Harold Butler's qualities were less those born with him than those developed and shaped by his education and breeding. A man to reckon with, in any case, and one whose creative spirit contributed powerfully to the birth of the new world civil service.

The other two in the set of the four men who created this civil service were Albert Thomas and Jean Monnet. This time, two individuals, if both well set each in his class. Short, wide-shouldered, almost square, stocky, red-faced, everything in Albert Thomas spelt strength; his big luminous eyes behind his large tortoiseshell-framed glasses, his vast forehead enlivened by rebellious locks, the square, powerful jaw, the large, generous mouth able to smile without weakness and to correct without ill-feeling, the boxer's trunk – all that concentrated power would have impressed the observer as a natural force, innocent and free from any particular direction, working through and above human beings, had it not been directed and mastered by as keen an intellect as ever came from the higher schools of France. Albert Thomas had been predestined by his natural gifts for the great rôle he was to play in history.

A son of the people, he never disowned his origin, which, in fact, would have been an impossible as well as a ridiculous thing, for his physique was plebeian in the extreme and he would have cut a comic figure in the rôle of a *bourgeois gentilhomme*, let alone an aristocrat. His laughter at the idea would have been stentoreous. For him class was too far away from nature, so that he was not prone to dwell on it unless a concrete social problem were at stake. That is possibly why his socialism was never acidulated by bitterness or resentment.

The soul of his straightforward nature was his spontaneity. He was straight, not like steel, smelted in that shape, but like the stem that rises towards the sky and grows and is born again every second every ring; straight not by method, tactics, incapacity of being otherwise, but with all the lightness, invention, ever-surprising newness of an essential gift that remains the same under any form.

It did not take him' long to reach the summits of power in France, where the first world war revealed him as the very man for the Ministry of Munitions, an office in which he won the admiration of the other genius for munitions in that war, David Lloyd George. But Albert Thomas was one of the all too scarce men of our times who burst the frame of his own nation and he did not come into his own until he became Director General of the Labour Office, and its first at that, entrusted with the task of creating it out of nothing. It was then that he took in hand a task on a world-wide scale.

Those who saw him at work know that he never resigned himself to work as a Secretary more or less General, invited to sit at the Council table by a friendly gesture of the President; but that he took in earnest his title of Director General and, from the first, ruled the new institution with a firm and sure hand. Thanks to him, the I.L.O. grew to acquire a world authority nearly as weighty as that of the League of Nations. Although logic demanded that the former should loom no larger than the latter, its staff was soon about as numerous as that under Drummond; and when I told him once that this fact was sometimes raised against him, he retorted: 'The I.L.O. is not too big; it is the League that is too small.'

When Drummond, later Lord Perth, left Geneva, his successor as Secretary General of the League of Nations should have been Albert Thomas? but he was dead, fortunately for all those who would not let the League grow out of the modest proportions Drummond had accepted for it: a club of nations, a co-operative of sovereignties in which the sum of national powers added up to international powerlessness. A civil servant was chosen, Joseph Avenol, Inspector of (French) Finances. He was an executor of other people's decisions. Albert Thomas was a creator.

He would certainly have declined to remain a Chief Rubber Stamp or a Grand Inkpot such as the Powers would have wished him to have been, for he thought that the Secretary General should become what he would probably have made him grow to be: a true World Chancellor. With his typical generosity, knowing how cordially I shared his ideas, he said to me one day: 'How many things we would have achieved together!' He certainly would, had he been given the chance.

Beside Drummond, Jean Monnet was the creator of the League of Nations. Yes, I know. There is the Covenant and the great Fathers, Wilson, Smuts, Cecil, Bourgeois. But these texts and these great names did little more than drawing-board work. The movement came from Eric Drummond and Jean Monnet. Monnet perhaps more consciously. But for his dreamy eyes, everything in him suggests the precision and order of a well-regulated instrument. Small but perfectly proportioned. Jean Monnet seems always to preserve that physical and moral balance for which the English have coined an admirable word–*poise*. Though a realiser Monnet is also a creator.

Albert Thomas was a man of the people. Jean Monnet is a *bourgeois* and will remain in the history of France as a model of all that the French *bourgeoisie* has given to France and to the world: positive intelligence, disinterested action, integrity, the sense of public service and responsibility. More cosmopolitan than Albert Thomas, open and friendly to the Anglo-Saxon world, Jean Monnet was in Geneva as international as Albert Thomas, less fiery but perhaps more aware of the obstacles in the way, just as tenacious and possibly more skilful. They differed as fire does from light: agitated, ardent, over-active the one, as much as the other was serene, calm and luminous; but they shared that intellectual passion which is perhaps the deepest feature of the French nation.

These four men were the creators of the two Secretariats, and history owes them a considerable debt. For they showed, each in his own personal and national way, a creative imagination without which the League and the I.L.O., the seeds of the formidable international bureaucracy of our day, would not have become alive. It was, I believe, Drummond and Monnet, with Albert Thomas and Harold Butler, who made true and effective what in President Wilson was little more than a fortunate literary phrase for presenting the League to the world: 'A living thing is born.'

Drummond had effectively barricaded himself against all foreigners by installing Frank Walters at one of his approaches and Miss Howard at the other. Walters had a first-rate mind and, as a person, was what one calls in England a thoroughly decent chap. But he certainly was not the type of Briton who easily gets on an even footing with foreigners (understood as identical with non-Britons). Indeed, after a whole lifetime of intercourse with Britons, I still wonder whether such a man exists. As for Miss Howard, she considered herself as definitely 'U', as the saying goes now-a-days: and I soon discovered a quiet way of irritating her. When asked to dinner at Drummond's, I would ring her up and innocently ask: 'White or black tie?' just to enjoy her almost offended: 'Why, of course, white.' She was certainly the most superior member of the Secretariat. Her English was good.

The keenest British intellect in the Secretariat, before Salter's arrival, was G. H. Mair who had been my chief at the Information Office in Victoria St. during the war. He had been an infant prodigy in Edinburgh, in Oxford and in Whitehall, where he was already a V.I.P. at twenty-eight. 'He must have sown his wild oats over his cradle,' one of his professors had written to another one. He was still at this delightful sport while supposed to be second man to Pierre Comert at the Press Section. A sad case of a near-genius who let himself sink in alcohol. But in those days, he was still gay, witty, all-knowing and nothing-believing. After reading a not very sharp report on Dantzig by a not very bright Dane, he wrote in the margin: 'A thing of beauty is a joy for ever' and with no further comment, sent it on to Drummond.

To round up and seal every access to his seclusion, Drummond had unearthed the most English of Englishmen one could dream of. Anthony Buxton incarnated that legendary Englishman who is supposed to have declared that the more he knew of men the more he liked dogs. He kept a pack of beagles, which the French, of course, delightfully transfigured into *bigueules*, and ran them after, I suppose, hares, for there must have been little else to tear to pieces in the Federal jungles around Geneva. He was also a keen bird watcher. He was tall, gaunt, rosy and ever smiling, and, for some reason or other, was in charge of the follow-up of action to be taken by the Secretariat after meetings of the League bodies. A less 'convertible' Englishman it would have been impossible to find.

That thoroughly English feature – the ability to keep the boy alive within the grown up – a feature without which no one can fully understand either a football match or a sitting of the House of Commons – was very much manifest in Tony Buxton's make-up. One evening round the fire, at the time when reminiscences break the surface of silence, he began to relate how he and a group of friends had hoaxed the Naval authorities in Weymouth into believing that the Emperor of Ethiopia was arriving and should be received with full honours. A telegram and a couple of telephone calls had done the trick. The phoney Emperor arrived (Buxton himself, followed by Virginia Woolf as an Abyssinian Prince), and he got a naval band, a red carpet, a visit to a dreadnought, a luncheon, a speech by the admiral and everything that goes with such events. The hoax was revealed just in time to prevent its explosion into publicity and that was the end of Tony Buxton's story.

Not, however, the end of the story itself. For the years went by and one evening, during the London black-out, I happened to be dining in Hans Square (if I remember rightly), at the house of a retired naval officer. We were very few guests, so that when the ladies left us to our port, only three of us were at table with the host; and they included Sir Walter Selby, who had been Ambassador in Vienna, and Sir Dudley Pound, the First Sea Lord. Before I come back to Buxton's story, I want to record one of the finest Irish bulls I have heard in my life, and remember that Irish bulls are at their liveliest when they are born before your eyes and ears. We talked, of course, about the war, and I put forward the view that, after Hitler, Stalin would be an equally hard nut to crack. Whereupon Admiral Pound pensively confirmed: 'Indeed, I don't see how we can win this war without waging another one.'

Pound's conversation, naturally enough, never wandered very far from the navy; so that I was not in the least surprised when a little later I realised that he was telling us Buxton's story from another angle; for he had been very much of a character in that comedy. After the laugh, he turned earnest, indeed grim, and went on: 'That was all very well, but there was the Navy. And we weren't going to let that pass. So we had them all thoroughly caned. All but one who had T.B. and a girl who was also a member of the gang. We arrived in their respective homes – they all lived in the country – told them to lower their pants and at them.' I remember how he described Tony Buxton's punishment in a hall adorned with beautiful china kept under glass.

I was fascinated to discover this last and supreme feature of Buxton's Englishry, this, after all, survival of the boy in the grown up not merely as a member of a gang of practical jokers, but as a boy ready to be flogged and submit. Who but an Englishman would have consented to such a thing without thoughts of murder? And yet, thought I, would England ever have lain down to thirty years of military dictatorship?

Buxton, however, did not mix very much with the crowd of foreigners who made up the Secretariat. There was another Englishman in Comert's section who tried to. His name was Cummings, and he was both able and attractive, endowed, moreover, with a lively sense of humour, a quality wihout which survival in Geneva was nearly impossible. For some reason or other, he frequented Henri Bonnet, one of the ablest minds of the French contingent; and it all may have been a conscious or subconscious endeavour mutually to improve their linguistic armoury, for Cummings' French was no better than that you usually get in *The Times* and Henri Bonnet's English had a long way to go before it reached the level that enabled him to become French Ambassador in Washington.

One day, seeing these two good friends of mine engaged in animated conversation, I drew nearer to join in their debate, soon to discover that while Cummings was talking about Landru, the French assassin who had out-Henry VIII-ed Henry VIII by murdering seven wives, Bonnet was talking about Irish Home Rule and the bloodshed it had cost to both countries. Such was the basis of many a Genevese understanding. Not till later years, during one of my trips to the United States, was I to be told the wonderful Goldberg story, so symbolical of our international encounters. Goldberg, an American on his first trip to Europe, sits at his first dinner on board ship at a table for two in his French liner. A young Frenchman opposite says 'Bon appétit', to which he, half-rising from his seat and bowing, answers 'Goldberg'. On the same ceremony occurring at the beginning of the following two meals, Goldberg seeks the purser for an explanation, and, loaded with it, awaits his table partner with a newly added composure. Hardly has the young Frenchman sat down, when Goldberg cheerfully sings 'Bon appétit' to him; whereupon the young Frenchman, rising and bowing, retorts: 'Goldberg'.

Next to the French and the British contingents, those of other nationalities mattered less. We were, of course, almost altogether deprived of an American contingent when the U.S. backed out of the League after one of the most disreputable campaigns of misrepresentations and deliberate lies in the history of that great democracy whose very progress along mechanical lines exposes her to the dangers of a pre-fabricated public opinion. I was so much impressed by this campaign and by the cynical, indeed inept, leadership under which the Republican party made the U.S. repudiate Wilson and the League that, in later years, the cycle of my official public life already closed, and with over two years of exile behind me, I published a poem in English, 'The Home of Man', of which I reproduce here one of the sonnets:

> Are you content, hard men, are you content?
> Cabot-Lodge, Mellon, Hearst, Frick, Harvey, Harding,
> Are you content? Behold, you saved the farthing,
> You saved the farthing, but the million went.
> You thought that money was the coin you spent,
> Goods, just things you were handling, watching, guarding,
> Services, claims that called for a rewarding,
> Your fatherland, a land that gave you rent.
> But all is life and there is but one life,
> By dooming foreign lands to storm and strife,
> To storm and strife you doomed your continent,
> By refusing to help build the World Order,
> By hoarding peace, you doomed e'en the peace hoarder
> To the wild beasts of war. – Are you content?

This sonnet as well as the other seventeen that make up the poem, written though they were in 1937–8 while returning from one of my many visits to the U.S., bears witness to the depth of my convictions in the matter of peace. As I now see them, these convictions owed more to an intuitional attitude to the problem of human relations than to the experience I acquired in Geneva during the fifteen years I spent there in one way or another; but this experience confirmed what my intuition had seen from the first. We were in for a long, a very long trek; but we had to persevere.

This was the attitude that inspired my centenary portrait of Woodrow Wilson published by the *Virginian Quarterly* in the autumn of 1956:

The top hat, the frock coat, the long jaw, the lofty forehead, all 'vertical' features, impressed upon the world the image of a straight, rigid, unyielding, unbending, highminded intellectual. But this came later. The crowd was enthusiastic. Paris, London, Rome shouted themselves hoarse when the great American President rode through their thronged streets. What a dramatic return! Neither Franklin nor Lafayette nor Pershing had risen to the size required to balance the figure of Christopher Columbus and to stage that mighty historical come-back. America discovered. America fully grown protecting its progenitor. One dreamt of Canning's dictum: the New World came to restore the balance of the Old; but in such a deeper sense! None of your miserable balance of power between nations jealously watching each other lest one leap at the other's neck (or pocket); but a balance of mind, a sanity at last found and ready to rise above the jungle of sovereignties towards a civilised Community of Communities. What those European crowds exulted at was the hope that the slogan 'the war to end all wars' would become true; that out of the turmoil and carnage of the cruellest war so far experienced by mankind a new era would emerge without fear at any rate from external aggression.

The crowds longed for that peace out of the misery of their war. The days of military 'glory' were gone. The word sounded now empty and rhetorical, nay false and hypocritical; something not unlike the round of rum or brandy handed to the troops about to leap over the parapet. Above the crowds but yesterday drunk with war a dream of reason was spreading its even wings. There must be some way for human beings to live together in peace.

Wilson, lofty, straight, unyielding, vertical, incarnated that popular yearning which rose towards the inner sky in man. The world of bleeding Europeans chose him as their prophet because he was an American, above their internecine squabbles; because he had resisted any drift of America towards war with a manly, stubborn attachment to neutrality; because after he had declared himself 'too proud to fight' when the *Lusitania* went down in the Atlantic, with one hundred Americans on board, he accepted the challenge and fought when the *Sussex* went down in the Channel. They chose him because in his Address to the joint session of Congress on January 8, 1918, he had laid down the Fourteen Points which were to stand as a basis not so much for the peace treaty as for the way of life

to be adopted after it; and because the last and most important
of the points ran thus: 'A general association of nations must
be formed under specific covenants for the purpose of afford-
ing mutual guarantees of political independence and territorial integrity to great and small States alike.'

This vision of an association of nations caught the imagination of the peoples of Europe. They saw in Wilson the
leader who would free them from that thraldom. They knew
that their governments had woven the war and the defence
against it with hidden diplomatic threads knotted into secret
treaties, and liked the more the first of the Fourteen Points
which laid down the new rule: 'Open Covenants of peace
openly arrived at, after which there shall be no private international understandings of any kind, but diplomacy shall
proceed always frankly and in the public view.' This was the
language to be spoken to a Europe wounded by its own folly
and dreaming of a new life of wisdom.

When that man's eyes drank in the clamorous crowds, that
divine clemency which blurs our future kept from him beyond
the screen of glory his defeat in Congress; his helplessness as
a paralytic hidden by his wife and doctors from his cabinet and
Congress; a victory for the most nationalistic and least distinguished of American Presidents; a refusal of his own
country to join the League; and as a direct consequence of this
refusal, the failure to restrain Japan in Manchuria and Mussolini in Ethiopia, thence Hitler and the Second World War.
He has often been accused of having brought about his own
defeat by his unbending character. But the testimony of those
who knew him well would not appear to warrant such an
accusation. Wilson was exactly what a Statesman should be:
unyielding as to principles but amenable to compromise and
advice on details. This failure must be explained in other ways.

And to begin with it was not his failure but the failure of his
day. When one peruses the Fourteen Points, and his 'Four
Ends' speech of July 4, 1918, one is struck by the boldness,
but also by the unrealistic nature of some of his ideas. Wilson
was the voice that uttered the dream of reason of an age of
folly. As such his plan was both too perfect and too abstract.

As for perfection, let me quote a number of items of the
plan he advocated. Point 3, for example: 'The removal, so far
as possible, of all economic barriers and the establishment of
an equality of trade conditions among all the nations consent-
ing to the peace and associating themselves for its main-

tenance.' This was an obvious counsel of perfection, unattainable in his day. Or again points 2 and 3 of his speech of September 27, 1918: 'No special or separate interest of any single nation or any group of nations can be made the basis of any part of a settlement which is not consistent with the common interest of all.' 'There can be no leagues or alliances or special covenants and understandings within the general and common family of the League of Nations.' This coming from the President of the United States, committed to the Monroe Doctrine!

It came from a man, moreover, who had sent marines to Santo Domingo and Pershing to Veracruz; who knew that there were forces in the United States which not even he had been able to hold in leash when an easy prey like Mexico lay helpless at hand; and who on the very masterpiece of his statesmanship – the Covenant – had felt bound to stamp the nationalist limitations of his own country by excluding Mexico from eligibility to the League.

As for abstraction, the very constitution of the League of Nations shows conclusively that the world of 1918 was not yet ripe for a sound organisation of peace. It sought to set up a kind of world government at one go. The 'realists' tried to prevent this error by whittling down the powers of the League and reducing it to a mere club of fully sovereign nations, a *league* and not a *society*. But surely the right way would have been to organise it from below in tiers of federations. This would have had two inestimable advantages: to keep all international institutions in close touch with their own local realities and at their scale, scope, and size; and to secure as the top authority a small but powerful and authoritative 'Council of Continents'.

No blame attaches to Wilson. He was a man of his time, the man of his time, his time made flesh. He sought to harness anarchy and anarchy kicked back and killed him. It is sad to think that when, discouraged by a violent come-back of European nationalisms, he returned to his country in search of moral support, it was his countrymen who administered the *coup de grâce*. And by what means! Distortion, downright occultation of the truth, pretence to back the League in order to secure the vote of the well-meaning American internationalist – no weapon was too low to strike the Leader with. These men who won the Harding election stand before History as the true begetters of our present-day miseries. On the day the American nation forsook Wilson, a long night of suffering began for mankind.

The betrayal of Wilson by his Republican countrymen was a hard blow; and its immediate consequence was the withdrawal of Raymond Fosdick, who had been appointed one of the Under-secretaries General. I was somewhat taken aback by this resignation and its acceptance. It seemed to me that the principle involved was wrong. Either Fosdick was the right man for the job or he was not. Therefore either he should not have resigned or he should not have been appointed. Evidently, all this top-heavy hierarchy of Secretaries General was based on nationalism. Fosdick gone, the chief American left was Arthur Sweetser, another of the two deputies to Comert in the Press Section, a charmer, a cordial, open-minded, friendly and shrewd journalist. He lived in a pleasant *campagne*, a comely house with a garden big enough to be styled a park and as he was not a good sleeper, he used to get up at dawn to kill nightingales with his revolver. I was callous about these murders because I had a grudge against those birds ever since I read that they had consented to act as a chorus for Heine's sighs.

The Italian contingent was led by a most untypical Italian, with the rank, of course, of Under-secretary General. Attolico had nothing of the refined, acute *finesse* one connects with Italians. He was a tall, thick-set, robust, peasant-looking giant, whose head seemed to speed backwards along the line of a receding forehead, while the body stood ready to push forward to the attack. A most dynamic person, whose eyes seemed always to be beaming out wonder behind his spectacles, while his thick mouth smiled in amusement at men's folly when it didn't swear malediction at men's infamies. He became much later Mussolini's Ambassador to Hitler, which broke him, for he was an honest liberal, and died as Ambassador to the Vatican. Of his countrymen in the Secretariat, the ablest was a more or less Americanised economist, named Stopani.

The Italian member of the political section was not quite true to type. He was fair-headed, rosy-coloured, intelligent enough, but not over-intellectual, and altogether lacking in that sharp, pointed intent which is so characteristic of the Italian genius and finds expression in the omnipresence of the letter 'I' (EE) in the language. He was kind, indeed famous for his fondness for old ladies; and that, combined with a certain way of walking as if he had a horse between his legs, led to the possibly unfair application to him of a French taunt: *l'hypertrophie de rien.*

Looking back, what strikes me most now – it did not then – is the importance of the Jewish contingent. The Directors of the Press, the Political, the Transit and the Health Sections were all Jews: Comert, Mantoux, Haas and Rajchmann, the first three most attractive, clever and efficient persons; Rajchmann at least as efficient and clever also, but not in the least attractive. He had one of those razor-sharp faces, in which eyes, nose, lips, seemed to have been honed to a cutting edge, so that a first glance was enough to detect in him a sharp brain and a determined will, but not much else. More than once it occurred to me that there was too much of a coincidence in this fact: that the French Jews were all attractive and the Polish Jews were not; and I was beginning to wonder whether this might not be due to Polish antisemitism, when I remembered that among the French Jews in the Secretariat – well, the argument would not do.

The contrast between all those French Jews and the English Jew in our midst was striking. Gerald Furtado Abraham was as perfect an imitation of a British gentleman as Pierre Comert and the rest of them were of French intellectuals. *Gerald* for English gentry, *Furtado* for Spanish ancestry, *Abraham* for Jewish blood, he was intelligent and cultured, suave and quiet, good natured and friendly, but determined to be sound rather than brilliant. For good measure of Englishry he lived at well over forty with, and under the thumb of, his mother, and was unmarried.

Gerald Abraham would not hear of super-state or world authority or any of the supra-national concepts. The Geneva organisation was a *League* and not a *Société*, and this difference between the English and the French names of Wilson's 'living thing' was by no means merely verbal. It did neatly describe the radical difference of attitude between the English and the French way of feeling its quality and destiny. This difference might be traced back to that between Plato and Aristotle, for we Mediterraneans have ever remained fascinated by perfect geometrical figures, while the Northern Europeans are deeply aware of the sad but nutrient fact that in nature all spheres are at best potatoes.

CHAPTER III

UPS AND DOWNS OF A CIVIL SERVANT

I was running myself in as an assembly official by following the work of the Second Commission. The rhythm of the Assembly was by now well established. After a general debate to let off the hot air accumulated during eleven months, the Assembly split into six Commissions, each specialised in one particular aspect of the League work; and when the Commissions, in all of which all delegations were represented, had adopted their resolutions, the Plenary Assembly met again to pass, amend or reject them. I was told to follow, from the Press point of view, the second Commission in which all technical matters were debated.

The Commission's President was a Senator Doherty, a Canadian who was under the impression that he could speak French, though the origin of this delusion is somewhat obscure. It had been agreed that, in order to save time, French would not be translated into English, though English would into French; for, in those days, French was more generally spoken than English. This put the interpreters in a quandary whenever the President spoke in what he thought was French, but in fact hardly differed from English. Still, there was the rule, until our old friend Monsieur Gabriel Hanotaux, who represented France on the Commission and sat far away on the right at the other end of the hall, after a fairly long Presidential statement in his strangely undefined Canadian, cried out: '*Traduction, s'il vous plaît.*' That settled Senator Doherty.

Robert Haas, whose leadership of the Transit Section hardly sufficed to consume his ability, had set about to organise a kind of Trade Union for the members of the Secretariat. We had a number of meetings which I attended, though as a matter of fact, I was not yet a permanent member of the Secretariat. When I drew Comert's attention to the point, he just laughed. 'Monnet has made up his mind. You'll have your permanent contract the very minute your temporary year is over.' I was struck by his assurance that Monnet's will was enough; I was entering that house if not against Drummond's will, at least without his blessing.

Curious as I was to see a white collar Trade Union at work, I therefore attended the meetings of Haas's Association as a mere observer – let alone the fact that I felt utterly sceptical about it. In the subtle way of nature, this situation was providing the raw materials for my first failure with Drummond. I had met him once, when I called to present myself to him on my arrival as a temporary official. The interview was pleasant enough, for Drummond was friendly and well mannered, and it went no further than the usual sparring for mutual acquaintance. But one day I received an invitation to dinner from Jean Monnet (black tie, Les Bergues) and on enquiry I discovered that it was an occasion offered by the Deputy Secretary General to Drummond and to all the heads of Departments. 'You will be the only one from the ranks.'

I was puzzled even more than flattered. But both feelings were to rise higher when I found that at the round dinner table, set for about twelve persons, the élite of the Secretariat, at which Jean Monnet and Drummond sat opposite each other, I had been placed at Drummond's left. 'Well', thought I, 'this is going to be like passing an examination. Must watch my step.'

Drummond and I got on fairly well for a good part of the evening and then fell to talking on Haas's Trade Union. I gave him a sceptical-humorous report of what I had seen, and concluded by describing how the meeting had debated at length on when they should meet again. I paused, then added: 'I got up and suggested February 30th.' He looked at me silently for a while, no doubt awaiting an explanation, which I did not provide, then surrendered: 'Why February 30th?' – 'Because there is no such date.' He smiled awkwardly: 'Oh I see. Sorry. I am so tired, you know!'

'I'll be ploughed,' I said to myself.

Well, I wasn't. Or was I? Events were to say, but then the language of events can be ambiguous. Just a year after I had begun work as a member of the Press Section for technical matters, I was appointed head of the Disarmament Section. My presence at that élite dinner had therefore been a piece of intelligent anticipation. Or, in other words, the French again, on the strength of my linguistic-literary ability and my technical training, had persuaded Drummond to entrust me with the most delicate post the Secretariat then had to offer.

This last aspect of things was not then worth the attention of a British gentleman; so, the appointment, a surprise for me who knew nothing about it until I was told by Drummond, confirmed my impression that the group of French *normaliens* who advised Monnet, and Monnet himself, had insisted on my promotion. It did not dawn upon me at the time that Drummond might interpret the event as a successful manoeuvring on the part of an ambitious young man; which is what I came to suspect later.

At any rate, though I was entrusted with all the duties and responsibilities of a Director, I was not made a Director, but a 'Chief of Service' (of which there were none then) with less gold braid and less salary; and, as if this were not enough, promotion to the same rank was bestowed the same day on Drummond's golf companion, a nice American chap, Huston by name, who saw to the Establishment, tables, chairs and janitors. It would have been ungracious for me to look so closely into the mouth of the horse I was being presented with, but there was no lack of candid friends who did.

Comert pointed out to me that my leaving his Section left him without a Spaniard at all. The fact is that when I entered the Secretariat by way of his section, Comert had already a Spaniard, to deal with public relations in Spain. He was no other than Luis Bolin, the same Bolin who, fourteen years later, was to organise Franco's flight from the Canaries to Tetuan, and so start our civil war. This person was, of course, utterly unsuited since he believed in nothing whatsoever. On his return from a mission to South America, where he was at the time of my entry, he resigned. What Comert was really asking me now was to find him a successor to Bolin.

I bethought myself of Plá, my London friend, a wise man, a good internationalist, fluent in both French and English, whose first career — he was a Captain in the Marines — would help in matters of disarmament. But there was a fly in the ointment. After years on the reserve list (unpaid) which he had spent teaching Spanish in London, Plá had received warnings from his old comrades in arms that his remaining in London while there was a war on in Morocco, was not welcome to the Marines. He gave up his London establishment and joined a fighting unit.

It was no easy operation to tear him from the grasp of the military authorities, though he had already spent quite a while at the front; but by pointing out that he would be serving his country if in a different capacity, I had my way.

I was supposed to hold my new post under a special subordination to Attolico. This arrangement, which, as it turned out, was purely theoretical, was meant to cover with a semblance of justification, the *capitis deminutio* that had been inflicted upon me by denying me the directorship; but also to put disarmament neither under Drummond (political affairs) nor under Monnet (economic and technical affairs), since disarmament was one of the chief bones of contention between Britain (i.e. Drummond) and France (i.e. Monnet). The fact that I was a Spaniard with equally strong French and British ties and connections had therefore also helped my promotion.

All this rubbed me the wrong way. I wanted a world government with a world perspective; and all I found was an inter-national organisation more national than inter. I had been forewarned. Comert, while I was still in his section, had held forth to me about Quiñones de León, the Spanish Ambassador in Paris and chief delegate to the League Council, and put me on my guard against any velleity of action that might interfere with his policy and diplomacy, 'for otherwise he will break you like glass.' And when I surveyed the landscape of my own new kingdom, I saw nothing but sheer nationalism.

My staff comprised a French Army man, a British naval officer, an Italian airman, and a South American jurist. The first three men were the Secretaries respectively of the military, naval and air Sub-commissions of what was known as the Armaments Commission, composed of the military, naval and air experts of the nations represented at the League Council. This Commission had successfully blocked so far any attempt at reducing armaments and its only practical utility was to examine the armaments of nations that applied for admission, reporting to the Council whether these armaments were justified or not.

In my new capacity I attended a number of these examinations, during which the chief delegate had to answer a number of technical questions. It soon became clear to me that the chief if not the only aim of the procedure was to provide one or other of the powers with an opportunity to get rid of an obstacle or to obtain an advantage in the process of admitting the candidate-nation; and that if no such thing was in the offing, the proceedings went through smoothly enough. One of them stuck in my memory because of the impressive and picturesque figure of the chief delegate, no other than the present Emperor of Ethiopia, then the Ras Tafari, heir to the throne. His blue cape and white trousers brought welcome relief from the drab European attire of all of us, and the marvellous conciseness of the Ethiopean language was dramatically shown whenever Colonel Lowe, who presided, asked the Ras Tafari a question about those two divisions or batteries or what not; for the Prince, glancing hard through the English colonel as if he were a brick wall or a load of fish, barked a long monosyllable that sounded like 'Hatrrrsh', whereupon his interpreter spoke in pretty fluent English for quite a quarter of an hour.

It had become obvious to the most obtuse observers that this Commission of colonels and rear admirals was not the right instrument for paving the way to complete and general disarmament; and so the Assembly decided to set up another Commission which would no longer be des Armements but du Désarmement. The military commission, whose title to exist was embedded in the Covenant, did not like the idea, and so demanded and obtained that while it was styled Permanent the intruder would be known as Temporary. This Temporary Commission would also be known as Mixed, because it would have both military and civil members, these last the more numerous. Its President was René Viviani, a typical French politician born in Algeria of an Italian father and a Spanish mother.

Aghnides, my Greek predecessor in charge of Disarmament Affairs, was terrified of him. 'Be careful,' he warned me; 'when he turns round on to me, I feel like a rat under a tram car.' Viviani was tall, hefty, powerful, the very image of the public tribune, and little used to opposition; but, in fact, as I soon found out, quite manageable, indeed as manageable as a good President should be for his Commission's Secretary. It was while working with him that I evolved that dictum, which among the many that have been attributed to me, happens to be genuine: 'A good commission is composed of a good president and a good secretary, and when I say a good president I exaggerate.'

It was precisely to take this job, that of Permanent Secretary of the Temporary Commission, that I had been put at the head of the Disarmament Section. The Permanent Commission, not illogically, tried to cold-shoulder me and rely solely on the three service officers in my staff. I solved the problem by ignoring it, and while I left each of my service subordinates to act as secretary of the Subcommission dealing with his own speciality (land, sea or air) I took my seat next to the President whenever the full Committee sat. Gradually I conquered the sympathy of all those soldiers, though, as I shall presently relate, not always their acquiescence in this or that; but in any case, we grew friendly enough for me to pull their legs on a memorable occasion.

Mathenet was not my first French assistant. He came to replace Monroe, who had studied with me at the Paris School of Mines and gone over to the Army.

He was the most capable of my aids, who was to rise to division general during the war and, after a period as a retired officer in Marraquesh, would return to Marseilles with his Moroccan orderly as his man servant, who stabbed him to death. Mathenet was too intelligent not to see the need for some incipient world government, though too wise to be sanguine about its early realisation. Leone, the Italian airman, held similar views. Arocha, the Venezuelan diplomat, was wholly indifferent to the issue. The two successive British naval officers never did as much as look at the thing. For them the British Navy was good enough. The first note I got from Paymaster Hodge was signed W. Hodge R.N. I sent it back with a request that he struck out R.N. which had nothing to do with his international job – and pay. He took it very well, gracious and unruffled, since, after all, everything, he, me and the League and his 'R.N.' and my striking it out, everything rested on the British Navy.

This world that had so far flourished as the PAX BRITANNICA was ruled by an aristocratic-bourgeois élite some of whose members came to Geneva to lead the League. The most picturesque of these aristocrats was Arthur Balfour. Towering by his mere stature above the average European crowd, whom he had to look down upon, he was unable to hide his superciliousness because it was too natural for him to be aware of it. He was scrupulously polite to that pack of foreigners; and scrupulously consciencious about his duties. His red face, white hair, piercing eyes behind his *lorgnon*, sceptical mouth, solid, unshakable demeanour, added up to a landmark in any crowd like a church tower in an old city.

His mordant wit was as active in public as in private. At the Council table, on hearing Tittoni demand a fairer distribution of natural wealth, backed with the acid remark that Italy was buying coal at the price of bread, Balfour countered by demanding a more equitable distribution of sunlight between Italy and Britain.

Léon Bourgeois was a French statesman of more weight and prestige in his day than he seems to have managed to retain with the passage of the years. He had acquired his reputation as the theoretician and ideologue of the French radical party, which he tried to endow with a lay philosophy on the basis of human solidarity founded on reason. The birth of the League, to which he contributed a good deal, caught him on his decline. He was already in his body a very old man, no matter his actual age, and while still a dignified figure, his noble features framed in silver hair and beard, he had to move slowly on unwilling feet, with the help of his faithful secretary, an old spinster who answered to the name of Mlle Million.

Little more than a glimpse remains in my memory of Tittoni, the aristocrat who then represented Italy in the Council and Assembly. I was much better acquainted with his successors, Salandra first and then Scialoja. On the other hand, I grew to know very well Quiñones de León, the nobleman who represented Spain at the Council though he rarely troubled to come to the Assembly. Typical of him, too, not that he was undemocratic or anti-parliamentarian, but simply because he thought that human affairs are best transacted between a cigar and a glass of sherry, *sotto voce*, and by as few persons as possible.

He probably was the most aristocratic of the lot; as his very name implied, for he was the scion of an old Leonese family who, early in life, had emigrated to Paris as the best place for him to spend his large fortune. He spoke perfect French, more distinguished than cultivated, and was as fond of the good things of life as he was indifferent to the joys of the mind. His favourite quotation was: '*Un peu de joie, un peu d'amour, et puis bonjour.*' But he was a shrewd, able, and nimble ma-noeuvrer, and there was little he could not achieve if he were given freedom of action and time. His reddish, round, chubby face, with a dumb mouth but clever eyes, was always welcome everywhere.

An anecdote will clearly convey the gist of his shrewd yet naïve per-sonality. Towards the end of a long morning Council sitting, when everybody round that table had been having hallucinations of caviar or other hors d'oeuvre, and as the President was on the point of declaring the sitting closed, Quiñones asked to speak. Everybody's eyebrows went up. Quiñones never spoke in public. All his Council work was done in hotel halls or private drawing-rooms. He noticed the fact and felt the cause of it; for he was as sensitive to a good lunch as every mother's son. So he appeased his colleagues in words that deserve a twig of immortality: 'Oh, Mr President, it will take no time. It is a matter of no importance whatever. A mere matter of principle.'

Now, the most remarkable thing about this remark is that no one laughed and no one was shocked. Everybody knew he believed in noth-ing but power and national interest. Yet, perfect diplomat though he was, he had gate-crashed into diplomacy by way of worldly relatives. He had served as honorary secretary at the Spanish Embassy in Paris for many years before the King took the bold course of having him appointed Ambassador; and he could tell many stories of the Paris he had enjoyed to the full as a wealthy young man. He lived then in Versailles from where he had himself driven to the office in his landau by a pair of wonderful chestnuts. He once told me himself, when I was his successor in Paris, how once, as a young secretary, having arrived at the Embassy an hour late, and as he tried to explain his delay to the Grandee, his Ambassador, as due to some amorous adventure the night before, His Excellency countered: 'That is no excuse, my young friend.

I am an older man than you are; and I serve the Ambassadress every night, yet I am at my desk at nine o'clock every morning.'

These aristocrats took their right to govern as a matter of course. They considered the Council as the Cabinet of the World and the Assembly as a nuisance. They were somewhat taken aback when the Assembly refused meekly to follow their plan that it should be split into commissions to work hard and talk little; and insisted on beginning with a general debate. In the end, the balance achieved between the two bodies was reasonable and worked well; a fact which may have been due just as much to the aristocratic resistance of the Council as to the democratic urge of the Assembly, not to speak of Drummond's skill.

While the aristocratic human element prevailed in the Council, its meetings were as simple as they were dignified. Room B of the Palais des Nations (the old Hotel National), elegantly but very simply decorated in blue, was the usual venue; at one end of it, the long table for the members of the Council and the Secretary General; a few chairs behind for officials both national and international, and within a couple of yards, the rows of chairs for the public. It was all almost like a private gathering. But lo and behold, suddenly Europe went left, and socialists turned up from everywhere. Lord Parmoor, Beneš, Vandervelde, Paul-Boncour, all socialists; and soon a silken rope separated the great from the crowd, the table was raised on to a platform at least two feet from the ground trodden by the people, and everything was grand and eloquent.

CHAPTER IV

CHIEF OF THE DISARMAMENT SECTION

I had never turned my mind on to the problem of disarmament until I was entrusted with it, indeed, in a way, to be responsible for it; for no delegation could be trusted to deal with anything *an sich*, since they all were conditioned by their national limitations; and while, up to a point, these limitations also afflicted the members of the Secretariat, we all felt a definite moral pressure to induce us to try to overcome them.

This moral pressure was more or less successful according to the nation and to the individual. It would be invidious to attempt a list of nations graduated from this point of view; but it is only natural to surmise that the most resistent to the internationalist drive were the nationals of the big powers, though nationals of small nations with a grudge could also be very dour.

It is only fair to record here the splendid example of world discipline Sweden gave then to all nations big and small in the matter of the Aland Islands; for while there were, of course, sound reasons to decide, as the Council did, that they should be awarded to Finland, no one disputed the fact that the Alanders were Swedes and wanted to belong to Sweden; so that a rebellious attitude on the part of Sweden would by no means have lacked supporters of a genuine, objective character. Sweden's self-denying acquiescence in the Council's decision did much to strengthen the young institution.

At the risk of falling myself into that nationalism I was criticising, I venture to suggest that we, Spaniards, were amongst the best prepared to enter the new era of world relations, owing perhaps to a combination of qualities and defects, and to the education to which we have been submitted at the hard school of history. After all, as I used to put it to my American audiences, Spain is an Empire builder retired from business, and knows many of the tricks of the trade, as well as the frustration that awaits even the successful imperialist. I have heard more than one American with a couple of decades of experience of the Philippines express admiration for the mere fact that Spain kept the island in relative peace for over two centuries. And the three centuries during which 'Latin' America was Spanish compare favourably for both peace and prosperity with the century and a half during which she has been

30

independent in name but fairly (or should I say unfairly) dependent on the U.S.

There is a quality-defect in the Spaniard that prepares him for world citizenship: his individualistic urge that tends to place him in an attitude of antagonism to collective pressure amounting to pre-rebellion. This feature combines with his tendency to neglect the middle stretches of life between the two extremes of the Self and All. A concrete example may impart substance and clarity to all this: twice in this warlike twentieth century, Spanish liberal opinion has been confronted with a mighty split among her friends; and twice, in 1914–18 and in 1939–44, the greater and the more enlightened part of Spain has sided with the Anglo-Saxons. Now the two Anglo-Saxon powers have been the most relentless enemies of Spain throughout history. This can hardly be denied. And yet, in two world wars, the more enlightened Spaniards sided with them, because these Spaniards were able to see the issue objectively, and came to the conclusion that, on the whole, the victory of the West was the lesser evil. This is one of the most remarkable cases of self-denial in the service of truth, yet one hardly ever hears about it, least of all from the two Anglo-Saxon nations that benefited from it.

Disarmament seemed to me a puzzling subject to bother about. I came to think of it as an unnecessary fuss, very much as if one took a lot of trouble to ensure that two lovers actually carried on Cupid's business. Let fear of war vanish and armaments will soon be discarded. No one goes about with a revolver in his pocket in the streets of Geneva, but one does sometimes in Shanghai or in Chicago. In other words, disarmament seemed to me a natural phenomenon which would occur of itself if the necessary conditions prevailed. But these conditions had nothing to do with armaments.

These conditions were political, not technical. And a glance at the picture Geneva offered then to the observer could only drive the point home. By and large, the British were the motive force and the French the chief resistance in the drive for disarmament. This was at first sight paradoxical, for there seems to be no reason why these two powers should not look upon disarmament in exactly the same perspective. This, however, may be the moment to relate that Austen Chamberlain, (he told me so, himself) when Secretary of State for Foreign Affairs, used to have on his desk my book on *Disarmament*, open at a particular page; so that, if need be, he could ask his interlocutor to read this sentence: 'it is not altogether impossible to bring the French and the British to see eye to eye – only their eyes are so different . . .'*

* *Disarmament*, Oxford University Press, 1929. p. 20.

From the time Spain abdicated as the paramount European power, Britain and France have led the historical evolution of Europe and, therefore, of the world. In the course of this co-leadership, cooperative in matters of the mind, inimical in political matters, France and Britain have developed certain habits, chief of which may be considered the French tendency to organise the nations of Europe as a ring of suburbs round Paris, and the British tendency to favour the second most powerful continental nation against the first.

Having fought the first world war on the side of France against Germany, in virtue of her chief acquired habit, this very habit demanded that Britain should now favour beaten Germany against France. This situation it was that provided the British drive towards disarmament with spirit and force; and it also explains why the British were so utterly unable to see why the disarmament they demanded on land should extend at all to the sea. The rest was arguing.

When it came to arguing, you could trust Viviani, one of the most successful of French barristers. When he took the Chair of the Temporary Mixed Commission, he devoted a powerful speech to a picture of the world in which every nation was anxiously watching her neighbour over the frontier, for fear of another war. When he sat down, knowing, no doubt, Cecil would not let that pass unchallenged, he whispered to me to let him have a quick translation of what the British chief delegate would be saying, without waiting for the official translation by the interpreter. I did so, and when I came to 'I don't see every nation entertaining such fears, and anxiously watching her neighbour over the frontier. Spain is not. Britain is not,' Viviani turned to me and asked: 'Has he really said Britain?' 'Of course he has.' He seized a piece of paper and scrawled: 'Why don't you let us build the Channel Tunnel?', and shoved it along the table.

It was an apt repartee. Indeed, Viviani hit the very bull's eye of the issue; for Britain's stubborn refusal to build the tunnel was, has been, is perhaps still, the symbol and the core of what was at stake in that strange, protracted duel between her and France on – of all things – disarmament. But was it about disarmament? Of course not. It was – let there be no illusions on the point – a duel about power. When that sitting was over, and the delegates were gone, only a handful of men remained around Viviani. All but I were Frenchmen; but my long life as a student in Paris often made Frenchmen forget that I was not one of them. Viviani gave vent to his feelings with no inhibition whatever: 'We have won this war, haven't we? Then, we have the right to do as we please.'

He was less inhibited in form than but not different in substance from

... I was going to write: Cecil; but Cecil was no ordinary Englishman and while, had I written his name there, my sentence would not have been altogether wrong, it would have required qualifications, which I have endeavoured to outline in a later chapter on his work and Murray's. The fact remains, though, that power was in those days no less the stand of the British than that of the French.

It was, of course, a duel strongly coloured by subjective attitudes; previous to and independent from disarmament itself, therefore, apt to manifest itself *à propos* of every other issue. In fact everything went on as if, for lack of any common adversary, France and Britain had chosen the League as the arena in which to fight each other. One of the most picturesque aspects of this rivalry was the two-fold struggle that went on for years between the crusade against the traffic in opium and the crusade against what in those days was known as the white-slave traffic.

Both fell under the general supervision of Dame Rachel Crowdy, a gifted and attractive English spinster, faithfully served by a strong, hefty, masculine and rather handsome Irish woman by the name of Figgis who owned a fine farm of Irish bulls.

Opium, however, was only in theory under Dame Rachel. In fact it was the diocese of Alfredo Ernesto Blanco, an incredible yet genuine Spaniard who had a truly episcopal way of rubbing his hands as if soaping them, in an unctuous and priestly gesture. He had come into the world in Bordeaux, spoke perfect French and English, fairly good Spanish and – I was assured – excellent Chinese, which he owed to twenty-seven years in the International Customs Service of China. Whatever hair he had kept was fair, his eyes were blue, his skin rubicund, his face chubby, and he displayed one of those mouths with fleshy lips ever gathered to a point as if to kiss which the French unceremoniously describe as *une bouche en cul de poule*.

There was little that Alfredo Ernesto Blanco did not know about China, and I suspect that what he didn't he just made up, which can hardly be done without a good deal of real knowledge as raw material. Once, on hearing that I was to receive General Hsu at 11 a.m., he rang me up asking to come and see me first. He told me that General Hsu was interested in disarmament because he had been sent by Chiang Kai Shek to buy arms in Europe; whereupon the Republic against which Chiang was fighting had suggested that he might also buy arms for them, a suggestion Hsu found most reasonable and conforming to the principles of Confucius.

He further told me that while warlord of one of the provinces, Hsu had invited his chief rival to lunch. Hsu gave him a sumptuous meal, enriched by those delicate improvisations in four lines of verse at which the Chinese are masters, and to which the rival guest responded in the same spirit with equally masterly poems. The meal over, Hsu put it to his guest that the least he could do to acknowledge such a feast was to let his, i.e. Hsu's, men cut off his head, since this head happened to be the only object that caused trouble in the whole province – a proposition which the gracious guest again considered reasonable and in complete conformity to the principles of Confucius. 'Then,' concluded Hsu, 'please step down to the courtyard, my men are ready.'

Hsu came and went (while I managed to keep my head on my shoulders), but a few months later, so Blanco told me, he had been received with enthusiasm by his victim's son, in some railway station or other in China, and had even been offered a sumptuous banquet and duly murdered at the dessert, everything, of course, according to the principles of Confucius.

Anglo-French rivalries, we must acknowledge, do not reach that degree of refinement, but they were just as keen; and in those days before the Soviet Union gained enough power to effect a forceful comeback, they provided the League with the dramatic force it needed to retain the attention of the press. Opium and women became the respective weapons of the French against the British and of the British against the French. The French needed the 'women' to relieve the tedium of their armies abroad; the British were in an awkward position over the repression of opium out of whose production and trade a number of their Asiatic possessions made handsome revenues. So did a number of French possessions, but then, the French were not advocating the control of dangerous drugs as a good thing in itself; but only as a counter-weapon against the English drive for the abolition of brothels.

The wave of idealism that had drawn the U.S. towards the League was both strong and genuine; so that when the Harding-Cabot-Lodge conspiracy succeeded in severing the nation from its dream, a vast sector of American opinion was left like the bridegroom whose bride has not turned up at the wedding. The halls and corridors of the League were always crowded with these frustrated lovers of the League.

Nor was this regular migration of American doves merely composed of sentimental admirers; for it included a number of capable, sensible and practical students of world problems as competent as they were disinterested, and whose knowledge of the particular problem they happened to be concerned with rested on solid work at home in one or other of the societies set up in the U.S.A. with that aim in view. The two leading ones were the League of Nations Union and the Foreign Policy Association.

This Association owed a good deal of its success to the backing of Thomas Lamont, whom I thus met in Geneva. Thus began an acquaintance that grew to a friendship based on my side on admiration for that quiet, yet profound and wise man. The Foreign Policy Association also enjoyed the advantage of Raymond Fosdick's leadership. Its specialist on opium questions was Helen Moorhead, a woman who seemed to have been able to combine a masculine mind with a feminine charm and manner. Her constant companion in her relentless anti-opium campaign was Herbert Smith, a wealthy American Jew, one of the finest and most generous minds I have come across.

But though Americans were the most numerous, the crowds one had to walk through when moving from office to bench, from meeting to session, across the thronged halls, were of course thoroughly cosmopolitan, and every nation in the world was represented, even though the Euro-American contingent would be then a good deal higher than now-a-days. Officials were especially sought and even when in haste one was apt to be kept standing by some member of a badly treated minority or a journalist in search of copy.

That is what I thought was happening one day when, cutting through the crowd on my way to my commission, I felt my sleeve pulled sharply. 'Romans. II. 3. That's what you should read. Remember. Romans. II. 3.' I had recognised the warm, slightly raucous voice of Nancy Astor. I tried to imitate one of those wonderful obscurations à la Drummond and look as if I hadn't understood a word. 'Yes. Romans II. 3. Don't you ever read the Bible?' – 'I never read bawdy books,' and before she could recover, I cut the painter and fled leaving her like a red rose all thorns out.

There was, no doubt, a chaotic element in the crowd which surrounded the League's work in those days; owing to the very richness of the trends, drives, pushes, causes and crusades that converged there, criss-crossing at all angles and pointing in all directions. But this simmering and at times bubbling and boiling, of so many opinions and abnegations witnessed to the fermenting power of the universal hopes that the mere birth of the League had awakened. Unknown to most of us, what was happening then was the beginning of a world public opinion, the dawn of the feeling of world solidarity which was to transfigure world affairs within a generation.

CHAPTER V

THE CIVIC MONKS*

MANKIND had been through its first world war, and was just awakening from a nightmare. Worse nightmares were still to come; but those men who gathered in Geneva to start a new era of peace were mercifully ignorant of that future that lurked waiting for them or their children. They had been called to the town of Calvin by another Calvinistic, upright, austere soul: Woodrow Wilson. And at his call, though in his tragic absence, they were trying to inaugurate the era of world co-operation for peace.

Though Woodrow Wilson had been the chief official architect of the League, the idea and the force behind it had been born simultaneously in many lands, neither last nor least in England. This idea-force could easily appeal to Englishmen as the extension or prolongation of their own familiar concept of the King's Peace. It was but natural that the desire to widen the scope of the King's Peace to world affairs should arouse the interest of that order of British society which by then had for several reigns led and administered the nation; an order which, at the risk of running counter to the egalitarian trends of our day, we might describe as its *aristocracy*, or in other words, its public-spirited and disinterested men.

Two societies for the promotion of the League of Nations were already afield in Britain by 1917: the League of Nations Society, led by Sir Willoughby Dickinson and Aneurin Williams, and the League of Free Nations Association, founded by David Davies, the untiring apostle of the International Force. They differed in that the leaders of the first were apt to stress the value of moral forces, while David Davies believed that moral forces were more forcible when backed with good guns. These differences, however, were not strong enough to prevent an amalgamation of the two bodies, and eventually the League of Nations Union was founded, with Grey as its President and Gilbert Murray as its Chairman. After Lord Grey's death, Lord Robert Cecil became President.

Thus began the collaboration between Murray and Cecil in the great work of the age. Though born in different stations, both belonged to

* First published in Gilbert Murray, *An Unfinished Autobiography* with contributions by Friends. London 1960.

36

the same élite, spoke the same language, felt the same feelings and took the same instinctive attitudes. They are both typical of a class, functional rather than social, the class which by discipline and devotion had kept intact, had indeed increased in the nineteenth and twentieth centuries the greatness of England, which much less devoted and disciplined generations had raised to eminence in the three preceding centuries.

We can watch them gradually expand their earnest cares and concerns from the mere foreign policy of their country to what amounted to the inner policy of the wide world. These two men and the group round them are not content with the old categories: power and patriotism, sovereignty and supremacy, command of the seas. Monks of a civic religion, they differ from what was perhaps the bulk of their brethren in their desire to widen the scope and concept of their deity. Their deity had grown with the centuries from England to Britain, from Britain to the Commonwealth; and now this forward-looking, possibly heretical group of British civic monks aspired to enlarge it still to . . . something wider, on which, however, their own views were not perhaps clear enough.

'I shall be glad to discuss the question of a League of Nations at any time you may wish,' wrote Robert Cecil to Gilbert Murray on June 27, 1918; and on January 4, 1919 he wrote again, inviting him to serve on the Phillimore Committee which he was setting up on the eve of his departure for the Paris Conference. In Cecil's mind, the Phillimore Committee was 'to discuss the draft schemes on which we are working in Paris and to supply us with criticisms and suggestions of its own on the various aspects of the subject.'

Such was the foundation of the fertile partnership between the two British civic monks most devoted to the organisation of peace. Alike enough to work in perfect unison, they differed enough never to make their partnership a boring pulling at the cart by two identical oxen. The gaunt, stooping, clerical figure of Robert Cecil seemed ever drawn forward by an eager zest which one fancied sharpened his long pointed nose and flashed in his powerful eye (only one: in Cecil the other eye did not matter). That cross hanging from his waistcoat pocket witnessed to the religious basis of his political faiths; but the sharp tongue, the determined chin, the large, powerful hand, the air of a man used to being obeyed, proud towards men if humble before God, did suggest that in that tall figure striding with his long legs the thronged corridors of the League, the levels of Christian charity were kept high above the plane of fools.

In contrast with that power in action, that forward motion and forceful drive of Cecil's, Gilbert Murray struck the observer by a quiet, smiling, indrawn strength. His spare figure would seldom be seen

moving about, walking from group to group or from office to office in
the daily weaving of activity; and when in motion, it would be at a
leisurely pace, with an air almost of resignation, and willingness to go
through it since it had to be gone through. One gathered the impression
that Cecil was rather the motor and Murray the brake. There were,
however, other differences, subtle and complex. Cecil was a Christian
and Murray an agnostic. 'Patriotism or any other version of the herd
instinct seems to me an entirely inadequate basis of virtue,' Cecil wrote
to Murray (October 25, 1948). 'Christianity is from that point of view
an explanation of and a support for an essential ingredient in man's
nature – far the best, though necessarily imperfect.'

In the course of a discussion by correspondence in 1943, Cecil writes
to Murray:

> I thought you meant that religious belief involved the sub-
> stitution of the ordinances for the moral law. That no doubt
> came to be true in a degree with certain of the pharisees, may
> be true in a degree with some Christians. But it is not true with
> the Xtianity in which I was brought up. To Xtians of that
> kind God's law and the moral law are and must be identical.
> Hence if it could be shewn that Pacifism was in accordance
> with the moral law I should have to hold that *all* war was pro-
> hibited by Xtianity. If on the other hand, it can be shewn as I
> think it can that there is no such prohibition by the Xtian
> law I cannot admit that the moral law forbids me to support
> my country in a just war.

This wide Christian basis for a civilisation of peace, though not perhaps in the forefront of Murray's thought, was possibly not alien to his
way of thinking as the European that he was. Yet a certain resistance
can be felt in his mind to any excessive, direct claim of Christianity or
Christian beliefs to consider themselves as a world-wide basis for peace
in a planet so full of men who are not Christians. After all, even within
a world of Christians, Cecil himself admitted in that very letter that
what he said about the identity of religious and moral law applied to
'the Christianity in which he was brought up', and not necessarily to
other Christians.

Lord Hugh Cecil wrote to Murray that the League should not be
entrusted with the administration of justice because justice is a matter
of sovereignty, and because the same principles of justice as applied to
individuals cannot be applied to nations. 'Justice between persons is
dominated by the strictly theological dogma that all persons have an
identical status before Almighty God.' And Lord Hugh goes on to say:

'I should like therefore to shift justice behind the scenes and substitute the happiness of human beings as the purpose of all international arrangements.' (Jan. 6, 1936).

Gilbert Murray's answer to this is typical of his stand and mind. First he grants an acquiescence on theory, which however he couches in such terms as to keep him a safe distance from theology. 'About justice: I remember that you took much the same position in your interesting little book on Conservatism for the *Home University Library*. I think, as to ultimates, I rather agree with you, and I should have thought your brother did too.' (Jan. 8, 1936). This reaction to the 'strictly theological' stand of Lord Hugh Cecil is characteristic. When dissenting on not very relevant points Murray would withdraw into silence, unless he were stirred out of his serenity by some strong provocation. Now this, curiously enough, could happen precisely when arguing about these matters of the impact of religious belief on the moral side of politics. Witness, for instance, this curious outburst to Lionel Curtis on how to rebuild the structure of world affairs, an outburst which leaves room for no doubt on the agnostic, or at least unorthodox character of the foundations of Murray's liberalism: 'There is one point where I possibly differ from you, and where I differ violently from Toynbee. He considers that the liberal principles of justice, co-operation, the brotherhood of man, etc., are worthless unless they are combined with a belief in the divinity of Jesus, the Virgin birth, and Lord knows what other bizarre and speculative beliefs. This seems to me pernicious rubbish, leading straight to a revival of the wars of religion and the persecution of heretics.' (Feb. 10, 1939.) Stern words, on so close and so much admired a friend, addressed moreover to the man who had written 'The Commonwealth is the Sermon on the Mount reduced to political terms.'*

So much for the definite differences between an agnostic if deistic Murray and an Anglo-Catholic Cecil as to the dogmatic-Christian bases of their respective endeavours for world peace. But the two other points of Murray's answer to Lord Hugh Cecil are no less worth recording. He begins with a statement of his purely empirical standards for not merely international but all political action: 'the real aim of political action must be something utilitarian: the happiness and welfare of human beings'; and finally, an acute, penetrating application of Lord Hugh's criterion of happiness, to show him how it must bring back into the picture that justice which Lord Hugh had rejected: 'I also agree that justice is often very difficult to define and the just line of policy impossible to discover. Still, psychologically, it makes an enormous difference

* *The Round Table*, December 27, 1930.

to people whether they feel they are getting fair or unfair treatment. . . .
Of course, it would be impossible to give every nation, or perhaps any
nation, what it chooses to consider its just rights, but I think people are
often calmed down, if not actually satisfied, by what they feel to be an
attempt at justice; e.g., if they are not allowed to state their case they
get wild with rage; if they are allowed to state it before a reasonably
impartial tribunal, and then lose it, they grumble but do not feel positively murderous.'

This stand is common sense itself, given at any rate the premise of
aristocratic rule. Common sense is a quality that will never fail Murray.
As late as 1942 and 1943 he was writing to Cecil: 'I am really rather
alarmed at the way people go on talking about the earthly paradise
which we are to achieve at the end of the war. Even Roosevelt's Four
Freedoms, which are all right as aims to work for, become dangerous if
they are treated as promises.' (May 23, 1942.)

One year later he is more explicit still: ' . . . all this talk about "freedom from want" etc. is not only unrealistic but dangerous. We are telling masses of people that, after the war, they are going to be rich and
happy. When they find that they are really poor and miserable, they will
turn against somebody.' (Feb. 12, 1943.) At no point in his public life
does he seem to have strayed from this empirical common sense line of
thought; unlike Cecil, who could be drawn by his impulsive, forward
temperament into rash courses and serious errors of judgement (such as
his advocacy of the International Peace Campaign, a red herring, *c'est
le cas de le dire*). And yet it is by no means certain that Cecil was of the
two the more faithful to principles. 'As you know, I hate principles,'
he wrote to Gilbert Murray. (June 13, 1944.) And though this impulsive,
sweeping statement should be taken with a grain of salt, coming from
a man of such integrity, it does suggest a difference between the two;
Cecil was more of an empirical politician and Murray more of a theoretical intellectual.

Both, however, took their stand on the moral law, and in everything
they did for the world this allegiance to the moral law is implicit.
Writing to Lyttelton about Neville Chamberlain's policy, Murray says:

> I am profoundly shocked at the way he absolutely ignores
> the moral element in politics. Germany and Italy break their
> treaties and announce their intention to make war whenever
> they like, and Chamberlain treats this as a mere difference of
> policy, morally indifferent, and claims that we should be equal
> friends with those who keep the law and those who break it;
> and when we suggest that the nations which mean to abide by
> their covenants should stand together and support one another

diplomatically, he says that is dividing Europe into two camps. (April 14, 1938.)

Murray took his attachment to the moral law very much in earnest, indeed almost passionately, to a suprising degree in such a serene man. There is a letter to Cecil at the acme of the Abyssinian crisis typical both of the depth of his feelings in such matters, and of his capacity to control them for practical purposes. He is writing about a meeting of protest which is being organised by the League of Nations Union. 'Thinking of the Albert Hall meeting, I am convinced we ought to make the subject Collective Security in the full sense, rather than an indignation meeting about Italy.' But he is careful to add a postscript in order to say: 'I may add that I am personally bursting with rage and indignation against Italy.' (April 4, 1936.)

It is doubtful whether any statesman ever went to the League of Nations meetings with a cleaner intent than these two men. Geneva, however, was to be for both of them a constant source of experience, bewildering at times, educating always if not always edifying. Geneva revealed to them nary a thing they had not suspected about the world and perhaps about themselves. The *League* of Nations, as the new institution was called in England, was in fact, as they were not long in discovering, a *society* of nations, as the French more aptly had named it; and this society, by its mere existence, gradually revealed to them the shortcomings of their own position, which they had thought so strong and unimpeachable: their insular prejudices, their aristocratic assumptions, their all too vague yet limited notions of what a permanent peace required.

These good English aristocrats had only thought the idea, not lived the experience, of a society of nations. When they arrived in Geneva, a most awkward discovery lay in store for them: the world was full of foreigners. Neither Murray nor Cecil nor that other upright, honest to God, sincere civic monk, H. A. L. Fisher, failed to register the shock. Fisher is at first delighted to be able to write to Murray: 'There are, so far as I can see, no intrigues, very few symptoms of log-rolling – though there are a few; and a very good tone and spirit in the whole Assembly. The debates have gone smoothly. There has been a general elevation of tone, and in spite of the fact that very few members knew anything of their colleagues before we met a fortnight ago, we are now very good friends and have learnt to work with one another cordially and harmoniously in the Committees of the League.' But he goes on to say: 'Of course, in the full meetings of the Assembly there are, as you would expect, a certain number of purely rhetorical and empty speeches. The Latin races love grandiloquent platitude'. (Nov. 30, 1920.)

Nothing irritates an Englishman more than what he calls sweeping generalisations, particularly when applied to the ways of human beings. Nothing however comes more easily to the Englishman abroad than generalisations about people he dislikes or shrinks from. Note Fisher's. More will be forthcoming. One year later, Murray, who to his regret had not been included in the first British delegation, was sent to the Assembly as a member of the South African delegation, by special instructions from Smuts. His letter to Smuts of October 8, 1921 records his first impressions with delightful freshness. Murray is particularly frank, genuine and even naïve when expressing his somewhat provincial, Nordic shrinking at the mere sight of foreign types: 'At the time one was conscious of many weaknesses in the Assembly: some intrigue, some loquacity, a rather large proportion of small dark Latin nations and so on.' That 'small dark' could not be more revealing. It will be outmatched by Cecil in a letter which with typical impulsiveness begins: 'Dear Gilbert: What lunatics foreigners are!'

All this was up to a point very natural. The civic monks, used to the society of Britain, a society undisturbed for centuries in its peaceful development behind the sea-moat that had protected the island, were bound to find the ways, the languages, the mannerisms of the other members of the incipient world society somewhat disappointing. They were not at first – some of them never were – in a position to realise how much of their disappointment was objective and how much was due to their own insular provincialism. More often than not, when meeting with suspicion, protest, indignation at British ways, they grew indignant themselves at what they thought to be an insult to the obvious disinterestedness of Britain and of her men at Geneva. Were they not transparently disinterested themselves? Was not Britain transparently disinterested, and a natural leader in world affairs just as they were the natural leaders of British affairs?

Read again Murray's opinions quoted above, about the aim of all political activity, and the relations between happiness and justice: 'the real aim of political action must be ... the happiness and welfare of human beings.' Does not this suggest a subconscious or unconscious division of the world between the receivers and the givers of happiness, and even between those who will have happiness defined and measured for them, and the definers and measurers thereof? I may be a heretic on this, as on many other tenets of liberalism; but I should have thought that the real aim of political activity would not be such an elusive, personal and perhaps illusory will-o'-the-wisp as happiness – a thoroughly unpolitical or apolitical concept at that – but liberty, a clear and political concept. So that public men should strive to ensure that every man is free to choose his own road, either to happiness if happiness is his particular hobby, or to something else if something else happpens to urge him on with more power.

The mere fact of selecting the happiness of men as the aim of political activity seems to me to smack of aristocratic government, i.e. a government by civic monks. Now civic monks, and in particular British ones, are admirable people; and I for one might conceivably be persuaded to admit that a government of such men as Cecil and Murray, were it possible, would be by far the best for Britain, and (provided they were able to shake off their subconscious national prejudices – a tall order, very tall indeed) for the world as well. But alas, the world won't have it – nor Britain either.

Similar conclusions can be drawn from the words to Lord Hugh Cecil already quoted: 'It would be impossible to give every nation, or perhaps any nation, what it chooses to consider its just rights, but I think people are often calmed down, if not actually satisfied, by what they feel to be an attempt at justice.' It is all excellent common sense, and perfectly impartial throughout. But in the background there lurks a picture of a world of big, motherly, powerful nations (including Britain, of course, in any case) enquiring what can be done about, and how much can be 'given' to, the 'small dark' ones.

The parallel holds good between the governing and the governed Britons on the one hand, and on the other between Great Britain and the 'lesser breeds without the law' which Britain was to bring within the pale. The assumption, the subconscious attitude was that Britain would rule the waves of international assemblies as she ruled the waves of the sea; that she knew best what was good for the happiness of other nations. And up to a point this was true. Britain had more experienced, more disinterested, wiser civic monks than any other nation that had congregated in Geneva. But other nations had their own ways of understanding what was good for them, and even an exasperating way of preferring freedom to happiness.

Murray's professorial origin and vocation, his lack of parliamentary and diplomatic experience, made it easy for politicians gradually to confine him to humanitarian matters. We can see him learning hard at the school of experience in the description of his work which he sent to Smuts on October 8, 1921:

> I was also made Rapporteur on two subjects: the International Organisation of Intellectual Work ... and the Traffic in Women and Children, which is the name now given to the 'White Slave Traffic'. I thought this was going to be plain sailing, but found it quite the reverse. The French obstructed hard from the first. Hennessy, owner of the brandy and many

race horses, obstructed on Committee, and after the first day
was supported by Hanotaux. Then Mr Balfour came to support me, and things were very exciting. They fought entirely
on points of form. Our position was quite straightforward.
There had been a Conference – very large and good, representing thirty-four nations – which passed unanimous recommendations. These recommendations were embodied in a
Draft Convention put forward by the British Government; we
wished the Assembly to express a 'vœu' that this convention
should be signed then and there by all those Delegates who
had powers from their Governments to do so. The French
wanted to do nothing till they had held another Conference
and got it to draw up a new Convention: to examine the exist-
ing Convention again clause by clause and see if it did not
need amendment or did not go beyond the recommendations:
they said the French and English texts did not agree, that my
motion was out of order, etc. etc. In answer to this I got two
judges of the International Court to sit on a Drafting Committee to see that the French and English texts did agree, and
that the Convention did not in any point go beyond the
Recommendations of the Conference. Then the French kept
proposing 'compromises' which consisted in putting things
off till after the Assembly had dispersed, and waiting till two-
thirds of the States sent in a request for a Convention, and
so on. All these we refused, Mr Balfour being adamant on the
subject, and eventually they brought the matter to the Assembly and were utterly beaten. The highest vote they ever
got was 8 out of 48. It was a mystery to us why they courted
such a rebuff, but Hennessy eventually confessed to me that
they thought the new Convention would hamper them in
running their *Maisons Tolérées* for black troops. However,
I do not think that the delegates themselves knew why they
were obstructing. They were really obeying orders from Paris.
Poor old Hanotaux was dreadfully cross and upset; and
Bourgeois sat silent and avoided the subject.

I did a good deal of work on the Opium Question also,
but thought it better to keep in the background, as I was
becoming *persona ingrata* to the French. The evidence from
India, China and Persia on the Opium Question was curiously
conflicting and interesting.

Now the fact was that the French, uneasy about what they considered the unrealistic policy of the British-led attack against prostitu-

tion, soon learnt tactics consisting in counter-attacking on the opium traffic, which they, rightly or wrongly, thought to be a weak spot in Britain's armour owing to her vast possessions in the Far East. These manoeuvres must have been an eye-opener for our good and pure civic monk; and a glimpse that something of the kind might be afoot would suffice to explain his remark to Smuts that 'the evidence from India, China and Persia on the Opium Question was curiously conflicting and interesting.'

Gilbert Murray's chief activity in relation to the League was, however, to develop in the realm of Intellectual Co-operation. The evidence he left behind shows how limited and provincially British was his approach to the subject, how readily and open-mindedly he learnt from his foreign collaborators and from the subject itself, and what a convinced advocate he became of this (in my opinion) all-important aspect of world affairs.

When quoting from his letter to Smuts, I omitted an incidental remark: 'the International Organisation of Intellectual Work – a somewhat hazy and obscure subject, on which nobody but a few cranks seemed to have any clear views. . . .' (Oct. 8, 1921). With these unpromising words did Murray begin his long career at the head of the intellectual wing of the League. Exactly one month earlier he had written to Lady Mary Murray a remark with which by inference and unwittingly he ranged himself among the 'cranks': 'I see they will put me on to the Organisation of Intellectual Work, a subject that bores me stiff, but I am one of the few people who know anything about it.' (Sept. 8, 1921.) And the next day: 'Today, I have the Assembly, and that beastly Intellectual Travail . . .' His repugnance was to remain as strong as ever throughout the Assembly, as reflected in his correspondence with Lady Mary. 'The afternoon from 3 to 7 was spent in a devastating and drivelling discussion on Intellectual Labour. A Serb . . . spoke twenty times, each time worse than the last. A Greek was mad, and Hennessy, the Frenchman, spoke about fifteen times. . . .' (Sept. 10, 1921.) 'Now I must go to the Assembly again, to report on Intellectual Work. This subject is almost a joke . . . I hate reporting to that indifferent Assembly on Int. Work!' (Sept. 21, 1921.) But is it not possible already to perceive in these words the first glimmer of a change? Here is an extract from the next day: 'On Intellectual Work . . . I had to make a longish speech to a tired and inattentive Assembly . . . I find I am getting interested in the wretched business, from having to explain and defend it!'

In the following year the Committee for Intellectual Co-operation has been constituted. Bergson has been elected President and Gilbert Murray Vice President. He writes to Lady Mary that he was 'impressed by Madame Curie'. He was soon working with his usual earnest zeal and even zest on this aspect of world affairs which he had approached with so much scepticism. To be sure, his humour is ever ready to sparkle over men and things in the company of wits, for as a true sage he is both in the game and out of it, interested and disinterested. Two letters to Isobel Henderson, written in July 1931 when he was already President of the Committee, are worth quoting at some length, for they make up as lively a picture as one might wish of that illustrious body.

> You always like to hear of the highest movements of the European intellect. The Sub-Committee of Experts on the Education of the Jeunesse Mondiale in the principles of the League after two peaceful days lost its temper completely over the question whether certain things were 'instituts' or 'institutions'. They had called themselves 'institutions' in English; so Gallavresi called them so in French. Then Rosset . . . put his hands to his head and cried *'instituts! instituts! Mais c'est ce qu'elles s'appellent elles-mêmes!'* . . . At last I had to ring my bell, and ruled that where their own words were quoted they were to be institutions, if that was the word they used, but where we ourselves spoke of them they were to be Instituts. This gave satisfaction.
>
> Yesterday . . . a really interesting and exciting discussion at the C. d. Lettres et Arts. Paul Valéry and Focillon and Strzygowski were the most original. Old Destrée thought he ought to make an eloquent speech. Looking like a bloated crocodile, with eyes half shut, he held forth on . . . *'le spectacle de la jeunesse moderne dévouée aux jouissances matérielles'* – just as Margaret Wilson, my Secretary, looking very Quakerly and clean, came in. . . . Destrée's secretary had been explaining to her with admiration what a dog Destrée was, how *'il aime toutes les bonnes choses, les vins, les femmes, la musique, les arts, les bonnes viandes'* . . . It was rather like a Shaw play. I persuaded Masefield to speak . . . (July 7, 1931.)
>
> Knowing your love for things of pure intellect, I have to inform you (i) that only once did Painlevé leap screaming into the air . . . to prove that the plan of the Comité d'Etudes was not a plan . . . (ii) that De Reynold, the leader of the Swiss Catholics, has been possessed by a devil. Thus: Mme Curie, *à propos* of nothing and entirely out of order, said that M. Paderewsky ought to be a member of the Ctee. of Lettres. I said she was out of order. Painlevé said *'Mais nous déraillons, nous déraillons absolument.'* But De Reynold, who had been looking at a new translation of the Kalevala . . . told Mme

Curie that he thought M. Kalevala ... would be even better than M. Paderewsky. She, nice woman that she is, said she did not know M. Kalevala. ... Whereupon De Reynold invented a wonderful Cursus Vitae for him. I hope she will never find out. It was a shame ... P. Valéry, Strzygowski, Thomas Mann, Focillon and Jan Masefield all enjoyed themselves. Hélène Vacaresco ... begged Jan to go and sit with her and form a Poets' Corner, but the Chairman (G.M.) instantly adjourned the meeting and Jan got out of the window. (July 19, 1931.)

There is a remarkable contrast in two letters dated December 14, and December 20, 1936. 'Tomorrow at 8.15 I start on my disgusting travels: two-and-a-half days of LNU Council in London, then eight of Int. Co-op: in Paris: for all of which – do you know old Mr Roberts, a tall and stately clergyman with aphasia, who was asked to say grace ... and said: "to all of which, O Lord, we most strongly object".' Thus on December 14th from Yatscombe. But on December 20th, from Paris: 'I am having five days of ten here, and am feeling some surprise that my colleagues really are very able men in their way ... De Reynold wanted us to cut loose from the League and be autonome. Julien Cain discussed how far we had differed from *"l'ignorance ou les caprices de l'Assemblée – je laisse le choix des noms à M. De Reynold."* De R: *"J'accepte tous les deux".'*

From then on his correspondence bears witness to his growing interest in the Committee and his growing conviction of the value of its work. He begins to object to the niggardliness of a number of Nations, notably the Dominions, towards the Committee; he worries about the effect of nationalism and vanity. He hopes that the appointment of Henri Bonnet as head of the Institute in Paris will strengthen and widen the scope of the work; on December 8, 1938, he writes to Smuts a letter of praise of the work of Intellectual Co-operation, and even says: 'I have often wished that you might come over and lead a philosophical *Entretien.*' And so convinced does he become of what at first he had sneered at that he writes to Isobel Henderson: 'Any malediction that you care to think out and utter against Lord Halifax will have a warm echo in my heart. He has again refused to contribute a penny to Intellectual Co-operation. They give £150,000 to national propaganda by the British Council.' (December 22, 1938.)

Such things as the inveterate tendency of the British Government to spend no money on international institutions of an intellectual kind would probably induce searchings of heart in the man who had gone to Geneva assuming that all would be, if not well, at least tolerably normal, when foreigners had been coached by British civic monks in the art of governing the world.

From this point of view the discussions on disarmament were typical. In those days, for Britons keen on disarmament the black sheep was France. That France should wish to ensure herself by her own means against another war (such an insurance was still possible then) did not seem to enter the heads of the disarmers. The size and power of the French army were a constant source of criticism and concern in Britain. Why exactly it would be difficult to say. But what made matters more difficult still in the international atmosphere of Geneva was the inability of the British to see the superiority of the British Navy at sea in the same light as that of the French Army on land. When Simon at the 1932 Disarmament Conference, discussing big tanks, said he could not define an elephant but he could tell one when he saw it, I asked him if he could tell a whale when he saw it. This was one of the points which made the English misunderstood, for the Continentals would not be content with less than 'hypocrisy' and 'dark designs'; while the real explanation was in most cases the happy incoherence of British empiricism.

Murray's mind was too alert to remain bogged by the conundrum of disarmament. With his usual intellectual honesty he writes to Wegerer (April 25, 1932) that there may be in the British attitude an element of 'unconscious hypocrisy'. This remark shows how shrewd he was apt to be when his attention was awakened. He was to experience at close quarters the difficulties raised in the path of the British at Geneva by this complexity of their attitude, particularly in the matter of disarmament.

The trouble with disarmament was (it still is) that the problem of war is tackled upside down and at the wrong end. Upside down first; for nations do not arm willingly. Indeed, they are sometimes only too willing to disarm, as the British did to their sorrow in the Baldwin days. Nations don't distrust each other because they are armed; they are armed because they distrust each other. And therefore to want disarmament before a minimum of common agreement on fundamentals is as absurd as to want people to go undressed in winter. Let the weather be warm, and people will discard their clothes readily and without committees to tell them how they are to undress.

Then, disarmament was tackled at the wrong end. A war is the *ultima ratio* in a conflict; a conflict is the outcome of a dispute that has got out of hand; a dispute is the consequence of a problem that has proved insoluble; a problem is born of a question that has not been tackled in time. Disarmers would avoid wars by reducing armaments. They run to the wrong end of the line. The only way is far more humdrum and modest. It consists in dealing day by day with the business of the world. It follows that disarmament is an irrelevant issue; the true issue being the organisation of the government of the world on a co-operative basis. Now this was one of the chief points on which the British in the League were adamant. The League was to be a League, not a Society; it was to deal with peace and war, not which humdrum facts and relations between nations. With the years Murray came to understand how wrong this position was. In his later documents he refers more than once to the necessity of developing the non-military, non-political aspects of the League, which the several governments, and particularly the British, kept starved.

But the years must also have brought home to him the inevitable developments of the stand which he and his brother civic monks had taken on world affairs. For the path is plain that leads from renunci-ation of war to that of the fruits of past wars which have to be kept by force or by threat of force. This, the ultimate lesson to be learnt by every sincere internationalist, no matter his nationality, was bound to be particularly painful to Britons; for Britain then had, and still has, domains acquired by active force and kept by potential force. In this process of self-enlightenment Murray was no doubt helped by three international tragedies: Manchuria, Abyssinia, Hitler. He was not always of the very first to see the red light. His best case was that of Mussolini; he was perhaps slowest with Hitler. His indignation about Mussolini has been recorded in the preceding pages. On June 8, 1931, he warns the Fichte Bund that their propaganda is causing great harm to the cause of Germany in England; but on October 10, 1933, he writes to Austen Chamberlain an astonishingly optimistic letter which deserves quotation:

> I have been very much disturbed by the educational policy of the Hitlerites; it goes, of course, dead against the under-takings which the members of the League have given, and my C.I.C. colleagues will, I think, make some representations about it. The best hope that I have is this: though the German people are kept quite in the dark about foreign opinion and about the doings of the Nazis, the German Foreign Office and Hitler himself must see that they are leaving themselves without a friend in Europe and creating all kinds of unnecessary dangers. Won't the result of all this be an order from headquarters to right-about-face? And the German nation, being accustomed to obey orders from above, will probably obey. I do not think all this mili-tarism is quite as dangerous or really deep-rooted as it would be if it appeared, say, in France or America. Most of the Nazis

I have spoken to seem not to like the Goebbels propaganda, but they do not dare to oppose it openly.

Three years later, however, he wrote to Crozier of the *Manchester Guardian*:

> By the way, I am getting really alarmed at the flood of anti-French feeling in the English papers. Hitler makes it quite clear in *Mein Kampf*, and has since repeated it to Brüning, that his policy is 'to bring France to her knees by the help of Great Britain', and I think he has chosen a very ingenious way of doing it. He breaks his treaty at a point vital to the French, where we are legally but not morally or emotionally bound. If we acquiesce here, what shall we do when he makes aggressions in Czecho-Slovakia or Austria, where we are bound by no special treaty? My own view is that we ought simply to have replied to him that by violating the Treaty of Locarno, Germany has forfeited the protection of the Treaty, whereas France and Belgium retain it. Thus, the result of this action is not to divide us from the French but to align us up with France and divide us from Germany. I believe that would have been enough, and we could have done it without any consultation.

For such a man the behaviour of the Nazi Reich on the one hand, and that of the Soviet Union on the other, was bound to act as a kind of spiritual rack. The world of nations was not just a society which had been somewhat given to disorder, and which a number of years under civic monks would gradually canalise into some sort of King's Peace; it was a meeting of rivers of passion rushing at each other from fierce and dark upper valleys, where the tribal totems still exacted human sacrifices. No one should blame Gilbert Murray if towards the end of his life he seemed to have returned to a more conservative attitude. In the notes, letters and speeches of his later years he insists on a somewhat (for him) new set of values: patience, tolerance of situations even if not so good as one would wish; inequality of men and nations. The civic monk has become a sage – through disenchantment.

CHAPTER VI

VARIATIONS ON DISARMAMENT

W HEN I left the League for the University, I kept faithful to the oddity of my very odd life by leaping from the directorship of Disarmament in Geneva to the Chair of Spanish Studies at Oxford; and so no one need wonder at the odd fact that my first book as Professor of Spanish Studies was one on *Disarmament*. Fresh from the struggle, I described its peripeties, and, referring to the difficulties encountered, I wrote:

> Let us imagine an international question theoretically soluble; an open fortress. The barbed wire of psychological differences would still remain to be crossed. For think of the composition of an ordinary League Commission. The discussions, carried on in several dozen varieties of French and English are fed by intellectual waters coming from all climates and lands – white, yellow and brown, Catholic, Protestant, Orthodox, Moslem, Buddhist, atheist, old tradition and new progress, the abstract, the empirical, the impatient, the traditional, the sceptic, the enthusiast, the obvious and the enigmatic; the soloist who commands the powerful blasts of French eloquence, the virtuoso who performs on the violin of Italian dialectics; the master who controls the fifes and drums of English persuasiveness, and the perfect artist who plays impeccably on the wide and subtle registers of Japanese silence.

But that picture was fixed in space. Complications were multiplied by the action of time. The great Bruno Walter told a story about a flautist whom he corrected on the phrasing of a melody adding to his correction: 'Let me take this opportunity to thank you for your assiduity, for here we are at our last rehearsal and you are the only one in the orchestra who has not had himself replaced by a substitute on one or other of our days of work.' To which the flautist answered: 'I regret, though, Sir, that I shall not be able to play at the public performance.'

This situation obtained only too often at the League. When a government had at last been convinced to play in tune with the others, it fell. The orchestra kept going but the musicians were often different and demanded different works. This was in particular the case with disarmament. The three steps towards failure which the League took – the Treaty of Guarantee, the Protocol, Locarno – were due to changes in the London leadership, a kind of ballet the League had to dance at the behest of the flighty public opinion of Britain.

When I took over, my first task was to gather and present to the Council and Assembly the answers sent to the Secretariat by the nations of the League to the most naïve of questions: Why are you armed? The answers amounted all to the same: 'I wish I didn't have to be, but my neighbours are such a nuisance!' They, of course, cancelled each other out. The leading spirit was Lord Robert Cecil. But during this first period, up to 1924, Lord Robert represented no one but himself, and even when he came as a British delegate he was given more rope than other delegates partly because his prestige in Geneva paid handsome dividends in terms of British prestige, partly because the State and its government tacitly reserved their right and power to disown him, as indeed they eventually did.

His first approach was politically and empirically sound, if lame in substance: France had only consented to give up a Rhine frontier in exchange for a guarantee that she would be defended by the U.S. and Britain if attacked by Germany. After the defection of the U.S. France did not consider the mere Covenant as a solid enough guarantee. Lord Robert proposed her a treaty in which this guarantee would be explicitly re-affirmed, but, as a *do ut des*, for a no less definite measure of disarmament. Such was the plan submitted to the 1922 Assembly through its Third Committee, of which I was Secretary, and which became the famous Resolution XIV. We worked all the winter on the treaty suggested by this resolution. 'We' were Cecil, Henri de Jouvenel, Attolico and I. We had to evolve a legal-diplomatic instrument that would embody the ideas of Disarmament and Security in close association. Cecil, stubborn though he could be when he believed he was right – which often happened and often rightly so – could be admirably supple in the seeking of formulas. Henri de Jouvenel was an easy-going, well mannered, good companionable sort of Frenchman, first and foremost a journalist, but in the grand style; not, perhaps profound or fond of exhausting any question that went his way, but shrewd and original for all that, as well as, like most Frenchmen, a master in the use of his language. Attolico was by then already oppressed by the new Fascist regime, which he disliked more than he dared say, so that he always kept a corner of his eye and half an ear on Rome. I was beginning to feel that my special usefulness to the League might well spring from my gift to fit other people's thoughts and intents into an adequate verbal expression in both French and English, a gift composed of a natural literary vein and of a certain neutrality or disinterestedness as to the issues in dispute, sometimes achieved not without some throttling of my own preferences.

This was therefore not merely a case of verbal intuition. I was already beginning to elaborate the parallel between the English, the French and the Spaniards that I was to publish in 1928, for which no more ideal laboratory could have been imagined than those long sittings watching the Englishman and the Frenchman at loggerheads, endeavouring to bridge over their differences by means of subtle, verbal girders. These differences did not hit my mind in an abstract sort of way: they broke the even surface of our talk on concrete issues of power and diplomacy; and by dint of 'solving' them with verbal ability, dexterity, trickery, juggling, I was generally led to a healthy scepticism on the very work that was absorbing so many hours of my life.

This work went on for months thanks to Cecil's persistence and driving power. The outcome of it all was the *Treaty of Mutual Assistance* which the Fourth Assembly (1923) examined, amended and approved. But when this text, so laboriously chiselled, arrived in London, the cabinet had changed. Ramsay MacDonald, the new Prime Minister, a pacifist, rejected the Treaty, and, what is more remarkable still, founded his opposition on the military shortcomings of the plan, using thereto arguments one had read before in French military criticisms of it. The mystery is transparent. MacDonald's negative welled up in him before any arguments had come to his head. He gave orders to have a negative letter prepared to send to Geneva, and his services relied for arguments on their military advisers, who, in their turn, looked up their French colleagues' well-reasoned texts.

It is my personal experience that the military, naval and air 'advisers' of the British Government were never more powerful than during that brief Labour spell. While waiting one day in the Council room a few minutes before the sitting in which the Council was to decide whether the Permanent Advisory Commission should or should not deal with a specific point (which the French experts wanted to discuss and the British did not), one of my British naval friends said to me: 'I warn you that, no matter what the Council decides, *we* shall not discuss the point for we have no instructions.' And I, pointing to Lord Parmoor who, being the representative of Mr Ramsay MacDonald and of the British Government on the Council, was in my innocent opinion the head of the whole British Delegation to the Council in Geneva, said: 'Why, just ask him.' And my naval friend: 'He won't do. Our instructions come from the Admiralty.' Mr Ramsay MacDonald's instructions came also from the Admiralty, and from the War office, when he signed that extraordinary letter of July 5th in which the first question he raised in connection with the Draft Treaty was: 'Are the guarantees contained therein sufficient to justify a State in reducing its armaments?' This sentence must have thrilled Colonel Requin of the French General Staff (Geneva Division). Mr Ramsay MacDonald is made to conclude that the Treaty is not effective from the military point of view, but, though that is bad enough, worse is still to come. 'His Majesty's Government,' he says, 'are persuaded after careful examination of the Draft Scheme, that if the obligations created by the Treaty be scrupulously carried out, they will involve an increase rather than a decrease in British armaments.' This, by the way, was sheer nonsense. And as it turned out, while the pacifist Ramsay MacDonald refuted Cecil's treaty on the ground that its military guarantee was not sufficient (i.e. the French argument) Herriot, who had succeeded Poincaré, accepted the treaty.

To *Disarmament*, Cecil had sought to add *Security* so as to appease the French. To Disarmament-Security, MacDonald insisted on adding *Arbitration*, and he found a willing co-operator in Herriot, whose liberal views made him sensitive to the issue. The Assembly of 1924, therefore, met under auspicious circumstances. Furthermore, the thorny problem of German reparations had just been solved in London – or so most people believed – and a bevy of Prime Ministers and Foreign Secretaries announced their intention to be present at Geneva.

The British Government having rejected the Treaty of Mutual Assistance, MacDonald had to make good in Geneva, and so the coming *Protocol* was hailed as the new Ark. The enthusiasm of the pacifists of the world was aroused even to dangerous levels, for, on the day Ramsay MacDonald spoke, I nearly lost my life trying to pierce the solid wall of them that blocked the entrance to the Salle de la Réformation. It was not a good speech. The insularity of the British was never more manifest than in their attempts at 'communicating' with the League Assembly. Balfour did not even try. For him, it was not worth the trouble. His distance was not merely horizontal, but vertical. He looked down his nose on all those Europeans and did not even see the others. Cecil was not haughty but he kept somewhat aloof and ironical, and he would hardly conceal his dislike for most of the lesser breeds without the law, least of all when he thought he was concealing it by wrapping it up in the tissue paper of his courtesy.

Ramsay MacDonald was disastrous. He thought it his duty to *demagoguerise*, probably imagining, in his simplicity, that by so doing he came *down* to the level of all that lot down there, blind to the fact that his audience was composed of hard-boiled diplomats, officials, lawyers and experts who held his cheap eloquence in contempt both in itself and because they felt it to be insincere and put on in the hope of pleasing them, so that while he vociferated arbitration and the rule of law, his audience wondered why he had not signed the Hague Court optional clause.

As ill-luck would have it, MacDonald was followed by Herriot, a heavy-bodied, indeed obese, but keen-minded and elegant French intellectual. He once owned to a friend that his secret ambition was to be an orator. 'Well,' the friend retorted, 'there you are. The best orator in France.' But, still disconsolate, he lamented: 'Ah! I should have liked to play the violin, and I have to play the big drum!' This was the man, self-critical and self-demanding, sad perhaps at his looks, for indeed, this professor of history and delicate word-artist looked like a *marchand de vin*. He would never have made MacDonald's mistake. Realising what sort of an audience he was addressing, he made a warm, even eloquent, but well-built and reasoned statement, cordially agreeing on the new emphasis on arbitration and therefore on the trinity of concepts on which our work was to proceed: arbitration, security, disarmament. The two leaders, ably seconded by Beneŝ and Politis, had soon drafted a plan which in the short space of a month, thanks mostly to Beneŝ and Politis who presided over two very hard working Committees, became the Geneva Protocol.

Nothing could be more instructive on the evolution of the political types that the mere creation of the League had initiated than the contrast between Ramsay MacDonald and Herriot on the one hand and Beneŝ and Politis on the other. The Protocol was born of the two speeches shot at the Assembly by the two big leaders amid much noise of rhetorical artillery; it was presented to the Assembly by two didactical men intent on explaining its purpose and architecture and carrying conviction.

In every other way, Beneŝ and Politis were as different from each other as were MacDonald and Herriot. Beneŝ, though an academic by profession, was a politician. Of the politician he had the empiricism, the flexibility, the willingness to bow to the facts of power and to the storms of crisis. An execrable linguist, he spoke many languages, all badly; but was fluent in them and clear in his mind, if not always in his expression. As the member of a small nation of doubtful internal stability and exposed to formidable foreign strains, he was a firm believer in the League of Nations. His nature and style, however, did not arouse him to eloquence, beauty of form, iridescence of ideals or dreams, indeed not even to the quiet but abstract level of academic theory. His was the world of facts and so even his facial features looked as if they were washed smooth by the stream of events, which he seemed both to accept and to oppose by a forward-stooping stance as if he were going out to meet them.

In contrast, Politis seemed to stand or sit back and upright, as if seeking to keep facts at a distance, both in front of and below him; while his features were sharply chiselled and hard, baring the bone-structure of his head and suggesting the articulated framework of his thought. After Beneš had described the set of forces, the political situation, the general picture of insecurity which the Protocol came to remedy, in a speech rich in political wisdom, Politis proceeded to a masterly legal anatomy of the new instrument during which he often referred to the text now of this now of that article, thus rebuilding what he was analysing, without a single note before him. It was a masterpiece of intellectual control. One verbal antithesis: *l'arbitrage ou l'arbitraire*; no fireworks.

The Protocol appealed to the Assembly because it established a, so to speak, automatic way of eluding war and, if hostilities broke out, of pointing to the aggressor. The Protocol, indeed, was a modern version of Roland's mare: it had every quality but it was dead. The U.S. were not yet ready for so much world discipline; nor the Soviet Union. And as for Britain, despite all his vociferous pacifism at the beginning of the month, Ramsay MacDonald did not allow Henderson and Parmoor to sign it even after France had done so. The Conservatives were misleading British public opinion into believing that the Protocol meant putting the British fleet at the beck and call of foreigners – exactly what Mr Shinwell said later of the Treaty of Rome; and in the end the Government fell, and Austen Chamberlain, the new Foreign Secretary, intimated that he wanted to play other instruments and change the score.

One morning, as I was passing from the old building to the new hall, I suddenly came upon him. He was alone, standing by, almost leaning on, a French Empire metal and mahogany desk, smoking a cigarette, his eye-glass on, whose truant reflections enlivened the glint of his eye. He was the very image of the upper class man born to govern. Not a shadow of doubt in his mind that Britain ruled not only the waves but the hills as well, and that the Chamberlains ruled Britain. His courtesy and perfect manners did nothing whatever to lubricate his stiffness, which was by far his dominant feature. He was good enough to explain his plan to me and he quietly but effectively gave me to understand that, for the time being, he would take over and the like of me could relax.

I was, on the whole, inclined to agree, not that any dissent on my part would have made the slightest difference. But I did feel more and more that the problem we all inaccurately and many misleadingly called Disarmament was at its core one of political relations mostly between the big powers, and that in so far as any progress could be made on it – about which I was growing more and more doubtful – it would have to come from an improvement in the relations between the big powers.

The Locarno system may be described as a local 'Geneva Protocol' minus disarmament. It comprised treaties of non-aggression, and of assistance if attacked, between Germany, Belgium, France, Britain and Italy; arbitration conventions between Germany and Belgium, Germany and France, Germany and Poland, Germany and Czechoslovakia; treaties of mutual assistance between France and Poland and between France and Czechoslovakia. These treaties and conventions were an improvement in that some of them were not merely alliances between friends but sets of obligations not to go to war between possible adversaries. The system, however, was defective in that Germany declared inviolable her western but not her eastern frontiers; while Britain and Italy guaranteed this inviolability in the west but not in the east. This was a decision inspired by short-sightedness rather than by prudence. At the time, I wrote: 'We are dealing with faith, which is one of the most delicate imponderabilia in politics, and Great Britain's action in this case, following closely upon her decision not to ratify the Protocol, was bound to result in disastrous moral effects. The first was a general and diffuse weakening of the Covenant guarantees; the second an encouragement to those who feel that the Eastern European settlement is too precarious. These two effects, combined with the fatal solidarity which links together European affairs, constitute a far greater risk of war for Great Britain than a definite pledge to go to war if trouble arose would have been, while such a pledge would have removed a violent solution of the Eastern difficulty from the field of practical politics.' This was written in 1928. Unfortunately it was confirmed by events, so that eleven years later I had to write: 'Because Chamberlain I would not give a fool-proof guarantee to Poland, in 1925, Chamberlain II has felt bound to give her a fool-hardy guarantee in 1939.'

CHAPTER VII

INTERPRETERS

THERE were in Geneva all kinds of interpreters, good, bad and excellent. Some, like Madame Angeli, of the illustrious Rossetti family, could take in a whole speech in English, French or Italian and repeat it in the other two languages without ever taking a note. These were best for Assembly purposes. Others, more used to short talk and swift repartee, were better for committees, and when endowed with tact and political acumen, for the Council. Parodi, for instance, one of the best of his kind, an Egyptian whose bulging eyes seemed ever to be wondering at what he saw, saved more than one situation. Once, when Cecil had allowed his holy anger to overpower his diplomatic reserve, Parodi coolly watered down his statement; and, the sitting over, was rewarded with a noble acknowledgement from the sensible and by then cooler Englishman. Another time, after a whole morning of acrimonious exchanges between the British and the French delegates, Parodi brought about an agreement by means of an obvious mistranslation. He was right; these were not regular texts to be protocolised for ever; but merely temporary verbal agreements between partners tired by their own obstinacy.

Caemerlinck, the interpreter for the Assembly President, had no less delicate problems to solve. Perhaps the most delicate of all arose during the Presidency of Cosme de la Torriente. This Cuban Senator should never have been submitted to the humiliation of having to preside over the League Assembly with as little knowledge of English and French as he could muster. Motta, the Head of the Swiss Political Department, i.e. the Minister of Foreign Affairs, was that year the candidate for the Chair; but owing to his persistent advocacy of the entry of Germany into the League, he had incurred the enmity of France. The French managed to deprive him of his otherwise certain election by providing a candidate with a safe block of votes behind him. This, in practice, meant a Spanish American. The Cuban? Why not?

Alas, he wouldn't do. Not only did he not speak intelligible French, he did not understand it either. He directed this or that, but the Assembly did not know what he meant. He invented a nation: '*La parole est à la Tchekoslavie.*' In the end, Caemerlinck struck on a solution. The President spoke and he, assuming it was French, translated what the President had said into English, then retranslated into French.

Little did I know that some day . . . But this story is for a later page.

Still, the most heroic episode in this lively world of interpretation was enacted by Russell. The story is almost incredible but it was told me by Albert Thomas, who was rich indeed in imagination but totally lacking in fantasy. It happened at the 'Conference' or Assembly of the I.L.O. Spain was then living under the dictatorship of Primo de Rivera, and the working class leader, Largo Caballero, accused the Spanish Government of I do not recollect what heinous crimes against the working class. The Spanish Government representative was a Count who will be designated in this page as J.M. He was, of course, fairly put out, and what with this agitation, the gravity of the issue, and the solemn nature of the event, his French, fairly fragile, went to pieces. He made a vehement speech in some language known only to him, which baffled the shorthand reporters, the précis writers and the translators. So, there they all were with a speech and no text.

'The Lord,' however, says a somewhat optimistic Spanish proverb, 'squeezes but does not strangle.' The interpreter happened to be Russell, and he, of course, was well provided with whisky. He had understood very little of what the minister had said, but he knew Spain, he knew the facts and he had a fairly good idea of the Spanish Government's attitude. Before his blank page, sensibly, he asked himself: 'What would I say in his place?' And he said it. Translators, shorthand writers and précis writers got moving with alacrity, and so J.M.'s (supposedly) French speech was saved for posterity in English.

At this point Albert Thomas's telephone rang. It was lunch time, but he was eating a sandwich in his office. J.M. explained that the speech was crucial for Spain and for his own political career, 'so please let me have a text at once so that I can correct it before it is cabled to Madrid.' Telephones rang and swearing was heard in many languages. A group of translators was set to work in order to revert into French what Russell had improvised in English. About an hour later, the text was sent to J.M. while everybody under Albert Thomas was kept waiting for the catastrophe. At last, the call came through from J.M. to Albert Thomas. 'Perfect. No corrections.' Russell drank another whisky. This time it was paid for by Albert Thomas.

In 1924, Briand became the French head representative. This event was capital, for Aristide Briand was then the best political head in Europe, and a firm believer in the Covenant as a positive instrument for the organisation first of Europe and then of the world. Many years later, when I in turn sat at the Council table, and we were all saddened by his death, I was requested by the *Journal de Genève* to write a column in his honour. I give it here in English as my tribute to this great man.

His figure stooping as if to welcome you, his voice, his eyes, where wit and wisdom shone, his powerful, almost tiger-like jaw, his hands as delicate as those of an artist (a subtle revelation of his statesmanship), his talk now grave now light-hearted but always earnest – for though witty he never was frivolous – his whole life, so rich in movement and variety, is still so near us that memory will not fix it, still less congeal it into one of those ancestral portraits, one of those great-man statues which death petrifies. No. Briand is not dead. Death lacks the power to kill those who have lived in their spirit, as this man did, both tender and powerful, 'softly obstinate' as he himself said in his immortal, moving speech to receive Germany into the League.

In Geneva, he was France. They know who heard him evoke the war that had devastated the sacred soil of his country, and cry out in a voice that came straight from his heart: *Arrière à tout cela*. Those who have not heard and seen him that day will never know how thoroughly one man can incarnate a whole nation. But in Geneva, he was also a new world, made of order and justice, of intelligence and understanding. He knew how to mellow the clarity and the logic of the countries of light with the practical sense, the intuition and the suppleness of the countries of mist. He had the breadth of views of a world citizen, the perspective of a historian, the patience of a wise man. But what made of him the leading spirit, the Moses of our moving and lively exodus towards the Promised Land of Peace, was his faith.

Briand brought to the Council a great intellect, simplicity and, often enough, wit. One day, after a longish intervention on the Saar, Stresemann wiped the sweat from his brow and searched his pockets – in vain – for a cigarette. Briand – a chain-smoker – opened his case and smiled: 'This is all I can offer you, Mr Chancellor.'

Wit, however, in those days was no rarity. Askenazy, the Polish delegate who often sat at the Council table to carry on, year in year out, the Polish-Lithuanian dispute, was so short-sighted that he had actually to rub the page he wanted to read with the point of his nose. The Brazilian Council member, Da Cunha, in very bad French remarked once at the Council table, during those five minutes of banter before business: 'I have met Madame Askenazy. I never believed a word Askenazy said, but now I do not even believe he is short-sighted.'

The French military were obsessed with the idea of *contrôle*. I write it in French because *contrôle* does not mean 'control'. This was one of the blessings and the curses of the League. (Blessings and curses are the heads and tails of events): words that should be the versoes of each other and aren't. The Frenchman expects 'all right' to mean *tout droit* and his all right goes all wrong. Now control really implies power, domination; while *contrôle* is a peculiar French concept which means checking up, verifying, making sure that what the other fellow has bound himself to do is being done. *Contrôle*, therefore, suggests not enough power or not enough confidence in somebody's power.

The Treaty of Versailles and its family – Trianon and the rest – imposed a limitation of armaments on Germany, Austria, Hungary and Bulgaria. Driven by the French Delegation, the Armament Commission prepared a Draft Convention to ensure that the military clauses of these treaties were actually applied. As soon as I read it, I realised that it was simply unreal. It was due mostly to a Frenchman, Colonel Réquin, the most intelligent and forcible member of the Commission, whose will power obviously had, in this case, betrayed his judgement.

I had always managed to keep excellent relations with him, for he was straightforward, indeed, forthright to a fault, and though his grey eyes could be as cold as steel, he often smiled in a friendly way. I may have taken an unnecessary risk, led astray by my incurable tendency for striking sparks of fun from the flint of life; for when he was promoted to General, I wrote him a line complimenting him as the first Colonel promoted on the score of Disarmament.

If he disliked my jest, he never showed signs of it. His promotion, moreover, was still to come when I drew his attention to the inadequacy of the Draft Convention; it was in vain that I pointed out to him that he was expecting the Germans to agree to surrendering to the Allied powers rights and freedoms they had not surrendered to their own Government. 'If the colonel of a German regiment keeps forbidden weapons in his bedroom, are you going to claim the right to enter it?'

Curiously enough, as soon as a mere civilian opposed one of them, the military of the Commission clubbed together; and the British, who would normally have opposed the French, even a Hungarian colonel who should have been on my side if for the wrong motive, since he was already being controlled, all joined in declaring the Convention the very thing that was wanted.

Thus blessed, it went up to the Council, which decided to discuss it in secret. This meant only one delegate per country and no one but Drummond for the Secretariat. The decision, by the way, was imparted to me, not without some glee, by an officious Miss Howard. That pleased me well enough; for though I was deprived of a spectacle which I had relished in advance, I felt that common sense was safe in Briand's hands, free from Réquin's whispers. Furthermore, Briand happened to be President. Yet, when I was in my room, comfortably rocking myself on this pro-con meditation, in ran a panting Miss Howard to tell me the Secretary General wanted me at the meeting.

As soon as I entered the small, quiet room, I realised what was happening. Briand, in his time-honoured way, knew nothing at all about the subject, and Drummond who knew about as much, and had relied on France's, i.e. Briand's, keenness to provide the facts and arguments, got cold feet on realising the President's state of blissful ignorance, and sought my help. In such cases, Briand's tactics consisted in letting everybody speak round the table, after which he knew enough to make up his mind. His conclusion was superb. 'Having heard you all, I must declare that though I do not consider myself as a jurist merely because I have often sat as counsel in civil or criminal cases; yet with what I have kept of law plus what still remains of my commonsense, I find that this Draft Convention is unworkable.' The rest was paper.

The fourth Assembly, 1923, saw the entry of Ireland and Ethiopia. I fancy myself as a candidate for a small niche in the history of the Irish Republic. During the heroic days of 1916, I often saw Art O'Brien and walked along the Strand with Desmond Fitzgerald, ever coolly indifferent to the fact that he was on the run from the British police. I was fairly well aware of the mood and policy of the British Government through Tom Jones, who had signified to Lloyd George his abhorrence of the Black-and-Tan war, and his determination to keep out of Irish affairs until that policy was scrapped.

One morning, my private telephone rang and Tom said: 'L. G. has just told me he has made up his mind. He wants to talk to the rebels.' It was 11 a.m. At one o'clock Tom and Art O'Brien lunched as my guests at the Spanish Club in Cavendish Square. That was the beginning of the Irish Treaty.

I have told elsewhere but cannot resist the temptation to repeat here how one day during the Second World War, I happened to dine next to an Irish author somewhere in Kensington on the occasion of a Pen Club Conference; and how, vain as I am, I described to him my share in the birth of the Irish Treaty. 'Well, you ought to be ashamed of yourself!', the good Irishman blurted out. I recognised the voice of my own people and so saved my vanity; for I have always maintained that the Irish are Spaniards who took the wrong bus and found themselves in the north by mistake. Hence their resentment. And if they are, after all, making good and drinking tea and whisky, poor things, instead of wine and clear, sparkling water, it is not merely because the climate has cooled their hormones, for it hasn't, but because they themselves have been anglicised to an extent they themselves are not aware of. Indeed, it is because they are anglicised that they are independent, for it is England who taught them that Ireland is more important than any Irishman. This principle, *mutatis mutandis*, few Spaniards will ever live up to even if they agree with it. I sometimes think the same fate might have overpowered us if Britain had patiently carried on pushing the frontier of Gibraltar northward while Spaniards were busy proving themselves more important than Spain, and so had reached the Pyrenees.

Oh dear, how far I have wandered from the admission of Ireland. I knew de Valera, who, by the way, could hardly be cited against my theory, for though he arrived in Ireland by way of the U.S. he was Spanish right enough; and I even remembered he had told me once that as 'a guest of H.M.'s' he had asked for a Spanish book to read and had been given the Bible in the translation of Cipriano de Valera. I believe he found (Eamon, not Cipriano, I mean) as much help and guidance as he could wish from this 'countryman' of his, more versed than he was in the corridors and alleys of Geneva.

CHAPTER VIII

GERMANY IN AND SPAIN OUT

THOUGH big and healthy, the League of Nations seemed at times to suffer from a weak digestion. Sickness developed often after she had swallowed a new member. The worst case was that of Germany. From the very first, Germany seemed disposed to be swallowed; but France and Britain, acting as the jaws and the palate, rejected the meal. This made Germany cautious and sensitive, and it was not until September 1924 that her leader, Stresemann, sent in an application of sorts, garnished with a number of ifs and buts, the most prominent, if possibly not the most important, of which was that Germany was to be made a permanent member of the Council at the very moment of admission. The general situation, however, was not favourable. We were then in the trough between the death of the Protocol and the birth of the Locarno treaties; and Germany was very punctilious about sanctions, for, being disarmed, she felt like a stark naked woman at a reception. So time went by, and it was not until February 8, 1926 that her final application was received in Geneva.

The properties of a great power in the League were two: a permanent seat in the Council and a member of the Secretariat at the top, i.e. either as the Secretary General, the Deputy Secretary General or an Under Secretary General. This second condition was easily fulfilled and Drummond, who visited Berlin at the time to adjust all these clocks, saw to it that his new German colleague should be confined to unimportant tasks, so Herr Dufour-Feronce was entrusted with Intellectual Co-operation. The German Government, unwittingly (I assume), helped Drummond by choosing a German with a French name and the manners of an English gentleman, but by no means as shrewd as even the bluntest looking sons of Albion are apt to be. Henri Bonnet, who was by then in charge of intellectual affairs, found it very easy to get along with his new chief.

My memories of Dufour-Feronce are all reminiscent of this short-witted, well-bred, a wee bit too forceful and not subtle enough, German. One day, Manning and I were standing behind the presidency as we often did, at a plenary sitting of the Assembly . . . Sorry, I must digress. So we were, but *another* day, when Manning, thin, long nose, a sun-tanned head sharp towards the chin, wide at the top, a fine mane of prematurely white hair, saw sitting on the edge of the central passage in the long symmetrical nave of the hall, the immense figure of Mlle

Vacarescu, the ugliest (and cleverest and kindest) woman on earth, a poetess of whom it was said that she very nearly caused a throne to crash by sitting on it, the King of Rumania having set his eyes on her – of which there was a lot to set one's eyes on – Manning whispered to me: 'A good thing she's in the middle of the boat.'

That other day, we saw Chamberlain and Stresemann come to the platform and sit facing each other at a tiny table, as tellers for an election to the Council. They looked so much like two mugs, so typical, less of their respective countries than of their caricatures, that the Assembly had to suppress a laugh. And I whispered to Manning: 'It is all very well, but how do we know they can count?" Dufour-Feronce overheard me and was actually furious. He took it as a national insult.

So much for the first condition Germany exacted in order to enter the League.

The other condition, however, led to serious trouble. Theoretically there were two types of members of the Council: the permanent members (i.e. the 'big' powers, who were not elected, since, so to speak, they belonged to the Council *ex-officio*) and the elected members, who normally sat for three years and then gave way to other nations on a more or less group basis (Europe, Commonwealth, Latin America, Asia, etc.). In fact a third type emerged because Spain and Belgium were always re-elected, and thus became *de facto* permanent. It was this group that caused the trouble when Germany was granted a permanent seat.

The storm began in Paris with a campaign in favour of granting a permanent seat to Poland for the sake of equilibrium. When this idea won the approval of Briand in public and of Chamberlain in secret, Spain put in the same claim and obtained the same backing. But Germany, rightly, it seems to me, argued that her permanent seat was one of the by-products and side-conditions of the Locarno treaty and could not be granted in a heap with other concessions to third nations. By then Brazil had put in a fourth claim for permanency.

A special session of the Assembly had been called (March 1926) for the specific purpose of admitting Germany; but the outcome was exactly the opposite of what we all had expected. The Germans, who had sent to Geneva an imposing delegation, had to return home unadmitted. A special committee had to be appointed to study the new composition of the Council. It would not be ready in time and Germany's admission had to wait until the normal September session. Her entry, however, saw the resignation of Spain and Brazil who both left the League while the September Assembly was sitting.

Yet, the report of the Motta Committee should have satisfied them. It proposed the increase of the number of Council members from ten to fourteen. True, Germany alone would become a permanent member; but a new status of no more than three elected members was created who, after their three years, could be re-elected, though by a two thirds majority of the Assembly. Brazil rejected the proposal dramatically and Spain discreetly.

Both were hopelessly wrong even on their own ground. As their Geneva men knew full well, behind their all too loyal silence, the new arrangement was more favourable to them than a permanent seat; for surely, a two thirds majority vote would invest them with more authority than a predetermined permanency which would in any case not suffice to confer on them the gold braid of being a 'big power'.

This, however, must be qualified in the sense that it applies far more to Spain than to Brazil. For Brazil based her stand on representing Latin America, which every one of the Latin American members denied by presenting the Brazilian delegate, de Mello Franco, with a collective request to accept the report; while Spain's claim, far more solid, was based on the fact that she had always been re-elected by a big majority and as a matter of course. Therefore, by insisting on a *de jure* permanency, she gave up this magnificent display which every three years confirmed her as a moral 'big power'.

Quiñones knew all this and knew that I knew it. He was heart-broken at the inept way in which Primo de Rivera had thrown away the strong hand history and nature had dealt him; and suggested that, as the King was to be in Paris on a given date, I should 'chance' to be there and put our case to him. I went to Paris, waited to be summoned to the presence, and at last was rung up by Quiñones who advised me to come to the reception in honour of Alfonso that night at the Embassy and 'we shall contrive something.'

It was a brilliant social affair in that beautiful embassy which owed so much to Quiñones's own taste; and when I was beginning to wonder whether I had wasted my time, lost among so many dancing couples, Quiñones turned up, took me by the hand and led me to a corridor, where, the King standing, his back to the wall, and I standing opposite him, with my back threatened every minute by unsteady trays of champagne, I put 'it' to H.M. He was, as usual, friendly and courteous, but aloof, cold, almost uninterested. 'Let's go through a period of distance. We shall see later.' I got the impression that he knew he was no longer No. 1 in Spain but just the decorative and historical appurtenance of the Dictator. And I thought 'Well, there he is with his back to the wall.'

It was a strange episode. When it came to voting in Geneva, I noticed, though no one else did, that Europe was split on religious lines: all Catholic nations had voted for Spain and all Protestant nations against. It was the first – though so far as I am concerned, by no means the last – time I was to see the ghost of Philip II stalking the hills and dales of Europe.

CHAPTER IX

TWO SO-CALLED DISARMAMENT CONFERENCES

ONE day, as I was busy preparing the International Conference for the Control of the Trade in Arms, Arthur Sweetser came to see me in my office, always smiling, half cordial, half mischievous. He explained that he was responsible for keeping American correspondents informed about the coming Conference and that he knew nothing about it.

I explained to him that the Conference aimed at a Convention controlling the trade in arms and armaments, but he asked at once if we had a draft text to start with. 'We have three,' I answered. 'The St. Germain Convention we inherited from the Peace Conference....' Sweetser cut in: 'Why not apply it?' To this I had to answer that, despite our repeated requests, the U.S. had refused to ratify it, mostly because it was too closely connected with the League. In those days, the anti-League feeling in Washington (though not in the country) amounted to sheer superstition. This point being cleared, I went on: 'a second one, on the whole bolder, proposed by Jouhaux, the Secretary General of the U.G.T. (French General Workers Union) and one, rather conservative, proposed by my countryman Admiral Magaz.'

Sweetser took a long, silent look at me. 'I put it to you that both Magaz's and Jouhaux's texts were written by you.' And I answered: 'You don't need to know so much to inform your boys.'

The President of that Conference was Carton de Wiart. Belgium has given the League excellent Presidents (Jansen, Theunis, Rollin, a number of others, and, of course, the best known of them all, Paul Hymans). Carton de Wiart was a star worthy of that constellation. I sent Blondel, Sweetser's Belgian colleague in the Press section, to meet him at Basle, so that, on his way to Geneva, he would have time to read the opening speech. I need not say it was a mere suggestion for the President to accept, reject or alter; but I do need to say that I had had it roneoed in English and French, in the hope that he would pass it unaltered, which he did, indeed with many congratulations, when we met at the station.

The Conference went smoothly enough until one day Allen Dulles, the Secretary General and live wire of the American Delegation, sprang a surprise on us. He suggested to me that an amendment to the Draft Convention should forbid all trade in chemical warfare materials and

68

implements. I told him it was out of the question. He retorted that Representative Theodore Burton insisted on it. This, for Dulles, was final. Burton, who had been a Senator and was then the Chairman of the Foreign Affairs Committee of the House of Representatives, was a very big noise in Washington. I reminded Allen Dulles that the U.S. had officially shared our preparatory work and had never mentioned the subject; and that we in Geneva thought it vital never to confront nations with issues on which they had not been forewarned. 'A conference,' I explained, 'should be a dining-room, never a kitchen.'

Dulles, of course, very much preferred to argue with me than with Burton, so he fought back. 'Very well, I'll appeal to the President,' I retorted. I put it to Carton de Wiart and I reminded him that the point – no surprises – had been put quite clearly 'in the Presidential speech.' He was good enough to agree with me fully and added: 'You are right. The point was made in my . . . in our speech.' Burton pressed on. We compromised on a protocol recommending the prohibition that Burton would have made compulsory. It was eventually rejected by the American Senate.

In spite of this episode, I want to say I always found Allen Dulles an excellent companion and friend, as well as a shrewd observer of things, for which he counted on a good provision of humour. In later years, when he became far more important, and rose to be the head of C.I.A., he remained the same good friend though no longer companion, and I seldom passed a few days in Washington without looking him up.

Such is the play of forces – national and personal – that complicate world affairs. The Conference worked hard and we, of the Secretariat, harder than any. The last night when the last proofs had gone to the printer, at about 11 p.m., and all seemed fair, we got a call from the British Delegation. 'Adhere' will not do. Wherever you have printed 'adhere' you must print 'accede'. It was no good arguing that the British delegates had passed 'adhere' in the first draft, in the second, and in the sub-committee, in the Committees, in the plenary Conference and in the first and second proofs. All we could do was to ring up the printer, who bowed before the might of Britain as all of us had done. Then we asked the printer what it would mean in time. He wouldn't be ready until 3 a.m. The night was fine, and Arocha, our legal expert, had a new, open car. We went for a moonlight drive.

At about 2.30 we were crossing the long bridge towards the Bergues on our way to the printer's. Right in the middle of the road, near the other end of the bridge, two men were talking. I said: 'I bet they are two Spaniards.' They were.

We drove on, corrected the last proofs and went home to a couple of hours' sleep, a bath and the last gala setting for the signature of the papers. The nations were printed in alphabetic order but Britain had demanded that the Dominions should appear in an alphabetic order of their own under 'Britain', but with a margin half an inch to the right. That half an inch, I thought, measured the sovereignty that remained to London, not much space for the Privy Council.

When Lord Onslow's turn came to sign he kept at it for so long that I asked Captain Mathenet to go and cast a furtive glance at what he was doing. He brought me the text of one of the several Conventions that were being signed that morning. On it, Onslow had scribbled a reservation several times repeated, once for every Dominion, and in every case he had used not the 'accede' prescribed by the Foreign Office but the 'adhere' we had had to strike out of our proofs.

Three aims and no hits. We had tried the Treaty of Mutual Assistance, the Protocol and Locarno, but Disarmament was no nearer. The chief cause of the trouble was no other than the fundamental error of tackling the problem of power and justice in international relations from the angle of disarmament, for disarmament is in fact a mirage or a will-o'-the-wisp.

Nevertheless, on we went and the Temporary Mixed Commission having demised, another Commission was appointed with the explicit purpose of preparing a Disarmament Conference. The Council took this decision on December 12, 1925, none too soon, considering that the Geneva Protocol had fixed June 15, 1925, for the opening of the Conference itself. The Preparatory Commission had a new look when compared to its deceased predecessor the Temporary Mixed. It was to be, no doubt, just as temporary, but it was more and better mixed. It comprised, of course, politicians, some of whom were apt to delegate their power and work to diplomats; but it was flanked by a Military, Naval and Air Committee composed of the experts who came with the members of the main Commission, and a Financial and Economic Committee the members of which were selected by League committees and by the International Labour Office, a considerable progress on national governmental appointments. Three new characters turned up: Paul-Boncour, Bernstorff and Gibson.

Paul-Boncour, to be exact Joseph Paul-Boncour (for there are many Frenchmen who suddenly choose one ancestor down the line and fix or perpetuate his Christian name by adding it to the family name), though small in stature, was built monumentally. His legs were pillars, his chest and shoulders a fortress, his head a façade, his eyes windows, his mane of hair a hill, heavily covered with snow. He was even more eloquent than Viviani, whose assistant he had been, and looked the part even more so than his master had. He was loyal, straight, courageous and a good friend. He liked the English, though he did not know them well and was a poor linguist.

Bernstorff must have been more impressive in earlier days than when he was sent to Geneva already too old. He was, I believe, compelled by the need to 'make good,' to reconquer for Germany the sympathies she had lost during the war, and to show himself as accommodating and reasonable as possible. He was correct down to his diplomatic stiff collar, hard tie and protocolarian air.

As for Hugh Gibson, he was a joy. He had that face, Anglo-Saxon by Red Indian, that one sometimes meets in the U.S., so often indeed that one wonders whether it is not due to the habitat shaping man's features back to the Indian style. It was a face in which arrogance did its best to hide humour, yet humour came through out of sheer strength. I believe it was this tendency to see and enjoy the comic in life that drew us together. After a distinguished period as Minister Plenipotentiary in Brussels, where, together with the Spanish envoy Villalobar, he had done wonders to help the Belgians during the German occupation, he had become Herbert Hoover's man and was Minister Plenipotentiary in Berne.

At the sittings of the Preparatory Commission, we sat very far from each other, I on the left of the President, he at the far end, close to the door, which always made me think of the way our satirical genius Larra describes the attitude of the Minister of War of a factious Cabinet, 'ready to run away at the first alarm'. I told him so and he enjoyed it greatly for he was as sceptical as a grown up should be on disarmament matters. We developed a correspondence. He had quite a talent for humorous sketching and the collection of those he sent me – very correctly, inside League envelopes by a janitor – was one of the treasures I lost in Spain, not indeed during but after the Civil War.

One afternoon, as we sat down after a late lunch owing to an aggressive, biting speech by Cecil on the French dragging their feet over disarmament, lo and behold, Paul-Boncour entered shorn of a good deal of his wonderful mane. I seized a piece of paper and solemnly wrote: 'Who is Delilah?', called a janitor and sent it to him, of course in a buff envelope. He sent it back. 'No Delilah. He tore it off after Cecil's speech.'

Cecil himself used also to exchange letters with me at the sittings, but he always sat at the end of the top table, on the left side, not far from where I sat. There was in those days a somewhat incredible Roumanian Minister in Berne, whose name was Petrescu-Commène. One day, someone else sat in his place. 'Who is that ruffian?' wrote Cecil. I sent the paper back after adding: 'Col . . . escu, replacing Petrescu-

Commène.' Back came the paper: 'What's happened to P. C. Have they hanged him already?' It was, of course, no more than banter fringed with a bit of British aristocratic insolence about 'those foreigners'.

There had been before my time a naval Conference in Washington aiming at limiting the expenditure of the big naval powers; and it had worked not without success, even if a modest one, because it had worked in fact as an Armaments Conference. This may take a little explaining. Since, in the main, it is not armaments that cause wars but wars (or the fear thereof) that cause armaments, it follows that every nation will at every moment strive to keep its armament in an efficient state as required by its fear, otherwise styled security. But being armed is a relative value, with a particular enemy in view. The U.S. must think of the Soviet Union, but Chile need only think of Peru or Bolivia. Therefore nations go into a 'Disarmament' Conference in order to maintain and if possible improve their relative armaments. That is why a 'Disarmament' Conference does not begin to talk sense until it sees itself as an Armaments Conference.

This is what the Washington Conference did. Hence its relative success; which was enhanced and possibly caused by a procedure the Japanese delegate seems to have appreciated. He was asked by newsmen what had struck him most. 'Your Government distributed the text of the inaugural prayers so efficiently that they reached the Delegates before they reached the Lord.'

The big naval powers lost no time in reminding the second line naval powers of the need to do something similar. The big powers were by no means anxious lest Spain, Holland, Sweden and the rest ruined themselves by keeping big fleets; but they, of course, expected the relative armaments of these cadet-nations to remain at a respectful distance from their own. So, I had to get busy on a Naval Conference to that effect.

It took place in Rome and it included all the second rank powers. Whatever the importance it might have been granted at the time, it was nothing more than an episode in the struggle, now time-honoured, to arm while seeming to be disarming and to keep an unsteady yet more or less permanent balance of power in terms of armament between all the nations of the world.

For me, its only memory worth recording was our meeting with Mussolini. As it happens, I saw him twice; for it had been arranged that the great man would receive first the admirals and captains with me at their tail, then the secretaries with me at their head. This gave me an opportunity to see the Duce on two different occasions. When the

principals entered the room, we found there, standing by his desk, a
rubber statue of Napoleon, his right hand on his heart beneath his frock
coat, an Austerlitz eye and an invincible jaw. He did not smile once.
The surface of his face, dark blue in the shaved parts, seemed to me
big enough to hold all the navies represented at that historic hour in
his room. There were two brief speeches, one from the Swedish admiral
who presided over our debates and another by the great man himself,
heavy with wisdom and political philosophy; then a few conversations,
a glass of wine and out.

Then we came back, and what was far more important, with our
secretaries, some of whom were pretty enough to disarm Mars in person.
They certainly disarmed his vicar in Rome, the Duce, for Napoleon
had vanished and in his stead there was as gay a dog of an Italian man
of the world as one could wish. Smiles and jokes enlivened and enlightened the occasion, and happy Benito seemed in no hurry to call
in his Who next?

As I left his room for the second time, I started thinking of the two
pregnant remarks of Pope Pius VII after each of the two phases of his
interview with Napoleon, the real one: *'Tragediante! Commediante!'*

CHAPTER X

THE SOVIET UNION PUTS IN AN APPEARANCE

THE directors of the several departments used to meet every week
with Drummond in the chair. The situation was reviewed and
discussed, and each director put before his colleagues the main features
of the League work from the point of view of his department. By then,
the Secretariat had acquired a good deal of authority thanks to its objectivity, efficiency, initiative and modesty, for it did the work but hid
its hand. In my case, I had got into the habit of presenting many a
report to the Assembly through an excellent Central-American delegate of good appearance, courtly manners and a shrewd mind, Gustavo
Guerrero, the delegate of the Republic El Salvador. Much as one hid
the fact, it did get bruited about, among other reasons, because of the
truth of Buffon's dictum: *Le style c'est l'homme.* So that when Guerrero
was eventually elected to the Council, the joke went round that he sat
as the representative of Salvador. . .de Madariaga.

We thus actually discussed whether the U.S.A. and the Soviet Union
should be invited to the Preparatory Commission for the Disarmament
Conference we were then setting up. Of course, all we could discuss
was what we were to advise the Council to do; but by then our advice
was usually followed. We were all agreed that both the big powers still
outside the League should share in the work of the Commission; and
it was then that my trouble began. Salter had been reading one of my
English books; and he suddenly sprang on the meeting that since the
letter to be sent to the Soviet Union would be a most delicate and hard
document to draft, he proposed that its drafting should be entrusted
to me, for he could not imagine anybody with such a command of
English. I saw Drummond frowning hard, as well he might for he was as
good a draftsman as anyone I have known. But there it was.

Still, you may say it is mere surmise and imagination. Wait a minute.
It happened that, some time after this meeting, Rappard, the Director
of Mandates, resigned; and we offered him a farewell dinner. We were
about a score of his colleagues round the table. There were to be three
speeches: Drummond's, mine and Rappard's. As Drummond ended
his, he looked at me, smiled his awkward smile and said: 'And now
I'll sit down for Shakespeare is going to speak.' I spoke in French.

Frivolously enough, I had concocted a speech full of jokes and puns
(some of them as bad as the worst in Shakespeare). The next day Rachel

Crowdy told me that, green with envy for my performance, she had related all she could of my speech to Miss Figgis; who forthwith produced another vigorous Irish bull: 'You could do just as well if you didn't mind how silly you sound.'

It is now so fashionable to embrace the Bolsheviks on both cheeks, indeed, *à la russe*, on the mouth wherefrom so many lies flow, that the actual way Litvinov and Lunacharsky were received in Geneva may seem incredible. Contrary to what had by then become a tradition, the Secretary General did not receive either in his house or in his office; nor did he offer them any hospitality anywhere. The Bolshies were then still 'those awful people', less because of their already rough treatment of their adversaries than because of their proletarian ways. Their bosses (one could hardly call them their 'leaders') went about as cloth-capped commissars, and had not yet become Homburg-hatted ministers. So that when Litvinov and Lunacharsky turned up, even though, for the occasion, fairly well disguised as what they actually were – *bourgeois* – no one in the Secretariat would move to offer them a hand to shake.

I took the initiative and gave the Russians a luncheon at the International Club. I invited the most interesting and the most interested of my colleagues. I had never met Lunacharsky, whom I was to receive in years to come as Spanish Ambassador in Paris when he himself had been appointed Ambassador to Spain (he was well versed in Don Quixote); but I knew Litvinov well enough from our talks and discussions in West Hampstead, where he lived before the 1917 revolution, and I well remembered how cool he could remain while Ivy Low, his wife, ran down Britain for all she was worth (somewhat irritated by my stout defence of British qualities).

During the luncheon, I overheard Litvinov answering Salter's suggestion that the Soviet Union join the League, with a broadside against the League in the usual Bolshevik style: instrument of capitalism and so forth (imperialism had not yet been minted at the Moscow Slogan-Mint). I turned to Litvinov and gave him a piece of my mind. 'That only shows that you have no idea of what you are talking about.' He enjoyed this throwback to our bantering days in Hampstead. 'Those errors of the League, if true, whose fault? Yours. Yes. Yours. For, if you were a member of it, you would see to it that we didn't commit them.' I thought he was beginning to sharpen his ears so I went on: 'You must understand something which has nothing to do with reports, dispatches and all that Chancellery nonsense, for it is life. When a big nation joins the League, the League dies and is reborn a different one. So, if you don't like the League, join it and so kill it and have it reborn.'

This was the first time I took it upon myself to invite the Soviet Union to join the League. I was to do it later, with more authority and more publicity in 1932, as will be told in due course.

That tiff with Allen Dulles over chemical warfare, closed though it was by the refusal of the Senate to fly with Mr Burton on the clouds of idealism, forgetting the needs of industry and the feelings of the Veterans' Union or whatever its name was, did nevertheless have a sequel. Feeling always ran high against chemical warfare, and as I write this, some students get rusticated in England for having drowned a lecture on war chemicals with irate protests, not merely verbal ones. In those days, the moving spirit was Lord Cecil, whose moving spirit was Philip Baker (as he still called himself in those days). For many less inflammable souls, the endeavour to prohibit all trade in chemical warfare materials seemed very much like a measure to secure the monopoly of such a nefarious form of war for the nations that manufactured the materials for it.

Nothing daunted, Cecil and Baker carried on their tenacious struggle under the aegis of the new Preparatory Commission; and I well remember one day Lord Cecil, who was one of those serpent-and-dove minds who never neglect caution, putting before me a speech he was going to read (which, on 'le style c'est l'homme' rule, I attributed to his friend and adviser) in which the committee members' flesh was meant to be made to creep by informing them that a recently discovered poison was so deadly that one drop on a man's tongue would kill him. I told Cecil that prussic acid could do that and had been known for generations. 'Has it really?' he asked, and out it went from his homily.

For once, Lord Cecil found a ready audience in the unlikeliest quarter, the French General Staff. The reason was plain enough: France was fearful of the power of the German chemical industry, while Britain had just discreetly declared her own as a key industry. What could the poor Americans do but forget all about the Hon. Theodore Burton? So it was decided to appoint a Commission on Chemical Warfare, whose terms of reference were modestly defined as setting up an international system of complaint and enquiry into alleged violations of a convention prohibiting chemical warfare. Here is what I had to report on this curious Commission and its work.

> The Commission which considered this question in its technical aspects was composed of a nucleus of what was known as the Joint Committee plus a certain number of experts chosen by the Commission and paid from League funds. In actual

fact, the choice was made by the usual method, i.e. in consultation, though unofficially, with the offices of the respective countries; yet it is well to bear in mind that the chemical experts selected were in Geneva as international and not as national experts. It was a curious Commission in more ways than one; the Italian expert was the only one who could be described as an Italian *tout court*. The British expert had a French name; so had the German; the American expert had an Italian name and was Cuban born; the Frenchman turned out to be an Alsatian who spoke French with a German accent. If ever a Commission met under good auspices to do international work, the Chemical Warfare Commission was it. What about results? Not so bad as results go. But the report which they produced should be read between the lines. The Commission had no difficulty in answering the first point. Chemical factories can be turned from peace to war purposes immediately in the case of gases such as chlorine and phosgene which are normally manufactured in time of peace; in a few hours or weeks in the case of other gases; and at most in a few months in the case of new products. But what about the methods of avoiding it? Here M. Jouhaux, who sat as one of the Joint Committee members, endeavoured to lead the way to the only reasonable solution in sight: an international chemical cartel which, being manned and managed by international employers and experts, would see to it that none of its branches went astray. A curious scene followed. Of the chemical experts present only one, the Frenchman, was a business man; the others were theoreticians, laboratory experts or professors; these intellectuals unanimously declared that 'the industry' would find M. Jouhaux's plan unacceptable; the business man quietly declared himself ready to accept it straight away. He favoured a loosely knit federation of national industries which would submit when necessary to the inspection of a 'syndic', and when the American expert objected to the plan on the ground of national sovereignty and industrial secrecy the French expert retorted that their works were already being inspected by American customs officials who came to control costs, so that what French sovereignty and French industrial secrecy had given up to help the American Treasury, American sovereignty and American industry would certainly sacrifice to help the peace of the world. The argument is here re-told for the sake of its inherent value, but as a matter of fact the Commission did not go beyond a timid adumbration of international understandings which would apportion the quantity of each gas to be produced in every manufacturing country according to the requirements of legitimate use. The question of control was treated with a little more courage: the Commission considered two kinds of infractions: by firms and by States. The first, it said, could be dealt with by the machinery of the industrial cartel envisaged. The second would require an international commission or preferably a single inquirer. The Commission did not see any difficulty in accepting such a procedure – an opinion of course limited to the strictly technical aspect of the question and leaving aside all its political implications and complications. Despite this reservation the American expert preferred to keep out of this part of the report. He was quickly followed by his Italian colleague.

What is the conclusion of this episode? The same which we have met and are to meet so many times: that questions of disarmament resolve themselves into questions of security and questions of security into questions of international organisation.*

* My book *Disarmament*, pp. 162–4.

CHAPTER XI

THE PREPARATORY COMMISSION

W HEN the Preparatory Commission began its work (May 1926) I had every cause for satisfaction so far as my standing in the Secretariat was concerned. There was – barring Salter and perhaps Rajchmann – no other head of section that could equal my record, and even Salter and Rajchmann were more in the limelight outside the League than within. At any rate, both were directors, but Drummond refused to raise my status and salary to the level of my colleagues, though I daresay some of them were 'sound', but by no means 'brilliant'. I use these words because candid friends had reported to me that 'brilliant but not sound' was Drummond's diagnosis for me. I had discussed the matter of my status with him, and he had upheld his negative stand with two observations: he gave Sweetser nearly double the salary he gave me because, he said, 'I must pay a man bearing in mind what he could earn outside', and when I asked him how he knew what I could earn outside, he coldly answered he did not know. His second point was more forthright. 'I am not sure you have all the qualities required for a director.' This was so outrageous, considering that, for years, I had been a director, but for the gold braid and salary, that I proceeded at once to prove him right.

These words of course do let loose a rather powerful Irish bull; but then, as a Spaniard, I have a right to give forth Irish bulls, and as for this one, I am going to run him at once for all he and I are worth. What really happened then, as it had happened before and has kept happening since, was simply this: there is (I believe) in every Spaniard a depth at which the thread of the screw suddenly shifts from one direction to the other, so that one turn more makes the machine snap. I had felt the screw turned harder and harder and suddenly it snapped.

When this happens, the Spaniard 'is against'. The counsels of prudence, reason, circumstances, relations of power, any argument relevant to the situation, suddenly twisted by that inversion of the thread of the screw, become irrelevant. One is against.

I had enough friends, some of them enthusiastic, to get a number of them to present a motion to the Third Commission of the Assembly, over which I had presided for years. . . . Sorry. This is of course a slip of the pen, yet in the right direction. For it is true that I had been for years not the President, but the Secretary of that Commission, yet not less true that I had put in circulation as my opinion that: 'a good commission consists of a President and a Secretary, and when I say "a President" I exaggerate'. So, as I was saying, I had so many friends in that Commission that I got a motion presented, proposing that in view of the importance of Disarmament, the Section should be put under a Director. This meant, of course, promoting me, and lest any doubt remained, the fact was pointed out by nearly every speaker in unmistakable terms during the debate. I say *debate* because such is the official name, but there was no opposition, at any rate, none vocal. Indeed, one of my most determined backers was Philip Baker, who, everybody knew, would not have risen without Cecil's approval.

William Martin, the able editor of the *Journal de Genève*, and a good friend of mine, dropping in while the debate was on, sent me a note: 'What! Are you having yourself plebiscited?' He had hit the nail on the head. It was an absurd move. Quiñones backed me, *ma non troppo*, just to show Drummond that Spain had nothing to do with it. This pleased me, for I always felt nations should not back their own men at the Secretariat; and although the motion passed with flying colours, Drummond killed it in his Budget Committee. This body was composed of one or two thorough financial experts (nearly always French) and a number of nonentities who depended on the Secretariat, i.e. on Drummond, for their appointment, a boring job for them, had they done any work, but one which served them well at home.

I was not promoted. The episode, however, proved useful. It revealed to me the shape of my own inner screw, from which I derived a good deal of satisfaction since it enabled me in later years – oh no, not to avoid such absurdities, that, never – but to understand them after they had happened; it taught Drummond how wrong he was, particularly after a conversation he had with Salter; and it prepared me to look towards the way out of that house in which I was successful with the delegates but unwanted by my chief. I was promoted the following year.

The President of the Preparatory Commission was Jonkheer Loudon, a handsome Dutchman who had been Holland's Foreign Secretary and spoke perfect French and English. We were on the best of terms; he was as efficient as he was well-bred and tactful. An excellent president. But he did not have to preside for long; for the Commission had soon to split into its two Sub-committees, the Military, Naval and Air Sub-committee and the Economic and Financial Sub-committee. These names gave rise to considerable trouble. The U.S. was then led by President Coolidge, a narrow-minded, indeed a downright stupid man; and he got it into his head – or whatever he thought with – that such names, in particular the first, sounded too much like League language so that he would have none of it. We were at a loss, until some genius among us suggested we call them 'A' and 'B', and the world was saved.

Saved it was, for these two Committees were to study every possible thing on earth preliminary to disarming; and please note that the ruling word here is *preliminary*. There is a Spanish story of a peasant who, having stood for an hour or so behind an artist who was painting a picture of his field and oxen, went away scratching his head and muttering: 'God be blessed, what a lot of things people can invent so as not to work!' How often did this scene come to my memory during those long months when the Military, Naval and Air Sub-committee as well as the Economic and Financial Sub-committee studied everything on earth in, on, about, under, over, this side or beyond disarmament!

Don't you go and think they were frivolous, those questions. How could they be? They had been formulated by the Council; and anyhow, here they are: How should armaments be defined? How could they be compared? Could offensive weapons be told from defensive ones? What were the various forms that limitation or reduction could take? Could the total war strength of a country be limited, or only its peace establishment? Was it possible to exclude civil aviation from the calculation of air armaments? How could such factors as population, industrial resources, communications, geographical position be taken into account? Could there be regional schemes or must reduction be world-wide?

This list was fairly comprehensive; but the Commission took upon itself to add two more items: the possibility of an international supervision of armaments and our old friend poison gas. It was a pity no one considered my plea that a number of other questions had been overlooked such as the influence of monotheism or polytheism on armaments and the beauty of princesses as causes of war (considering Helen of Troy); nor would any one see that, in view of this programme, another proposition of mine should have been considered: that all jobs having to do with disarmament should be made hereditary.

The proceedings were enlivened by temperament, personality and national prejudice. Thus, while the land officers of France and Britain had easily reached a state of peaceful coexistence, a permanent war was waged by the French naval officers against their British colleagues. The operations in this war were not commanded by the admiral, who was debonair enough, but by his spirited *locum tenens*, Captain Deleuze, whose sharp eye and powerful jaw betrayed the true aggressive spirit the British love in Nelson or Beatty but thoroughly dislike in any Frenchman.

The missiles in Geneva were merely verbal, but not less explosive and capable of wounding than atomic heads. Deleuze was a master at this warfare. One of his most memorable shots was his stigmatising as 'iniquitous' a proposal made by Admiral Aubrey Smith. Now this simply would not tally, for if there was a model of straightforwardness in Geneva it certainly was Admiral Aubrey Smith. On the other hand, Captain Deleuze's target was not the good-humoured admiral, but the British navy, and so, '*inique*' it had to be. The British sailors took it very ill, but Deleuze, nothing daunted, stood by his verbal guns, with as much valour as if he were at sea shooting real ammunition at a British frigate. The French admiral had to be called. He arrived flushed, hurried and harried, and was duly and simultaneously pumped gallons of information by Deleuze in French (through his port ear) and by Aubrey Smith in English (through his starbord ear); until he signalled himself fully stocked. The meeting was then called to order, and the French admiral explained, in the finest French Pickwickian style that '*inique*' was not meant and could not have been meant as an insult, since it just meant 'unequal', as every good etymologist would confirm. Aubrey Smith whose seamanship was much better than his semantics, wisely declared that if by '*inique*' Deleuze had meant 'unequal', he would declare himself satisfied. The incident was closed.

The President of Commission A was Senator de Brouckère. He was immense, red-faced, grey-bearded, bespectacled; behind his glasses, a luminous, wise, kind and generous soul peered out at the windows of his eyes. He was a wealthy socialist, who lived with the simplicity and austerity of a monk, and gave over his income to the Belgian socialist party to which he belonged. He had fought in the war as a sergeant and had refused a commission so as to remain close to his soldiers. One of the men I have most admired and one of the very few I might have envied. Add that he had a delightful sense of humour, which his presidency of Commission A gave him plenty of opportunities to tickle.

We had been discussing with the Air Sub-committee whether it was easy to turn a civil aviation into a war air force; one of those 'things man invents so as not to work', of which we had produced so many; and after weeks at it, we decided to request the Governments represented at our Sub-committee (all military air experts) to send civilian air men to discuss the matter from the other end. (Lengthening the sauce, the French call this.) It was also decided that the civil aviation Sub-committee would meet at Brussels, where de Brouckère lived. So, there I repaired with my staff, to meet my President and my brand new Civil Air

Committee. And when we gathered for the sitting, keen was our plea-sure at seeing round the table of our Brussels Civil Committee the same friends with whom we had so often sat in Geneva as an Air Military Committee! Thanks to the wisdom of the governments concerned, the meeting could be described in the Spanish saying as 'the same dogs with different collars'.

We heard their arguments put the other way round, wrote their report, dismissed them, and with our President embarked for London, where we had to study another item on the mighty subject how not to disarm: 'how to speed up the meetings of the Council in case of a threat of war', for it goes without saying that if the Council can meet at once, this in itself increases security and therefore decreases the need for armaments. Isn't that neat?

We went to bed in our cabins at Antwerp and I requested my steward to wake me up at seven as we were to land in England at eight. Next morning when I woke up nearly at eight, I rang for my steward in a pretty bad mood. He explained we were still in Antwerp – fogbound. An admirable illustration for the subject we were supposed to begin to discuss in London.

When we eventually did meet, with a paltry twenty hours' delay due to fog, we put it to Lord Cecil whether the building of the Channel Tunnel should not be added to our programme. That Channel Tunnel seemed to be butting in from the very beginning of our work. The Italian member of the Committee, unable to come, had been replaced by the Military attaché to the London Embassy, to whom our persons were about as unknown as our subject, and that is saying quite a good deal. We had two workers' delegates, a Fleming whose name I forget, a humorous, well-fed and hearty man, and Léon Jouhaux, the French C.G.T. (General Workers Union) leader, whose long, heavy-cheeked face, ill-humoured mien, large, unfriendly eyes and black moustache and 'imperial' goatee greatly impressed the Italian colonel. At one turn in the discussion, the Colonel, who had no idea who Jouhaux was, respectfully addressed him as *mon général*; very much to the enjoy-ment of Jouhaux's Flemish colleague, who since then always addressed his old friend and colleague as *mon chénéral*. No one explained any-thing, and Jouhaux accepted the title without a smile. His promotion was the only net result of the meeting.

We worked hard throughout that year on our Byzantine enquiry. What is a weapon? You might think that question easy enough, but when looked into, it revealed unsuspected subtleties, and the mere fact that they are unsuspected for us shows how undeveloped the civilian mind is. Thus, a gun is war material. So is a gun carriage. So is a gun carriage wheel. What about the grease for the carriage wheel? A military kitchen is war material. What about a military bed, uniform, pair of boots? It required the courage of a military committee to penetrate this labyrinth of subtleties and distinctions and with such success that, for instance, it gave as its considered opinion that the steel and the wood that go to the making of a rifle are war material, but the complete rifle, stored in an arms depot, and not in actual service, is not. There it stands in choice French and English in the League of Nations Disarmament Records.

But why spend so much subtlety on mere definitions? It is indeed one of the characteristics of military debates. The military mind is used to the gradual conquest of *positions*. The soldier begins by taking a first line of advance; he fortifies himself there; with the advantage thus acquired, he attacks the second position and so on to the final planting of his flag on the summit which was his aim from the beginning. The masters of this strategy are of course the French. Their admirable method, their dogged perseverance, their intellectual capacity for classifying questions by order of logical precedence, enables them to fight their way in debate step by step. Time and again in Geneva a resolution presented, pressed and wrenched from a Commission by a strong French delegation was seen to blossom forth months or years later in altogether unexpected consequences – unexpected, that is, by all but the French. This tendency which is pretty general in the French is naturally akin to a military psychology, and Sub-committee A took the French hint with the utmost alacrity. So that the questions submitted to them were treated exactly like successive lines of trenches for dialectical fights; generally speaking, these lines were: first, definition; then, comparability; then, limitation or reduction. In each of these lines the battle was fought on strictly national grounds; each delegation was always ready to vote for the general principle, if, when applied particularly, it resulted in an increase of the delegation's own relative armaments.

Such is the background which gives its dramatic and even its comic value to the famous duel on naval categories. It began on the trench of definitions. Could naval units be defined in separate categories? The English, the Americans, and the Japanese wanted navies limited by categories; the French, the Italians, in fact practically every other naval power, preferred the total tonnage method. But this was the summit to be conquered. The first trench to be won was definition. The Naval Sub-committee fought Homeric fights on that trench. One day the British naval delegate with the frank, somewhat blunt, sincerity of his nation and profession put the matter in a nutshell. 'Is it possible,' he asked the Sub-committee, 'to classify naval ships in categories which the expert can discern?' and he asked for a division. The Naval Sub-committee voted and there was a majority of noes. To add insult to injury, the French delegation hurried to another room to fetch a Czech general who, as the 'naval' representative of his land-locked country, had a right to vote. I turned to my English friends in the Committee and sought to allay their feelings by comic relief: 'It serves you right. Why did you allow Shakespeare to give Bohemia an access to the sea?'*

When the Plenary Commission met again (March 1927), I had stuffed de Brouckère's pockets with mischievous and explosive statistics, that enabled him to congratulate the Naval Sub-committee on having used enough League paper to allow the Polish Delegation to return on foot from Geneva to Warsaw treading on League paper all the way.

But the extensive work performed by its sub-committee left no room for the Commission itself to waste any more time. There were attempts, though; and it all reminded me of a Spanish story: the young peasant telling his girl, 'Your father away ploughing, your mother in church and you in your nightgown. To hell with all these obstacles!'

Whereupon, Lord Cecil presented us with a Draft Convention, soon followed by a similar gift from Paul-Boncour. Empty frames, though, into which the disarmament terms and figures would have to be registered – when agreed upon. Yet, even empty of substance, both were full of intention and national style. The French text suggested that all effectives should be limited, but the British thought that sea effectives should not; throughout the discussion, the trends of nations crisscrossed each other on any and every subject animated by the same inner law which, by the nature of things, turns every disarmament endeavour into an armament achievement.

Thus, for instance, on the chapter of men, the first difficulty was how to define a comparative unit; the Committee solved it by adopting the man-day, on the proposal of the Spanish delegation. But when it came to who, where, how long, was a man-day, trouble began. Trained reserves: were they to be counted? No, said the French. Yes, said the

*My book *Disarmament*, pp. 168 *et Seq.*

British. Seamen serving on merchantmen, were they to be counted? No, said the British. Yes, said the French. When it came to war material, similar troubles arose, and it soon became evident that private manufacturers were too strong to be ousted, and that the United States would never agree to giving up the pull on Spanish America that she could exert by giving or refusing armaments. The problem of the supervision of the Disarmament (?) achieved (?) was no less thorny.

CHAPTER XII

THE UNCO-OPERATIVE CO-OPERATION OF THE U.S.A.

IN the recess between the second and the third sessions of the Preparatory Commission, President Coolidge bethought himself of the advantages of a separate conference, and he issued an official inquiry to the British, French, Italian and Japanese Governments (February 10, 1927) to ascertain whether they would be disposed to empower their representatives at the forthcoming meeting of the Preparatory Commission to begin negotiations towards a limitation of naval armaments. The government of the United States acted exactly as if the work done in Geneva to date had been transacted in a language utterly unknown to them. Once more, official America remained isolated, impervious to world influences, unable – or unwilling – to learn from the experience gathered by other nations. There were at the time well-meaning and ardent international workers who felt drawn by their offended emotions to attribute all kinds of unworthy motives to Washington. We heard about playing at party football with the peace of the world and what not. The League Commission on disarmament was strenuously grappling with the difficulties of the subject. True, it was not getting on; but, leaving aside the fact that one of its difficulties, perhaps the greatest, was precisely the isolationistic attitude of the United States, the work of the League had already achieved two definite results: the first, to prove that there is no hope of making any headway in disarmament without· dealing simultaneously with land, sea and air; the second, to show that disarmament is indissolubly linked with the growth of international institutions. Both these results were, or should have been, clear to Washington. Both were no doubt unpalatable. But that was not a reason for throwing them unceremoniously overboard.

Nor was that all. For there is no question that the calling of an international conference of five Powers to discuss one of the points which twenty other Powers were already debating with them was, to put it mildly, an unexpected action. There were some Americans at the time who, anxious to help, tried to put the best possible complexion on the singular step taken by their Government. But explanations could not alter the essence of the position.

Yet nothing succeeds like success, and if what came to be known as the Coolidge Conference had succeeded, all these thorns of reproach would have turned into laurels. Yes. But the fact is that success was impossible. For the Coolidge Conference aimed at limiting the vessels not dealt with in the Washington Conference, and the Washington Conference had succeeded precisely because those vessels had been left out of it. It is easy to drive the hollow in a deflated india-rubber ball from one point to another; it is less easy to round the ball up altogether. The Washington Conference was able to reduce or at any rate limit certain types of vessels by allowing the states all freedom to develop their navies in other directions. A limitation of all the navies in all directions is another matter. The Coolidge Conference had to bow before the law which governs all so-called Disarmament Conferences which meet before the political preliminary conditions for their success have been fulfilled. Ostensibly a Disarmament Conference, it became fatally an Armament Conference.

Let it be quite clear that though it took place in Geneva and was even for a time housed in the League of Nations building, the Coolidge Conference had nothing to do with the League. I was then Director of Disarmament of the League Secretariat and was only invited to the three public meetings which took place during the whole duration of the Conference. But as a sight it was fascinating to the specialist. On coming to grips with the subject, every delegation chose its ground regardless of previous attitudes. The Americans, for instance, who in the general Conference had been adamantine defenders of the faith in naval categories, suddenly discovered that the British were most bigoted on this point and, being converted to the excellences of French logic which they had cursed in the Preparatory Commision, claimed the right to apportion their total tonnage as they saw fit. But the most dramatic conversion was that of the British. They had been for years most impatient with the French obsession for security. When the French reminded them of the many invasions France had had to suffer, their country overrun with foreign troops, her towns destroyed, they listened with respectful boredom and took most of it as political rhetoric. But when it came to cruisers, Mr Bridgeman in most emphatic terms pronounced immortal sentences which the French loved to repeat. Security, security above all.

And yet, the French after all could point to a traditional adversary just over the border. But what were the English afraid of? The answer to this question is enigmatic and we should respect enigmas. But any one who saw and heard at close quarters what was done and said during the Coolidge Conference knows quite well that the war which was used as a working hypothesis for the discussion was the Unthinkable War. It was a pleasure to hear Lord Jellicoe who, as the New Zealand representative, was an expert in Channel naval problems, explain how seventy cruisers were an irreducible minimum for England, since a hundred and forty cruisers had been hardly enough to save England from destruction during the last war. And still more pleasurable to hear Mr Gibson, the distinguished American delegate and President of the Conference, argue that if a delegation came to Geneva determined to put forward absolute and immovable claims it was useless to meet in conference at all – which is exactly what everybody had been saying for six years about American Delegations.

Anglo-American relations were never more strained in recent years than they were then. Why should an endeavour to disarm have led to such heated situations? It seems that a difference in method as to how to do away with armaments should never lead to suspicion and controversy of the bitter character which obtained then. But, of course, under the vocabulary and gestures of Disarmament, what was at stake in the Coolidge Conference was Armament. The three nations there present, and particularly the United States and Great Britain, were ready for any reduction of *absolute* naval power all round which would result in leaving their own *relative* naval power stationary at any rate and if possible increased. The arguments exchanged in Geneva have no meaning whatever unless they have that meaning. 'Your case is a very strong chain hanging from a very weak nail,' an international observer said then to one of the British delegates. True, if England did not control the sea-roads she might be starved in a fortnight. But the argument applies to Finland just as well; moreover, who wants to starve England? Where is the enemy? And as to the United States, true that, having no naval bases dotted all over the world, she would be put in an inferior position if she were forced to build her total tonnage in the form of small cruisers – but in an inferior position towards whom? In what kind of conflict?

In Geneva Great Britain and America spoke thoughts of power in the language of safety. With, however, this all-important difference that England was psychologically entitled to a certain 'security-complex' in sea matters as France was on land questions; while it is difficult to explain America's naval policy except as a very human tendency to reap in the naval field the harvest of her financial and political superiority. The difficulty plainly shows the importance of armaments as instruments of policy. It was not so much actually in order to shoot her guns at England that America wanted her cruisers; nor to defend her supplies from American cruisers that England was so particular about her superiority at sea. It was because naval pre-eminence means international prestige; preponderance in the counsels of the world; authority in troubled areas such as China; power to have one's own way; political backing to financial, economic and commercial penetration.

Hence, a partial attempt at solving the problem of Disarmament such as the Coolidge Conference can end only in two ways – in sheer failure or in an agreement of a political character apportioning the power available between the parties, i.e. an agreement to pool armaments between the two nations concerned, which in its turn is only possible when a pool of power of all kinds, and particularly of political power, has been previously set up between the partners. For let it be said again and not for the last time, the only solution of the problem of disarmament lies in the organisation of the World-Community in such a way that power may be used only as the weapon of the World-Community against law-breakers.

During that conference, I happened to be beginning a game of golf one afternoon when I saw in the distance Hugh Gibson playing home. We hailed each other and I asked him how his Conference was going. 'D'you know the story of the little New York Jewish boy? He went to a shop and changed his dollar into quarters, then to another, where he changed his quarters into dimes, then to another, into cents, then to another back into one dollar again and so on all over again; until one of the shopkeepers recognised him. "Why do you keep this game up?"' – "Zome time, zomebody is going to make a mistake and it isn't going to be ME!"''

The U.S. of those days dealt with Geneva in a curious way. After the Coolidge Conference, launched as if the League Disarmament Conference wasn't there at all, the Kellogg Pact was launched as if the Covenant did not exist. There is little need to discuss here this largely futile episode on the way to disarmament. The idea behind the Kellogg Pact had been conceived by Briand as a strictly bilateral treaty with the U.S.; it was made multilateral by the then Secretary of State, who, nevertheless, frowned out of court a proposal to make its discussion as multilateral as its aim. In actual fact it aimed at barring permissible wars, i.e. wars that remained possible even after the Covenant had been applied; but not so-called 'defensive' wars which were efficiently prevented by the Covenant. Therefore it tightened the ring inside which the League members were enclosed, while leaving non-member States free to go to war under the flag of defence.

The chief attraction of the Pact for Mr Kellogg and his friends was that it enabled the U.S. to contribute an 'unqualified' idea to the peace movement without paying a cent in loss of international liberty and independence of conduct. The Pact aimed at peace and co-operation, but by ways founded on power and isolation. The U.S. was ready to sign that she would not go to war unless she wanted to, and that she would submit to arbitration whenever she thought fit on the points her Senate would define; but she was not going to give up one inch of her sovereignty in world affairs. She took back in the spirit what she gave away in the letter, and in the Kellogg Pact, showed the world a magnificent example of splendid isolation and power couched in terms of verbal idealism.

The result was felt soon enough. The President, having congratulated himself and his nation on the idealism of the Kellogg Pact in outlawing war, proceeded to advocate a strong navy to guarantee American defence.

The U.S. nation and people have made immense strides along the road of world understanding and co-operation since those days; an achievement mainly due to a growing realisation of their responsibility but also to a certain descent to the realm of human common sense from that of puritan cant. If only to record the fact with accuracy, I shall copy the words with which one of the prophets of the Kellogg Pact Movement, Charles Clayton Morrison, wrote on it: 'Mr Kellogg launched a new idea when he made his offer of a general treaty renouncing war. The idea had taken root in certain circles of American peace thinking but was wholly new to Europe. . . . The fact that America has defined the issue between peace and war in simple unambiguous terms and has chosen peace spells the doom of war. . . . If Christ was standing among us it would be like him to say, "I see Satan falling as lightning from heaven". . . . It is, we say, the natal day of peace. The peace movement has at last been born. There has been no peace movement until now.'*

For all the cold reception he met with at Geneva, Litvinov was too shrewd not to realise that the Soviet Union was welcome there. By whom? An interesting point. By that elusive Ariel of international politics known as *the spirit of Geneva*. Contrary to what was happening in a number of nations of the League, the League of Nations felt no aversion towards the Soviet Union nor did it show that undue haste in thawing her and drawing out smiles that might eventually blossom out into $s or £s. Geneva saw the need to bring everybody in. True, the spirit of Geneva had not read Hamlet and did not know that one may 'smile and smile and be a villain'.

Our endeavour to that end was thwarted for a time by a somewhat irrelevant tragedy. A Soviet diplomat had been murdered by a Swiss. The jury found the assassin guilty but by less than a two thirds majority, which in Swiss law meant that he was set free. The Russians took it very

* Quoted by Mr Kirby Page in *The World Tomorrow*, New York, May 1928.

ill and it required all the patience and good-will the Swiss are capable of to turn this obstacle. The episode proved how mistaken the Soviet Union was then in declaring that the League was a diabolic machine for isolating her.

She was isolated, but by her own doing. And so her representatives arrived in the midst of the most sophisticated gathering in the world with nothing less than a plan for a complete, immediate and universal disarmament. Litvinov came to see me and asked me whether the Commission would reject it. 'They will do something much worse than that,' I answered: 'they will consider it very carefully.' In their naïvety, these Russians imagined themselves appearing before the world as the angels of disarmament, falling in to the midst of the Devils of War.

The bourgeois devils grinned. They knew too much. (The Devil, an old Spanish proverb warns, doesn't know so much because he is the Devil but because he is very old.) Paul-Boncour, in a tone half paternal half brotherly, upbraided his two fellow-socialists, Litvinov and Lunacharsky. 'That is how we began, my friends, but we have already walked all the way to Warsaw on League paper.' The next day, the true debate began, with a speech by the British delegate, an Ulsterman by the name of Lord Cushendon (which Deleuze was not long in translating as *Cochon d'âne*). The speakers were many, and they all performed a kind of verbal war dance around the Soviet plan without ever actually touching it, for it really was taboo. The taboo in it came from a very simple fact: armaments being but instruments of policy, no one can disarm but the communists; for communist policy could at a pinch do without international war since its method consists in subversion.

True, the case of Budapest 1956 seems to destroy this view. Yet what was then destroyed was the moral authority of the Soviet Union. If the Soviet Union is faithful to its own faith, subversion should suffice to convert peoples to communism and to keep them there for good. *C'est la lutte finale.* The Soviet Union had not yet swallowed half of Europe by brute force.

This first rough-hewn plan presented by the Russians was doomed to rise to the Purgatory of Draft Conventions, by then already made illustrious by the presence of the Treaty of Mutual Assistance, the Protocol, Locarno and what not. But Litvinov and Lunacharsky had another card up their sleeve. This second Draft Convention sought to achieve disarmament by applying a new principle: nations would reduce their armaments at a pace the quicker the stronger they were. States would be classified into groups according to the size of their armed forces: group one would undertake to reduce their armaments by one half; group two by one third; group three by one fourth. In naval armaments there would be only two groups; and chemical warfare would be prohibited. The Commission read the plan and commended it to the Governments concerned. That, of course, was safe enough.

In so doing, the Commission did not mean business. Its members knew only too well that the basic element for such a thing was missing: the *unit*. If we want to reduce in an equal proportion a number of quantities, they must be comparable. On what basis? How can we compare the man-day of a compulsory service nation with that of a professional army nation or with that of a citizen, rifle-at-home, army nation? The second Draft Convention presented by the Soviet Delegation joined the Limbo of ghosts.

CHAPTER XIII

SPANISH TRAVELS

A chance discovery of a private letter dated April 14, 1926 enables me to describe one of those strenuous trips I now and then took, now to this now to that country, 'preaching the Gospel of the League'. I do not recollect when it was exactly that I preached such a gospel to an audience consisting of the one and only person of Alfonso XIII, King of Spain; but I do know that I was summoned to the royal presence one sunny day and thought it indispensable to don a morning coat and top hat. I possessed no such hat, but found one in a fairly good state (it had belonged to my father) somewhere in the lumber room of our house; and while it was not quite my size – whether by defect or by excess, I cannot recollect – I bethought myself of the saving dilemma that I could not wear it in the royal presence and I need not wear it in the royal absence. So, both I and the top hat arrived at 10.45 at the main entrance to the Royal Palace, both resting on the seat of an open cab. I seized the hat and walked up the magnificent grand staircase.

There was no waiting. An A.D.C. waved me into a small room not very much wider than any of the large windows one can see from the Plaza de Oriente. A small desk, a chair for the King, a chair for the visitor. That was all. And suddenly the King himself, eyes smiling, mouth forbidding more out of natural shape than of mood. He sat down at his desk and bid me sit opposite, which I did, not without some hesitation as to what I was to do with my monumental hat, which in the end I held on my knees in unstable equilibrium. Soon I found myself forcibly arguing for the League with such eloquence and vigour that I thumped the top of the hat with my impatient hand as if that polished surface was the very soul of a belated and benighted nationalism. The King was rather amused and seemed at times to fear for my hat.

This audience must have taken place during one of the very earliest years I spent in the Secretariat. By 1926 I had already led the Disarmament section for four years and had successfully piloted the Conference for the regulation of the traffic in arms. I was less dogmatic, less enthusiastic, yet, if possible, more 'convinced' about the League and its predestined part in the tragicomedy of the world.

But the trip was not to be all work. Before I launched into my somewhat heavy duties, I spent a few days with the Mostyns at Lord Wellington's estate in Illora, near Granada. Mrs Mostyn had a daughter by her first marriage who was no other than that Diana Cohen who had been my first secretary at Victoria St. and who had graced with her non-chalant presence the Barcelona Transit Conference in 1921. Mr Mostyn was the manager of Wellington's estates in Spain. And this is what I wrote to C.H.M.A. on April 14, 1926:

> Good weather at least. [I meant at any rate.] The colour of this landscape is a dream. It seems as if it has been painted with new colours that have never been used before.
>
> Lord Gerald Wellesley, the Duke's second son, who is here, wished to visit the Soto de Roma, the other (and bigger) part of the estate, and off we went yesterday in two horse-carriages through terrible roads. The way is most beautiful. At the village, where we had tea in the manager's house, a couple of minstrels came to serenade 'the Lord', and it all ended in a dance. This item being over, we left the crowded village, Lady Mary Thynne on horseback riding like a man and in riding breeches, which created a tremendous sensation. The Thynne[s] brother and sister, are charming, simple people, and as for Lord Gerald he was most graceful and danced with the manager's wife who is a perfect Moorish type, and with her cousin who is as white as a lily and as flame-haired as a Titian lady. [Indeed I was so inflamed by that hair that I actually wrote *flamme*-haired.]

Five days later I left for Granada, where in the evening I had to de-liver a lecture at the Ateneo. Of this lecture I remember nothing. But I do remember that I stayed at the Washington Irving Hotel and this detail brings to my memory so vivid a figure of those days that I shall have to digress. He was a Persian delegate who answered to the grand name of Arfa-ed-Dowleh, and looked it. He was (as we say in Spain) 'older than his mother', but tried to conceal it by insisting that his hair and moustache had to be as black as nature allows and art can ensure; save that when he happened to sit with his back to a window and one's glance fell on his nape in a direction perpendicular to that of the in-coming light, his hair was apt to take on every possible hue the rainbow is capable of. He was a delightful companion and conversationalist so that once at a big banquet in Geneva, he got so immersed in conversa-tion with his partner – who happened to be Amelia Azcarate – that they both went the round of the huge U-shaped table three times before he found where he was supposed to be sitting – which endeared him the more to all of us, for they made a lovely couple, as she was most elegantly attired, and he crowned his evening dress (bejewelled with incredible stars and orders) with a black astrakhan fez.

He had also slept at the Washington Irving, though many years earlier – I should say forty at least; and he told me himself that one night, half asleep, half awake, he half-dreamt half-thought that he was dead and actually in Mahommed's paradise, for the scent in his room was inebriating and the music was divine – until he finally woke up, went to the window and found that a nest of nightingales was playing and enjoying a concert in a bush of jasmine that crept up to his very bedroom window.

That day, he went on telling me with some wistfulness, he had lived a dangerous hour. He had hired an open horse carriage to visit the Albaicin, in company of a young couple, a Belgian secretary at the Embassy in Madrid and his wife; and, of course, the lady sat to his right i.e. Arfa-ed-Dowleh's, and the husband by himself on the front seat facing them. A Gipsy woman took her chance as the carriage stopped for a while, and after a good look at Arfa-ed-Dowleh's hand, she told him that in due time he would still have five more boys to add to the one he had already by his charming wife, sitting by him – which did not seem to be as comic to the Belgian husband as it did to his wife.

I hold no very strong opinion as to Gipsy prophecies, but I do as to jasmine and birds under your window in an Andalusian spring, so that if Mohammed's paradise does not deliver that kind of bliss, I for my part will not change over, and frankly prefer to have to tune my harp with Adenauer's and Barthou's than my tambourine with Nasser's and Boumedienne's. Meanwhile, I was still on this planet, trying to earn my right to choose my heavenly instruments, and after my lecture at the Ateneo on the 19th, I had lunch with Falla the next day.

I had met him many years earlier, when his *Three Cornered Hat* had been offered to London by Diaghilev with vivid stage-decorations by Picasso, and I had been struck by the contrast between these three first-rate artists, two of them super-sophisticated, while the third, Falla, went through life with the ascetic simplicity of a monk. I had seen and heard the puppet show of his Don Quixote produced in Zürich, and I had been impressed by the depth and purity of the emotion that Falla had been able to express in his music. Indeed, I believe to this day, that while most of the work of Falla is so Spanish that it can be nothing else and one feels its Spanishness from the very first bars, *El Retablo de Maese Pedro*, the least outwardly Spanish of his works, is perhaps the most Spanish in depth.

Music does not escape the natural law that empowers the national character to impress itself right into the texture of all the creations of a people, and true though this is of any music, it is truer still or more immediately true of Spanish and of Russian music. But the very ease with which Spanish forms, melodies and rhythms come out in Spanish music may at times detract from their universality and cultural value, unless they are handled by as great an artist as Falla; and it makes it easier for composers foreign to Spain to write 'Spanish' music as Lalo, Chabrier, Rimsky-Korsakoff and *tutti quanti* were able to do. These thoughts occupied my mind during those days when I heard the *Retablo* in Zürich, and admired the more how vigorously Falla had succeeded in rendering the profounder spirit of Spanish music while hardly ever having to lean on the usual Spanish melodies and rhythms.

My visit to Falla was not altogether disinterested. I had written a fantasy for the theatre which, though not precisely a comic opera, did require enough singing to have to be played by actors who could sing. Its title was *The Golden Fleece*, and its setting was an imaginary country in which no one's memory can hold facts for more than five days. Though written in the early thirties, it reads like a premonitory satire on the Marshall-Plan (which, as I shall relate some day, I also anticipated in yet another and a more direct way). Prince Tirabolo, the reigning sovereign of a happy country, has a Minister of Finance who explains that the accounts of the State are quite simple: what comes in goes out and nothing remains, nor are there any debts either, because every year something happens, which, of course, he does not remember, that refills the coffers of the State.

This was the fancy I brought to Falla. I found him in his 'carmen' on the side of the hill that rises towards the Alhambra, sitting at the piano and playing to himself a page out of *Così fan Tutte*. He was enchanted with it, and for a while we did nothing else but Falla play and I listen to his enthusiastic comments, which pleased me immensely for I can consume any amount of Mozart. But while we were thus swimming in the purest, most diaphanous music that ever was written, something warned me within, at another floor of my human building, that I should fail in my main purpose. Falla's voice, his saintly, lean body, his grave eyes, those eyes whose very smile was so earnest, his mouth free from any worldly desire, could one dream of a human being more distant from Voltaire, to whom I felt so close?

Shall I? After lunch, in the sunny afternoon, we had gone out to sit in the garden. Without having answered my question, I found myself relating to him the story of *The Golden Fleece*. Being a genuine saint, Falla had a lively sense of humour, but he would not, of his own, tune himself to humorous things. He declined my offer of collaboration, but put forward another one. 'When I knew you were coming,' he said,

'I made up my mind that you were the man. It had not occurred to me before, I believe, because you were sunk in foreign affairs and I had not put two and two together. But now I know. I should like you to write for me a poem on the discovery of America.'

I was taken aback. What was it, I thought, that made men of such eminence connect me with an event for which I felt no interest whatsoever? A few years earlier don Ramón Menéndez Pidal, on assuming the editorship of a monumental history of Spain, had proposed to me that I take on the reign of Ferdinand and Isabel. I had written nothing historical yet, and though he had been impressed by C.H.M.A.'s essay on the emancipation of the serfs of the Abbey of Ste. Geneviève, and his offer was to both of us, I had felt more puzzled than honoured by Pidal's offer and had declined it. I declined Falla's.

Yet these two men had seen in me what I had not and yet was there. Fourteen years later, I wrote my life of Columbus and my poem of the Discovery of America; and if I had accepted Falla's offer I might have guided his *Atlantida* into better channels. As it was, Falla, led by his religious zeal, wrote his musical composition on the Discovery on the basis of a poem in Catalan by Verdaguer, a priest, a good poet, but one whose poem was not really good. Passages of beauty there are no doubt; but his *Atlantida* lacks that without which there is no true poem – unity. It is pagan tradition leading to Christian myth or vice-versa or both; and this lack of poetical unity raised, I believe, a fatal obstacle to the composer's inspiration.

Fernando de los Ríos, who was soon to be one of the most prominent leaders of the Republic, was then in Granada where he held a chair of Jurisprudence in the University. He was in his element, being an Andalusian through and through; and I saw a good deal of him. One morning we had arranged to walk together in the grounds of the Alhambra. He arrived with a young man of wide, deep eyes, a swarthy complexion and a supple, youthful body. 'Our local poet,' he said to me. His name was Federico García Lorca.

CHAPTER XIV

I LEAVE THE SECRETARIAT

ALL this went on during 1927, which was to be my last year of service in the Secretariat. Why I left? As usual in such cases, moved by a knot of circumstances, some of my making, some caused by others, some perhaps determined by forces within me of which I was not fully aware at the time. One of these, I am certain now but I was not then, was the growing strength of my literary vocation. In those days I underwent two of the three experiences I have had of books springing unannounced, unprepared, un-thought-of, out of my mind, like volcanic eruptions. One was *The Sacred Giraffe*, a story that takes place six centuries ahead of us, when Europe and the white peoples have disappeared in a cosmic catastrophe and the world is ruled by a black, feminist people. This fantasy is still awaiting an intelligent film producer. I shall say no more about it save that it gave me an opportunity to provide a literary outlet for the experience I had acquired as a draftsman of pacts, during the Ethiopian dispute, as will be told at a later stage in these memoirs.

While I was busy writing as quickly as I could this story that came forth so easily, I had to put it aside altogether, because another volcanic eruption came through. I happened to have Lol on my knee, and had read to her 'The Little Boy Lost' and 'The Little Boy Found' which had moved her deeply, and to free her mind from that emotion, I began to improvise a description of the 'Bird of Paradise':

> This is the Bird of Paradise
> Such a fine bird you never saw.
> Two stars of heaven are its eyes.
> It holds a half moon in each claw.
>
> Its beak is made of emerald;
> Its wings are made of velveteen;
> Its head is big and round and bald;
> Its tail is yellow, red and green.
>
> Its mouth is made of ebonite;
> It has a tongue of chocolate;
> And when it feels great appetite

It gives its tongue a hearty bite
And thinks its meal is truly great.

It makes its nest under the curls
Combed in the hair of little girls.
Its song is like the strings of pearls
Worn by the wives of dukes and earls.

Only with gold can it be slain.
It must be boiled in turkey's milk,
Kept in a dish of porcelain
Placed on a cloth of crimson silk.

If served on slices of roast lamb
On which the bird can nicely sit,
It has a taste of strawberry jam
Before you've had too much of it.

Children below thirteen
Should not, however, eat the wings of velveteen.

I got stuck now and then, and then the idea or the rhyme turned up and on we went, until the bird was there complete before our eyes. Then Lol, who was great at questions, asked whose the bird was, and I answered that it belonged to the Lord Privy Seal; whereupon she asked who the Lord Privy Seal was and I answered that he was a powerful man who owned a seal of his own that he carried in a bath-tub on wheels.

That set me going, and I had to write *Sir Bob* while *The Sacred Giraffe* waited. Lol always claimed co-authorship on the ground that one of the lines describing the Bird of Paradise had been supplied by her. I have had no other case of a volcanic book, for, though I write my fiction books quickly I dream them slowly.

The Sacred Giraffe was too whimsical to find a publisher easily. It went from pillar to post for some time. I spoke once to MacKinnon Wood, gave it to him to read, and he, who as a racy Scot had a good dose of sense of humour, saw the point. He advised me to write to John Murray, of Oxford, who was then in the publishing business under the name of Martin Hopkinson and Co. I seized a piece of blank paper from my desk and wrote Murray a line.

He had not heard from MacKinnon Wood, had never met me, had not seen the MS, but answered that he would publish the book. I was nonplussed by my own success; for it did not seem to me business-like; and my puzzlement was not to vanish into the free air of rationality . . . well, a rationality of sorts, until long after *The Sacred Giraffe* was out. It had a fair success. Tom Jones made what may still be the most objective valuation: 'It just misses being a great book.' I am not sure, though, about that 'misses'.

Other circumstances contributed to my resignation from the Secretariat at a time when I was perhaps at the top of my form as an international civil servant. One of them certainly was my dissatisfaction with the policy of Britain and France about the League. Britain openly and at times brutally, France more subtly and hypocritically, were firmly opposed to any supra-national tendency in Geneva; while I was persuaded that the very idea of the League as a mere co-operative of unlimited sovereignties would suffice to sink it; and therefore, that the best future for the world lay in a gradual growth of a supra-national authority. That is why I saw in the Secretary General a mere prefiguration of a true World Chancellor.

That was exactly what Drummond neither was nor wished to be. Indeed, he had evolved backwards; for, with Monnet, he had created the Secretariat, and it was thanks to him that the Secretariat was an international body instead of a conglomerate of national offices; so that his spontaneous and initial attitude could not have been more enlightened. Yet, whether through weakness, scepticism or fatigue, his stand veered and actually ceased to be what his position required. The crucial change came, I believe, after his visit to Mussolini. When he allowed the Duce to force him to accept as successor to Attolico, the Duce's own personal assistant, Paulucci di Calboli Barone, the very essence of the Secretariat was compromised. I saw no future for the League after that day, none beyond a certain utility as a diplomatic gadget, which is the highest level of vision Austen Chamberlain's political intelligence would reach.

I also felt Drummond's personal hostility, the cold draught of which chilled me even after it had passed through the warmer air of Frank Walter's climate. Thus I could see British, French, Scandinavian Directors sent travelling to all lands on more or less important missions; but when I presented what seemed to me a well-grounded proposal for a political tour, I was met with a definite refusal. The pattern of League allegiances was fairly clear. The Nordics were British clients; the *Petite Entente*, French clients; the 'Latin' Americans were wooed by both; Italy and Germany were big enough in themselves; Spain was alone, and not big enough to stand on her own. And, against all logic, this pattern of adhesions did in fact prevail in the whole Secretariat. I was popular – possibly the most popular of the Directors – with the Secretariat, but not with my chief.

There was a reshuffle of top rank people and I was told by Drummond that the new Japanese Under-secretary General Sugimura would be head of the political section and, as such, would supervise Disarmament on the political side. I should have plenty to do with its technical aspects.

I said that I viewed the proposed change with deep misgivings; for in Disarmament, there were no technical aspects worth bothering about, since the problem was merely political; and I should have to consider my position very carefully. Drummond was full of sympathy for my point of view: he stood to win both ways. If I stayed, I was diminished. If I left, good riddance.

I began to look around for other fields. Then, the way out was suddenly opened. I got a letter from Henry Thomas, at the time head of the Spanish-Portuguese Books Department at the British Museum. It was handwritten in dark ink on blue notepaper. It informed me of the fact that a new chair of Spanish Studies had been created at Oxford; that he was a member of the selecting Committee; and that he had been requested to write to me that if I answered his letter privately assuring him that I should accept, the chair would be officially offered to me. As he knew me well, he let fall in passing that the Chair would be known as 'King Alfonso XIII Chair of Spanish Studies' and that the salary would be £1100. This amounted to about half of what I drew in Geneva, where, moreover, I paid no taxes. I accepted by return of post.

The crown and sceptre over my professorial chair were not at all in my way. I have never attached much weight to whether a nation called itself a monarchy or a republic, mere labels for a wide variety of political forms and substances; nor had I ever declared myself either a republican or a monarchist so far as Spanish affairs were concerned. Furthermore, I knew the British love to dedicate their chairs to patron saints, so that my colleague for French Literature was decorated with the name of 'Marshal Foch Professor of French Literature', and, therefore, I knew I should no more be expected to become a courtier in Madrid than Rudler would to become an adept of Foch's strategical ideas. And, again, I soon learnt that neither Alfonso nor the Spanish Government had contributed a cent to the funds towards the new chair, that owed its existence mostly to a wealthy Chilean diplomat of Welsh-Jewish extraction. The royal name attached to it was due to the prepossessions of Colonel Bedford, an English military doctor who knew no Spanish but, for some reason or other, became interested in the Chair, fought, travelled and collected money for it, and wanted a Spanish grand cross which he got in due time.

All this was plain and straightforward; but not easy to explain to my political friends in Spain; and, while at the time it didn't matter very much, it was to allow the flourishing of all kinds of attacks on my republican loyalty during my time of public life in Spain, which as yet was very far from my thoughts or even imagination.

Thus the pattern of my life asserted itself. I seemed doomed to enter professions and institutions through the window; I was apt to become a 'great noise' while I remained; and I was evidently pre-destined to leave not very long afterwards, in order to jump through another window that seemed more attractive. This time, my departure raised a wave of general sympathy in the Secretariat. The subscription for a farewell present grew and grew even after the sum to pay for the gold watch had been well covered; and preparations for its presentation had to be altered as the room required became bigger. Drummond con-veyed a private message to the Committee that he wanted to deliver the gift himself and in his study, no one else present. And so it was done.

But he could not prevent anybody who would pay for his ticket to come to the farewell dinner, which took place in a large room at the International Club. Of this dinner, I only remember the general mood of friendliness, well expressed in several speeches, and three points in my own speech. One which I have noted already on water in the land-scape; another one on nationalism, in which I alluded to the banner of Geneva half of it occupied by an eagle the other one by a key, showing, I said, that at least half of our nationalism had better be kept locked up; and the third, a prompting that led me to say that one always returns to Geneva and that I was sure I should return.

I believe that this doubt about what I was doing was the dominant mood in which I left Geneva towards the end of 1927. I had plunged into the League adventure in an unquestioning, naïve faith, not in the possibility of bringing about some sort of world government, but in the actual coming of such an event. Despite my sobering experiences during my noviciate at Barcelona, and the sceptical mirth they often raised in me, I was as convinced a world citizen as ever breathed in Geneva. In fact, I had never analysed, never indeed looked at the roots of my belief. It was, I suspect today, an off-shoot of the conviction that if men see that the better road is better, they will resolutely choose it – a rational rather than a reasonable conviction.

I find a trace of this state of mind in an article I wrote in the *Journal de Genève*, on the building of the new headquarters for the League. The very form in which this dismal business had evolved should have warned me against enthusiasm. No important nation seemed able to bear the humiliation of being passed over in the choice of an architect. Styles, persons and states were being dealt around and mixed and cut like cards for a gamble, and the end was a hybrid affair contrived by a bunch of architects in the purest Swiss Federal Railway Station style.

I had foreseen this unhappy ending to the compass and rule intrigue, and so had written an article in which I asked for a building that would leave a profound trace in the history of architecture, as a fit expression of our faith in a world of reason, and I asked that the new palace be given a tower rising as high as our hopes towards the sky. And I signed it 'Weltbürger'. An eminent and most respectable old Genevese Elder Statesman wrote to the *Journal de Genève* a letter in which he protested against such extravagance. I liked this old man, for he was a clean image of a clean generation, but he seemed to me plainly mediocre for all that, and unable to see the scope of our modern world; so I was sorry when the city gave his name to the Quai which until then had been known by the liveliest of names: Quai des Eaux Vives.

I was particularly fond of this quay because of its name, which was more than justified by the Spout – the water-geyser that rises towards the sky, with a powerful impulse, in which I probably felt the surging optimism of our faith in the coming era of reason. I had, furthermore, identified it with the minuetto of Mozart's *Venus Symphony in G. Minor* whose rising rhythm and cadences appealed to me as almost identical with those of the 'live water' in the spout; and all these dreams, that music, those events, happening between the two endless blue spaces of the blue heavens and the blue waters, moved then in my inner self as the living waters of hope.

Nor can I say that, when I left, all that light-air-water had vanished. Far from it. Its charm resisted the cold, grey, sarcastic, diabolic winds of disbelief that blew in my inner being day after day, night after night, during those tedious negotiations for – what? A text. Or, as I put it in my *Sacred Giraffe*, the common frontier to which we of the Secretariat could manage to drag opposite delegates to agree while they remained obstinately each on his own side of the verbal frontier and as far from it as possible.

I put it to my friends of the Secretariat that the four pillars of the League of Nations were by no means Faith, Hope, Charity and Truth, but 'so far as possible', 'eventually', 'in principle' and *'au fur et à mesure'* which really works better in French, for it is in French that it is most inscrutable. Drafting was the top virtue. I believe it was my skill at drafting that was the chief cause of my success in Geneva; though I grant that such a skill is not merely literary, springing as it does from a certain aloofness as to the issue.

Aloofness there was, but of two kinds. One was due to the very small-ness, the backwardness of many of the disputes. Without in the least feeling out of sympathy with the parties, that had grown into their respective attitudes through centuries of their history and tradition, one felt that actually the problem was due to their enmity rather than their enmity to their problem; and one sought to find a link at a higher level.

Of course, the grim, final demonstration of the fact that we were dreaming was yet to come. But by the time I left Geneva the six years of experience had fermented my optimism without actually killing it. My book *Disarmament* is not the work of a sceptic, though it is no longer that of a dreamer. In my own personal perspective, it had led me to write in the *Sacred Giraffe*: 'Each man is to himself his best friend, his worst enemy and his only teacher'; and when challenged on my philosophy, my answer was: 'I am a pessioptimist: Considering how bad men are, it is wonderful how well they behave.'

Then, Hitler.

Part II
Academic Interlude

CHAPTER I

MY DISCOVERY OF AMERICA

B ETWEEN my days as a League Civil Servant at Geneva and my days as professor at Oxford, I discovered America. Dodging the *far niente* of holidays, I stuffed them with a visit to the U.S. which I financed by a lecture tour as the paid guest of the Foreign Policy Association and the League of Nations Union. During my Geneva days I had made a number of American friends who, in one way or another, were connected with that admirable institution; notably Thomas Lamont who was one of its patrons. He was one of those Americans whose handsome smiling image usually comes to my memory when I hear Americans denigrated and even slandered; for he would have honoured any country by merely belonging to it. I had early realised his sterling qualities of brain and heart, and we soon became good friends. His prominent position in the Morgan Bank made it possible for him to be the protector and the patron of a number of public spirited but privately financed institutions such as the Foreign Policy Association, and to act as host to many European visitors in his New York home.

I have elsewhere told how on boarding the *Dresden* at Cherbourg, I came across Keyserling. We had met at Geneva where he had delivered a lecture which I attended; and we ripened an acquaintance during this trip. He was a huge man, so tall that his length concealed his breadth. His features were definitely Slav. His weight, both physical and intellectual, was definitely teutonic. But I hold that he has been unjustly neglected by his country, for he had a first rate brain, which he used with marvellous speed. I once wrote that he made me think of a heavy lorry propelled by a Rolls-Royce engine, which pleased him immensely. For everything he did was huge.

When we were sailing close to the territorial waters of the U.S. most of the Americans on board vanished. Keyserling, a heavy drinker – indeed he looked like a huge tankard on legs – but never drunk (the stuff had to travel too long to get to his head), explained to me that the vanished Americans were holding cabin parties to imbibe as much liquor as possible before the bars and cellars on board ship were sealed in accordance with the prohibition laws.

This was my first experience of prohibition. I had to live through many more. It was a disastrous experiment, due I believe to a miscalculation of the strength of the addiction to alcohol in the people of the

U.S. I am not saying that the matter of alcoholism had better be left to itself; but I do say that prohibition was not the answer, because among other reasons, it added the attraction of the forbidden to the other lures of that particular devil. College girls drank eau de cologne or hair tonic, and the cocktails one was *made* to drink through sheer insistence, could be repulsive when not dangerous.

I have often wondered at the tendency to drink in the Anglo-Saxons and the Nordics. The first time I saw an upper middle class woman utterly drunk was at an international dinner in Copenhagen. She was a Dane whose beauty and distinction made the sight even sadder. The first time I saw an upper middle class man utterly drunk was in Stockholm, at 3 in the afternoon. I am speaking with no sense of superiority, for I have a feeling that, had I had a liver able to stand alcohol without turning sick, I might have been a drunkard myself. My hunch is that the Nordics and the Anglo-Saxons are held too hard by reason while at business and work, and need to release themselves from their fetters when at play.

'We are not breaking the law' – Florence Lamont said to Keyserling while Metcalf, her wonderful English butler, served some Chablis. 'We bought dozens of it before the Amendment.' For all Keyserling cared. . . . Seeing her gambit had failed, she tried another subject. 'Do you like oysters, Count Keyserling?' while Metcalf presented a plate of oyster stew. 'I never take them but raw,' vociferated the giant. Florence stole a dispairing glance at me.

A few days earlier she had wired to Chicago asking me whether I was to be in New York on such a date and if so, could I lunch with her. (Her house was my base during my American tour.) I answered I was arriving in the morning and leaving in the evening, and accepted lunch. When I arrived I found a note begging me to call on her at once. She told me, somewhat dumbfounded still, that she had asked Keyserling to lunch and he had answered he would only come if I came also.

We went to have our coffee at the Lamonts' handsome library, and Keyserling began to hold forth on wisdom, which seemed to be his speciality. On and on he went on this rich subject when he was suddenly blocked by Florence's courteous and slightly frightened voice: 'But Count Keyserling, what do you mean by "Spirit"?' He shot a glance at her which was meant to kill her instantly, and drily and finally cut: 'I never explain!' Then, over poor, defenceless Florence, the Rolls-Royce lorry rolled on.

I left in the evening to carry on my lay preaching for Our Lady of Geneva, and when I returned a week or so later, Tom and Florence gave me a full and animated report of the dinner they had given to the Foreign Policy Association Executive in honour of Keyserling. It all began with an invitation which Keyserling accepted 'on condition he sat between two pretty women.' I seem to remember, though I do not vouch for this, that Florence, who though no longer young was still handsome, gave up her right as a hostess to place her guest as he had demanded, between two peaches; and the dinner went on beautifully, the great guest being adequately supplied with champagne by the inimitable Metcalf, who (something never seen or above all *heard* before or after in that house, where service was as perfect as it was silent) every time he passed and refilled the ever thirsty glass, would ask in an audible and spirited whisper: '*More* champagne, Sir?' Whereupon, the table was graced by a garland of smiles.

'When are you going?' I asked Keyserling one day I happened to be in New York, soon after, and he rang me up. He wanted in fact to know about an article Harper's had asked me to write on the U.S. He answered: 'Tomorrow. You see, I've been here a fortnight. Far too much. If I stay longer, I shan't be able to write about this country.' I was delighted. I told him that at my first lunch-cum-Press Conference, organised by my sponsors, I had begun my short address by saying to the press boys: 'Gentlemen, I landed from Europe at eleven. Our lunch began at twelve. It is twelve-thirty. So, you will please excuse me if I haven't yet written my book on the U.S.' He laughed. 'It is all very well, but I will not write my book until I've read your article.' And I must say that he kept me at it by letters and cables until he got his copy.

I believe I am a type of mind not unlike his was – who picks up things rather than plods at them, and trusts impressions more than he does statistics. We kept a good relationship and exchanged a number of letters. Most of those in my possession were lost with my library and files, not during the civil war and the siege of Madrid, but when the forces of so-called law and order took over the town, and not during the more or less excusable disorder of the first rush in, but during the cool, quiet time that followed.

While a professor at Oxford, I once received a cable from a ship on which Keyserling was crossing the ocean from New York to London. He asked me to accept an invitation to dinner I was to receive from 'Guinness' for he was to be the other guest. It turned out to be a dinner for six: the two Guinnesses, man and wife, Keyserling and his very charming wife, C.H.M.A. and I; in a private room at the George in Oxford. The host and hostess, handsome and in the best simple, well-bred style one usually enjoys in Britain, enquired what we would drink, whereupon Keyserling, with as much authority as voice, laid it down:

'Champagne, of course, but let's begin with beer.' The Scots woman and the Spaniard were too well disciplined to show the slightest sign of distress; the Guinness couple were perfect; as if such an abomination had been the inveterate custom of the British Isles since Alfred the Great, they ordered the stuff; and throughout the whole evening Keyserling kept transmuting the two gaseous liquids which he imbibed by the gallon, into a regular geyser of philosphy, wisdom, wit, gaiety, anything but hiccups.

CHAPTER II

LAY PREACHER OR SALESMAN IN THE U.S.A.

WHEN he learnt that I was going to the U.S.A., Sweetser began to nurse me carefully. He was so conscientious, so keen on the League, so concerned about the unscrupulous means some American republicans had used to bamboozle their countrymen into leaving it in the lurch, that he wanted to make sure that my trip would be a success. Most of his advice was more invaluable than I could even appreciate, owing to my lack of experience; but one piece of it I flatly turned down. We were then struggling to bring the U.S. into the Hague Court; hoping that its strictly legal character would appeal to a Republic that had made of its Supreme Court the keystone of its Constitution. But Sweetser and his friends took a tactical line that did not appeal to me: they played down the connection between the Hague Court and the League, even though the budget of the Court was part of that of the League, and the judges were elected by a simultaneous vote of the League Assembly and Council. This did not seem to me fair to the American public opinion nor indeed realistic either.

In my talks throughout my lecture tour, I insisted on the organic unity of the Court and the League. The American public understood this language. They were used to the relation between the three powers in any state, and saw the logic of my picture. I was soon able to satisfy my sponsors on their choice of lay preacher. I was earnest in substance more than in form; I never read, but always improvised though on a carefully prepared frame of thought and argument and I enjoyed the cut and thrust at question time, which I called 'retaliation'. One of the newspapers that reported my talks coined a flattering sentence: 'a Spaniard who looks like Julius Caesar and speaks like Bernard Shaw'. My New York agent, Mr Feakins, an excellent person who became a good friend and organised all my subsequent trips, said to me: 'You know, doctor [they always called me doctor in America, I don't know why], you are a bit of a swindler.' I saw he was friendly and joking, so I just asked why. 'I come to listen to your lecture and at the end I find you have sold me an idea I didn't want to buy.'

That, by the way, introduced me to the O.B.M. (omnipresent business metaphor), possibly the chief difference between the English and the American languages. It rests – in this use, at any rate – on a curious inversion of the actual process. Your commercial traveller convinces his would-be customer of the advisability of buying his toothpaste, motor car, steel works or what not, and as a consequence of your being convinced, you buy his stuff. The language inverts the order, and to say that you are convinced it says you have bought the idea. This moreover assumes that you can get nothing from another person unless you buy it from him, or, in other words, that there is no human relation other than those based on money transactions. Man to wife: 'I find you have sold me a baby I didn't want to buy.'

Utterly alien as I feel to all this, I don't dislike it because I like Americans. You like or dislike people. If you like them, you like their ways, even those you don't like. (This sounds like an Irish bull. Perhaps it is one. But it won't hurt. Irish bulls don't usually charge.) I was ready to own to myself that their way of life was not mine, nor were most of their bodily, mental or intellectual tastes, nor their jokes, nor their egalitarianism and 'keep smiling' and general verbal style and – what else? Granted. But the sum total of this dissent was a curious assent, not of the intellect but of the heart. I liked the Americans.

I keep turning this paradox in my mind round and round, wondering why. Why, my usual hobby, watching national character at work. I believe I was fascinated by the humility and the utter lack of envy I observed in the men and women of the U.S. Their humility seemed to me astounding. Often, not so much in public lectures, but in the more congenial environment of an academic social evening or seminar, I felt like Jesus in the Temple answering questions put to me with a sincere desire to hear my opinion by men whose intellectual power and knowledge of the subject, I feel certain, were as good as mine, if not better. And in such cases, I had the feeling that my opinion sounded better and more profound merely because I was able to use language in a crisper way.

Only once, in many years, after having crossed the country four times or five from New York to San Francisco, Chicago to S. Antonio and Boston to Los Angeles, was I the victim of an unpleasant, downright rude verbal attack by a woman, backed by her husband. They turned out not to be Americans, and they were communists. But I was in danger once, and also from a woman. This weak sex! The occasion was one of those luncheons with a speech the Foreign Policy Association used to organise, and the place one of the best-known hotels in New York. The hall was packed and the speaker's table was very long. I spoke, there were some questions, everything went, as they say in America, like a house on fire, and most of the guests had gone, when I found myself discussing points of the speech with eager guests, standing on the edge of the top table platform, close to Pierre de Lannux, a French man of letters who knew America well. A relatively young woman came forward, eyebrows knit, lips tight, military step, a three-cornered hat at a menacing slant. 'How long, she began in a true Catilinarian style, and all mouths stopped and all eyes were on her: 'How long are you going to stay here corrupting the youth of this country?' – 'Well,' I answered, 'it is a slow job, you know! I shall stay until I have done it.' 'Do you realise . . . ' and I noticed a clarion-like burst of voice as she put her question . . . 'that there are forty-eight States in this country?' Then the Devil stole onto the stage. Tennessee was at that time facing a liberal campaign of criticism for having prohibited the teaching of Darwinian theories. Why the odd idea should have crossed my mind, of bringing this issue into the debate, I don't know. I answered: 'No, Madam. Only forty-seven. Tennessee does not count.' The Devil was in it: 'I come from Tennessee!' she shouted and her three-cornered hat shook in a frightening way. Pierre de Lannux had to grapple with the virago.

Next to their humility what charmed me most in Americans – and still does – is their total freedom from envy. This is a precious virtue in a nation; for it enables the more capable man to rise without feeling the envious ones below pulling him down; but, quite apart from this utilitarian aspect, it makes life so much more pleasant when those who shine can do so under the sunlight of a general smile instead of under the yellow-black clouds of ill-humoured jealousy. It may well be that this freedom from jealousy the Americans enjoy is the reward of another of their virtues: their ever awake inventiveness. Gadget-minded, someone has called them. They are far more interesting than that. They are the ever active pioneers, the men out there on the edge of the unknown. They accept, indeed, assume the possibility of everything, even of the things that to the more conservative-minded Europeans might seem chimerical. For instance, to write down instruments and voice inside a wax cylinder and have the whole thing read by a steel needle. A perfectly absurd idea. As absurd and as sensible as going out to cross the ocean in three little more than fishing boats and discover a continent.

It is this refusal to admit the impossibility of anything that has not been tried, this looking out and forward, this feeling that tomorrow's world is there uncreated, that liberates the American from envy. His neighbour's achievements, far from saddening him, spur him to attempt his own.

Nevertheless, I found none of the tremendous sense of activity which in our youthful days in Hampstead, Ezra Pound used to sing to me, his eyes shining behind his glasses. 'The other fellow, you know, he just walks through you!' I found nothing of the kind. Indeed, my impression – perhaps because I expected too much – was rather of a certain underlying indolence, ever-ready to take over from whatever burst of activity it had to be interrupted with, for it is, I still think, indolence rather than activity, that is the normal state of the American. And under the indolence, a core of boredom. One might even suspect in that eagerness to fly to the moon a desire to flee from the boredom at home.

But whence the boredom? Possibly the very surfeit of affluence; the certainty that every desire can be satisfied. For otherwise the Americans have been as successful as any nation in achieving a gracious society. No more unfair accusation can be levelled against them than that which would represent them as boorish and uncultured. Weaker brethren there are among them as among any other nationals of any other country; but the general level of culture and refinement is high, taste is usually good and at times excellent; and, what to my mind is most invaluable, a good-humoured tolerance and a courtesy of the heart is found to flourish with a gratifying frequency.

This last gift was, I found, the most equitably distributed in all the classes, for otherwise the varnish of culture does not lie evenly on the surface of the nation, and it rises steeply with comfort and education. (I am not sure about education though. I knew an American woman who was a lawyer and had not managed to master the difference between *consul* and *counsel*.) I remember having read in a Spanish book that a group of young European graduates, travelling on a goodwill tour organised by some Foundation, being received by the Mayor of a middle-west town, was being introduced by their leaders: 'Monsieur Durand, French, señor Martínez, Spanish, Mr Patridis, Greek.' Whereupon the mayor's face brightened: 'Ah, Greek! Indeed! Ancient Greek or modern Greek?' I happened to know the author of the book, one of our finest humorists, Julio Camba, so I took it as a joke; until I told it, as such, to my friend Aghnides, who had preceded me in Geneva in charge of Disarmament and later made a good career at the United Nations. He protested. 'A joke? No joke at all. I knew Patridis. He told me so himself.'

CHAPTER III

AMERICAN SUBTLETIES

O F course some of these observations may have become obsolete through the evolution of the Americans themselves. Their access to top rank in world affairs may have made them arrogant, thus super-imposing arrogance – a collective sense of collective superiority – on their individual humility; but some of their features do remain. They differ from the English but do not like to think they do, unless the English assume they don't. The English will delight in building fences thick and high to keep off their neighbours' curiosity and feel really at home; while the Americans keep no fences at all between garden and garden; withal the American feels very English still, only he must not be found out.

I believe it was during that first visit, that I was led to dramatise this situation one lovely day in California. I had been entertained at lunch in a beautiful house in the vicinity of Los Angeles, and we all sat in the garden sipping our coffee in the sun. As usual, the assembly – all Americans but one, Lady Willert – soon turned me into an oracle spin-ning out parables of wisdom to quench their thirst for that brand of ambrosia, when at a sudden quirk in my argument, I happened casually to drop a statement that made everybody sit up. 'You Americans, despite Washington, Jefferson and all that, are still at heart the subjects of the King of England.' Up war. 'Yes. The umbilical cord has not snapped yet.' I was challenged to make my assertion good with a con-crete example. 'Here it is. When you speak of the King of Spain, you say: 'the King of Spain', and of the King of Sweden, 'the King of Sweden'. But when you speak of the King of England, you say 'the King'. It was so, then. I can't speak for to-day. Perhaps they call the Queen, 'Our special relative'.

For change there has been, and considerable at that, mostly in the realm of foreign relations. During my first tours I found a good deal of humility, indeed of naïvety, and occasionally a challenging, almost offensive aggressiveness (rare though this was). The background was still that of manifest destiny and unashamed imperialism, at any rate within the continent; the spirit of Theodore Roosevelt, blustering, jingo and no nonsense. I still remember one day, at the old Spanish Club in London, in Wells St., during or soon after the first world war, a young, tall, handsome American diplomat wearing a black frock coat,

117

to whom I had just said that in my view Puerto Rico and Cuba should federate, answering in proud, determined terms: 'What we have we hold.' And that was that. Nor was Theodore Roosevelt less forthright in his declaration of intent, made in his private correspondence, that every European nation would be ousted from the New World by the U.S.

After all, remember it was Wilson who deliberately barred the door of the League to Mexico – a situation I took the initiative to put right later, and it will not be the least lively story to be told in these pages. While that kind of mood was no longer active, at any rate in the gatherings that my name and assignment congregated, it was still there in the background and nearly everywhere. I did not attack it head on; but I did a good deal through humour, and trusting the debonair spirit of my audiences. It was then that I devised certain verbal coins that have rolled a good deal since. 'Yes. You are imperialists. We Spaniards understand. Spain is an Empire-builder retired from business.' This went down very well.

Of course it led to conflicts of conscience between the would-be imperialist and the would-be pacifist, or at least, internationalist living within the same skin. I watched many a case of these schizophrenic League fans, and it led me to another verbal coin. 'His conscience,' I told one of my audiences, 'does not prevent the Anglo-Saxon from sinning, but it prevents him from enjoying his sin.'

Thus prepared, my kind victims were ready to hear what I had to say on the Monroe Doctrine; and I was not remiss in letting them hear it.

There are only two things I hold for certain about the Monroe Doctrine, I told them: the first is that no American knows what it is; the second is that no American will tolerate that it be touched. Now these two features do not define a doctrine at all. What they define is a dogma. And, sure enough, a close examination will reveal to us the dogmatic character of what goes by the name of Monroe Doctrine. Instead of one dogma, we discover two: the dogma of the Immaculate Conception of American foreign policy; and the dogma of the Infallibility of the American President.

They took it very well, for they were courteous and I said it without malice; but also, because they felt it to be true under the banter. It is always a wonder for us, grandsons of Rome, to discover how easy it is for Britons and Americans to hold within their brains contradictory opinions and even opinions contrary to the facts. The sincerity with which Americans believe that the history of their country is one of peaceful progress is only equalled by the profound conviction Britons hold of having always fought for the freedom of every European nation as well as for the freedom of the seas. And yet, the very name they have chosen for their country is revealing: United States *of America*. They subconsciously see the whole continent as their domain; and such is in fact the root of the Monroe Doctrine.

I must quote Camba again. 'Yes. A fine country, indeed. A pity she has no name. No. United States of America is not a name: it is a description. It is as if that pretty Mary, you know whom I mean, instead of calling herself Mary, was known as "the blonde girl in the second storey".' To which I retorted: 'Ah, but look at the letters on the lapel of American uniforms. That is a grand and a proud name: *U.S.* That is a true name: "We, of the herd". And instead of "Americans" which is a usurpation, or "North Americans", which, besides being a mouthful, abolishes or annexes Mexicans and Canadians, or "Yankees", which forgets the South, the Middle and the West, we ought to know them as "Ussians".'

This proud U.S., WE, inherited from Britain, (nay, from England, the strongest herd in the world, for it is so by nature and needs no help or sting from any shepherd) this proud U.S. gained a wonderful impetus during the two world wars; but in a less original nation, it might have given rise to mere jingoism and presented the world with an enlarged vision of Theodore Roosevelt (an appalling thought); while instead the U.S. has evinced a growth of her world conscience parallel to that of her world power. This was by no means certain to happen; indeed, there was a time when the expectation was the very reverse. Once I was told by Dr Marañón, a prominent expert in the science of internal secretions, how, one morning, he saw a strange football scramble enter his study. Four hefty men were forcing in an unwilling patient who looked like a young man in his twenties. One of the older men said: 'Doctor, I am this child's father; these three are my brothers. The boy's age is five; his body is twenty. He is very strong. No girl in the village is safe.' I leave off the biological conundrum to switch back to world affairs. I cut Marañón's story to point out: 'The United States, isn't it?'

We are lucky that this quip turned out to be unfair, at least between any two presidential elections. For, as I once put it in a letter to *The Times*, the world is like a passenger car running along a road that winds through perilous precipices turning hairpin bends, whose driver goes every four miles through a nearly total blackout. Let us hope we are going somewhere. Still, no one who has known the U.S. of the early thirties can but be thankful and glad at the impressive strides the American people have made in world affairs.

It is generally believed that the U.S. has come as nearly as any nation can to the phase of development so eagerly sighed for by socialists: a classless society. There is something in it – but not that much. The down-the-nose effect one often gets in England, the insolent treatment of the humbler sort one is pained to find still alive in Italy or Spain, are of course not to be found anywhere in the U.S. save perhaps in the south as between Whites and Blacks – a point I shall discuss later. While on this note, let me say that in my experience, the foreign visitor has at times to endure as much arrogance in New York as in London shops – but of a different character and flavour. A visitor to a big store in say Regent Street will never understand what is happening to him unless he realises that every shopman, and even more so, every shopgirl, in that street is a member of the Royal Family who, owing to unfortunate circumstances, happens to have landed on that shore behind night-gowns and other feminine what-nots, a fact which must be conveyed to the intruder before any transaction is considered. A would-be customer in New York, if found out to be a foreigner, will soon discover that patience is short and enquiries unwelcome and questions frowned at as insults to the land of the free.

You may say that this stand-offishness towards the foreigner is also a feature the Americans inherited from the British, and I should, of course, agree. Gibson told me once how his mother, a wealthy New-Englander, once saw her English butler come up to her with a very long face and give notice. 'Madam,' he explained, 'your staff have insulted me.' Asked in what way, precisely, he answered: 'They have called me a foreigner.' Mrs Gibson patiently and tactfully tried to make the offended Englishman see the light; but her long lesson was rejected by a firm and irrefutable argument: 'The fact remains, Madam, that I cannot be a foreigner, since I am an Englishman.'

The English, as we all know, owe their strength to their sticking to the facts. What, however, saves them is their sense of humour, and in this particular aspect of things, one of them has cleansed his people from their insular arrogance with the sheer fountain of delight fusing with the luminous air of laughter and reason:

> And resisting all temptations
> To belong to other nations
> 'e remains a Henglishman!

The far less humourous attitude of some shopkeepers – in my ex-perience a small minority – who will be rude to the visitor raises the problem of foreignness in the U.S. It is, of course, ubiquitous. The country is composed of successive waves of foreigners, even though the number of Americans who descend from the Mayflower contingent is impressive. So impressive indeed that in my fantasy *The Sacred Giraffe* I turned the Mayflower into a mythical ship that symbolised reproduction and multiplication, as her very name suggests.

I read not long ago that the American melting pot was really treble, its parts not mutually mixable,. or, at any rate, not yet mixed; the Protestant Anglo-Saxon, fed by Dutch, German and Scandinavian immigrants; the Roman Catholic, made up of Irishmen, Italians and Poles, and the Jewish. I suggest that, if we are to tackle the problem of classes in the U.S.A., it is from this angle we must approach it. We must forget all about Marx. In that America, supposed to be the most money-minded country in the world, money has little or nothing to do with classes. Define? Well. No one would do such a thing. *Always feel, seldom think, never speak*. That is the golden rule about classes. Now, the Christians feel above the Jews; and the Protestants above the Catholics, and that is that, and only an unmannered foreigner writing his memoirs would ever dream of mentioning it.

This leads in a subtle way to another class difference, never spoken of, seldom observed. The Republicans as a class are above the Democrats. This became apparent to me during my first trip. I noticed that, if I came across a Democrat, I knew I should be treated to an explanation: 'Yes. I am a Democrat. But, of course, all my family, as a matter of fact, have always been Republicans: still, I am a Democrat.' I have never met a Republican who offered the inverse explanation. The chap who owned that he was a Democrat was on the defensive lest I thought that he rose from the ranks instead of descending as he no doubt did from the apex of society i.e. from the Protestant Anglo-Saxon, Northern European pool, far above the Polish-Latin-Jewish rabble he had joined on becoming a Democrat. This experience seems to me an irrefutable proof that social, if not economic, classes are going strong in the U.S.

But hasn't the fact more than a purely American relevance? Isn't class a far subtler concept than the paltry income-affair economists and socialists are only too prone to see in it? 'Ah', some will argue, 'but the non-economic aspects of class are but the flowers of its one and only sap, which is money, from which comfort, leisure, culture, manners, charm will in due time flourish.' No. Class is so subtle and universal that it turns up even within classes. A community is the richer for the variety and subtlety of its feeling of class. There is in England a concept, a feeling and a word – 'exclusive' – that has always appealed to me as utterly silly; and one which, in itself, would turn every man but a saint into a hater of the very idea of class. It corresponds not to class but to *clique*. Class is natural; and in countries endowed with a highly developed moral sophistication, it is apt to proliferate into a number of hills and dales, so that the same person may be upper in one light and lower in another, in a gently undulating social landscape. The American social landscape is far less sophisticated, and yet, one can perceive in it all kinds of ups and downs, pride and superciliousness, humiliation and loneliness, comradeship, recognition, coldness and warmth – the whole well wrapped in the transparent plastic of American courtesy.

At bottom, the Negro problem, or as people say now-a-days, the Black problem, contains many of the elements of class. The very change of name is part of it. After all, *negro* is Spanish for *black*, and the objection to the word today is less due to the letter than to the music with which it used to be sung for centuries, and still is in many parts of the U.S.A.

I owe to that shrewd, beautiful, generous and faithful friend, Helen Moorhead, my first 'live' experience of the Negro problem as early as January 1928, during my first visit to the U.S. She took me to an evening in a house in Harlem, where a number of Black intellectuals and artists had been gathered for a purely social evening – no lectures, no talks, nothing but just to meet and converse. It was delightful in every way. Men and women of intellectual distinction, most of the men in black-tie attire, all the women in elegant, gay, yet unostentatious evening frocks; most of them, men and women, handsome and some of the women beautiful; a lively conversation, neither too highbrow nor too frivolous – in one word, definitely an élite.

Then an idea seized my mind. There wasn't a single man or woman there who, in the Spanish world, whether of the new or of the old, would have been described as black. They were all mulattos. This seemed to me significant in more ways than one; so significant indeed, that I devoted some attention to the fact in every one of my later visits to the United States. The 'fact' could be put in this way: 'Most, if not all, the American Blacks whose culture and education raise them above the mass, are half-caste, or, more concretely, show some white features.'

I may be wrong, but I believe this to be a fact, with one important exception, to which I shall come presently. Whenever I have come across an American Negro out of the common, the white blood was evident somewhere, either in his features or in his colour; he was, in short, a man who in any Spanish-speaking country would not have been styled a negro but a mulatto.

The only pure Negroes definitely out of the common I have met were Cubans and Haitians. When I was at school in Paris, 'J.J.' a Haitian pure negro, was the handsomest and one of the cleverest in our class – not perhaps in our actual studies, but as an all round, powerful, self-possessed, wise creature. And when I worked on world affairs in Geneva, I met two Haitian delegates who were capable men, and one of them as good a speaker (in French) as any Frenchman.

But I have not had that luck in the U.S.; so that I am led to the conclusion that one of the factors that has created the unhappy situation known as the Black problem in America is the peculiarly wide definition of who is a Black that prevails there. I have known a secretary of an important pro-Negro association who was grey-eyed and whose hair turned white from fair and not from black (i.e. was silvery and not steel coloured), and whose name, to crown it all with sarcasm, was 'White.'

CHAPTER IV

MY DISCOVERY OF OXFORD

NOW that I look back on it all with a better knowledge of Oxford and of myself, I realise that when I arrived there at the end of January 1928, I was bound to be looked upon as an intruder in more ways than one. I was a foreigner, indeed, the most foreign of foreigners for a world as essentially English as Oxford, since I came from Spain, and Spain, despite the years gone by, has remained for Englishmen 1588 and all that; I was an upstart, a mining engineer turned man of letters, a humanist with no Greek and little Latin, a professor of Spanish with no standing in philology; finally, I was a total stranger to the ways of Oxford, those subtle forms of behaviour, things taken for granted, items of esoteric knowledge, acquaintances, who's-whos, meanings of silence, which shape the human pebble well rounded off by the waters of habit. Once again, I had entered through the window another profession and another institution.

My own chief impression was Tibet. I felt as if I had suddenly landed in a lamassery. Exeter College, where I was housed for a few days – until I fled in terror to the Randolph Hotel. Yes. And when I arrived in Oxford from the U.S. I discovered that the colleges – Exeter at any rate – had not yet reached the stage of one man one bathroom. I was given a bedroom whose only claim to heating was the somewhat theoretical one of a chimney in which an enormous cube of coal hid its one and only red face by turning its five other black cold ones to the room and its dweller; and when the next morning I asked where the bathroom was, I was told I had to walk across the quad and go downstairs and follow a corridor and then I'd better ask again.

This is not my *ain hoose*, thought I, remembering those overheated American rooms which weren't my own house either, but which at any rate did not expose one to the risk of dying of pneumonia or going bathless for a week. I daresay these obstacles on the way to my daily bath increased my Tibet feeling. In those days, Exeter College was led by a set of old scholars, thoroughly cured by immersion in sherry and port (whose colours still ran in rivulets over their complexions), self-possessed, sure of themselves, their eyes safely set within deep sockets, lit by flashes of wit, disdain, humour, everything but surprise, eyes that had read all there was to be read and could bear no more sadness. They walked slowly, spoke slowly and thought slowly; but they knew everything. Lamas of Tibet, whose gatherings ran in the bed of time like a slow, murmuring river going nowhere, over which now and then burst, like the call of some exotic bird, the boisterous peal of laughter of a young carefree voice soaring above the frozen Himalayas, Balsdon, the sub-rector.

He took me to All Souls to be inmatriculated, or something to that effect, by Pember, a dignified figure in his vice-chancellor's robes; and then I was told I should be made an M.A. by decree. Admirable England! They first chose the man; then they put on him any academic labels he might need in order to circulate along the main channels and the nooks and corners of officialdom. I could remember countries much less wise.

Yet, the question might be, indeed was, put: had they chosen the right man? My appointment had been due to the meeting of two circumstances: a scarcity of Hispanists at the time in Britain; and the feeling which my books had fostered that I should be a good professor. Both these 'circumstances' turned out to be wrong. When I left, Entwistle was appointed, and while his spoken Spanish was by no means perfect, he was a fine Spanish scholar and a first-rate scientific linguist. As for my own qualification for the chair....

Modesty and vanity keep quarrelling about this. They had better be told to be quiet and let us get on with *das Ding an sich* ....Would Christopher Columbus, Marco Polo, Stanley, Livingstone or Captain Scott have been good professors of geography? I am an intuitive explorer of things, mostly of human nature; not a didactic mind at all; universally curious but averse to concrete knowledge. I was bound to interest my students more but to teach them, if not less, at any rate fewer things than a regular academic professor. And this inherent shortcoming is one which the Committee that chose me did overlook.

Did they, though? Some of the men in it were too shrewd and too experienced to have missed such an obvious fact. It is likelier that they saw the risk and chose to run it, which says a good deal for their imagination and courage. How often have I admired the spirit in which my appointment was dared, even if in actual fact, fate, hazard and character were to work against its success. When I compare the free dom from bureaucratic fetters and nationalist prepossessions that presided over my choice, I feel full of an admiration lined with envy.

CHAPTER V

PROFESSION VERSUS VOCATION

THIS struggle between my profession and my vocation soon reached the surface of Oxford daily life. On the one hand, I felt a certain amount of friction in the Department; I was not warned about this, I was not made aware in time about that; and the trouble obviously came from a passive opposition to the upstart professor; on the other hand, I was often requested to speak on all kinds of occasions, at meetings of undergraduates' clubs in particular.

For my part, I was not always helpful. Instead of behaving so as to win my forgiveness as the housebreaker that I was, I took pleasure in showing off my sin. One of the first dinners I attended has stuck in my memory because of my talk at table with Lady Mary Murray. She wanted to know what I had been doing before I had become 'King Alfonso XIII Professor of Spanish Studies' at Oxford. She first asked me whether my appointment had anything to do with the King of Spain. I laughed. She was puzzled. 'The King would not have minded me but his Ambassador would.' And I went on to explain that neither the King nor the Spanish Government had had anything to do with the founding of the Chair. 'Why his name then?' she asked. I conveyed to her that the man who had collected the money, an English Army doctor, was eager to become a Knight Grand Cross of Something in Spain.

That avenue now closed, she bethought herself of her first query. 'What were you doing before you came here?' I rapidly recited my *curriculum vitae*: primary, secondary education in Spain; secondary education again in France; Ecole Polytechnique, Ecole Nationale Supérieure des Mines; four years in a railway company in Madrid, five as a journalist in London; six as head of the Disarmament Section of the League of Nations ... 'and (diabolically omitting my books of essays) here I am.' She was dumbfounded. 'But ... but, when did you learn Spanish literature?' 'Well,' I answered, 'never; you see, I never needed it. I am going to learn it now.'

Of course, there was nothing systematic or preconceived about it. This kind of thing bubbled up nearly always when the talk came close to my profession-vocation complex. It came perhaps from deeper levels than I was able to fathom then, from that mistrust of concrete knowledge that always has been – as I now see it – one of the strongest though an instinctive feature of my mind. At one of the clubs where

I spoke, as I was asked for the title or subject of my address, a thing I always hate to answer, I suggested: 'On everything'; and my lecture was devoted to showing how and why everything was the only thing I was a specialist about. I remember another dinner-cum-speech at which I was the chief speaker. One of my friends warned me the club was notorious for the high number of communist undergraduates that belonged to it. I was already – indeed I always have been ever since Lenin kicked the Duma to death – an adversary of communism; but the idea of these wealthy Oxford young bloods being so silly as to applaud was too much for me. So I told them about a fascinating short story by Gabriel Miró: An angel sent on some mission to the earth lingered on, liked life down here and in the end lost his wings. Another angel was sent to fetch him back. They had a long talk on the sunny side of life down here, which was concluded with these words from the wingless to the winged one: 'If you only knew how sweet life on earth is so near heaven!' Then I added: 'How sweet must life be for a young communist on 400 a year!'

The biggest show of this kind I remember was the Rhodes Trust Dinner organised by Philip Kerr, then warden of Rhodes House and head of the Trust. He was one of the bunch of minds gathered around Lloyd George mostly through the industry of Tom Jones, for I do not believe Lloyd George, out of his own natural gifts, would ever have discovered the value of brains. Of this group Kerr and W. J. Adams were, in my opinion, the most alive and the most human, a fact that showed even in their luminous and open faces. These men – this type of man – are the salt of Britain. I add, with some diffidence, that they are often Scots, Irishmen or Welshmen, for there is something inhibiting, stand-offish and insular in the unadulterated Englishman which chokes his communication channels with human beings, or at least so it strikes me. Witness Lionel Curtis, a man whose handsome face expressed a spirit far less endowed with a true, universal humanity than he perhaps thought, and whom I could never stand after he wrote that 'the British Commonwealth was the Sermon on the Mount reduced to political terms.' This kind of cant-trash would never have occurred to Tom Jones, to Philip Kerr or to W. J. Adams. One always came across Philip Kerr or W. J. Adams with genuine pleasure.

Philip asked me to be the chief speaker at the Rhodes dinner, or rather, should I say, one of the two, for the other one was to be Barrie the playwright. I agreed with pleasure, for that is one of the few things I feel I can do well; and when the day came, I found it really was a big occasion to judge both by the quantity and by the quality of the guests, so that I could not help feeling that Philip Kerr had conferred upon me an outstanding distinction.

Out of that oration I only remember the story of the elephant, which
came to my mind because the elephant happens to be the emblem of the
Rhodes Trust. It was one of the many stories told us one evening at
Cliveden during the first world war by Dmovski, the head of the
National Polish Party. A competition is on between the nations of the
world and the subject is: the definition of the elephant. The Briton goes
a-hunting for three months and presents a book, lavishly illustrated
with photographs, under the title: 'Elephant Hunting in Somaliland'.
The Frenchman visits the Jardin des Plantes in Paris, tips the *gardiens*
on the ways of their wards and publishes a yellow paperback (as we
would say today) on 'The Elephant and his Love Affairs'. The German
studies for three years in many universities and laboratories, and offers
a three volume thesis entitled: 'Introduction to the Definition of the
Elephant'. The Pole wrote off the cuff and presented a pamphlet on
'The Elephant and the Polish Question', and the Russian sent in an
article on: 'The Elephant, does it Exist?'

This was the story as told by Dmovski. I added to it two other
nations: the American put in a memo on 'The Elephant: How to Make
it Bigger and Stronger'; and the Spaniard didn't bother to compete.

On reading it all, two things strike the mind; one is the permanency
of the national feature alluded to, and therefore, the constancy of the
national characters of the European nations; and the other is the exception to the rule if it really is an exception; for it is curious to think
that a Pole, in 1917 or 18, should give as the prominent feature of
the Russian character the tendency to doubt the reality of the obvious;
and one wonders if this feature might not be after all lurking behind the
highly unrealistic regime which prevails in Russia today. If that were
so, it might add to a number of other features that bring together
Spaniards and Russians, since both would evince a tendency to deny
reality any right to interfere with or contradict what they themselves
think of it.

The meeting with Dmovski and his Polish stories that evening remains one of my best memories of Cliveden. It was, of course, Tom
Jones who took me there, and I soon became a fairly frequent visitor
to that house as well as to the Astors' London home in St. James's
Square. Dmovski felt inspired that night and told story after story, the
best of which seemed to me that of the narrative of 'the' battle by a
Polish wounded soldier to his friends in the village. 'We were marching
along a road; there was a meadow on our right with a cow in it, then a
ditch, then a hill. The colonel ordered us to take the hill, so we marched
across the meadow, and the cow was on our right. We were thrown back
by the enemy and ran back to the road, and then the cow was on our
left. The colonel ordered us to attack again, and the cow was in the

ditch for I could see her horns, and then I was wounded and I don't know what happened to the cow.'

It is the best description of a battle I have ever heard and the truest. His other 'battle' though was *ben trovata se non vera*. An Austrian regiment, commanded by Austrian officers but manned by Italian subjects of the Dual Monarchy, was waiting in the trenches to go over the top. The Colonel drew his sword and shouting: 'Avanti Savoia', he moved forward to lead them out. Not a soldier budged. The Colonel tried a second time, with the same success: and finally a third time, raising his sword, his voice and his enthusiasm: 'Avanti Savoia!' Whereupon the whole trench broke into loud applause: 'Bravo, Colonello.'

Next to Dmovski, the most inspired story-teller that evening was Nancy Astor herself, sitting on the floor, not, I gathered, very much to the liking of the Court ladies (both London and Commonwealth) who sat very prim in their armchairs, and one of whom answered a query about the latitude of a Canadian city: 'It is the same as that of London. I was told by one of our best scientists.'

Nancy Astor enjoyed this mixture with all the longitudes and latitudes of her irrepressible spirit. I noticed a curious look in her eyes as she glanced at the chorus of dowagers and I felt some mischief was coming. 'You know,' she said, 'King George is very worried lest people think he is hen-pecked like Tino of Greece; so poor Queen Mary can't say a word about politics without his hitting back: "What do you know about these matters, Madam?"' She was rewarded with a garland of frowns.

The Astors had built a Canadian hospital in the grounds of their beautiful park, neat but, of course, made up of temporary huts. It was meant mostly for convalescent men, so the death rate was very small; yet there was a cemetery and this was a masterpiece, an elliptical arbour of greenery of simple and moving beauty. One evening, at sunset, a few of us had gathered there; the moment was so instilled with quiet harmony that one felt as if an inaudible bell called us to meditate: then, we heard the noble voice of H. A. L. Fisher: 'Ah! England will never be the same again. After this war, we shall have to work hard from week-end to week-end.'

CHAPTER VI

SUMMERS IN GENEVA

FOR my holidays, I worked in Geneva. My chief occupation in Geneva brought me back to my days as an international official; for it amounted to teaching young Europeans and Americans the art and science of international relations. During the first summer, I taught in a school run by Alfred Zimmern who was run by his wife. Zimmern was a first-rate mind, and an excellent soul; his looks followed the almost conventional type of the Jew, very short-sighted and thick-lipped, stumpy and fleshy. So was she, who had first been the wife of a French professor whom she had divorced to marry Zimmern, a move sharp wits would put to the credit of that acute French intellect.

Mrs Zimmern had every gift but tact. She was clever, quick, hardworking, a good musician, though very selective as to who was worthy of hearing her Debussy; but she simply could not manage to move about without bumping into this, upsetting that, being sorry for yonder and having profusely to apologise – which she did readily even when not asked for. She once came to me almost in tears, swearing to God she had not meant it and how sorry she was and I must surely know she was above such things, and that as soon as she had realised it she had done her best to put things right . . . and I hadn't the faintest idea of what it was all about – nor do I know to this day.

While working with Zimmern, a more than fair proportion of the youngsters I had to deal with came from the London School of Economics. They all bore the imprint of that brilliant chatterbox Harold Laski. He was a mini-philosopher, micro-economist, of such an easy talker that, when listening to him, I often thought of that wistful beginning to an after-dinner speech I once heard in Barcelona: 'I should like, on this occasion, to have been endowed with the wisdom of Socrates, the intelligence of Plato, the eloquence of Demosthenes or the powers of observation of Aristotle; but lacking all these gifts, I should be content with the facility of the gentleman who has just sat down.'

Laski's facility was served by an incredible memory that enabled him to sandwich into his speech – whether tuitional or conversational – whole pages of Locke or Burke (his favourites), and when I say 'incredible' I mean it, for a good half of his memory was rooted in imagination, so that, if need be, he could complete an eloquent page of

Burke with a few beautifully flowing paragraphs of his own best vintages (which could be very good).

These, however, were his minor, fringe gifts; for, after all, he was also a substantial, if not always consistent, political thinker; and his mind was so sharp that he could marshal an imposing array of arguments in faultless formation against any view before plunging for the view he had been attacking. Liberals could safely go to him for arguments, if not for conclusions.

Laski was graced with the finest gift a teacher can aspire to: he charmed his students. They all swore by him, and often adduced his word as proof of this or that 'truth' plucked from the tree of his wisdom. He belonged to that Left which, in a Britain carefully divided in horizontal layers by English snobbery, injected that most un-English, indeed, non-British feeling – envy. In his students, I often detected the question prompted by envy rather than by an objective observation of what was there. 'Why' – asked an Australian student of his – 'are there so many political families in the bourgeois parties of Britain?' He was ready with Laski-provided statistics. The answer was obvious; but I preferred to let it evolve by the students themselves. In point of fact, as both the answer and the facts converged in showing, the number of Labour political families was by no means less high.

The following summer I worked with an international organisation animated and made to work by an American woman. Mrs Hadden was a tall, very handsome and domineering woman, whose big, black eyes were too earnest to consent to shine. She was wealthy, used to being obeyed, courteous and good-mannered: yet executive and almost masculine, though her beauty was by no means lacking in feminine charm. She was generous, disinterested, devoted to her work, and, from the fact that she had migrated to world affairs from a foundation for saving girls who had turned awry, some wag had concluded that for her the world was just another girl to be rescued.

There were, in fact, lots of girls in her seminars, though whether they felt any need to be rescued it was not for me to investigate. These American girls often were able to bring to our studies a fresh, commonsense approach, let alone their looks, which as the French (for once understating) say, *ne gâte rien*. Sometimes they tried to play with their looks. I well remember one, profusely adorned with good looks by nature, who tried to pretend that she was just a stupid girl bent only on lipstick and all that. I knew she had as good a mind as any in the seminar. One morning, as I was apportioning tasks, oral or written essays, as I came to her, I pretended to change my mind, after having defined her subject: 'No. You'd better leave that for someone else. You just listen and comment.' This and my condescending tone did the trick. From that day on, her work became first-rate. She was first-rate; and in a very few years made her mark as a novelist: Martha Gellhorn.

This work of education in world affairs was carried out in Geneva by a number of devoted Anglo-Saxon agencies – for they were all Anglo-Saxon, and witnesses to the public spirit of these two peoples, the British and the Americans. It would be hard to say how far it succeeded, and whether it meant anything tangible for the future, considering that such a future is now our present. A certain amount of it was diverted to communism. Many of these young people were attracted to the simple, uncompromising creed of a total revolution. Some went through their red measles like Martha herself; less acute minds never recovered from them. I remember how in New York a young Englishman, then in charge of the Oxford University Press, introduced me to a young German communist, in the hope that I should understand why he had reported against publishing a book of mine which he did not find red enough for his taste; this good young English bourgeois in love with Moscow came to see me in my modest hired cottage in Switzerland, where I cooked my own meals, leaving on the road his sumptuous car. This was the time of the drawing-room communist. It still is in some ways and places.

It is not a type that appeals to me. One of my first arguments with an eminent Spanish intellectual who had espoused socialism (though by no means communism) turned precisely on this question, or rather on the principle that is implied in it. I believe a man should not merely think but live his opinions. In those days, it was the rule for a middle class, liberal-professional family to have two resident domestic servants. 'I am a liberal, and therefore, I am consistent in having two girls to serve my family; but you are a socialist, and should live according to what you think.'

It may be, though, that our losses on the frivolous-idealistic Left were not so substantial after all; the fact is that a whole generation of time, devotion and expense provided by our Anglo-Saxon friends in Geneva was followed by a remarkable conversion of the American people from the Washingtonian tradition of isolationism and mistrust of foreigners to an intelligent attitude of world-wide interest and observation of the world, without which they would not have been able even to grasp their responsibilities in the world of our day.

CHAPTER VII

SHAW AND EINSTEIN

IN this task, insofar as it was performed by Geneva, we were helped by a stream of world characters that passed through that city. George Bernard Shaw was one of them. I had met him many years earlier and well remembered his strenuous endeavour to walk on all fours sideways the length of the Gymnasium at a Fabian Society Summer School somewhere in England we had visited together. He took several photos of me and also of C.H.M.A. who, on protesting that she was not 'famous', was answered: 'Ah, but you are beautiful.' Not a usual side light in G. B. S., this Versaillesque politeness; for he was apt to prefer the role of candid friend with the stress on *candid*.

I had added a visit to my Geneva (Hadden) summer school to his programme when I knew that Zilliacus was bringing him over anyhow; and Zilliacus told me that on alighting from the train G.B.S. had met him with an 'Ah, but you are a man. I thought you were a telegraphic address!' He was late for his appointment with my students, some of whom, anxious not to waste their time, put a question to me: 'How does G.B.S. define an intelligent woman?' (For the *Intelligent Woman's Guide to Socialism* was just out.) My answer was that whatever G.B.S. answered when we asked him that question, would be my answer too.

He turned up when the young people and a number of less young ones drawn by the scent of celebrity, were already tense with expectation. His face, beaming mischievousness as well as a dash of ferocity, was pinker and fresher than the pinkest and freshest girl in his audience, and his pale blue eyes drank in the light of popularity with a zest that made him look younger. There was something unsexed about him, a diabolical light-without-warmth, which turned a meeting with him into some kind of other-worldly experience. The question was put to him at once. 'An intelligent woman,' he answered, 'is one who realises that it is in her interest to spend 15/6 on one of my books.' I acquiesced.

Then someone put to him the question I had once debated in Copenhagen with Senator Douglas, a sensible Irishman (there are lots of them, far more than the average Englishman thinks). Should the Irish go in for Gaelic as a national language? He rose to the occasion and developed the subject with common sense, skill and his usual vivacity. He was indeed a living example of his own theory. If the Irish are so gifted and

capable of forcible expression, they had better bring their gifts to bear
on a universal language, such as English, than on a language such as
Irish known only by very few. They will soon evolve a way of talking
and writing English that will be original, but universally original, instead of a mere provincial curiosity. 'So,' he concluded, 'if any one asks
you Irish (there were some present) to leave English and seek expression in Irish, just put the man in the dustbin, dump the lid on and sit on
it.'

Another lion Mrs Hadden hunted for us was Albert Einstein. The
rooms were packed with young and old; for this man performed the
miracle of becoming a world star for all peoples and classes on the
strength of a couple of notes on mathematical concepts far beyond the
grasp of any but a tiny minority of human beings, mostly physicists.
He wandered about cutting through waves of gaping admirers, his
forehead and white hair like a sail in the wind, his eyes wide open with
a glance of wonder, as distant as a horizon. He said very little and would
not address us. My mind was at the time busy with the schism in the
scientific church between Niels Bohr and Einstein. Too eager to realise
that the moment was not opportune, I got gradually into a conversation
on Bohr's views with the great man, and so was led to ask him about
determinism, which, it seemed to me, the physics of the day was losing
sight of. Einstein gave me an answer that went a good deal beyond what
I had expected. 'More knowledge will bring it back.' The answer in
itself surprised me less than its tone. It was a certitude, obviously not
based on science, but on faith. When I was on the point of putting that
very thought to him, an old American lady, with a charming smile,
broke in. 'A cat may well look at a King,' she pointed out with characteristic modesty. Einstein, not yet used to American ways, not sure
of having understood that cat-King business, nor its relation to determinism, just fled. He left me with the cat-King old lady in her grey silk
dress, and with my thoughts. 'Determinism!' thought I. 'What event
could have been less pre-determined than that one!'

Such was the concentration of great men that converged on Geneva
as moths drawn towards the light, that I found myself one evening
having to dine with Rabindranath Tagore and also, at another place,
with H. G. Wells. In my usual absent-mindedness, I had accepted both
invitations. I disentangled the conundrum by dining with Wells and
going to have coffee with Tagore. It was a curious experience. Both
were by then world figures with a considerable following in every continent; but how different they were! How typical of the East and the

West! And within this contrast, perhaps how un-typical as well! Thus one of the elements in the contrast was unfair to the West, for while Tagore was nobility incarnate, Wells was vulgarity at its best-worst.

Now this was not altogether fair either to the West or to England; and, while I was still 'living' the contrast so to speak, I kept thinking on that supremely dignified, yet simple, quiet, in one word, noble, Rudyard Kipling, I had met once in his room at Browns Hotel, when I was translating some of his poems. Mon Dieu, thought I, unwilling to say 'my God!', how complex is life. Here is Wells, the democrat, the egalitarian, the world citizen, in all his vulgarity and yet superciliousness, as the spoilt child of success; and there was Kipling, the staunch English jingo, a model of modest courtesy and simple distinction. What would he have thought of Wells?

Wells, however, had his own fascination, and in a parallel with Tagore he was by no means the loser; for he did, at least, hold his own. Tagore, sitting in an ample summer chair on which he spread his vast figure and flowing robes, looked the picture less of poetry than of eloquence. Flowing drapery everywhere. He spoke well, with a beautiful voice and natural images which he did not tease into existence for they came of their own to his lips. His theme was the unity of mankind, and his argument, forcible and convincing, led to the need for developing the League of Nations into a world government.

But when I listened to Wells, whose talk nearly always covered the same ground, I could not help preferring the Westerner's concrete, direct, original approach, to the Easterner's more vapid, general and, so to speak, goody-goody preaching. Wells was ever at his best in the context of action, cause and effect, mechanics of society, evolution of production and consumption, strains and balances between nations and the vast avenue of progress his mind opened for men out of the (then) present mess. Perhaps, would I then think, his very vulgarity helps to make it taste more modern.

CHAPTER VIII

LOVE AND SPORT

MUCH as I enjoyed those summers in the world-wide atmosphere of Geneva, I always returned with pleasure to the secluded and insular air of Oxford; where the world beyond the Channel was never evoked without a smile. 'What lunatics those foreigners are' as Cecil, once, wrote to a friend. And, indeed, while in Oxford, one was tempted to sympathise with this view. 'England', once wrote Churchill the Great, and, of course I quote from memory, 'still is the best country for a rich man to live in.' What remained but to become rich and enjoy life in England? But was wealth really necessary? No. Seen from Oxford, the foreigner did seem a lunatic, or at least somewhat foolish to insist on remaining a foreigner. English life was undoubtedly a good thing.

The more I watched it, the less I misunderstood it – and that is, after all, the least and the most you can do. I had become a member of one or two London Clubs, and I kept comparing them with the Oxford Colleges, which I frequented, mostly my own, Exeter, as well as All Souls. It was pretty obvious that they owe a good deal to each other, Clubs to Colleges, or Colleges to Clubs, I was not sure I knew which. Possibly a common ancestry.

Perhaps the view was true, after all, that both Clubs and Colleges were for the average Englishman refuges in which to protect himself from his women folk. For I had come to the conclusion that the English, men as brave as any in the world, fear no one with the exception of their women. This revelation came to me (no doubt after many foreboding intuitions) one evening when I heard an Exeter don exclaim with a mixture of fire and tears in his voice: 'That happened before Oxford was *dishonoured* by the admission of women.'

My trained ear detected the fear behind the indignation. I came to think that this fear and this indignation might well be due to a twofold cause. On the one hand, to the fact that English women have always evinced a far greater capacity than men for the amenities of civilisation. Left to himself, the male is no better in England than in other lands; he will rejoice in sweat, mud, tobacco, gunpowder, whisky, and all the ill odours of food, drink, smoke, bodily miseries and forms of dirt of which nature is only too prodigal. At this level, just a cut above the pigsty, would the English man have remained till Doomsday had his wife, mother or sister not seen to it that he was cleansed from his earthly proclivities.

At the point where I must pivot round to the second objection to women I detect in Englishmen, a story comes to my mind which will act as a perfect hinge. Marlborough was away at his wars. He returned after his usual victory, landed somewhere, leapt on a horse, rode to London, and, his wife writes in a letter to a friend: '. . . arrived and without taking off his boots, possessed me twice.' That's the stuff to give them. But . . . is it? Aye. The whole problem is there. What came first, the egg or the hen? The not-so-fond-of-women male or the not-so-feminine-female, the she-man or the he-woman? Courage is not in it. I well remember being told by Marañón (whom I may have to quote again in these variations on the theme of Middlesex) that during the first weeks of the Spanish Civil War, a regular army artillery Captain became the hero of his men for his tremendous courage which, in the usual male Spanish parlance and belief, they identified with the size of his testicles. Eventually, he came to call on Marañón professionally. He had no testicles whatever. Add to it the magnificent physical valour women of all nations, especially British women, have often evinced, and we shall be able to conclude that this aspect of the question may be safely passed over.

Now, since there is but one human species, giving forth male and female out of the same stem, it seems natural to assume that on the same stem, the more masculine the women the more feminine the men; or in other words, that if in a particular region, nation, province, the women are apt to be masterful, the men may be apt to be homosexual.

This way of thinking may require further study. As the subject is delicate, I crave for some freedom in order to state my views with clarity. I understand the woman who acts woman for a woman; it is the easiest case; also the woman, who acts man for a woman, the reason being of course that her hormones are mixed up (masterful mother? weak father?); for similar reasons, I understand the man who acts woman for a man. Where I stall is at the man who acts man for a man. Why, when there are women? I have not solved that conundrum, save for those cases in which for long periods there are no women available (sea life in the days of slow ships, armies) and perhaps by a psychological extension of the 'law' I laid down a minute ago: the son of a masterful mother may acquire a horror of women. As I write these lines the press tells of a man who at 35 had never tasted but baby food, so strict was the life his mother made him live.

I suspect though that the prevalence of homosexuality in Oxford and Cambridge is due to other causes. One is the clerical tradition and the abnormal congregation of men, young and less young; and the other is the predominance of classic studies, homosexual habits having never reached a higher degree of philosophical dignity than in the great classic centuries, especially under the Greeks, in whose eyes a woman was fit for maternity but not for love. This strange aberration was not shared by the Hebrews, who, more ambitious than the Greeks, would take nothing below angels for their pleasures.

In the days I am now remembering, the shadow of Oscar Wilde still darkened this aspect of English life, and one did not speak of such things, let alone write about them; but England has evolved a good deal since the Victorian and Edwardian days, in deeds, in words both spoken and written; one can even read reproaches at the lack of frankness of a biographer who does not mention that the great man whose life he writes had hired a flat in London to enjoy a 'man' friend of his whom another more or less great, more or less man, was also interested in. One rubs one's eyes.

Or ears. I was once asked to take part in a debate in Cambridge on whether a religious faith was an indispensable basis for a country; and in the course of it, the undergraduate who shared my opinion in the affirmative told a story the mere telling of which plainly showed what a long way England had travelled since the Victorian era (this happened in the 1950s): a traveller takes a room in a London hotel, finds a Bible in the night table drawer, and opens it. There are some scrawls on it. He reads: 'If you are fed up with sin, read Isaiah II.2; if you are not, ring up Paddington UXYZ.' (I have to take refuge in Algebra lest the quoted number complains.)

This permissive trend has become scholarly. We have read an erudite article in an intellectual review, in which the head of an illustrious college went thoroughly into the question whether Lady Chatterley's gardener entered her estate by the front or the back door; and beautifully argued proofs have been put forward to establish the arrant nonsense that Shakespeare's Sonnets have nothing to do with physical love, his interest in the boy to whom they are dedicated being purely platonic.

This is one of the pet manias of the queer community. Love between men, they will insist, is a higher and purer form of love than love between man and woman. The subject is fascinating but hardly open to discussion without unpleasant sidelights, if the word fits, which it doesn't. By and large, it is not by its spiritual aspects that it propagates.

I hear that a Spanish Jesuit, who received a high decoration for philanthropy, was asked by a group of journalists in Panama what philanthropy was about, and on his answering 'Love of men', he had to stand to a wave of loud laughter followed by: 'But, Father, that is what we here call buggery.'

CHAPTER IX

ON DICTATORS AND HERETICS

BY 1923 the deed was done, and King Alfonso committed the heaviest blunder of his reign. Perhaps he thought that there was no danger in such a light-hearted general, but if so, he was soon going to discover his mistake. Primo reduced the King to practical impotence and made him feel so. In the process, when confronted with a conspiracy to oust him, in which he suspected the King to have shared, he let out and put in motion a phrase in which a new verb became instantly popular: '*A mí no me borbonea nadie* ('No one is going to Bourbonise me!'), and coolly put before the King a decree sending the chief conspirator, a rival general, to study the military organisation of a couple of countries in the Balkan peninsula.

In accordance with a pattern that Franco was to imitate, Primo de Rivera appointed as his *locum tenens* in case of absence, not a general but an admiral – both a friendly bow to the Navy and a precaution against rival ambitions. This admiral was no other than the Marqués de Magaz whom I knew well from our Geneva disarmament debates – when he used to endeavour to persuade H.A.L. Fisher of the wisdom of some Spanish idea which Fisher would admire, consider, contemplate, promise to study, commend and bear in mind but of course never accept.

I tried to make use of my good relations with Magaz to touch up the course of the dictatorship. Primo had an Andalusian idea of government; and saw himself as a kind of Harun al Rashid dispensing peremptory justice under the sun at the gates of some Alhambra. On hearing that there was some surplus in some State account, he had it handed out to those who had pawned their clothes and had no money to buy them back before the winter. That was his style. In seven years of dictatorship, only one Spaniard lost his life for his opposition to the regime, which in Spain today sounds well nigh incredible.

Even so, I was of course, 'against'. I told Magaz so, and explained that, while I was too much of a man of my century to be scandalised by experiments on the parliamentary system, I was sure that nothing good could come out of anything unless the press was left free. He wrote that I only insisted on freedom for the press because I wrote for it, but that the almost totality of Spaniards didn't care a bit. I retorted: 'If you hold a man's head under the water, the almost totality of his body may remain dry, but the man dies.'

I will concede that Primo was entitled to a certain scepticism on the freedom of the press, which he blurted out, at least once, with characteristic breezing zest. Faced with a series of harsh articles in *Le Temps*, then the premier paper of France, he sent to the papers one of his famous *notes* marked FOR COMPULSORY PUBLICATION, in which he began by stating that it was well known that the Spanish Government and the French paper had signed an agreement whereby the one guaranteed a minimum of publicity for tourism and the other a minimum of comprehension of the political problems of Spain, an agreement recently fallen in abeyance because of higher claims put forward from the Paris partner.

This was part of Primo's style. He was as much of an extravert and talkative as Franco is an introvert and silent. When he decided that Spain was to leave the League of Nations, he published in a newspaper a long, whole front-page article explaining why he did not believe in such things as 'Leagues of Nations', and defining instead what, in his view, should be done – which amounted to exactly the same – only he did not know, never having read the Covenant. It was in this article that, wishing to describe some institution that was to act as a link between two other ones, he wrote 'trade union' instead of *'trait d'union'*. It was all one to him.

It made him popular in fact. He would not lurk behind guards and safety locks in a distant palace, but lived a bachelor's life at the War Office, right in the centre of the city, and used to go for a walk after a (late) evening meal, along the streets of Madrid never more crowded than late at night, then repair to his headquarters (both private and official) at the War Office, and ring the bell for some ham and sherry, and it was then, in the small hours of the dawn, that he would spin his immortal notes out of his head – or utter his heartfelt phrases: 'Oh what a bore. I wish I could go back to my little whores and my champagne!'

I believe it was my correspondence with Magaz that set me thinking on a curious political paradox: the strong attraction dictators feel for plebiscites and the direct universal vote. The method within this madness consists in pulverising the structure of the institutions of the people thus reducing it to a formless mass, and to count heads only after they have been emptied of their ideas and deprived of their frames of reference. I was thus led to formulate my chief political belief: *a nation is not the arithmetical sum of its individuals but the integration of its institutions*. And by a logical conclusion I came to think that a number of notions that pass for truths even in free liberal democracies are but fallacies.

I do not intend to develop here what I have written elsewhere; but I may record that for me liberty is a primary need of the spirit of man, while democracy is but a set of rules that vary from one democracy to another. For Bernard Shaw, it meant a system that ensured that no one was governed by his betters; the pessimistic side of which was, I believe better put by Raymond Aron when he said (I quote from memory) that the qualities that go to the making of a good statesman are hardly ever the same as those required to reach the heights of power.

Liberty then was, is and ever shall be my chief concern; and, though Primo's dictatorship was a much lighter affair than Franco's, indeed incomparably so, I was worried because the minister in charge of what dictators call law and order, which is in fact neither, was the notorious General Martínez Anido, well known for his unscrupulous ways in the use of force. One day I chanced to read some news about him that made me fear for the worst. In these cases I have learnt from experience that the only consideration that will or may stop a dictator on an evil way is publicity abroad. I published an article in *The Observer* drawing attention to the activities of the nefarious minister and calling the attention of the King himself to his responsibility.

The Spanish Ambassador was furious. He was a very stupid man, Merry del Val by name, very much liked in Britain both because he spoke perfect English and because he was stupid, a feature the British do not dislike in a foreign Ambassador; and he wrote to me a letter which he meant to be insulting, adorned with sentences such as this: 'I shall limit myself to pointing out that when one has the honour to hold the Alfonso XIII Chair and one has to one's great satisfaction eaten the bread not so long ago provided by the regime whose chief carries the same name as your own post, one resigns before attacking the August Person.' The poor man did not seem to know that I had never 'eaten Spanish official bread' since my League post was international and the Chair bore the name of the King but owed nothing to him. But there he was, unable to rise higher than this kind of manger talk.

And yet he could not have forgotten an episode which should have enlightened him on my attitude to official money. I had, a few years earlier, stood as a candidate for the King's College Chair of Spanish vacant on the death of Fitzmaurice-Kelly, and I had failed, I suspect, owing to his veto. I was then at the end of my tether, having thrown away my very promising technical career in Spain to take a job in England for the duration; and when I was wondering where to turn I got a letter from Merry del Val asking me to call on him. He proposed to me to become the P.R.O. of the Embassy (as we would say today) at the salary of £400 with freedom to make more with my pen. I turned the offer down and took care to let him know that I was at the time jobless and penniless.

I will say this for him: I made his life hard. Here is an example. *The Times* had published an article on the third centenary of the discovery of the circulation of the blood (May 1928), on which I wrote to the Editor:

> Sir,
>   In his admirable article on Harvey, Dr Singer, dealing with the precursors, cites 'the Spaniard Michael Servetus, a fellow student with Vesalius, who was burned alive for his religious views in 1553'. These words might be interpreted as meaning that Servet (as we call him) was burned by the Spanish Inquisition. This institution can afford to have it made clear that Servet was burned alive by Calvin, in Geneva. I have no doubt, however, that if Servet had remained in Spain, he would have died at the same temperature.

And, as if this was not bad enough, I signed as I never had before and never did since: King Alfonso XIII Professor of Spanish Studies, Oxford. Merry del Val, incensed, wrote to Madrid and had me attacked in one of the right wing papers as a man who did not know what patriotism was, and so forth. To which I made answer in another Madrid paper that my job as a professor was to stand up, not for Spain but for truth.

This enabled me to add, not without some authority, that Dr Singer's article was too reticent. The correspondence that ensued was revealing in this respect; for a Protestant woman wrote that Servet had also been sentenced to die at the stake by the Inquisition of Vienne (in France) and, mind you, by slow fire, while Calvin, a good soul, made him be burned by quick fire. (In point of fact, the wood was green and his torment was long, but the lady in question did, nonetheless, reveal the delicacy of the Protestant conscience, for which all of us who feel a certain proclivity to heresy should be grateful.)

CHAPTER X

PRIMO AND UNAMUNO

SPAIN was then, as she is now, wondering what was going to happen when the Dictator fell. Primo was as indifferent to (or unaware of) the issue then as Franco is now. The opposition was then led by two men a good deal to the right of their present day corresponding figures. Francisco Cambó, the head of the conservative wing of the Catalan home rulers, was a wealthy financier, an able man and perhaps more of a statesman than a politician. Santiago Alba, a Castillian-Leonese, was a prosperous barrister, the *bête noire* of Primo de Rivera, a liberal to the core. These two men, neither of whom had kept good memories of King Alfonso, were nevertheless anxious to save the monarchy and ready to play a role similar to that which Cánovas and Sagasta had played during the previous reign and the Regency; which amounted to letting the monarchy drive on its two wheels, the Conservative and the Liberal party.

I used to call on them whenever I passed through Paris, where they both lived; and in one of our conversations on the ever-recurring theme of the future of Spain, they had asked me to enquire on the actual relations between the King of England and his ministers, in the hope of being able to use this as a model for the monarchy they were dreaming of. I remember I felt like answering them that no such enquiry was needed, for I was sure of what my conclusion would be; but I bethought myself of the unwisdom of such a step, since it would undermine their confidence on a judgement so swiftly reached; so I accepted their request and promised to write to them.

I consulted Tom Jones and I went to New College to H.A.L. Fisher, who was then Warden and had had a good experience as Cabinet minister with Lloyd George. These two interviews confirmed what I had all along been ready to put before my two friends. To whom I wrote more or less as follows: The British practice in this matter is worse than useless for you; it is dangerous. You complain that the King of Spain, caught in a net of constitutional rules, breaks the rules to act as an almost absolute monarch; but the King of England does the very reverse: he acts as a strictly constitutional King, but his language is absolute. If he wants to see a Cabinet minister – which happens very seldom – his secretary tries to find out when the minister can come, and once this is ascertained, the Cabinet minister receives a command

to come. In Spain the words are constitutional and the deeds are absolute; in England, the words are absolute and the deeds are constitutional. Alba and Cambó saw the point. And in any case, it was too late.
Nothing could save the monarchy, since the King had taken sides.

Those were the days when I grew familiar with the team that launched *Le Quotidien*. It was to be a pure, idealistic, liberal newspaper.
It was mostly financed by one of the French members of the Hennessy
family and among its moving spirits was Caspar-Jordan, a kind of
French Don Quixote, who had thrown away a promising career in the
French Protestant Church because he found the French colonial regime
in Madagascar too difficult to swallow. I had struck up a good friendship with him in 1909 because he had then taken a quixotic interest in
the Ferrer case and became Ferrer's widow's lawyer. Ferrer was an
honest, not very intelligent, schoolmaster, who was shot for his alleged
responsibility in the events of 1909 in Barcelona, for which little if any
could be attributed to him. This common interest, an almost abstract
indignation at the sight of injustice, brought us together.
    It so happened that at this precise time, Unamuno was in exile in
Fuerteventura, the least fortunate of the islands our ancestors called
Fortunate and we Canaries. It all began with a private letter Unamuno
had written to a well-known Spanish professor then on loan to an
Argentine University, in which letter Unamuno had let himself go on
the virtues and vices of Primo the then Dictator of Spain. Somehow or
other, the letter got to the columns of an important Buenos Aires paper;
the Dictator was wroth, and he exiled Unamuno to Fuerteventura.
    More easily said than done. Primo, who was no fool, realised that he
had blundered, and gave orders to the Police to let the prisoner escape.
That, however, did in no wise conform to Unamuno's style. When the
police came to his house in Salamanca to fetch him, he refused to
budge. He had to be conveyed to the taxi and to the train, where he was
left unescorted in the hope he would vanish. He didn't. And so all the
way through Madrid and Cádiz and the boat and the island.
    Years went by; and Unamuno had had enough of the dry, sunbaked
island. By then *Le Quotidien* was in full swing; and, as a publicity stunt,
the team conceived the idea of rescuing Unamuno and making a big
splash of his return to freedom, of course, in Paris. Everything was
prepared in strict secrecy, so that no one really knew anything about
the plot ... except Primo. And when the elegant sailing yacht sent by
Le Quotidien was in sight of Fuerteventura, it met another sailing boat
in which Unamuno was sailing towards France.
    Well, never mind. It was a splash all the same, and *Le Quotidien* kept

making a noise for as long as it possibly could. To begin with, the banquet prepared at Cherbourg to receive the hero did take place, and Unamuno did make his speech of thanks. What *Le Quotidien* and its team did not realise, what they could not even conceive, as the intelligent rationalists they all were, was the depth of irrationality out of which Unamuno used to speak.

Those brilliant French left-of-centre intellectuals were all to a man patriotic, almost chauvinistic men, who had passed through the army as recruits, most of whom were officers in the Reserve. On the other hand they, all to a man, were *laïcs*, i.e. deadly enemies of any clerical influence on politics, and above all on the schools; most of them, moreover, were atheists. Now Unamuno's ideas ran counter to most of this, so that, barring a common dislike for dictators and a common love for freedom (a word and a concept that they would have probably interpreted in very dissenting ways from Unamuno's) there was hardly anything in common between the fierce Spanish exile and the crowd of keen French intellects that were drinking his health in Cherbourg; and when he rose to speak, the fighting Basque, fully aware of the situation, went at once to the attack and declared that, in his experience, there was far more sense in a Cathedral Canon than in a lieutenant colonel.

This was a mere beginning. With the same mixture of naïvety and generosity, the team of *Le Quotidien* offered Unamuno the place of honour on the paper. They were looking forward to brilliant, clever, liberal, Left articles. It was pretty obvious that they admired him on trust but had never read him. How could they even imagine that Unamuno would send to the paper his usual tortured, tortuous, self-exploring, self-doubting, labyrinthine essays, crammed with puns, half puns, inversions of the usual meaning, juggling with every word, turning it upside down or dismissing it with an intellectual flick? Odd in Spanish, the stuff was quite unintelligible in French.

The usual leader-writer was in despair. 'But, Monsieur Ünamünó, one cannot say that in French!' – 'I can,' Unamuno retorted proudly. In the end, they came to a compromise. Unamuno would write his articles in Spanish, and the Frenchman would translate them. It didn't work either. Unamuno felt his bristling prose combed down and flattened out as if with some hair grease, and suffered agony. He spoke to me about it, very pleased with himself because he had beaten the Frenchman with one of those verbal gadgets he enjoyed so much. 'So I told him: "Now, monsieur, you will agree that I know French better than you know Spanish." And he answered: "Oh oui, Monsieur Ünamünó." But then I said: "But you will have to agree also that I know Spanish better than you know French."' That seemed to afford him deep satisfaction.

It would be difficult to imagine a man less likely to understand the rational, clear, disciplined French genius than this anarchist Basque intellectual so deeply influenced by the Castillian spirit of the sixteenth century. He hung about in Paris, unable to take it in, lionised at first, given up later as a crank or 'unoriginal'; and in the end, he left it to settle in Hendaye, where his eyes, at least, were able to rest on Spain every day. The first time I went to call on him in Paris after his liberation, he was living in a very simple yet modern and comfortable *pension* not far from the Arc de l'Etoile. He arrived in the waiting-room, shook hands, produced out of his coat pocket a brown paper that seemed to me of the kind you pack books with, unfolded it once, then again, then again, and so on many times, until in order to hold it he had to stretch his arms as far as they would go, and began to read to me one hundred sonnets written in exile. They were all good and some superb. When he had finished he said goodbye and vanished.

In Hendaye he settled down to a rôle of head of the opposition to the Dictator, a quixotic task for which a Sancho turned up in the person of Eduardo Ortega, the less known brother of the philosopher. A story dating from the heyday of the Spanish monarchy will place this no more than well-meaning man. A minister of Education, Julio Burell, whose formation as a journalist had taught him much of that practical wisdom known in Spain as 'dusky grammar', had got into the habit of speaking in a very loud voice. This he did so as to frighten favour seekers whose whispered requests he would loudly repeat. One day, Eduardo Ortega came to his ministerial door and gave his name to the usher, who half opened the *sancta sanctorum* and announced 'Señor Ortega y Gasset'. – 'Who,' vociferated Burell, 'the philosopher or the fool?' And, so the story runs, Ortega peeped and piped at the door: 'The fool, Mister Minister.'*

Eduardo Ortega was a mediocre mind and therefore not a very brilliant journalist. He lived mostly on a name made familiar by his father and world-famous by his brother. He fought next to Unamuno; and with him and under the protection of his family name, he published a small periodical which was widely distributed in the Spanish territories close to the frontier, from where it could be easily smuggled into Spain.

One day, someone asked Unamuno whether he had noticed a man in a brown suit who every afternoon came and sat close to his table at the café Unamuno visited to relax after his lunch. He had. What about him? 'He is an agent sent by the Spanish government to spy on you.' Next day, Unamuno arrived and ordered his coffee at his usual

---

*The least bad of the biographies of Franco published in English, mistaking the one for the other, writes Eduardo but means José.

table, and soon noticed the spy who came and occupied the table close by. Unamuno rose, went to the other table, sat opposite the spy and asked him: 'Do you know what a whore is?' The other man, with an awkward smile, answered: 'Of course, I do.' – 'Very well. Your profession is even worse.' This done, he went back to his table and sat down to his coffee.

It was in his Hendaye retreat that Francis Hackett and Signe Toksvig met him. The Irish novelist and his Danish wife were on their way to the discovery of Spain; keen on it since I had explained to Francis that the Irish were Spaniards who had taken the wrong bus and found themselves, much to their discomfiture, in Northern Europe, where they do not belong. I am not sure Francis was very convinced, but I had a retort to whatever doubts he might harbour, namely that in the course of the years and the centuries, the English had strongly anglicised the Irish by good, less good and downright bad means; and that insofar as he could not see my first point, he was confirming my second in his own person. This would usually bring him round to a reluctant acquiescence. Not that it mattered very much, because Francis Hackett was irrepressible and his true self would come back and reconquer the field with an ironic glance of his keen eyes and an inimitable smile, and that Irish uncombable mane.

It took a Danish girl to tame such a wild goat, but Signe did it, I surmise, by never trying. They were a perfect pair, and they easily got round Unamuno's inhibitions with strangers. The most remarkable thing about these visits may well have been that the Spaniard and the Irish-Danish couple seem to have understood each other. Unamuno was immensely well-read in English. He seemed to have read everything published on both sides of the Atlantic, and while Francis found he had read *Rural Rides*, there are evident traces in his works that he read English books of sermons. It was to Unamuno that I owe my own discovery of *Moby Dick*.

But it all came to pieces when Unamuno insisted on reading Shakespeare aloud. Francis and Signe were treated to complete scenes of *Hamlet* or *King Lear*, read with tremendous energy and rhythm, but pronounced as a Spaniard would who knew no English. This was probable due in part to Unamuno's not quite sufficient knowledge of the language, but mostly to the fire he put into the tragedy, which made him throw to the winds all those rules of pronunciation he had learnt in books.

This 'just not enough' of which we nearly all suffer if not here then there, betrayed him once into a bad howler which, to my knowledge, no one had the courage to point out to him – possibly because it was too late. He had taken 'the rest is silence' as his text for a poem in Spanish;

but his poem was entirely devoted to elaborating that rest is silence and silence is rest. The rest is silence.

All these stories and more or less small events were but the approaches, suburbs, perspectives towards a truly great spirit. Unamuno was not a man of action – and his one error may have been that for a brief moment in his life, he dreamt he was. He was not a man of thought either, strong and original as his thought always was. He was a man of passion – in the sense in which I have endeavoured to outline this type of mankind to which all Spaniards belong*, indeed almost the perfect model of the type. To no one better and more than to him would the principle apply that he had laid down: that it was the man Kant and it was the man Nietzsche that mattered and, indeed, explained, their respective philosophies. He thought with his heart and let the Devil take the hindmost. The quotation he loved most and made his own was Walt Whitman's: 'Do I contradict myself? Very well, then I do contradict myself.' Others may have written as existentialists. He lived as one.

His looks, glance, stand, were aggressive. He seemed always ready to leap on his adversary; and in some cases, this aggressive attitude led him to write pages that his civil war experience may have made him rue; for at his core, he was a liberal (one of his many contradictions). It was, no doubt, this irrationalist 'man Unamuno' that led his steps towards Kirkegaard. But he turned Kirkegaard into a Spanish anarchist, such as he was himself, and heated up the intellectual blood of the Nordic to raise it to the fever of Spain.

Unamuno's style is a strange mixture of spontaneous almost formless lava and of self-conscious word-play. He hated and despised puns but wrote little that was not encumbered, spiced, animated by word-juggling, which reminded one of his ever-creative hands, sculpting all kinds of animals, from butterflies to pigs, out of pieces of paper. It was again another of his contradictions, that this man, a volcano of hot feelings seeking to become thoughts on survival and God, should turn so much of his lava into capricious *figurines* fit for a museum. With all his contradictions, though, Unamuno remains one of the greatest writers, thinkers and word artists of the twentieth century.

*I refer to my book *Englishmen, Frenchmen, Spaniards*.

CHAPTER XI

MEXICO

I was by then bored with my chair; at bottom, possibly, because teaching is not my vocation, indeed as I slowly came to realise, while in Oxford, it is one of my anti-vocations, for I frankly detest it. Yet, it was not that deep-down reason that came to the top then, but other shallower if more irritating experiences, chief of which were the administrative side of academic life and the elementary level of most of my students.

One may sometimes be pardoned for fancying that events are carefully matured and timed by some occult master-hand that sees to it that they tally and converge towards a comprehensive end. I was bored and discouraged, but it never occurred to me that the thing to do was to leave Oxford for good. There was a tremendous lot I liked in it, in particular, the company of men and women of a polished mind and a civilised way of life such as could be equalled but not excelled anywhere; and, in any case, I was not then aware of being dissatisfied as I now can see in retrospect I was. All the same, I eagerly seized an opportunity for a change that was offered me then by Federico de Onís, the professor of Spanish literature at Columbia University.

Onís was now an American. He had been a Spaniard, though, and even a *noble beard*. Accurately speaking, a noble beard in the classic Spanish theatre was the actor in charge of the noble, steady characters (the Commander in Don Juan, for instance). The Spaniard does not normally like beards. History shows that, left to himself, he shaves it off. In his long history, he has had three waves of beard-epidemics, the three of them coming from Germany, where the best beards come from, in harmony with flowing rivers and symphonies. In the Middle Ages, the Visigoths bearded Spain – as can be seen in *El Cid*, whose long, golden beard had to be tied to his neck by a silk cord lest an irate or scornful adversary pulled it. By the time of Ferdinand the Catholic, the beard was a thing of the past and the Spaniard had returned to his shaven self. But his grandson, Charles, Emperor of Germany, wore a beard, not so much because most Germans did so but because his lower jaw was so big that it disfigured his otherwise handsome features; and so, all Spain wore a beard again. Yet, this beard became less and less prominent as the dynasty fell down the three Philips to the Second Charles who had no face left able to support a beard at all. Time went by, which

Spain spent, of course, beardless, until during the second half of the nineteenth century, a Spanish professor of philosophy fell under the sway of a third-rate German philosopher named Krause; who, of course, sported a beard; and Spain became bearded again. Yet, this time, much less so; for only the intellectuals of what then was a left wing took to the fashion; so that when I was a boy, wearing a beard and being a republican were almost synonymous.

Onís belonged as a young man to this philosophical-bearded Spanish tribe, and his deep-set dark eyes and aquiline nose were adequately framed within his black locks and beard, and bestowed upon him the air of a profound spirit and a steady thinker. All was dissipated in America. He changed from introvert into extravert, from silence to talk, from a certain saturnine moroseness to slapping backs, 'keep smiling' and outbursts of laughter. His energy seemed either to increase tenfold or to explode, and anyone who heard him conducting a choir of his students singing Spanish popular songs felt he had been trained for the next revolution.

I knew I was leaving my lambs in good hands and that their temporary shepherd would knock their British introversion out of them during my absence abroad; but I did not know that I was leaving Oxford for good. Nothing, in fact, was further from my thoughts, when, shortly before Christmas, I left Britain on my way to the U.S., Mexico and Cuba.

CHAPTER XII

HERNÁN CORTÉS AND CUAUTEMOC

THE plan agreed upon with the University of Oxford was that Onís was to take over my duties as professor for the Hilary and Trinity terms, during which I was to lecture for three months as a freelance in the U.S. and as a guest professor in April in Mexico City and in May in Havana. I arrived in New York shortly before Christmas (1930) and made my headquarters at the Lamonts'. I lectured mostly in the West and South West, and on the last day of March I entered Mexico by Nuevo Laredo.

No planes in those days. In the excellent and comfortable trains of the U.S. one had time to reflect. What occupied my mind in those states was the vast dimensions of that country and the omnipresence of Spain in her past. It was hard to imagine that such a distant and relatively small nation should have been able to cope with the immense lands she had to administer. Savannah, whose cemetery was a stone catalogue of Spanish names, St. Augustine with its fort, Atlanta, New Orleans, where the Spanish and the French memories mix without blending; and on to S. Antonio where I happened to arrive on the bicentenary of the foundation of the city by the Spaniards. The layer of Spanish culture under the present American layer was plainly visible, indeed often still alive.

Why did the citizens of S. Antonio celebrate in 1931 the bicentenary of a city founded in 1718? Possibly because the 1718 founders were a military expedition from Mexico, while the 1931 founders were Canary Islands immigrants whom they were free (more or less) to represent as swarthy as their imagination would paint them, white though they were since they were Spaniards. This procession of Canarians gaudily dressed and heavily bronzed, was one of the picturesque ceremonies to which I was invited; another one being a banquet that has remained engraved in my memory mostly because the chief speaker, a judge, in the course of his address, happened to say: 'We, politicians . . .' A judge, a politician! I felt a shiver down my back.

The train was American, and the engine reeked of petrol. Everything else was Spanish. Mexico had been New Spain while it had remained a Kingdom of the Spanish Crown (a colony it never was); but, on becom-

ing independent, had returned to her Indian name. It certainly is, of all
the once Spanish Kingdoms of the New World, the one that most
hauntingly reminds one of Spain. This is strange, for in Mexico the Indian element is far stronger, both in quantity and in force, than in all
but one or two of the remaining nations of the continent; and the Indians do modify the Spanishness of the country in many ways: colour
(not merely of skin but of clothes), accent (a certain sugary feeling they
manage to put in what they say even at their fiercest), ways of living and
eating (hotly spiced food, strong alcoholic drinks); and in spite of it
all 'New Spain' did deserve her name; possibly because of a certain
likeness in the landscape to those of the central high plateau of the
Spanish peninsula, that feeling of dry heat, that predominance of ochre
and yellow, that metallic quality of the earth that seems to make sounds
rebound and reverberate.

My sponsor was a Hispano-Mexican Society of culture, led by a Dr
Perrín; and the times were those dominated by Pancho Villa, a self
made 'general' half-politician half-bandit, whose chief job consisted in
making it easier for the American oil-adventurers to exploit Mexican
petrol at their ease. Villa was known to be a trigger-happy man. Perrín
told me that, having made a few hundred prisoners in one of his battles,
he explained to them that they would be packed in a field separated
from another field by a narrow lane. He would let them run from one
field to the other through the lane, at the end of which he would stand
with a rifle; and shoot. If they escaped alive, they would be free. One
did. The others were left to die on the ground, while Villa rubbed his
finger.

Perrín told me this story as a prelude to another one. He was once
awakened at three a.m. in his house in the city of Mexico, and told to dress
quickly for an urgent case; he was refused explanations, and wafted
away at top speed out of the town and blindfolded. Presently, at dawn,
he found himself in an isolated house in the country and ushered into a
room in which sitting on an armchair he found his 'case'. A glance sufficed
for him to recognize Pancho Villa. One of his arms was badly wounded
and broken. 'But the other one', he pounced at me in telling the story
'was free, and he had a formidable revolver at his hip.' My friend found
it a most trying experience to operate on a man known for his irate
and volcanic reactions. All went well and on his return – under the same
melodramatic conditions – he was royally rewarded.

Dr Perrín advised me not to make too much of Hernán Cortés
while in Mexico – in fact to keep him out of my lectures altogether. The
Mexicans had chosen to put their pride not in Cortés but in Cuautemoc,

the leader who, after a gallant resistence, following Montezuma's death, had to surrender to the Spaniards. The same advice was offered me by a number of other Spanish friends. I was, of course, aware of this strange psychological situation, which persists to this day. But it seemed to me that the case was far richer and subtler than that which the advice of my friends suggested. My opinion was based on a number of observations I had made in the U.S., where I had gradually come to think that the more Anglo-Saxon (wasp, they call them now) an American was, the more Anglo-Saxon he wanted to be . . . and the more anti-English he was. Newcomers, Roman Catholics, Jews, Eastern Europeans, Italians, were more or less indifferent to the issue; but if a man said his 'people' had come over in the Mayflower, you knew what to expect; English ways, manners, tastes, even clothes, but these 'damned Englishmen' whenever it came to politics.

With different condiments, of course, and stronger spices, this was, I felt, the situation in Mexico. Treat a Mexican as a White, a Spaniard, and he will react as an Indian; do but suggest that he is an Indian, and he will react as a Spaniard. What about the pure whites or the pure Indians? The answer is that, if the man is literate, he will always be a mixed blood even if he is a pure Indian or a pure white. For a man is not a mere animal (hence the inadequacy of the word *race* applied to human beings). The spirit of Mexico is half and half, Spanish and Indian.

These intuitions, strongly held, prevented me from accepting the advice of my countrymen – let alone the fact that it amounted to recommending caution, an attitude I am not very good at producing at the right time. Before or after the event, I am cautious enough. At the time, though, caution is apt to evaporate.

These were the thoughts I rolled in my head when I drove to my inaugural lecture at the University. The new buildings were still waiting in the uncreated future, and the lecture was to take place at the old, stately and traditional house. Dr Perrín had come to fetch me with an astonishing punctuality, so that when the taxi stopped it was exactly twelve-thirty, the hour I was supposed to begin my lecture as announced on posters and in newspapers. He pulled out his watch, hesitated, and at last lamented: 'Twelve-thirty. Not very polite to be so hard on the dot.' And then, to the driver: 'Let us go for a drive out into the country.'

We had a pleasant drive in the vicinity of the Mexico of those days, which means over hills and dales that are now streets and squares, and at one-thirty we were again at the door. Up we went, I rather hurriedly, leaping over two steps at a time, Dr Perrín leisurely and relaxed. On our way to the rector's office, we had to cross the lecture room, in which about half a dozen persons were waiting, which seemed to me pretty well disastrous. We entered the Rector's office, found him talking to a visitor, smiled back at his smile on seeing us (no trace of a surprise at our being so late), and waited until he bid farewell to his visitor. This done, he came to us, and as unhurried and relaxed as Dr Perrín was, began a conversation on this and that and the rest. It was two o'clock when he opened the sitting with a short speech. The room was crowded.

So the moment for decision had come. I began by rapidly painting a picture of my trip north of Río Grande, its huge distances, its Spanish milestones everywhere; recalling how my S. Antonio hosts were also celebrating the founding of San Francisco by a party of their own, four hundred of them, trekking all the way from one saint to the other, a six-month march, no dead and a number of new born on the way, and the choosing of that wonderful site for their city, and much more on that note, to conclude: 'And when after that long and ample experience, a Spaniard arrives in Mexico, his plain duty is to burn his ships.'

This done I devoted the whole lecture to a portrait of Hernán Cortés, as I already saw him, with no blurring of outlines, no diluting of colour, to please or displease any one; and I explained how he had been the first Mexican citizen and the first Mexican author, whose letters to the Emperor stood as the first Mexican classic, and I depicted him as an oak whose roots delved into Spanish soil but whose trunk and foliage blossomed in Mexico. And the audience were enthusiastic.

CHAPTER XIII

WAR IN THE BLOOD

NO wonder. They were living in a country which the genius of Spain has strewn all over with beauty; indeed, so many are they, the buildings that deserve to live for ever, that the country is no longer – if it ever was – in a position to pay for their upkeep. Radicals and liberals will have to reconsider their anti-clerical policies, which by expelling or impoverishing the religious orders, have left so many splendid works of art defenceless against the deadly hand of time. Mexico, in particular, so rich also in pre-Colombian monuments that require attention and expense, is particularly exposed to the danger. We have the same problem in Spain where, to quote but the most glaring example, the beauties of Salamanca are threatened by decay and ruin, which is certain if nothing is done to save them.

But in Mexico, the danger that threatens her Spanish heritage is increased by the anti-Spanish prejudice that prevails in certain intellectual sectors. It is thoroughly irrational and leads even persons of pure European descent to identify themselves with Cuautemoc against Cortés. A distinguished English art critic, writing in *The Times* on the new Anthropological Museum of Mexico, described, not without an ironical smile, how one of the elegant young women who act as guides had lamented to him: 'See what the Spaniards have done with *our* culture,' and she was a one hundred per cent blonde European.

This attitude goes with a certain amount of make-believe or even *make-unbelieve*. The grim sides of the Aztec culture – the tearing of panting hearts out of the chests of victims – the human sacrifices – are subdued, suppressed, denied. The sacrificial stones are exhibited but by no means described. History is adapted to the untenable anti-Spanish prejudice. For, in fact, one can tell the story of the Conquest of Mexico in an entirely truthful way, without having to denigrate either Aztecs or Spaniards – by merely placing every one in the context of his day. But Mexico has not reached yet this detached perspective. It is still quartered by antagonistic tensions.

There were then a few men of letters and professors of history devoted to this systematic misrepresentation of the facts to which Mexico owes her existence; but none as powerful as Diego Rivera, the greatest

155

of modern Mexican painters. I called on him once. I did not return. Nothing was said the actual words of which could have caused my impression of the man; but I have seldom experienced a stranger sense of repulsion in the presence of a human being. It began with a thorough dislike of the house and studio in which he lived, designed (I was told) by himself, and it ended in my being there, standing in the middle of his studio, having nothing to say to him.

When I called on him all I knew about him was a story Andrés Segovia had told me. Vasconcelos, as Minister of Education, had asked Rivera to decorate the patio of the ministry with frescoes; and one day, as Segovia arrived at the building, he saw Rivera standing on the scaffold, brush in hand. 'Why those two pistols at your girdle?' asked Segovia. And Rivera, with his bitter-sweet Mexican accent: 'As a guidance for critics.'

Looking back through the years, I surmise that what put me off was the feeling that there was no love in him. His face was ferocious. It was also lacking in sincerity, shifty. And so I was able to understand his sordid inconsistencies. He had accepted a fat fee from Dwight Morrow (who should have known better) to decorate the house of Cortés in Cuernavaca. He actually used this opportunity to cover those historic walls with slanderous pictures of Cortés himself and of the Spanish conquistadors – which in the general atmosphere of the period might be excused – but also of Spanish monks, which is really inexcusable; and, in the same year when the State of California denied the use of its schools to Mexican children, he also accepted a commission to decorate the San Francisco Stock Exchange, which he did with scenes depicting the American biologists studying the trees of California. Why, I kept wondering, did he call himself Diego Rivera instead of Ahuitzotl or something to that effect? But then, that is the constant paradox of so many half-castes. Unable to rise above the war he carried in his blood, Diego Rivera wasted undoubted talents as a painter to express passions some of which he could not help uttering, for they overpowered him.

There were some minds in Mexico, though, who had conquered this limitation, if they had ever felt it. One of them was a clear-sighted, scholarly and friendly old man, the patriarch of Mexican anthropology, named Dr Ezequiel Chavez. It was to him, I do believe, that I owe the revelation that every one in Mexico, no matter his look, is a half-caste. This seems to me a profound intuition. It confirms that human beings are less the products of genes than of a common life and history, and 'life together' what we call in Spanish *convivencia*; and that with the passing of the years, the blending of mental-moral or psychical forces is bound to count at least as much as that of the merely biological ones.

Dr Chavez was one of the wisest men I have known anywhere in the world.

He was by no means unrepresentative or untypical. The Mexican intellectual class have always been outstanding, as Humboldt was already able to note. At the time I am sketching (1931), one of its leaders was Alfonso Reyes, one of the finest writers in the Spanish-speaking world, well known for the limpidity and depth of his essays and poems. Reyes was also a man far above the anti-Spanish superstition that afflicted lesser men; which, of course, by no means implies that one should look at things with a pro-Spanish prejudice either. Reyes was a free, universal mind.

A third man equally emancipated and universal was Dr Torres Bodet, whose career at the head of the Federal Department of Education would suffice to ensure for him a lasting memory in the history of his country; but who with his term of office as Director General of UNESCO became a world figure as well in the world of culture. What is perhaps less widely realised is that Torres Bodet is one of the finest masters of the Spanish sonnet writing poetry in our day. This makes of him by no means a pro-Spanish writer or public man; but he certainly is a mind above the battle.

All these attitudes for, against or even-minded, towards the Spanish past and present seemed to take little account, indeed to play no part in the relations between individual Spaniards and individual Mexicans. The Spanish colony in Mexico has always been strong, probably by natural selection, since those who came over, by the mere fact of coming, evinced a certain degree of enterprise. It was my good fortune to meet and appreciate a few of these new conquistadors in a modern garb, chief of them the two Prietos, uncle and nephew, who by then led the paramount steel works of the country, the Fundidora de Monterrey. Don Adolfo had arrived in Mexico in 1890, at 23, a young lawyer, just out of the University of Madrid. He soon made his mark in banking and within twenty years was a power in the land of his adoption. He was known above all by his creativeness, his omnipresent activity and his new ideas about salaries, housing, education, hospital and maternity institutions for his workers and families. Yet, his popularity went far beyond what one would expect, considering he was, after all, a capitalist; and the cause thereof was not known until his death, when the amount of his secret donations to private people in need came to be known. The financial wizard and masterly organiser harboured in his heart a secret saint.

When he died in 1945 he left the steel works in full swing. But not even he would have been able to prophesy to what heights of productivity and prosperity his nephew and heir was to raise them. Now this heir, Carlos Prieto, is not merely an up to date managerial master, who, as a holiday from his steel works, developed the most successful orange grove business in the country, but an artist as well. When I met him in Mexico in 1931, talking of music one day, I happened to mention Mozart's *Quintet for Strings in G minor*. 'You'll hear it to-night,' he said. I was expecting a record. I actually heard five musicians, led by Carlos himself on the first violin. He later married a French woman born in Spain, also an excellent musician; and I often, in later years, enjoyed very good Mozart or Beethoven in that admirable house. More years went by, and the quartet was completed with the two sons of the family, both first rate technicians technically formed in the M.I.T. and the London School of Economics.

I will not say that a family of such outstanding quality is to be considered as typical or normal of the Spanish colony in Mexico; but I do say that such an excellent level occurs fairly frequently, which explains the high performance of Spaniards in the growth of prosperity and culture in Mexico; to which should be added that, the two countries being so close in spirit, the second generation of a Spanish family settled in Mexico becomes totally Mexican.

This inner struggle within the Mexican soul, this perpetual reliving of the Conquest that goes on in it may well explain why the country lives with so much intensity. Measured in terms of what after all matters most – the intensity of the present – no country with the possible exception of Andalusia – can rival Mexico. Here again, the two strains in her people collaborate in opposition. On a background of Spanish baroque, itself strongly influenced by the Indian spirit (as admirably shown by Sacheverell Sitwell), the people move in a magnificent pattern of colour. The Spanish baroque is already pretty lively; but in Mexico it seems to boil over with movement and form. And the source of all that energy is there for all to see.

The people. And in the people, first and foremost, colour. It all begins with the colour of the skin; for the Mexican Indian is the colour of copper and some of them (I remember in particular a handsome Mexican Consul I once met in Chicago) seem to be lit from the inside. It is one of the most glorious human colours in the world, and, if the features but help a bit, it can rise to great heights of beauty.

This Mexican Indian complexion shares with the African Black the quality of enhancing all coloured objects. Driving once on a country road in Brazil, I came suddenly upon a roadside fruit market. The sight was such as to drive a painter to dispair or delight. The reds, purples, yellows, greens, indigos of the fruit, the perfectly chosen colours of the clothes the women were wearing and the noble bronze of their faces, made up an unforgettable sight. This kind of sight can be enjoyed daily in any Mexican city. In no other country that I can recall, is one oftener led to stop and turn back to follow with one's eyes an old woman just to enjoy for a few minutes longer the colour of the shawl she is wearing.

The fascination of Mexico is hard to analyse. Negatively, it may be due to a total absence of vulgarity. It may be simple, primitive, wild – it never is vulgar; and in these vulgar days, when vulgarity can rise to the heights of power and wealth, this is a quality to be thankful for. Another element in this fascination may well be the obsession with death which the Mexicans have inherited from the Aztecs and blended with a similar, yet very different, streak in the Spanish character.

Death is an active character in the dramatic life of the Mexican people. During my first visit there, I was told that the officers of Villa's army, when they met to dine together in a festive way, would gamble, with their lives for a stake. All tables and chairs were removed from the room; the guests stood round the room, their backs to the wall, and one of them standing in the centre, all lights out, pivoted on his toe and shot. Then the light was switched on and the loser's body was removed.

This is an illuminating case; for it shows how the essence of living for the Mexican is a gamble with his own life as the stake of the game; undoubtedly an attitude inherited from the pre-Cortesian days, when there was such a narrow connection between religion and the sacrifice of life. This attitude is bound to cheapen life in the eyes of the people, one's own and one's neighbours; and so it is that Mexico is a country of very brave people, who are prone to be reckless with everybody's life, including their own.

Everybody who has been in that wonderful and fascinating country knows what an incredible blend of anarchy and order public life in Mexico is apt to be. Outwardly it works so well that (despite occasional outbursts of violence) it would be difficult to find a more orderly republic in the world. A closer look baffles the mind. For in Mexico nothing is what it seems to be, *and yet is* somehow in the end. That is the crux of the system. The one and only party is not single, for it allows two or three more. The Federal States are not as free from the central power as they are supposed to be, yet do manage to be freer than they are supposed to be. The press is supposed to be free but cannot afford to behave as if it were, yet does at times behave as if it were free and as if it feared no reprisals from the top, which it knows full well it has every reason to fear; the police are perhaps one of the most corrupt in the world, yet keep the country in a tolerable state of order though they must be wise about whom they persecute to the bitter end; and the President is not really the President but, as it was once put to me by a shrewd Mexican, a synthesis of the Spanish Viceroy and of Montezuma. Hence his omnipotence, which no one admits and everybody not only respects but assumes.

All this may well add up to an unexpected conclusion. Mexico lives in a magic state. Most of what happens in it is due to magic forces; and when the visitor observes it with his logical kind of mind he cannot understand a thing. The happenings of Mexico do not unfold in a chain of cause and effect; they turn up all of a sudden and all together, like the roses and thorns in a rose bush, by virtue of a sap coming from the earth and presenting the whole lot of them simultaneously.

CHAPTER XIV

A TRADE UNION POTENTATE AND A PRESIDENTIAL
LANDOWNER

W HAT happened in all this to our old friend class war? How could
we understand, let alone describe, the dominant feature of modern societies according to the gospel of Karl Marx? That was the question I put to a keen, clever, Frenchman who owned considerable textile
mills in the country in which he had been settled for almost a lifetime.
He smiled and answered that the best way to understand this question
was to *live it*. That seemed admirable to me, and on my saying so, he
asked: 'Do you know Morones?' I didn't. Morones was a typical Mexican, for he came from Spain, was born in Asturias and had emigrated as
a young man. In about ten years, he had built up a Workers Union, a
powerful instrument which he managed, indeed ruled, as a dictator.
While everybody agreed that this Union had certainly increased the
bargaining power of its members, it was common knowledge that it
had raised Morones himself to the status of a potentate.

My French friend was on the best of terms with him; and through
the mists and screens of discretion, I was able to gather that many a
strike could be settled by means of unsung subsidies to the head of the
Union. Other friends confirmed that (in those days, at any rate) the
practice was pretty general in Mexico, as indeed it used to be also in
the U.S. The upshot of it all was that Morones gave a kind of festival in
my honour at his country estate.

This estate was worthy of a potentate of ancient days, which no modern tycoon could rival; for it rested on the existence of an unlimited
supply of servants of all kinds. The house was huge and offered to the
owner's guests rooms galore beautifully furnished; enormous garages,
stables vast and populated with fine native and foreign horses; while
every other comfort or luxury had been thought of and provided, from
swimming-pools to tennis courts; and there was a theatre.

We must have been about two to three hundred guests, and the food
and wines were first-rate. There was good humour and gaiety all along,
and after the lavish meal we were bid to walk over to the theatre where
a variety show was put on, composed of a well-balanced ensemble of
comedy, sketch, ballet, singing and folk-lore, prolonged into the small
hours of the morning. When I expressed my appreciation to my French
friend, the textile manufacturer who was at the origin of it all, he smiled
again: 'Much more had been prepared. But he got cold feet while

161

talking to you and he gave up the idea.' 'What idea?' I asked. 'You have missed an orgy in the grand style. He does that very well. A night of drink, women and song never to be forgotten.'

There is a distich well known all over Spanish America:

> Here lives the President. The Boss
> Lives over there, right across.

It applied to Mexico during my first visit. The President was an Ingeniero Ortiz Rubio (Rubio: fair headed) who was said to have beaten Einstein hollow at relativity, because he was relatively fair, relatively married, relatively *ingeniero* and relatively president. The boss was his predecessor, Plutarco Elías Calles, of Turkish Sephardi origin, a forcible and capable politician, if somewhat limited by an old-fashioned nineteenth-century radical political philosophy.

As I harboured a plot in mind, I asked to call on him, and he received me on his estate close by the capital. I had been told that this estate had belonged to one Noriega, a Spaniard, who had bought it cheap because it was a worthless swamp, and had transformed it by hard work, skill and money into the splendid thing it then was; whereupon he had been deprived of it by law, by revolution or by a combination of both, I don't remember. Anyhow, now it belonged to Calles.

My plan was to win over the Boss of Mexico to a somewhat complex and delicate operation aiming at receiving his country into the League. When the League was founded, Mexico was in the bad books of the U.S., and, strange though it may seem today, even as lofty a man as Woodrow Wilson had proved unable to rise above this utterly biased and nationalistic attitude. So narrow-minded was he on this point, that he had embedded into the Covenant an automatic and permanent exclusion of Mexico, by means of a single device: an article in the Covenant declared the League open to any State included in a list in an Annex, a list from which Mexico had been excluded. Naturally enough, Mexico took this as an insult and always turned a deaf ear when anyone suggested that she apply for entry. The acme of absurdity was reached when those very Americans who had caused the trouble that kept Mexico out, kept Wilson out as well, so that both Mexico and her adversary remained outside the League.

My purpose was to convert Calles to a plan to solve this conundrum. Mexico would not apply; but when everything had been privately agreed, Spain would launch a proposal to invite Mexico to come in, and the speech of the Spanish delegate, amounting to an oral invitation at the Assembly, would be followed by similar statements from all the big powers, i.e. the permanent members of the Council.

This was my plan. How to put it to Calles was another matter. I was a private individual, an Oxford professor on leave. I had no other authority than that of my name, by then fairly well-known as a political lay preacher in three languages and two continents. When I was chewing in my mind how to get around that difficulty, Genaro Estrada invited me to dine. He was the Foreign Secretary of the Mexican Republic, a man of letters, a word artist, a person whose mind, manners, education, sensibility appealed to me by their balance of simplicity, good taste and common sense. I knew him well.

He had been of course the first man to know of my plan, and he had liked it from the first. It was he who had arranged my meeting with Calles; so that I was naturally led to think that he wanted to talk to me about it. But no. We were alone, face to face, at a table just like any other, in a well-known restaurant of the city. Hardly had we sat down when Estrada produced a paper out of the inner pocket of his coat, put it on his plate, his two hands on top, and began to speak:

'You must know that tomorrow [April 14, 1931] is the inauguration of a new tradition we are starting: the day of the Americas. It will be celebrated every year, and it will aim at strengthening our links with the United States. All the States of Spanish America are in it, as well as Brazil. Tomorrow, then, the Mexican press all over the country will carry on its first page the message Hoover addresses to all of us and this message from Ortiz Rubio which is my answer to him.' He handed his paper to me and said: 'Please, read it now. I want you to be the first to know it here.'

I was not in the least surprised. This had always been his friendly and confidential manner with me. His massage was excellent, clear, substantial, without pedantry, hopeful without undue optimism, free from verbosity or false eloquence, inspired by a sincere cordiality towards the U.S. expressed, though, in dignified if warm terms.

When I got the papers next morning, I searched in vain on the first page for the two presidential messages. They had been exiled to the last page. The rest of the papers was devoted to Spain. The King had abdicated. And I was shocked to find that the Spanish revolution, though peaceful in Spain, had produced such an effervescence in Mexico that many people, as many as fifty of them, had been wounded. It seemed to me a bit thick for a foreign colony, albeit so intimate with Mexico as ours was, to behave in such a way; but when I spoke in that vein to Estrada over the phone he retorted: 'There wasn't a single Spaniard among them.' The temperamental Mexican had seized the opportunity to go in for a holiday from order.

So, when that day or the next I went to call on Calles, the political landscape had changed; but my place in it hadn't. I still was a private man, an Oxford professor with a vocation for political lay preaching. And I found Calles very much of a stuffed shirt. We talked and talked, but I could not see a spot where I could pierce the armour of ... no, not self-importance, but official solemnity which kept him at such a distance. He showed me a herd of lovely goats.

That rang a bell. I should explain that the Spanish language has two words for *he-goat*, one just it and the other one now become a term of abuse no one should utter before ladies. I began to see some possibilities, but they turned out much better than I had expected. 'President,' I said, 'now that we are going to become a Republic, you must be very pleased.' He smiled mischievously. 'You know,' he answered, 'what interests me in Spain is not her politics but her goats, the best in the world. And Spain won't allow them to be exported. So now my aim is clear. I want to bring over three hundred Murcia goats.' I saw a light. 'But sir, couldn't you bring over also three hundred *cabrones*.' He enjoyed that and celebrated it with a robust laughter: 'Ah but you know we have far too many here, as it is!' The ice was broken and my plot was safe.

CHAPTER XV

THE ADVENT OF THE SPANISH REPUBLIC

THE news from Spain flooded the newspapers. The revolution had been so complete and yet so quiet that people were talking of the Spanish Republic as 'the pretty girl.' It sounded too good to be true. (As it turned out so it was!) The dramatic element was provided by the names of the new men – the very men who had been in and out of prison for years. When the 'ins' go out and the 'outs' come in, the element of gossip is added incentive to the news. The papers soon began to adjudicate the more important Spanish embassies to literary men.

This was but natural. The career diplomats were nearly all tainted with a suspicion of monarchism; and the natural reservoir of good linguists acquainted with foreign lands was the literary world. It was soon known that Ramón Pérez de Ayala, the novelist, was going to London, Américo Castro, the philologist, to Berlin, and a career man with literary proclivities, Danvila, was transferred from Buenos Aires to Paris. On this, rather scanty, basis, the imagination of journalists built up a complete list of 'ambassadors' leaving out but a very few names. This was too much for Julio Camba, one of Spain's most entertaining yet most substantial humorists. 'What is wrong with me?' he wrote. 'I have good evening clothes, I know French, English and German, I write in the newspapers. I even write books, and no embassy for me?' Then he went on to provide his own explanation. He happened to be in New York at the time. So he suggested, the Republic had sent all those authors abroad in order to get rid of them, and as he happened to be abroad already, an Embassy had not been found necessary in his case.

That seemed also to be the case for me, though I did see my name mentioned once or twice. I carried on my duties as agreed for the rest of the month, and went to the Spanish Embassy to renew my passport, in view of the change of regime. The ambassador had resigned and gone, and the chargé d'affaires was no other than my old friend Gallostra who, once in Barcelona, had let loose the tongue of my dumb deputy-chief delegate by repeated applications of sherry. Gallostra transmogrified the royal formulas of my passport into Republican ones, and, thus armed, I took a ship for Havana, where I was due to take on an assignment for the whole month of May.

After an uneventful voyage, I landed in Havana on May 1st and read in the newspapers that the American Secretary of State, Mr Stimson,

165

had expressed his pleasure at my appointment as Ambassador in Washington. I was dumbfounded. No one had said a word to me. No one knew whether I could or would accept the post. No one had troubled to explore the pros and cons of that step – least of all I. No one in fact, knew whether I was a republican or a monarchist, for the simple reason that I had never written or spoken on this alternative, which seems to me more verbal than real.

Still, there I was, in Havana, officially appointed Ambassador of the Spanish Republic in Washington, and professor of the University of Oxford on loan to the University of Havana for a month. And it was up to me to make up my mind, choose, take the consequences and face the music they would make either in Oxford or in Madrid.

Fortunately, there were no aeroplanes in those days and the first ship available, the Spanish steamer *Cristóbal Colón*, would not leave before the 8th. I had a week to think things over. And there were lots of them. I was very favourably impressed by the exemplary way the changeover had taken place, the more so as it had proved me wrong. I had never believed that a change of that calibre could come about at all in Spain without the Army organising and leading it. The fact that it had not intervened either for or against, and that, nevertheless, the regime had changed in perfect order, seemed to me a very good omen.

My decision, though, was reluctant. The material side of things did not worry me, though it should have done so. What worried me about accepting was the feeling Oxford might have that I deserted her. I had begun my duties late in January 1928; gone away at the end of 1930; and here I was in May 1931 turning my back for good on a chair I had left on leave of absence hardly one year and a half after my inauguration. This lay heavily on my conscience, for the University could not have had the slightest advance notice and did not know, could indeed hardly imagine, that I had had no previous notice either.

Looking back on those days in Havana, it occurs to me that when I made up my mind to leave for Spain, via New York, on May 8th, instead of at the end of the month, for Oxford, my mind was already made up; even though I kept thinking that my decision would be taken in New York after a phone conversation with Fernando de los Ríos, the new Minister of Justice, the man in the new team I was best acquainted with. And I also suspect that under the more or less 'moral' considerations such as backing the Republic and so forth, one of my strongest, if subconscious, motives must have been that the chair bored me. That helped me to keep somewhat muted the theme of the material sacrifice I was making in launching forth on an uncertain diplomatic-political career leaving a certain and illustrious academic one.

When I boarded the Cristóbal Colón I felt for the first time that I was a true Ambassador and not a fanciful one, just as Don Quixote did when he was so ceremoniously received in the Duke's mansion; 'and that day was the first when he through and through knew and believed himself to be a true knight errant and not a fanciful one'; for the Captain offered me the best cabin in the ship – mostly, as I later discovered, because it was the only one he had vacant. It turned out handy when we were sailing into New York harbour, for with one of the service boats (port, health, mail or what not) that come out to meet the incoming steamers, a host of press reporters invaded my cabin with lively waves of tittle-tattle topped by a foam of 'Mr Ambassador.' I looked around the cabin and said: 'Gentlemen, I can see no Ambassador in this cabin.' They were taken aback. 'But you are the Ambassador to the U.S.! . . .' – 'I am nothing of the kind. No one has told me.' – 'Can we go and say that?' – 'Of course you can.' They vanished.

Why did I behave in that odd way? I wonder. There are men who plan first and then behave, more or less as planned. I seem to behave first, then think it over and wonder why. My surmise is that I was giving vent to a subconscious protest against those who had used me as their tool. I was still busy in my mind with this inquiry when we docked and presently the staff of the Washington Spanish embassy invaded my cabin, brandishing cables and papers. There it was, black and white, official and sealed. I was the Spanish Ambassador in Washington.

From the Spanish Consulate General in New York I rang up Fernando de los Ríos. I was somewhat cantankerous. 'You might have at least warned me if not consulted me. You are a professor yourself. Can you see yourself in the shoes of the Oxford Vice-Chancellor?' Of course he couldn't. But at least he knew of the existence of such a dignitary, which is more than can be said of the man who was to be my chief, Lerroux, Minister for Foreign Affairs. In the end, Fernando pleaded comprehension for a revolutionary cabinet, and I accepted and announced that I was arriving in Spain within a fortnight on board the Cristóbal Colón.

During these two days I spent in New York I was not able to see Tom Lamont. He was in Athens, from where he cabled congratulations; but I soon heard (if I remember right, from him) that not even my appointment could console him for the fall of a regime to which his Bank had just made a loan of sixty million dollars. I do believe he was eventually able to recover his peace of mind, at any rate on that score.

CHAPTER XVI

FAREWELL TO OXFORD

O N leaving New York I had to be transferred to the barber's shop transformed into a fairly comfortable cabin, for the one I had occupied in Havana had been booked by my predecessor as Ambassador in Washington, and so we travelled together. As fluke would have it, Padilla, my predecessor, a capable professional, had a Scots wife, so that, on that score at any rate, there was to be no change at the Spanish Embassy. His son, Ramón, was one of the Secretaries and, unlike his father, he remained in the service and I kept him in my embassy, where he was most useful. Time, the shaper of many a change, was to turn him into the diplomatic Secretary of the Pretender Don Juan.

S. S. *Cristóbal Colón* called at Vigo before it did at Coruña where I had meant to land. I changed my mind, left my luggage on board, and landed at Vigo, to drive on to Coruña later. My chief attraction was Compostela, on the way. In that lovely old city and shrine of the Catholic world, where Spaniards got their inspiration to gain Heaven by killing Moors, it was both sunny and raining. Nothing unusual. The drive Vigo-Coruña was dry but Compostela was wet. Owing to some trick of nature, it rains in Compostela more than in Bergen or Glasgow; but it is a sunny city, nevertheless. The explanation was once given to me by a native who knows Europe well. 'Our clouds', he said, 'are honest-to-God, hard-working clouds. When they are there, they are doing their job, which is to rain, not just lazily to obstruct daylight, as they do in other cities. When they've dropped their load of rain, off they go; and the city can enjoy the sun.'

La Coruña is a sunny city without explanations, and one of the gayest and prettiest of Spain. I had not visited it for a very long time; and as now I was an important person, my fellow Coruñese suddenly discovered that I was a great man, which they had not noticed before. I was asked to give a lecture at the chief Club in the city and the mayor himself announced that he would preside. He was a somewhat impressive figure, the owner of one of the biggest shoe manufactures in the city; a prominent republican, as could be seen even at a distance, because of the imposing size of his square, pepper-and-salt beard.

I do not recollect what I spoke about, nor do I think the subject mattered very much; for the chief point was the pride of the city in the native's success; so, everything I said was celebrated and received as

168

gospel truth, which it probably was, though it would have been received as such even if it hadn't been.

Madrid was bathed in pride and joy. Pride for the generous, good-humoured, civilised way in which the change-over had taken place. Joy because the people had at last got rid of the 'traditional obstacles' that stood in the way between them and political happiness. As an example of the first, everybody related to me how, when the King had gone and his wife and children spent their last night in the Royal Palace, the workers of the U.G.T. had organised a civic guard and closed the Palace with a human wall behind which that family could sleep in peace. Or again how, while the Queen and her children were waiting behind the station at El Escorial, one hour north of Madrid, for the train that was to drive them to exile, a lorry bursting with young, enthusiastic Republican workers of both sexes drove past the spot and, on seeing the vanquished family, all spontaneously grew silent and passed them with signs of evident human respect.

These first days were the finest of our short-lived republic. They justify the optimism of those who claim that the Spanish people, left to itself, is wise, humane and reliable. Unfortunately, it was not left to itself, and on May 12th, when the Republic was hardly a month old, the burning of churches began. Whose was the criminal hand? Let the search be guided by this two-barrelled observation: in Spain the extreme Left always betrays the Left, and the extreme Right always betrays the Right.

One sunny morning I walked up the Calle de Carretas and entered the shop of a French tailor there. 'How old are your records?' I asked. 'Have you got any of about twenty years ago?' Monsieur B. was surprised but by no means put out. 'Certainly. Here is 1911.' – 'Very good. Look up November.' Although from where I stood I saw the page upside down, I soon spotted my name. 'See. An evening suit for me. Wonderful. You have all the measurements. Make me another one.' Monsieur B. put his glasses on, read the name, took a good look at his customer ... 'But then, you are the new Spanish Ambassador to the U.S.?' – 'Of course. Do you think that I should otherwise have gone and ordered another evening suit?'

By the time I arrived in Oxford, the emotions caused by my unexpected appointment to the Washington embassy had been becalmed partly by time partly by the news that I myself had known nothing about it. Dr Dudden, the Master of Pembroke, then Vice-chancellor, received me with the utmost cordiality and asked me to lunch. This, of course, was an honour offered to the Ambassador, not to the professor; but it was gratefully accepted by both. The Master insisted on my having a glass of port, which I hesitated to take in the middle of the day; I had to accept, but asked, in exchange, to be revealed the secret of the excellence of Pembroke port; to which he made answer that no port could be drunk in the College that had not slept thirty years under its learned roof. This I have often quoted as a good example of the continuity of British institutions.

Soon, we left Oxford, (as we thought) for good. As we were actually going, the old, wonderful city pulled at the strings of my heart. Many years later, after another and much longer stay, thirty years of it, I tried to utter what I then felt. Here it is:

> Here, the stone that had slept between sheets of chalk and hardened clay for a long night whose minutes were centuries of centuries, woke up quickened by the breath of man. From passivity and lack of purpose, the stone, once dead, rose possessed of a purpose and pregnant with a meaning; so that with the passing of the years, a community of stones alive grew to perfect harmony and achieved that glory we call by the mysterious name of beauty. Movement animated it, and order shone on its face like the light that shines in human eyes; and on its surface, once flat, flowers blossomed and arabesques meandered, and Solomonic pillars spiralled, and saints, knights, scholars and gargoyles populated the stage.
>
> Down on the pavements, some of those saints and knights, scholars and gargoyles deambulated in dignified leisure, removed from transient vulgarity to an almost Tibetan serenity by their gowns and mortarboards (the mortarboard symbolising thought ever tangent to reality); and while some, overcoming their dislike for explosions and revolutions, adopted the new-fangled machine-propelled carriage, most remained faithful to strange and recondite conveyances; so that one would sleep-walk himself from Long Wall to Lady Margaret holding on to a poem of Pindar, while another would sail from Merton to the Bodleian on board a theory of Einstein, and a third one would vanish under the Bridge of Sighs lost in thoughts of Platonic love.
>
> But beware. Those Tibetans were no fossils incrustated on the cliff of time. In spite of their roof-of-the-world air, they might, for all you know, have explored the earth in search of antique monuments, or been parachuted somewhere in

Europe to fight with a stout heart and a keen brain against some vicious windmill, or ruled with advice some outlandish, far-off tribe afflicted with modernity; and there would be among them, those who could fluently speak (with the right upper-class accent) an archaic language now dead for centuries, and those who were able gently to redress a slightly twisted orbit by a delicate treatment based on differential equations; and those who could grind statistics to a dust from which they could distil economic fancies; and those who could analyse to a hairbreadth the balance of Catholic and Protestant promptings in the conscience of Henry VIII when he sent Ann Boleyn to the block. Most of them, if closely watched, would betray a lively corner in the otherwise indifferent eye, where one would detect the spark of sherry or the power of port. If the observer happened to be a Spaniard, pride would be set alight in his own eye at the thought that while English culture was based on Oxford and Cambridge, these two great cities floated on sherry and port. This warning thought would send the observer's imagination wandering towards the convivial halls where, after dinner, in the subdued light of candles, tinged with moonshine by the omnipresence of table silver, the priests of Euclid and Newton and the priests of Herodotus and Tacitus, and those of Plato and of Virgil, would sink their differences in ruby-coloured waves.

Over it all, the noble frontages wrought by men and polished by the centuries, stood in dignified, silent eloquence; and the stone in them rose higher and higher, thinner and thinner, until it thrust at the elusive skies its rigid, ever tense, arrows of desire.

Part III

On Stage for the Tragedy

CHAPTER I

LOST: AN AMBASSADOR

Y stint as Ambassador in Washington lasted about seven months on paper, and about seven weeks in fact. I presented credentials to Herbert Hoover, a man I only saw once – at that ceremony – and for whom I conceived a thorough dislike. The cause of this feeling was plain to me. In the half hour our ceremony lasted, I never saw his eyes. He managed to look anywhere in the room but at the face and eyes of the man he was conversing with. I came to the conclusion that he could not be straight. I hope I haven't been unfair to him. I have ever been puzzled since by the mere fact that such a man could have reposed his confidence in Hugh Gibson who, though endowed with the reserve, acumen and even guile of his profession, was a true human being, as sincere, open and transparent a mind as could be desired.

My chief problem while in Washington was to defend my stock of sherries and whiskies. This happened in the era of prohibition; and, under the guise of tourism, embassies were apt to be invaded by car-fuls of thirsty tourists on the chance of finding a convivial Ambassador. National festivals were especially dangerous days from that point of view. The kitchen and domestic staff had acquired quite an experience in dodging plain, forthright requests for a drink. If the leader of the invaders happened to be a V.I.P. resistance was apt to be weakened.

The ever present colour bar led to no trouble with us. C.H.M.A. caused a sensation by shaking hands with the Negro cook as she visited the kitchen. The cook had never seen such a thing happen, while C.H.M.A. had never imagined that she would produce such an impression by a gesture so matter of course. One day, driving from Washington to New York, we pulled up at an eating-place somewhere, and asked the head of the dining-room to see that our driver got his lunch. 'White?' was the answer-question. White he happened to be. But these were for us very strange problems.

A Spanish American distant acquaintance happened to know that I was coming to stay for a few days in New York. He persuaded me to stay at the Sherry-Netherlands, where we were given an immense flat, five or six bathrooms and (I counted them) seventy lamps to switch off at night – for a sum which by dint of being moderate, was absurd. We spent our first millionaire night in blissful silence on a very high floor of the tower; then at about eleven in the morning, we went for a walk in the Park. On arriving at the opposite side of the Avenue, I happened to look back at the tower we had come down from, and to my horror and dismay discovered that, no doubt in my honour, the hotel had flown the old flag of monarchist Spain. I went back, talked the matter over with the management, and – oh wonder, on a Sunday morning, too! – within half an hour, a huge silk banner of the Republic was proudly beating in the wind, up the tower where I lived.

My chief purpose for that trip to New York had been to meet the Spanish colony, which I did in some building or other where there was an auditorium for about 500 persons. It was very well attended, indeed packed, much to the concern of one of two friends who knew that we had had wind of some plot for an attempt on my life. A sixth sense had assured me that there was no danger, that indeed, it was more likely to be a sour grapes rumour put about by the monarchists – but those who knew of the threat were soon to be recognisable, for they all grinned when they found in the first row of the Republican audience the robust figure of Paulino, the Basque heavy-weight boxing champion.

One day, after a few weeks in office, I received a letter from Tom Lamont. It merely said that he thought I should be interested in the enclosed correspondence. This correspondence is one of the treasures I lost when at the end of the civil war, the forces of law and order occupied and emptied my house which had weathered unscathed the three-year siege of Madrid. I quote from memory. 'My dear Mr Lamont,' the Secretary for Labour wrote from Washington, 'Just before Christmas last year, an alien by the name of Salvador de Madariaga arrived in New York and gave your house as his address. He said he would stay in this country for three months. There is no trace of him in our records. Could you give us his present address?' To which Lamont, of course, obliged.

I sent copies of both letters to the Under-secretary, Castle, Stimson being then abroad, and I added: 'This is all very well, but the fact is that I left the U.S. as promised, on March 31st by New Laredo.' Mr Castle's answer was the best of the lot. He informed me that the papers had been sent to his colleague of Labour and added: 'One thing I can assure you, Mr. Ambassador: you shall not be expelled the country.'

What is the use of passports? I had passed the frontier at New Laredo in March (stamp); entered New York in May (stamp); and re-entered as an Ambassador in June; and the immigration authorities did not know where I was. What is the use of passports? To let the police go to sleep. The general trend of even the most liberal democracies points to a sacrifice of individual rights for the convenience of the bureaucracy. Human beings should circulate freely without passports or documents –

as Europeans did until 1914 from Lisbon to Stockholm and from Athens to Dublin. The requirements of the nation, mostly a guarantee that no one actually settles in it without its consent, could be met by strict injunctions to the visitor to report to the authorities after a three-month stay, under heavy penalties for failing to do so. This is obvious. But it is obscured because of the natural tendency to absolutism in all countries, and, sad to say, most of all, in the two Anglo-Saxon chief powers.

There's the rub. For when Britain or the U.S.A. have gone crazy on anything, it may be the parliamentary system or drugs, jazz or long hair, divorce or abortion, the whole world follows the craze. Hence, a curious paradox: the world has suffered, suffers and shall still suffer untold misery because of the political genius of the two Anglo-Saxon nations. The mechanism of this conundrum is plain. Britain and her New World offspring have been endowed by nature with a political genius of such eminence that they have been now for nearly two centuries the most successful political communities in the world. Their admiring observers attribute such a success to the constitutions of these two countries, and so, they all endeavour to copy them. The facts, however, should have led to exactly the opposite conclusion. The Anglo-Saxon political genius is of such a calibre that it has been able to turn into a practical success the two most absurd constitutions that were ever dreamt of; and the last thing the world should have done is to imitate those two models of absurdity.

The food and agriculture expert in my embassy was a competent Basque, Echegaray by name. We had some trouble with the Ministry of Commerce, the details of which I forget, but the whole thing seemed to me pretty futile. Then Echegaray told me a story which confirmed me in my dislike of Herbert Hoover. Apparently, during his tenure of the Commerce Department, Hoover had developed a kind of protectionism camouflaged as precautions against risks to the health of the American people, and this system was, of course, still in force during his term as President.

During my predecessor's tenure of the embassy, a cargo of Spanish tomato tins arrived in some American harbour, I believe, New York. This, of course, was a threat to the Californian producers; so it was turned into a threat to the health of the American man in the street, and the cargo was condemned. Echegaray called at the Ministry of Commerce and was told the cargo had to be destroyed because it was infected with botulism. So, he pursued his advantage home with much tenacity, and forced the ministry to recognise its error. The cargo of tomato tins was saved.

I happened to mention the subject to my Argentine colleague. He snorted. 'We don't go through so much science and laboratory work. I had a cargo of meat thrown into the sea because of some bug or other it was supposed to have; and within ten days, the Buenos Aires sanitary authorities found a shipload of Californian apples so deadly that down they went to feed our fish. Since then, Argentine beef has been found perfectly healthy here.' That was Herbert Hoover's style.

I did not cherish the prospect of being accredited to such an administration; and by the time I found myself in Washington in late July, I did not like the idea of remaining in that climate either. I was not, however, thinking of a change in assignment. Relief, however, came, I should say, from the nature of things. The League Assembly was due to meet in September; and this, the first international gathering it was to attend, was for the Republic a matter of great importance. The issue was causing some anxiety to the shrewder members of our foreign Service, and in particular to Oliván.

The Ministry of Foreign Affairs had been left in the hands of don Alejandro Lerroux, than whom fewer Spanish public men could have been found less competent for such a task. This unfortunate circumstance could normally be left to rot in a discreet penumbra, but when it came to representing Spain in Geneva, at a kind of World Parliament, it amounted to a disastrous risk. It was felt in Madrid that I had better come to the capital to take in hand the organisation of the Spanish delegation and the definition of its tasks. I left Washington for what I believed would be an absence of three months. I never came back as an Ambassador.

CHAPTER II

FOUND: A VICE-PRESIDENT

MEANWHILE I had been elected a member of the Constituent Assembly and even one of the four Vice-Presidents of that august body. How one could be Ambassador in Washington, chief delegate in Geneva (as everybody saw I was bound soon to become) and Vice-President of the Assembly, it is hard to imagine; but then, all politics is beyond not merely logic but imagination as well. I had never voted in my life – nor have I to this day; nor had I ever belonged to any party. But a fellow Coruñese, Santiago Casares Quiroga, had founded a party of leftish liberals, whose specific programme was home rule for Galicia. I liked him. There seems to have been some physical resemblance between us, because more than one visitor to the flat I then took in Madrid, on seeing the bust my brother had sculpted of me, took it for a portrait of Casares Quiroga.

I had met him in our common birthplace when I landed there from the U.S. and I was impressed by his forthright ways. As a good Gallegan, he was well provided with a sense of humour. His party, known as O.R.G.A., was the most popular in Galicia. I was elected *in absentia* and all I had to do for it was to pay 5,000 pesetas for the party funds – which I thought was very moderate.

The Constituent Cortes was a curious assembly, flooded by new men, a mixture of idealists, zealots and adventurers, adorned by such lights as Unamuno, Ortega, Marañón and a score of other intellectuals, watched by a few remnants of the Cortes of old, led by the bellicose Romanones, and trepidating with the impatience of many radicals and socialists eager to solve the problems of Spain now that the 'traditional obstacles' had been swept away.

The debates on the law for the prosecution of King Alfonso as responsible for the Moroccan disasters gave me an occasion to deliver my, what the English quaintly call, 'maiden speech'. I was by no means keen to speak then, but I felt I had to. The bill that was being discussed provided that for the purpose, i.e. the prosecution of the ex-King, the usual guarantees granted by the Spanish code of procedure to the defendant should be suspended, i.e. not applied. I was incensed.

As I had by no means foreseen that I should have to speak, I had prepared nothing, I mean in my mind, for I never read what I have to say; and (what, as I knew later, worried my friends even more, and notably

179

Besteiro, the President of the Chamber) I was sitting on one of the seats of the first or lowest row, which had no desk in front of it, so that the speaker is left with no table to rely on and rise above, a position no experienced parliamentarian would ever accept for speaking. I was no parliamentarian experienced or otherwise, and I plunged into my subject going for the Commission for all I was worth.

'How dare you propose such a legal monstrosity? What is the Republic? Not only must it live according to the law, but the Republic is the law. And you propose that it should begin its official life by committing a scandalous crime against national law, by depriving an accused man of the guarantees our law provides for him.' I won my case, and the misguided proposal was withdrawn.

But even in these very earliest days I soon began to perceive the accents and the envious silences of reserve and mistrust, the evil interpretations of my best-meant utterances. Oddly enough, I was apt to find in Madrid a mistrust that reminded me of Drummond's attitude: a tendency to imagine or suspect that, when I expressed an opinion or took an attitude, I was thinking of self-advancement. In both cases, this struck me as odd, because my spontaneous nature has always led me to express views that in most cases were bound to be harmful to my personal interests or advancement.

I well remember, for instance, a conversation I had with a well known M.P. and journalist, a friend of Azaña. I was then still Ambassador in Washington on paper, but was living in Madrid, working both as an M.P. and as the man in charge of Geneva affairs. I was impressed by the fact that our theoretical idealists were writing an inordinately long constitution, in which everything that everyone proposed was shoved in, with the result that there were far too many articles, far too many debates, while the country was waiting to be governed. I said so to this friend of Azaña's and concluded: 'Scrap all that verbiage, write a pithy, short constitution, and govern.' It was not long before I heard he had concluded that I was impatient to become a cabinet minister!

'That kind of thing', I thought, 'is sure to kill this experiment.' I began to wonder whether the Republic would last. Then, I bethought myself of an aspect of it all that I had to consider. If Drummond and Azaña's friend – two persons as far from each other as one could imagine – made the same error, surely there must be some responsibility on my part. It so happens, moreover, that, by instinct, I incline to believe that in any trouble between human beings, it is safe to adjudicate roughly half of the responsibility to each side, unless one is dealing with abnormal persons such as lunatics or criminals.

I came to the conclusion that, in this particular sector, the cause of the trouble was a hasty impulse to express the judgement I form on things, driven by the wish to improve the objective position and oblivious of the effect on my subjective position my words may have. It is sometimes hard for the man of action, or at least immersed in action, to imagine that anyone may wish to express an opinion for the sake of understanding what is there. This impulse is spontaneous and disinterested in the man of thought, but not in the man of action, who only utters opinions loaded with action- interest. From this contrast, most of the struggles between politicians and intellectuals originate.

As it happens, by one of 'life's little ironies' that spice it so often, I committed a blunder in which thought and action were balanced and blended. I had proposed that the Constitution of the Republic should include an article whereby Spain would explicitly renounce war as an instrument of policy; and the Committee in charge of the Constitution asked me to draft it – which I did. Before it reached the Committee, Azcárate, who had remained at the League Secretariat, read my draft and put forward a few criticisms which seemed to me very well founded. So I begged him to redraft the article and give me his text, which I should then present to the Committee in answer to their request. He did so, and I found his draft excellent. But the Devil saw to it. A clerk from the Committee came breathless to some corridor where I stood talking to someone and requested the text in a hurry, for the Committee were waiting. I fished the text out of my pocket, handed it to him and went on talking. Later, I found it was the wrong pocket and the wrong – i.e. my – text. By then the Commission had passed it *nemine discrepante*, and that was that. 'Well!' said I to myself, 'well!'

Here is another of life's ironies, but by no means little. When a regime tends to abuse its power (and which doesn't?) it is the next regime that suffers most; because it is sure to be born loaded with a number of biased ideas and resentful passions that deprive it of its objectivity. In Spain, for instance, the tendency of the Crown to play ducks and drakes with its right to dissolve Parliament was responsible for one of the most absurd articles of the Constitution of the Republic – the one which prescribed that if the President dissolved Parliament twice within the duration of his mandate, the third Parliament would have to begin its work with a debate on whether the second dissolution had been justified; and if the vote went against him, the President resigned.

Something similar happened with the State-Church relations. Under the monarchy, the Church had behaved in such an unwise fashion that she had alienated public opinion. The world outside Spain, nevertheless, entertained on Spain and her Church extremely old-fashioned ideas, inherited from the days of the Inquisition and all that. A description of State-Church relations in Spain in the days of my youth would not be a mere black and white postcard. It was a complex and subtle affair, not only because the country was by no means uniform on this as on any other aspect of her life, but also because the Church was not a monolith but rather a house more divided within itself than met the eye.

The big cities and the East were on the whole indifferent. Church-going was not strong; opinion and custom were rapidly moving away from the clergy. In the countryside and the West, the clergy was strong. On the other side, the religious orders were rich and unpopular; but the priests were miserably paid; and democracies being what they are, this fact created a prejudice against the regular and for the secular clergy.

When it came to matters of freedom of behaviour, again, the situa-tion in Spain was not easy to define. There were cities and country places, notably in the West and North-West, mostly, in fact, in the Old Kingdom of León or in the Basque country, where one had to live an orthodox life or be ostracised; but in the rest of Spain, and above all in the big cities, religious freedom was complete and, I should say, at times more so than in certain parts of the U.K. or the U.S.

When the part of the future constitution dealing with religion came up for discussion, I felt impelled to oppose it. I prepared a speech cover-ing the chief points on which I differed from the Committee. First: separation. I argued: if you believe that bishops and priests are less important than editors and journalists, you don't know Spain; but if you do believe it, what you are proposing here amounts to letting the Vatican decide who is going to edit and write the Spanish press.

Then the abolition of the budget for the salaries of Spanish priests, which our fierce anticlericals insisted on cementing into the constitu-tion. The item amounted to six or seven million dollars a year. Why abolish it? And why enshrine the measure in the Constitution? Pure prejudice and anti-clerical superstition and no attention to the facts. I made bold to suggest an increase of salary for every Spanish priest by as much as ten to one, which would have firmly anchored the Republic into the heart of every Spanish priest, shamelessly exploited as they all were by the upper clergy.

Finally, I fought against downright dogmatic and vexatious measures such as the excluding of the Orders from teaching; for their co-opera-tion was both necessary because the State did not provide enough schools, and useful as a competitive stimulus to the State. I also critic-ised other petty measures on marriage and burials, which were no more than images on a mirror of the equally vexatious measures the Church had too often practised against agnostics while in power.

This speech I had prepared in my mind would have added up to the most heretical utterance to be heard in that fiercely anti-Church assembly. I was fully aware of it. But I knew my Spain; and so I had planned to wind up by a sentence more or less to the effect that, before any of my colleagues began to refute my arguments, he was requested to declare what I there and then declared myself: 'I was not married in Church and my children had not been christened.' I surmised no one in that House would have been able to say so. Unfortunately it all came to nothing because on the Saturday afternoon when Besteiro, the President of the Cortes, was to call on me to speak, I had to leave in a hurry for a League meeting.

Meanwhile, the government very wisely thought that something had to be done about my inability to serve my American assignment. They began to realise that their choices for the several embassies had perhaps been a bit hasty and amateurish, and in particular that, when they had sent me to the Washington embassy, they had overlooked the value of my considerable experience of League affairs. Fortunately, they found that the ambassador they had appointed in Paris, a career man, Danvila, transferred from Buenos Aires, preferred for private reasons to return to his previous post. I was thus transferred to Paris, the new appointment to be effective from January 1, 1932.

I happened to be in Madrid towards the end of the year, already 'agreed' by the French government, when I received a cable from Lord Robert Cecil. There was to be a huge gathering of League of Nations Unions or something at the Trocadero in Paris, and 'Spain' was not represented. Would I come. I did and the trip was worth the trouble.

The old Trocadero was a kind of Albert Hall but still more so. We were to be twenty speakers, and I was to be the nineteenth, with Henri de Jouvenel the twentieth. Herriot was to preside. France was then tense with the struggle between right and left, exacerbated by a strong undercurrent of fascism intent precisely on measuring the tension. One of the 'pushers' rather than 'leaders' of this fascism was a Corsican, Chiappe, then Préfet de Police, later to lose his life in a most timely air accident as he flew to take charge of Vichy's interests and forces in the Levant. It was generally assumed in Paris that the Trocadero events had been organised by his hidden but efficient hand.

So, speech after speech began and, at last, ended; and I, sitting on the left of Herriot, noticed a frail girl standing on the floor of the hall, typing on her shorthand machine which stood close to the speaker on the platform on which, a short distance behind, the presidential table had been installed. Gradually, the audience became restive; and as Louise Weiss was speaking, an ass of a fascist shouted: '*Ça sent la choucroute!*' ignorant of the fact that sauerkraut is not a German but an Alsatian dish. That, however, was the atmosphere; and at one time in the proceedings, a squad of three or four fascists noisily entered a box somewhere in the immense circle and forced everybody out by means of lively and skilful boxing. This kind of sport went on nearly throughout the meeting, though, of course, in later cases, better resisted and ending in the victory now of the fascists now of the league fans.

The tumult grew worse and worse, louder and louder; and the German speaker could hardly make himself heard. The turn of Scialoja came. He was one of the shrewdest and sharpest of the Italians known to the international political stage, nose, skull, eyes, fingers, everything in him pointed and as if sharpened by a knife as one does a pencil. He instantly realised that no one would listen to him in that hall or madhouse, since fighting is far more tasty than listening, but that an immense audience was listening outside, for the proceedings were being broadcast live. So, he drew the microphone close to his mouth and he made an excellent speech in almost a whisper of a voice. It was a wonderful performance.

He was the most sensible of us. I the most insensate. When my turn came, the fight was at its most violent and the din infernal. Never mind. What I was then thinking I don't know. But I was so incensed that I scrapped the speech I had in mind to deliver, and in a voice far more powerful than I, or anyone there who knew me, ever imagined I possessed, I began to apostrophise the fascist mob in the most aggressive manner I could conceive. 'The bee is silent because it knows what it is after, and goes about it and does it; but the ass brays aloud because he has no idea of what should be done and informs his master far away, and so he grows long ears to hear his master's voice.' That was about the mildest I had to offer them; and Herriot, delighted, forgetting that a microphone open to the whole of France stood close to him, kept enthusiastically egging me on: 'That's the stuff, "Mada", on at them!' Next day I had no voice whatever left in my aching throat.

This circumstance enabled me to think things over. I had sinned against common sense and twice. First, in that I had excited that facist crowd, instead of endeavouring to calm it; in other words, I had satisfied my anti-fascist passion, in a manner worthy of the fascists I was attacking; and then, because at the moment when I was already an accepted Ambassador, due to take charge of my embassy within a matter of very few weeks, I had taken sides in a public quarrel that, strictly speaking, was a matter of internal French politics, egged on by a first rank French statesman!

I believe that, had it happened in Britain, this scene would have put

an end to my diplomatic career. But no. It could not have happened
in Britain. It was again the case of that Frenchman who did not like
haricot beans, 'and I am jolly glad, for if I did I'd eat them, and I just
can't bear them.' While in France, it happened, and no one thought it
odd at all. Why, to detest fascists and tell them to their face, was every
man's right; and as for me playing at French politics, why not? Wasn't I
one of them? No one criticised me – save, of course, the fascist press –
but did it matter even if that press was right? Evidently not, since
they did not find me wrong because I was *wrong* but because I was *me*.

Let me come back to the Trocadero though, for the best remains to
be told. Henri de Jouvenel began to speak. He made a splendid speech,
well argued, strong, and delivered in a voice that mastered the noise.
But I was even more fascinated by his feet. For he did not move them in
the twenty minutes or so that his speech lasted, and they stood close to
the shorthand typing machine on which the young secretary kept typing
with as much calm as if she had been taking down a sermon in a cathedral. Her own feet stood calmly on the floor. Right and left and behind
her, men were having their ears boxed, some fell, some rose again, some
rolled down together embraced in their struggle, but down and up her
fingers went faithfully taking down what de Jouvenel was saying. A
sight of rare elegance and of heroical devotion of which the heroine
herself seemed to be totally unaware. Suddenly, there was an assault at
the presidential table, and a counter-attack by the liberals. No blood
was spilt, but the bottle of water flooded the green baize and Herriot's
and my hands and shirt. Henri de Jouvenel's speech was over, and the
little heroine with her bundle of shorthand script left very prim skipping over those who lay on the ground.

Another scene of this preliminary period, when I was already Ambassador designate to Paris but had not yet presented credentials, comes
to mind, no longer in the agitated atmosphere of the Trocadero, but in
the elegant environment of the Spanish Embassy. This embassy had
been housed, decorated and furnished by Quiñones de León, and so it
was the finest in Paris, with the one exception of the British. The British
Embassy, however, owes its distinction to the historical value of the
Palace it occupies and the treasures it contains; while that of Spain
was in fact the creation of Quiñones, advised by that gifted Catalan
painter decorator, Sert.

My predecessor was Danvila, a polished diplomat, a good historian,
a man who, owing to his long period of service in Argentina, had become almost a Creole in appearance and accent, and who, unable to
resist the attraction of his favourite land, requested to be sent back to

his old embassy. (It was said in Paris that, in Hamlet's words, he had found there metal more attractive.) This circumstance had enabled Oliván to persuade Lerroux to bring me over from Washington.

Danvila asked me to lunch and I soon found myself at a table of about twelve persons in animated conversation with the most famous poetess of France, la Comtesse de Noailles. She was already in her third or fourth youth, yet still attractive owing more to her lively face than to her unfairly fair hair; and she had begun her pleasant offensive even before we sat down, by saying to me of me: 'But he speaks as one breathes!' I did not realise then, how ominous this remark was.

As we began to nibble at our *hors d'oeuvres*, the lively Countess landed on Napoleon; and Napoleon it was still when we were enjoying our ice and strawberries. The subject seemed to stimulate her eloquence and for the whole meal I was submitted to a torrent of admiration for the famous Corsican. I had no chance to put in a 'but' or a 'nevertheless'. She spoke too well and too continuously, and she seemed more willing than I was to sacrifice Danvila's good fare to her theme. So, after all, I had my compensation, for Danvila's cook was good. But when I least expected it, she stopped for breath, and I seized my first opportunity to counter-attack, I will own it, rather viciously. 'Dear Madam, I do not like Napoleon. He was vulgar.' She very nearly fell from her gold and wicker chair. 'Show me one to equal him,' she challenged. 'Madam, the finest man of action Europe has produced is not Napoleon, but Hernán Cortés.' She eyed me in silence for a while, then: 'How do you spell that?'

CHAPTER III

BACK TO GENEVA

'ONE always returns to Geneva'. With these words I had closed my farewell speech to my comrades of the Secretariat in December 1927. Who could have guessed that I was to return to Geneva as Spanish Delegate in September 1931? Certainly not I. My promotion had been the outcome of facts beyond my control. Yet the ascent had been so meteoric that there were no lack of disgruntled critics eager to reproach me for it. Envy has ever added its bitter, stringent taste to the cup of success whenever life happened to raise it to my lips; and this envy came sometimes from the most unexpected quarters.

Though I have suffered from envious people all my life, this has seldom if ever upset me, owing to a number of circumstances, the chief of which may well have been my own ruthless objectivity. I have but a very modest estimate of my worth and feel seldom pleased with my performance; even in cases in which I know I am doing what I can do best – for instance, public speaking, when I can see the effect on the audience. This again is the outcome of my conviction that if gifts are gifts – as indeed they are – they are given us, therefore they cannot be of our own creation. Finally, to come back to my return to Geneva as Spanish Delegate, I was sustained in my struggle against the envious swarm by my chief assistant Oliván, later Ambassador in London; for Oliván, by far the ablest of the Spanish diplomats of my day, was free from envy and thoroughly objective, as he was soon effectively to prove to me.

I was mercifully unaware of all this melancholy, indeed sordid, aspect of life when I prepared the delegation and its instructions for Geneva. My chief problems were two: how to present the Republic to an international parliament used to the ways of the monarchical delegations; and how to minimise the ill effects of a wholly inadequate Foreign Secretary. Indeed, when the Spanish political leaders who ousted the monarchy apportioned their several portfolios of the future State to themselves, they evinced a singular provincialism and a shocking neglect of the importance of the world image of the Republic when they chose Lerroux as Foreign Secretary. 'The only department we could trust him with,' they used to whisper. But what about the effect abroad?

In my official days, I have known only one or two efficient and capable Foreign Secretaries; chief of them Fernando de los Ríos, but at the outset he had been confined to the Ministry of Justice; while Lerroux, a shrewd politician, a bold demagogue turned conservative in his later years, was a man thoroughly ignorant of world affairs, not in the least interested in them and endowed with but the shallowest knowledge of French, his only foreign language, for the little it was worth. He came to Geneva as head-delegate, followed by a host of journalists in charge of his publicity in Spain.

As luck would have it, I had to precede my delegation because there was going to be a meeting of the European Commission just before either the League Council or Assembly were due to meet; and this gathering was the first that I attended as a representative of the Spanish Government. This European Commission was very much of a distant relation of the little girl who was born the same day as her sister but they were not twins. 'What are you then?' – 'What remains of triplets'. It was what remained of the United States of Europe, the dream that Briand (inspired I believe by Coudenhove-Kalergi) had been pursuing since 1929. Strongly backed by Stresemann, as he was, Briand might have conquered the objections of Great Britain, who was dead against, while Stresemann saw at least a monetary, postal and customs union; but he died, and Briand was getting older, and the idea was allowed to decay into a Commission of Enquiry, the opium of moribund institutions.

It was this somnolent affair I attended when I first represented Spain in Geneva, at the beginning of September 1931. Not so sleepy though that day, for my friend Litvinov was putting forward one of his half-business half-propaganda proposals and I was one of those who ventured to oppose him. As I sat down, I saw a distinguished red-haired man rise at the opposite side of the table, walk round its circuit and come to me. I rose to greet him, and he spoke thus: 'I am Colijn, the Dutch Prime Minister; and I wished to congratulate you, but not only on your speech. I have read your new book *Spain* and I was very much interested in all you say, above all, in what you write on Philip II; for we, Dutch, do need to hear another side to our usual way of seeing him.' I thanked him with all the cordiality this warm tribute merited, then, the Devil took charge. 'As for Philip II, Mr Prime Minister, we Spaniards are very impartial and objective. For us, he was a pure Dutchman . . . his water-eyes, his straw-hair . . .' I had to hold his hand, for I was afraid he was going to faint.

Before we left Madrid, Lerroux and I, with Oliván, had agreed on our strategy; and it had been decided that on the occasion of the general debate in the Assembly, Lerroux would read a speech (that I was to write) on the Republic and what it hoped to achieve at home and in world affairs. I wrote the speech and he read it, not too badly, and he had a great success. It was not a very happy assembly. It met in the shadow of a serious economic and financial crisis, that was going to force Britain out of the gold standard, and in the midst of a period of tension in the relations between France and Germany, always the core of European political life. The peaceful, hopeful change-over in Spain, the quietest and happiest revolution Europe had registered in her chequered history, was in fact the only rosy patch in a somewhat sombre picture; and the forthright assertion of fidelity to the League and its Covenant that Lerroux's speech proclaimed was extremely well received. I congratulated him. He was courteous enough to thank me for my part in his success, but I felt that Oliván remained very reserved.

I soon found what worried him. A number of points had been missed and would remain fallow unless people read the speech, which they certainly would not do. No man can do justice to the speech of another man. In fine, it had fallen far short of what it would have been if I had *spoken*, i.e. not read, let alone his reading it. That seemed to me pretty obvious but inevitable, and I cheered him up – or tried to – by pointing out that the Commissions and the normal work of the Assembly would afford several opportunities to put things right. One or two days later, Lerroux himself asked me to address the Assembly also in the general debate. I saw, of course, that Oliván had been at work. I begged for time to think it over, and went to talk to the master plotter.

I was objective enough – vain enough, if you prefer – to agree that, from the point of view of the Republic, it might be a good thing to let me speak to the Assembly for half an hour or so; but I had a number of objections to raise. It was not usual for a delegation to speak twice in a general debate; I was sure to be given an afternoon hour, when no chief delegate ever came to the Assembly; Lerroux's speech trumpeted forth by his team of reporters had had a clamorous success in Spain; so that no one would understand in Madrid why I spoke after he had spoken; and it was a bit hard for me to believe that Lerroux was really keen that I should speak; I thought he was just trying to please Oliván, whom he liked and admired. Oliván did not attach much value to any of these objections, and seemed confident that he would get the Secretariat to make room for me in a morning sitting.

Well, he didn't. And I was put down for an afternoon. Then, the unexpected happened. Briand came, shook hands, and told me he had come because he wanted to hear me. With a friendly smile, he gave me a photograph of himself, I had asked for the previous day. Soon, before I was called, every chief delegate was in his seat, so that the Assembly took on the air of its morning sittings. I was cordially received. I devoted my speech to an analysis of the issue of peace and war from a not merely or necessarily Spanish 'but international and objective' point of view. In the course of my statement, I said: 'I am at times tempted to attribute [the delays and obstacles I had been describing] to an attractive virtue observable in our most useful collaborators, I mean the modesty of our jurists; for being in most cases the draftsmen of our texts, they evince a tendency to attach the bare minimum of value to these texts they have themselves drafted. So that as soon as the Covenant had been launched into its international career, we saw the beginnings of an effort of interpretation which, curiously enough, always ended in a reduction, never an increase, of the value or its text.'

I tried to offer to the Assembly, in words which, I do believe, were new, a picture of the world concrete enough yet large enough, and as high above any merely national perspective as the world parliament required and should expect; and the Assembly reacted accordingly and most generously. One tribute, that of Aristide Briand, was particularly precious to me.

Oliván was vindicated and the day brought a good harvest for the Republic outside Spain. But it was my turn to be reserved. The effect in Spain – as I had forecast it – was not good. The point of a second speech by the delegation was not appreciated; the move was attributed to my 'ambition'; and the fact that a spoken speech always goes down better than a read one, was explained as a Machiavellian conspiracy on my part, for I had *written* a bad speech for Lerroux and *spoken* a good speech myself. Those who satisfied their passions in this odd way forgot that a few days earlier, they had acclaimed my written speech as a master-piece of Lerroux's own eloquence.

I was told these things by more or less candid friends; for I seldom read the press, a fact that was to lead to a somewhat comic scene with Paul-Boncour to be told in due time. My weak points were due mostly to features of my character that do not tally with the diplomatic profession; chief of which, my tendency to rejoice at the comic aspect of life, and to laugh when I can't help it. Words of mine had a way of circulating, doing a lot of damage in their orbit. A prominent member of the 'great chorus' that surrounded the Assembly was an Eastern European journalist who had settled in Paris and wrote articles for a Parisian newspaper. He had a huge forehead prolonged and enlarged by an enormous bald head. I was unwise enough to say to a friend I thought discreet: 'When one has a head like that one should put trousers on it.' There was no reason why my friend should have been more discreet than I had been. The quip came to the ears of the Big Head. It did not help.

My worst case in this respect was an access of uncontrollable laughter

I went through after reading a paper that was passed to me from behind, as I was sitting at the Council table. I do not recollect the motive of my mirth. I only know that it was so overwhelming that I shed tears of laughter while fully conscious of the scandal it must have caused, for Massigli was speaking while I laughed. Of course, my laughter had nothing to do with what he was saying, but it plainly showed that I was in no state to listen to serious business. It did not occur to me to leave the hall. Comert, who had sponsored my entering the secretariat only ten years earlier, sent me a stern note of rebuke, which I fully deserved. Eventually, I regained my peace. Massigli was perfect, and to this day, through many years of friendship, never mentioned that subject to me. I never again went through that awkward experience. Luck perhaps, discipline not likely; on the whole I rather think the change may have been due to the sheer weight of the responsibility I had to carry. I had been till then a mere spectator at the stalls. I was now on the stage.

I had known Massigli for years, as the permanent Secretary General of the French Delegation, and I liked him as the good friend, keen intellect and loyal negotiator he always was; but Eden was new to me, and my first encounter with him was by no means an augury of the good and cordial relations we were to enjoy for years. He came as the Under-Secretary in charge of League of Nations affairs at the Foreign Office; and the British Treasury had briefed him to demand a reduction in the League budget. I found this attitude intolerable. I spoke after him, and made the point, among others, that the League budget was more modest than that of the municipality of Barcelona, then a city of 400,000 inhabitants. The fact is that the insular trend in Britain – the same that even now, is so active against a European Federation – had never truly accepted the League.

When I ended my speech in answer to Eden's, Paul-Boncour, who represented France and sat not far from me, only with the Italian delegate between us, passed on a note to me: 'I am surprised to hear the Spanish Ambassador to France speaking in English.' As a matter of fact, in Geneva I always spoke in French; but I chose English that time because I wanted the Anglo-Saxon press to take in what I was saying; so, I wrote back to Paul-Boncour: 'There are times when one calls Paris, Paris, and times when one calls Paris the Capital of France.' (signed) 'Pascal'.

His note did, however express some uneasy feeling in French public opinion. Paris had been used to rely on Quiñones de León to behave almost as a mere second French voice in the council whenever a Spanish interest was not directly concerned. With the advent of the Republic all this had changed. True, the new regime was no less friendly to France. It was, indeed, a good deal friendlier. But by a decision which was in fact my own and so natural and instinctive that I was hardly aware of it, the Spanish Delegation in Geneva now acted on its own, without consulting, agreeing or combining with anybody. This was felt in Paris very keenly indeed; and Paul-Boncour's note was but one of the signs of this uneasiness. The cloud of journalists that surrounds the delegates of great powers didn't like it either; and the French contingent staged once a protest stamping the floor with their feet (an apt manifestation of herd feelings) when I began to speak. It was promptly put down by a few strong words from the President.

CHAPTER IV

THE RECEPTION OF MEXICO

THE time had come to reap the harvest of the good seed I had sown in Mexico when I had called on Calles. I was determined to bring Mexico into the League, and to that effect, had gone the round of the chief delegates of the permanent members of the Council. The plan consisted in inviting Mexico in a very special way, since her exclusion by Wilson, not only as a founding member but as an eligible member, had been downright insulting. Since the method was to be unusual, indeed explicitly so, it had to be publicly justified, and therefore, the old story had to be alluded to; but since it was in no one's interest, not even in the interest of Mexico, to offend the U.S., the story had to be left shrouded in a discreet cloud as a thing of the past. We thus decided that the speakers would be limited to the Spanish delegate, who was the promoter of the plan, followed by those of the powers, i.e. the permanent members of the Council. Nothing could be more reasonable.

All went beautifully, until the last of the agreed speakers had delivered his message – praise for Mexico, regret at some obscure injustice she had suffered in the past, hope of her prompt arrival (the delegation was just waiting outside the hall), and for the rest, a smooth, diplomatic discretion. But the trouble began when the South American delegates whose nations happened at the time to belong to the Council, rose to speak. Who could stop them? The President could not take refuge in the wise political blindness that is apt to afflict the Speaker of the House of Commons. So both spoke, and kept to the rules beautifully. Then, the floodgates were open, and not a single Spanish American State remained silent. Worried, at first, the plotters were pleased to observe how carefully even the most ardent friend of Mexico navigated the diplomatic straits of the debate. But we had forgotten Restrepo.

He was one of those fortunate men whom every one likes no matter what they do or say. A Martian appearance, i.e. a red face framed by a steely helmet of grey-white hair, a hooked nose, the most appealing, attractive smile you could imagine, he went about never too busy, never inactive, an ever good-humoured half-companion half-observer of those about him. He was at the time the chief Colombian delegate, and his peculiar form of spontaneous eloquence had grown into a legend among Spanish American delegates. A story went around that at a banquet graced by the presence of many women, Restrepo had risen to speak on the ever reborn theme of the historical achievements of Spain in Spanish America, a theme on which he was known to bestow the best gifts of his eloquence. So there he was soon soaring in the heights of a steep sentence raising ever higher and higher the praises of 'mother Spain' until, his emotion overcoming his vocabulary, his admiration burst forth into an unprintable word. The shock imposed a split second of silence, instantly followed by a storm of applause.

This was the Restrepo we all forgot about while preparing our delicately balanced scheme. He went up the steps to the tribune, smiled his best brand at the audience, and began a passionate attack on the U.S., on President Wilson, on the oil pirates and on the infamous behaviour of those who had closed the gates of the League of Nations for a nation as worthy and noble as Mexico. And it was the best applauded speech of the day.

Spanish America contributed all kinds of delegates to Geneva; excellent, good, mediocre and bad. It would be invidious to try to give marks, but seen in retrospect, the most capable and the one who proved ablest to express himself in the idiom of the League was Dr Eduardo Santos, of Colombia. His handling of the dispute between his country and Peru was exemplary, and it often made us think that a number of men of that calibre among the delegates of the most cantakerous of the European countries would have been a boon to all concerned.

There were a number of good linguists among them; and this circumstance, combined with the geographical distance of their countries, made them often useful in cases of European strife. Chileans came often to the fore in this respect, save that one was never sure what they were until one actually did verify the fact; for Chileans are often of mixed European stock and I remember a year when their three delegates answered to the names of Edwards, Waddington and Mackenna Subercaseaux. Chileans they were, though, and very proud of their nationality.

There were two brilliant Uruguayan brothers, Juan Antonio and Enrique Buero; who still very young had reached the heights of their diplomatic service; and Juan Antonio was to become one of the Undersecretaries General, when, as I shall later relate, I forced open the gates of such high levels in the Secretariat for the citizens of other than the great powers.

But the usual representative of Uruguay used to be Dr Guani, a small, wiry man who led for years the Uruguayan Foreign Office, and who gave all of us a good deal of work to do owing to a dispute with the

Soviet Union. What this dispute was about I am not certain; but I know it was very important, though it seemed at no time to have threatened the peace of the world. Still, it was deemed weighty enough to have been entrusted to the care of Titulesco, as *rapporteur*, as I remember only too well; for, having one day suggested to him and to Guani a form of words to get it settled – at any rate on paper – I was suddenly awakened at 3 a.m. or so by someone stentoriously singing *Aïda* or *La Traviata* or whatever it was, at the foot of my bed. It was Titulesco, who was in the habit of working until dawn and used to sleep until lunch time. He wanted to know whether I thought that a slight change in the text, the Russians wanted, would be acceptable for Guani. 'Why don't you go and ask him?' I enquired. And Titulesco: 'Well, you know, he might be asleep.'

In the end, the mighty conflict between the Soviet Union and Uruguay was settled to the satisfaction of both parties and Eden celebrated it with a poetical outburst which he sent me with his compliments. I found it among my papers, patiently waiting until I was ready to pass it on to posterity:

> The Government of Uruguay
> Decline to prove a word they say.
> The Russians, far from feeling slighted
> Declare themselves to be delighted.
> This air of mutual satisfaction
> Entitles us to take no action,
> And we, I think, can all agree
> *Solvuntur risu* tabulae*.

> * i.e. titters.

The advent of the Republic was hailed with elation in all Spanish America; and for the first time, the image of Spain as the Mother-Country or (odd though it sounds) *la madre-patria*, i.e. the Mother-Fatherland, passed from the Right, ultra-conservative sectors of Spanish America, where it had lingered since the Viceregal days, to the centre and left, the true heirs of the 'patriots' and emancipators of old. A warm feeling of confraternity, a hope perhaps of some political collaboration not unlike that which was later to appear in the British Commonwealth, seemed to inspire a number of Spanish American delegates. Some of them had spoken to me in those or similar terms more and more as my own moral authority in the League was increasing.

The Spanish delegation was in the habit of offering a banquet to all the Spanish American delegations on the day of the discovery of

America (October 12th), when the Assembly was nearly always still in session. Some blockhead sometime somewhere, almost certainly in Spain, proposed to describe that day as 'the Day of the Race', and, as it often happens with silly slogans, it soon became both popular and official. I detest the word *race* applied to human beings; but when it comes to Spaniards and Spanish Americans, the name and word are not only silly but inaccurate. What race? Are we to abolish the Aztecs and the Incas? And do we wish to forget the strong proportion of Spanish Jews that settled in the Indies – as Américo Castro so aptly has pointed out? And The Waddingtons and Mackennas of Chile? And Christopher Columbus who was certainly a Genoese and, I do believe, of a Spanish-Jewish family? Day of the Race, indeed!

So, while I was in charge in Geneva, the menu said: *October 12, 1492* and no nonsense about races. As it happened at the first banquet over which I presided, I had right and left, for protocol reasons, two wives of Spanish American delegates, who were both French and one of them, I suspect, Jewish. They were nice women to talk to rather than to look at; and when I rose to speak, this theme of the new role of Spain as seen by some of the more enthusiastic of our friends beyond the seas, was busy in my mind. I told my friends how the Chief Spanish delegate would now-a-days hear the witches of Macbeth urging him to crown himself King of the Old and the New Worlds, and how he would never do such a thing, for we were all equals and it was by remaining equal that we would remain together, which was what mattered.

We flocked out of the dining-hall and Castillo Nájera, the Mexican delegate, seized my arm: 'Why did you drag in your two neighbours into your speech?' – 'How "drag in" ...?' – 'Yes. That yarn about the witches of Macbeth.'

CHAPTER V

THE CONSCIENCE OF THE LEAGUE

A S luck or ill-luck would have it, my emergence as a Spanish delegate in Geneva coincided with the opening of that disastrous
period which was to end in the torment of Europe and the destruction
of the League. I will not claim that I was as wise before those events
as we all have become since about them; but I do claim that in the three
most important, the Manchurian and the Ethiopian crises and the Disarmament Conference, I saw further than the delegates of the big
powers.

It is true that I was particularly well placed to become (as Sir John
Simon said of me one day at the Council table) 'the conscience of the
League'. He said it. Did he think it? I do not believe he did. It was
wonderfully acted, but it was acted. His memoirs prove that he did not
care a brass farthing for the League; so 'the conscience of the League'
meant nothing to him. But he aimed: first at flattering me, then, at
posing as a League believer, which very few British politicians indeed
were then, one of them Lord Cecil. Yet Simon was acute enough to
sense that public opinion did then see me as the conscience of the
League, and shrewd enough to realise that it was useful for him to say
so.

The combination of circumstances that converged on me was indeed
exceptional in the extreme. Alone, perhaps, in that gathering, I was not
a politician but an almost pure intellectual. I put in that qualifying
'almost' to save whatever attraction for the actual carrying out of my
ideas may have instilled in me the very force and faith with which I held
them. But I soon became convinced of my lack of political vocation
when I realised that I hardly ever read the press, not even the day after
I might expect to be in the news.

One day, as I arrived for a Council Meeting, I saw Paul-Boncour
waiting for me, with a very long face. I wondered what was amiss. 'I
assure you, my dear friend,' he burst forth at once, 'that I was furious.
I summoned him an hour ago and thoroughly washed his head. You
must not bother about him. He is a vain man, full of himself . . .' and
more to that effect. I had no idea what he was talking about. He was surprised at my surprise. What! It was 10 a.m. and I had not read Pertinax's
lucubration for that morning? I hadn't. I never read Pertinax or any
one else. Now, the vain, clever, French political commentator, furious

because of my independent ways, had treated me with even scanter courtesy than his very modest usual, indeed with insulting contempt. For all I cared!

That definitely separated me from my friend Paul-Boncour by a whole Sahara of difference; for in a like case he would not have slept for a week. He was a politician, and I wasn't. He saw everything from the point of view of the political career of Joseph Paul-Boncour. I do not in the least suggest that he would have bartered his principles for a ministry. In fact, he had more than once proved to be a public man singularly faithful to his principles. But he had to make his behaviour fit in with a certain framework of national shapes and forces, a need from which I was free. For it never had occurred to me that I could have a political career in Spain. True, I was in politics, but it was none of my doing. It had happened to me.

At a later stage, one of Lerroux's jack-o'-all-trades had taken me aside in Madrid and confided in deep mystery that, if I became a freemason, and registered myself as a radical, Lerroux would eventually hand over to me the Radical party and retire. I turned the offer down, of course; and for no reason; but for something more fundamental, primitive and unutterable: a powerful refusal of all my being ever to accept any label of any kind. In my official position, representing as I was the Spanish Republic, I remained loose and unattached; unlabelled and unlabelable.*

This brings me to another of my odd circumstances: I never got any instructions. Lerroux never tried to give me any, for he was too painfully aware of his incapacity; but even when the F.O. in Madrid happened to be in less incompetent hands, no one ever thought of writing to me: 'Do this.' 'Don't do that.' I believe I was the freest chief delegate that ever went to Geneva – an ideal position for an intellectual who has made a study of world relations and has a faith.

And that is what I was. I did, of course, realise that Spain was not in the moon, and that we had to insert her policy in the natural frame-

---

*When I had hardly taken on my duties as professor of Spanish Studies at Oxford, I received a neatly printed list of the Roman Catholic members of the University of Oxford and, not without some astonishment, I saw my name on it. This annoyed me exceedingly; and I record the fact as yet another of those reactions of the essential anarchist that I am. The man responsible for the list was Francis de Zulueta, a Basque Spaniard nationalised British, who held the Chair of Roman Law at Oxford. I wrote to him thanking him for having solved an enigma I had been unable to solve myself from the days of my first (or maybe second) Communion – namely: whether I was a Catholic or not. Nevertheless, in view of the earnest nature of the problem, I begged him to let me know how in so short a time he had come to a conclusion that had evaded my grasp for so many years.

work that fitted her general interests; and to that effect, I did often check my own intuitions and feelings by confronting my opinions with those of Oliván, a technician of diplomacy; but owing to the freedom and trust allowed me by the governments that succeeded each other in Madrid, I was able to do what no other Spanish representative would have done in my place: take a strong line for or against in matters that did not directly or indirectly affect Spain – a behaviour most Spaniards would have rejected pointing out that there has never been but one Redeemer, and He was crucified.

This truly exceptional situation enabled me to espouse at every turn the true cause of the League of Nations. And as I had the gift of grasping essentials, the gift of clear exposition, and at times even, the epigrammatic gift that coins phrases easily put in circulation, my place in Geneva soon rose to what Simon described as 'the conscience of the League'. Thus I came to incarnate and concentrate the hope of multitudes of League fans, more especially in the U.S. and in Britain, who saw in Geneva the dawn of an era of world peace. My correspondence grew considerably, as I became the recipient of claims and complaints for justice on the part of every possible breed of underdog. I was even eventually to receive from Cecil himself in at least one case confidential documents in such circumstances as to suggest that he very much hoped that I should protest in Geneva: he evidently could not do this without inculpating his own government.

This singular position that I came to occupy in Europe at the time might have been of some use towards the consolidation of the Spanish Republic. It hardly was so for a number of reasons. One of them was that at the time few persons realised the fact in Spain. The general public had been so often told that the great man in Geneva was Lerroux that half of them believed it and the other half, knowing it to be impossible, were not ready to believe any reports, no matter how flattering, about anyone else; indeed the more flattering, the less credible.

Then the enemies of the Republic had already begun their campaign of slander against the new men. When from New York I phoned my agreement to become the Republic's Ambassador in Washington, I had written to my family: 'A good, clean name will soon be covered with mud.' Miguel Maura, one of the front bench men of the Republic, told me a story of the first days of the Republic which suggests how ready the sorely tried Spanish people were to receive any criticism on that score. He had gone a-shooting partridges in the grounds of a friend whose staff he knew well. He stopped to talk to a foreman. 'Well, Julián, what do you think of the Republic?' 'Sir,' was the answer, 'the other lot, who are out now, were already dressed and shod. We shall have to wait until the new lot get their clothes and shoes.' I was fully aware of this ingrained scepticism of the Spanish people and, of course, I knew for certain that slanders would soon fly about and that some would stick.

And so it was. An extreme right reactionary politician of little import was allowed to deliver a lecture in the Madrid Athenaeum (of which I was a member) in the course of which he asserted that I was pocketing an astronomic sum a year. He obtained this sum by putting down as my salary in Paris the whole budget of the Embassy; by adding my salary as professor at Oxford, which he naïvely assumed Oxford went on paying me while patiently waiting until I consented to return to the duties of my chair (this being the custom in Spanish universities with political professors); a salary (for the quantity of which he suited his own fancy) as Spanish Representative in Geneva, which he again naïvely assumed the League paid me, and I don't know how many more items to round up the sum. An extreme left anarchist promptly reproduced the slander in Oviedo. Years went by, and Ilya Ehrenburg, true to type, reproduced the sum and the slander in his Memoirs.

Furthermore, the administration in Madrid was not equipped for adapting their policy to mine. They had no policy. They lived from hand to mouth; and as my policy at bottom implied a radical change in our perspective for the whole system of our international relations, the problem was not even grasped, let along formulated. All I felt in Madrid was either a total vacancy, which I was expected to fill up with my ideas and doings, or a certain amount of distrust lest I carried the Republic to dangerous adventures – a legitimate and responsible if not justified attitude, which I found at times in Azaña. There was mistrust also in Alcalá Zamora, but of a different and less objective kind.

This may have been the reason why I never was the Republic's Foreign Secretary, though then and later I was often to be so described. I was in Paris, at the Hotel George V, already agreed as Ambassador to France, but not yet in office, busy with the Manchurian question, when at 1 a.m. a telephone call woke me up. Azaña, in the throes of Cabinet making, offered me the Ministry of Finance. Azaña had many qualities, but respect for competence was not one of them, as I was to know later to my regret. The idea of making me Minister of Finance of all things! I said: 'Don't you know I don't even know how to manage my own financial affairs? How can you expect me to govern those of the State? And when I am already agreed as Ambassador, and in the thick of a League crisis!'

He realised his error; but next morning, as I told Oliván, he, using his logical head, said: 'You will get the F.O.' We had to leave Madrid in any case, and I remember very well how puzzled we both were when nearly the whole day went by in the train, and no news from Azaña. In the morning, at El Escorial .we got a newspaper. The Foreign Secretary was Luis de Zulueta. No experience whatever. But why not I? We did not see it then; but my accumulated experience in the end gave me the answer. Azaña was not a convinced League man; not (I surmise) through lack of faith in the Covenant, but because he was too earnest a man to risk a crisis when he did not believe that the Spanish armed forces were ready for it. It was therefore a mistrust, not of my person, not of my ideas, but of the means the Spanish State possessed to back the Covenant in case of need.

Meanwhile, though, my activity at Geneva put Spain on the map of international relations in a way it had never been before; and this of course meant a considerable increase in work, for, contrary to what happened in the days of Quiñones de León, Spanish policy was based on public opinion, mostly that of the world, and not necessarily of Spain; and therefore, on the Assembly rather than on the Council, and when on the Council, on the public sittings rather than in the discreet penumbra of the corridors. Yet, at no time did I lose sight of the frailty of my basis; and, often, in our private talks, Oliván and I would refer to this fact. Any change of Cabinet, any attack on the Republic, any personal incident, would demolish my public person, and with it my policy which was supposed to be the policy of Spain. I found myself in the paradoxical position of having endeavoured to found and pursue an objective international policy wholly based on a subjective situation, and to depersonalise the foreign policy of Spain by entirely personal methods and criteria.

Such were the thoughts that Oliván and I were ripening when we were both suddenly projected into the limelight by the Japanese attack on Manchuria.

CHAPTER VI

THE MANCHURIAN CRISIS

THE Manchurian crisis is often seen as a Sino-Japanese dispute. It really was a dispute between Japan and the League, the first conflict in which a member of the League openly violated the Covenant. It was the true cause and origin of Hitler's power and of the Second World War. The responsibility of the permanent members of the Council, notably of Britain and France, was heavy; that of the United States, appalling; and the leadership of her Secretary of State, Stimson, inept.

Such is my honest view on this sad episode. The big powers had carved for themselves exorbitant privileges within the League organisation, on the ground of the heavy responsibilities they assumed; but when the case came for them to discharge these responsibilities, they were not at home. The Manchurian crisis was the first case in which the Covenant had to be applied in order to uphold the Covenant against a truant big power; and this was not done – for that is the fact: it was not done – because great powers don't eat great powers, just as dog does not eat dog.

It was bad enough to begin with, that such a blatant offence against the Covenant should have been committed by a big power, a permanent member of the League Council, whose chief delegate, the elegant and distinguished intellectual, Adatci, had just been elected to the Permanent Court at the Hague. The world was astounded on reading on the morning of September 19th that, the previous day, the Japanese army had attacked Mukden in Manchuria on the usual trumped-up 'incident'. To add insult to injury, Japan did not hesitate to break the Covenant while the Assembly was sitting.

But when we say 'Japan' whom do we really mean? The answer is neither easy nor quite certain. There are three possibilities: that a united and disciplined Japanese State had decided to go for it and did; that the Army went for it in defiance of the Cabinet; and that the local Japanese Commander in Manchuria went ahead in spite of restraining orders from the Tokyo General Staff or government. The solution of this riddle lies in the files of the Japanese State departments concerned. Our stand is – mine at the time – that a big power is no such thing if it is not disciplined enough for the League to assume that the government is responsible for the actions of its soldiers.

This is no mere theoretical stand; the western big powers let themselves only too willingly be persuaded by the blandishments of the Tokyo politicians who lay all the blame on those foolhardy soldiers whom it was best not to irritate; and that kind of trick, merely aimed at putting the League off the scent of true and effective action, was only too readily accepted by experienced public men who should have known better; who, in fact knew better, since it was obvious that it was not for the League to spare foolish generals but for the Emperor and his ministers to sack them.

This by no means suggests that the dissensions within Japan were a comedy to deceive the West; on the contrary, my remarks presuppose such a disagreement. The Manchurian case is a clear example of a conflict caused by an imperialism that has nothing to do with the materialistic interpretation of History so dear to Marxists. Marxism as the rationalist philosophy it is, tends to overestimate the value of common sense in man. As a selfish member of a 'privileged' class, your capitalist will make a war to make sure he goes on making money out of your depressed race or colony or what not. But in most cases, things do not work that way. Your capitalist is getting on nicely swallowing the new country in perfect peace, spreading as he goes on enough new wealth in the new country to ease the shearing of it, when a number of young bloods in uniform, who do not care two hoots for dividends, but are thirsty for glory, butt in and bring down the whole capitalist edifice with a crash.

This is what happened with Manchuria in 1931, and in 1914 when France was quietly being swallowed by German capitalism until the Kaiser's young bloods demanded a 'joyous war' and led their country to a humiliating defeat. In 1914, however, there was no League; but in 1931, the Covenant was there, the League was sitting, and a pack of young Japanese would-be heroes (after murdering two prime ministers in the process) destroyed in a few months the remarkable economic power that the Japanese bankers and technicians had patiently been building in Manchuria.

Manchuria is one of those lands around China whose relations to China proper have ever been vague, claimed as part of the Empire by the Chinese but not always accepted as such by itself or by others, as in this case, Japan. It was then held under sway by a dictator, Chang Hsueh-Liang, as tyrannical as, but not as efficient as, his father Chang Tso-Lin had been. It was being developed by Japan; but as an inevitable outcome of this development, it was being rapidly populated by immigrants, mostly Chinese. It is hard to see how such a conundrum could be solved by war; but the Japanese State thought otherwise – and so I, acting for Lerroux, President of the Council, with my faithful Oliván as companion, went on January 19th to call on Mr Yoshizawa at the Hotel Métropole in Geneva.

The very selection of this man as its permanent representative in Geneva seemed to me, as time went by, a sign of the evil intentions of the Japanese Government; for both before and after these events, Japan had been represented by open-minded, smiling delegates who spoke the two League languages well; while Yoshizawa was an arrogant, negative, closed-in sort of Japanese, who smoked his cigar, listened to arguments in obvious boredom and was content to answer (in Japanese – French): 'That is not the opinion of my *Govelment*.' I will say he was nothing like as negative when we called on him, and I, in the name of the Council, asked for explanations. But he was not very forthcoming either, and he limited himself to saying that he had no news and would ask for it and put it before the Council as soon as he got it. Nevertheless, we both left in a pessimistic mood.

In all but one aspect, which I put to Oliván thus: 'This conflict seems to have been contrived by an archangel who is strongly in favour of the League; for Japan is the arch enemy of the U.S. and the League is weak because the U.S. is not in it. Therefore, if the League upholds the Covenant with a firm spirit of world solidarity, it will, indirectly, be serving the interests of the U.S. Therefore, the U.S. will help the League; and so the League is bound to win. This might then bring the U.S.A. into the League.' That is what should have happened if, again, men behaved rationally. But the opposition of the Republican Party of the U.S. to the League was not rational; and everything went on in a manner favourable to the aggressor and contrary to the interests of the League, of the U.S. and, ultimately, of the Japanese people also.

The issue evolved in a manner not unlike a classic minuetto in which the movements of the dancers, though not utterly devoid of the novel and unexpected as to details, remain faithful to a preconceived pattern. The first movement of the conflict had to be played while Spain occupied the chair of the Council, and this meant Lerroux. Unfortunately, Lerroux spoke very poor French, though no worse than other presidents the Council had known; and, worse still, he did not understand it, particularly when spoken by other than French people. His chairmanship was soon found practically out of the question. Even when provided with a sheet of instructions to guide him step by step he would make bad mistakes. Most of the Council's sittings on this were, however, not merely private but secret.

This meant one man per delegation plus the Secretary General, one interpreter and one précis-writer. It was nevertheless tacitly agreed that I should be present and sit next to Lerroux; and by the sheer weight of facts and circumstances, I had to preside as if Lerroux had not been there, save that, if I had to intervene in the debate, in matters either of substance or of procedure, I would begin: 'The President thinks . . . or says . . . or rules . . . ' though it was obvious to any one that Lerroux and I had not exchanged a word. It was most trying; and every day I hoped that Lerroux would give it up, return to Madrid and let me work; but he could not (as I realised later) because he had trumpeted his League 'successes' in the Spanish press, and no one would understand his leaving the scene of his triumphs when the League was tackling such a grave issue, and his presence in Madrid was by no means necessary. When the session was at last adjourned and all was over for the time being, as we left the League building together, Lerroúx said to me: 'Sometimes one must accept a ridiculous situation for the sake of the country.'

Cecil represented Britain. His position was not enviable. At home, he was apt to be suspected of unrealistic idealism; and by a diabolic concourse of ill-luck, on September 21st, three days after the Japanese aggression, Britain, in the throes of a grave financial crisis, had come off the gold standard. Ill-luck, I said; but there may have been more to it than that. The Japanese government may have been better informed than we were, and have known that precisely then Britain would have plenty of more urgent troubles to think about than a quarrel between Japs and Chinks at the other end of the world. This would help to explain that Japan should have launched her attack at such an otherwise inauspicious time, for the League Assembly was then in session. China, elected to the Council by that very Assembly, was represented by Alfred Sze, an attractive and intelligent diplomat, who was ready to assure the Council that his country would endeavour to remain calm and avoid any reprisals against Japanese subjects. Yoshizawa spoke little and played for time.

The trouble was the lack of news under which the League laboured. From those very first days, I began, so to speak, to touch with my fingertips what was perhaps the chief fault in the League structure: her eyes and her ears were not her own; she had to borrow those of her member States, which in practice, nearly always, meant those of the big powers. This schizophrenia was to be the chief disease of the League, and, as the narrative unfolds, it will provide the subject of at least one significant scene. Our only direct source of news was Japan herself; next, though less reliable, the diplomatic and military services of the big powers, none of which proved ready fully to inform Geneva of what they learnt.

The only sensible thing to do was, therefore, to send to Manchuria a Commission of Enquiry. This was proposed by the Secretariat; and then the fat was in the fire. Only a few months before the Japanese attack, it had been decided that Article 11 of the Covenant, the chief League instrument to deal with aggression, could only be set in motion with the consent of all the members of the Council, including, therefore, the aggressor. This made nonsense of the Covenant, but suited the big powers; so, nothing could be done to circumvent Japan's aggression but what Japan herself was willing to accept; and the taciturn Yoshizawa had an easy answer to every one of our proposals: 'It is not the opinion of my *Govelment.*'

Furthermore, our proposal to send a Commission of Enquiry was fiercely blocked by Stimson, who was persuaded that such a step would make it impossible for the Japanese Government to control its army young bloods – a favourite delusion of the American Secretary of State. Not content with holding fast to his error, he confided it to the Japanese Ambassador, which of course, made Yoshizawa's position the stronger. Some of us began to think that Stimson should come to Geneva and attend our debates, which would have settled the Manchurian question and instilled so much strength into the League that the disastrous Second World War would have been almost certainly spared to mankind.

Yoshizawa assured the Council that there was by then, no military occupation and no plans for a future conquest or annexation – all, of course, contrary to the facts; that evacuation had begun and would continue, and that all Japan wanted was to talk things over with China without any League interference. Since Sze assured the Council that China would respect the life and rights of the Japanese in Manchuria and in China proper, the Council passed a resolution registering these assurances, reported somewhat optimistically to the Assembly, and dispersed. (September 30, 1931)

CHAPTER VII

ENTER VANSITTART

WITHIN a week it was plain that those of us who had insisted on the underlying solidarity between the army and the government were right. Chinchow was bombed by Japanese planes on October 8th and General Honjo, who commanded the Japanese army at Mukden, declared that Japan no longer recognised Chiang Hsueh-Liang. The Council was recalled for October 13th. Lerroux did not come; but I was determined to take no risks again. I felt, of course, quite capable of handling the business from the Chair, but I reflected that Lerroux might change his mind at any time, or come to a later meeting (since, by then, it was plain that we would have to meet almost continuously); and it weighed upon me also that, since our request for Stimson to come and sit at the Council table would soon have to be formulated, it would be more impressive if signed by a well-tried statesman. So my mind was made up that I would open the sitting and request France (next on the roster) to assume the Presidency. That meant Briand.

Stimson was disappointing. All he would do was send brave words about vigilance, reinforcing whatever the League did and invoking the Kellogg Pact. Meanwhile, the Japanese delegate raised constitutional questions about the presence of a non-League member at the Council table and even spoke of sending the matter for consultation to the Hague, a well-known form of delaying tactics much favoured by generals in a hurry; but the Council members were against such a trick, all but the German delegate. It was, indeed, if I am not mistaken, during this session, or if not, during one of those we had to grind through that autumn, that Beck, the Polish Foreign Secretary, reported to the Council that, according to his Ambassador in Tokyo, the German Ambassador there had assured the Japanese Government that the German Government regretted the militant action of the Council on behalf of China – which the Council members were being pushed to adopt by the delegates of Poland and Spain. That Spain, or at any rate her delegate, had won the right to be thus mentioned, I should be the last to deny; but the perfidy of the German government in adding Poland to the advocates of China, or that of Beck in making it up, was a masterpiece.

We debated the invitation to the U.S.A. in the knowledge that it would be both accepted and poorly accepted; and brushing aside

Yoshizawa's legal quibbles, we voted it by a majority vote, as a mere matter of procedure. But our victory was almost indistinguishable from a defeat: Stimson sent his Consul General in Geneva. Now Prentiss Gilbert was as nice, efficient and amicable a man as one could wish; but it took the American Government of those days, a Hoover and a Stimson, to be asked to come to Geneva to stop the first challenge to the Covenant and to world peace on the part of a big power, and to send a junior official as the yardstick of the interest of the American nation in the issue. The mealy-mouthed words in which American ways are usually commented upon by most of those who, for ideological reasons, don't bark at them with an equal if opposite bias, has too often obscured the gravity of this episode. It was downright stupid, and nothing, not even his fear of an adverse public opinion, should have prevented Stimson from coming where his plain duty, his country's interest and plain common sense, required his presence. What could Gilbert do but keep to his instructions, parrot pious platitudes about the Kellogg Pact, and keep out of any League decision? Even so, Stimson, frightened to death lest the anti-League superstition of his fellow republicans had him burnt at the stake, would have withdrawn Gilbert before the end of the session, had he not received better and strong advice from France and Britain.

We had frequent secret meetings. Officially we could not meet without the presence of our Japanese or Chinese colleagues; in practice, Briand turned this difficulty by inviting us – all but the two parties – to a cup of tea in his hotel room. One secret meeting has lingered in my mind here from an anecdote Briand told with his inimitable *bonhomie*: 'I asked the Japanese Ambassador to come and see me in Paris. I said to him: "*Monsieur l'Ambassadeur*, I have a friend who is a boxer. A very strong man. And he once said to me: '*Monsieur le Président*, I fear no man, nothing ... nothing ... but an eiderdown; for you punch and punch at it and it does not care.' Well, *Monsieur l'Ambassadeur*, think it over. China is an eiderdown." We talked about the Japanese complaint about the abundance of banditry in China. I said: "Ah, *Monsieur l'Ambassadeur*, there is nothing harder than to tell a Chinese bandit from a Chinese patriot. Particularly when they are running away."'

If only this wise man's views had prevailed! In the end, after much talk, mostly useless, Briand had a resolution prepared, which began by summing up the terms of our September 30th resolution but insisted that evacuation of Japanese troops must begin at once and be ended within three weeks of the date of our next meeting; and that the two parties must enter into immediate negotiations. Although this second condition was in fact a concession *from the League* to the aggressor, Japan voted against it. This was the harvest Stimson got for us.

Next to the attitude of the U.S. the Council was fettered by that of Germany, whose tendency to recover her military predominance over Europe was re-emerging, as well as by the financial troubles the whole West, Britain in particular, was then afflicted with. But, if one peruses the memoirs of the period, Vansittart's autobiography, Simon's or Paul Boncour's, one soon realises that the rot delved deeper than the events, and was perhaps symbolised by the way Britain, France and the U.S. had forsaken the League in one way or another. For the French, the League was a mere instrument for mobilising a number of nations for the rescue of France, in case of an attack by Germany. For the British, it was an illusion of non-Darwinian idealists with no sense of reality and the survival of the fittest. What was Germany to conclude? If Britain had a right to an empire, why not Germany? This was the thought no British head seemed able to hold, for they were so used to overlording the world that they had in the end mistaken their para- mouncy for a law of nature. And yet, it was that thought that was ruling everything we did or did not do.

Vansittart, for instance, a brilliant coiner of epigrams, so brilliant indeed, that one reads his memoirs skipping from epigram to epigram without ever touching the soil of facts, dazzled into obscurity by so many sparks of wit, Vansittart is unable to see that his prescience of the German danger he so often boasts of, is purely due to British bulldog feelings that differ in nothing from German expansionism; and that when he advocates a strong Anglo-French-Italian alliance (even with Mussolini) to keep Germany at bay, he overlooks that the frontiers of nationalism are just as spiky in the case of the three nations he would unite as they are in that of Germany, and would therefore make such an alliance impossible or unworkable. Our trouble was that we were still led by an old-fashioned nationalist diplomacy that mistook for realism an obsolete view of world affairs, and for vapid idealism an intelligent endeavour to organise the world in the spirit and mental habits of our century.

What this old-fashioned diplomacy did not see was that the unseemly 'grab and retain' scramble for colonies, territories, phosphate islands and what not that followed the 'war to end the war' was the true cause of the aggressiveness of the three nations which for historical reasons too well known to be re-stated, had come of age in 1870 instead of in 1500–1600, as Spain, France and Britain had done; and that, if a few 'idealists' like those Vansittart so heartily dismissed as fools had had a say at Versailles. Europe would still be today the strongest continent in the world, instead of finding itself split into a crowd of beggars and a drove of slaves.

The root of the evil was the Lie. And the Lie was the Covenant. For the official diplomatic establishments did not believe in the Covenant and lacked the courage to say so. It was this combination of lack of faith and lack of courage that ruined Europe. The tangible proof of this was to be the Manchurian case; and a scene that occurred in Paris, in Briand's room at the Quai d'Orsay, where the Council met many times, was to illustrate the fact.

By then, Simon had replaced Cecil. He was a handsome, tall, giant of a man, who bore himself with proud mien and a good deal of self-satisfaction. At first sight, he looked like Balfour, Rappard, Restrepo and a number of other League characters, a martial type, a reddish face capped by a silver helmet of hair; but it did not work. His silver helmet was burst open by a bald top that shone in the light. The fact that he had to stoop to talk to most people made it natural for him to be or seem to be condescending. I believe he was an honest and kindly man, indulgent in the extreme towards the vagaries and errors of others, for, after all, what else could you expect of others but vagaries and errors. He had soon brushed half Europe the wrong way – which, as is well known, never fails to generate electricity.

CHAPTER VIII

THE RULE OF LAW

ONE day, after a long sitting, while we rose for a brief respite, I drew Simon to a window, from which one could enjoy a view of the Seine peacefully flowing, and Montmartre rising towards the sky. Since Beck's revelations about the confidences of the German Ambassador in Tokyo, I had inklings of similar, if much less crude, endeavours by European powers to keep in the good graces of Japan. I did not directly allude to this sorry fact in my talk with Simon, but I did say that it seemed to me our tactics with Japan were all wrong, in fact the very reverse of what we should be doing. Publicly, we condemned and even threatened Japan; privately, there were members of the Council that sought to soothe the Japanese Government by minimising their part in what we were doing. We should, on the contrary, never hurt Japan in public, but send one man, one only, as the Ambassador of all of us, and, in secret, make the Japanese Government understand that a League armed *riposte* would be inevitable if the Covenant had not been complied with within thirty days.

Simon listened with his usual overdose of politeness; then he asked: 'And if it came to blows, would the Spanish fleet co operate?' My answer was: 'Sir John, the Spanish fleet will be by the side of the British fleet whenever the British fleet will be by the side of the Covenant.'

This is what Vansittart makes of it all: 'Leaguers and pure spirits like Madariaga could not see over their ideals to the nakedness beyond. "The smaller powers were ready", he declared. With what for what? "The Spanish fleet will always be by the side of the British fleet," he said to Simon, "whenever the British fleet will stand by the Covenant." The Señor had forgotten his Sheridan.

> The Spanish fleet thou canst not see because
> it is not yet in sight.

To have pitted the *quincaillerie* of the Smaller Powers against the Japanese would have been massacre worse than Tsushima. If only we had provided Tokyo with such sitting ducks, ran on the optimist, "public opinion in the United States would have swept Mr Hoover into Geneva, and there would have been no Hitler." With such inconceivable rubbish we had to contend then and long after!' (p. 438).

Vansittart is no longer here, so I shall refrain from drawing conclusions. I shall, however, say that it was not cricket for Vansittart to expect more from the second rank nations than he was doing from the big powers. True, he stoutly fought for bigger arms for his country, but he did so as a British Jingo, which he was, and he himself wrote why Britain would not uphold the Covenant: 'John [Simon] displeased him [Stimson] by [...] showing no disposition to fight Japan for Russia's benefit, no enthusiasm for China where British exports had been viciously curtailed' (p. 437). The man was living in the nineteenth century, and might just as well have been in command of a gun boat in the Yang Tse to force the Chinese to smoke opium. It was this kind of honest enough, clever too much, downright Jingo that led us straight into Hitler's war; and the tragedy was that he was one of the few men who saw the Nazi danger in time; but he never understood the function of moral force. 'To my knowledge, he [Stimson] harped only on moral force, and harps are the instruments for those who rely on it' (p. 437). He never saw the one or two episodes during this crisis when even Japan had to fear the effect of a universal rejection of her stand. He was right in many of his forecasts, yet worse than useless, for he was a fossil diplomat unable to realise that the era of small nations was over and that Britain was fast becoming a small nation.

His jibe at the Spanish fleet shows that he failed to see the true purpose of my suggestion, which was not to intimidate Japan with our *quincaillerie* and the steel of the big powers, but to confront Japan with a firm and credible demonstration of solidarity. His memoirs bristle with epigrams, good, ordinary, mediocre or recondite, many of them barbed and darted against moral power and public opinion. What else have we to-day? He writes of F. G. Smith: 'He could no more keep off wit than spirits. Neither did him any good' (p. 333). Evaporate the spirits from the sentence, and it fits Vansittart like a glove.

He sees that 'Nothing but a change of heart can avert another catastrophe' (p. 480), but he means a change for the Germans, not for the British, and he does not even *adumbrate* that there was no reason why the Germans should give up building a German empire while the British never ceased hugging theirs. His insular arrogance burst forth throughout his book: 'When I warned him [Arthur Henderson] of foreigners he rejected my *dossiers* as unfeeling' (p. 398). And this man, intelligent, refined, kind and thoroughly honest, a poet of sorts, head of the Foreign Office, will write in complete unawareness of the gravity of what he reveals the following paragraph on the Austro-German attempt at Anschluss in 1931: 'French, Italian and Czechoslovak prompted reference to the League, which passed the onus to the Permanent Court of International Justice, which by eight opinions to seven pronounced the union illegal. With the United States, Japan, Germany – of course –

Holland, Belgium and China, we [sic] voted for this obvious danger. Fortunately France, Poland and Italy found Spain, Rumania, Colombia, Cuba and Salvador to vote against it – a wiser and less reputed team just good enough to beat us.'

This crack reveals the very heart of the arch-imperialist Briton, thoroughly unable to see beyond power and the *raison d'Etat*. It is obvious that for Vansittart a Hague Court judge was but a civil servant of the Foreign Office of his country who was supposed to turn into legal jargon whatever he was told at home to think. This would explain the tendency of some big powers to present their Foreign Offices' legal advisers as candidates for the Hague Court; but the paragraph quoted is an insult to most of the Hague Court judges of those days. I knew Altamira, the Spanish Judge, and the idea that he would adapt his views to a government directive is simply unthinkable. I should say the same of Anzilotti and of the Spanish American judges at the time. For, even on his assumption, how would he explain that countries like Colombia, Cuba and El Salvador, politically so dependent on the United States, voted on the other side? This episode and the way he tells it suffice to show that Vansittart never lifted his eyes above the level of the herd. ('We', 'us'.) The fact that, in this case, he was against the opinion of the herd is irrelevant. He was thinking in terms of what was good for the herd.

This herd instinct dominated Vansittart's attitude even more than he was aware of, as shown in the passage in his book where the foundations of his stand on Manchuria are at last revealed. He is discussing the Ethiopian crisis (to which I must come back later) and has been putting forward the obstacles for British action due to military unpreparedness (his strong point, on which he was right) and he goes on:

'There was a moral catch too: we were not as earnest as we thought. In my youth, we were called hypocritical by aliens' which angered me. Ageing I found the old malice but a new truth never admitted. More years passed, and I did admit it – but only to myself. In the thirties there was no denying it. We assumed postures contrary to our intentions, as in 1931. If, by some miraculous departure from character, the Americans had then fought the Japanese over Manchuria, they might have fought alone – as we in 1935 – since nobody in Britain thought seriously of sacrificing her sons for yellow men. In such matters unavowed racialism prevailed. We felt indisposed to die for white men in 1938.'

It is clear that Vansittart never understood that the risk of war in 1931 would have been incurred not for yellow men but for the rule of Law. And this error – then widespread in the West – was the true cause of the rise of Hitler.

CHAPTER IX

DON QUIXOTE OF LA MANCHURIA

DISPERSED on October 24, 1932, we, of the Council, met again on November 16th. These frequent meetings made manifest the uneasy feelings of all the Council members, not precisely on the poor help we were granting China but on the gradual deterioriation of the very principle on which the League rested. The interval between our two meetings had, of course, seen a steep rise in the aggressiveness of the aggressor State: jingoistic parades and other outbursts of nationalism in Japan; open military invasion, occupation of Tsitsithar and even battles in the region of Tsientsin. At our Paris meeting, Gilbert had vanished, and Stimson had sent (oh, not to Geneva! but to Paris) his Ambassador in London, General Dawes, better known as the banker who had given his name to the Plan for German Reparations. Dawes set his office at the Ritz Hotel, and never came near the Council for fear of contamination; but he had us members to lunch with him one by one.

Dawes may have been an ace at finance; on the business of peace, war and the League, he knew little and understood less. Japan kept her deaf-and-dumb Yoshizawa at the Council table, but sent also to Paris her Ambassador in London, Matsudaira, a first-rate man, related to the royal family, to whisper powerful hints in embassies and hotels.

On November 19th Stimson surpassed himself. He told Dawes that, if the Council decided on sanctions, its action would be overwhelmingly supported by public opinion in America, and the United States would not interfere. Little wonder Dawes made no use of this message.* Had Stimson added: 'And we shall be the first to apply the sanctions' the aggression would have ended there and then. In any case, the mere fact that even Gilbert had been withdrawn from the Council table was bound to act as an encouragement to the aggressor, and we all realised it at once.

There were Council members who thought the time had come to invoke Article 15 of the Covenant, which would put the matter before the Assembly; and, considering China could always do so on her own (as she eventually did in fact) this course seemed indeed reasonable; but the majority of the Council was reluctant, and, in any case, Yoshizawa

---

* Walters, p. 479, footnote. Based on Foreign Relations of the U.S. 1931 vol. I. pp. 498 seq.

showed signs of having recovered his voice. He now put forward the very proposal against which he had fought so gallantly for weeks: a League Commission of Enquiry was to be sent to find out all about Manchuria . . . and China, but not, of course, Japan. We talked on this for two days and were assured that this idea – which a few weeks earlier was thought dangerous by Stimson for, he thought, it was sure to excite the bellicose mood of the Japanese army – had become a very good one because it was thought by Stimson to be sure to act as a moderating influence on the said Japanese army. On November 21st Yoshizawa presented his idea at a public meeting of the Council, knowing it would pass muster; yet it cost us weeks of palaver to agree on a text that would suit the now exacting Japanese.

The view here taken to the effect that it was the lack of firmness on the part of the Council and of the U.S.A. that ruined this unique occasion of consolidating the peace institutions of the world received a signal confirmation when, on the news that the Japanese army was actively preparing an attack on Tsientsin, the Council reacted vigorously and resolved to send a group of big power military attachés to Chinchow to establish and maintain a neutral zone. Japan would not recognise them as forming a League Commission. What happened? Stimson, left high and dry by the firmness of Geneva, had to honour his own repeated promise to back the Council; then, faced with a firm stand by Geneva and Washington, Japan gave up her military plans.

At last, on December 10th, the Council was able to pass a unanimous resolution deciding to send a Commission of Enquiry to Manchuria. It was all we could do, but it was by no means enough. The Commission would study and report but would not be empowered to stop the fighting or to negotiate. Japan had signified her intention to take or continue to take military action against 'lawless elements', and retained her freedom to do as she thought fit no matter her obligations under the Covenant.

This resolution did much harm to the League. It inflicted a grievous humiliation on – whom? On the League of Nations, certainly. But what was the League of Nations but the Nations of the League? And what could the smaller nations do if the big Nations did not stand up to one of them? This resolution marked the beginning of the end of the faith in the League. The representatives of the smaller powers in the Council raised a determined opposition to the Resolution until the very end, and only voted it because they had to bow to the inevitable. The U.S. backed it the very day it was voted.

There is little doubt that this resolution inflicted a heavy blow on the biggest French statesman of the day, and the most genuine believer in the League that not merely France but Europe then possessed. I say so with some hesitation thinking of Cecil; for though Cecil's faith in the League was genuine and deep, he was not a leader of governments, as Briand was in France. Shaken in his health, he resigned in January 1932 and died in March. As I visited his mortuary room, I found my predecessor Quiñones de León wandering disconsolate among the crowd of mourners. We commiserated, not on Briand, now free, but on the world he left behind.

The big powers being responsible for the failure of the League, it was to be expected that they would reserve for themselves the membership of the Commission. This aspect of the matter was not well received by European public opinion. The *Journal de Genève*, then led by William Martin with outstanding intellectual distinction, printed the news with the following comment: 'Once again, the permanent members of the Council have shown that, in their eyes, their small power colleagues are inexistent or unimportant. The explanation has been put forward that Japan would not have accepted for the Commission members of countries having no extra-territorial rights in China. But then, what about Germany? Let alone the fact that this subservience to the will of a State that has set itself outside of international law is, to say the least, singular.'

My countryman Plá, who had succeeded me in the Press Section when I had gone on to lead the Disarmament Section, and was still there, sent me this cutting from the *Journal de Genève* (January 11, 1932) with a note of his own: 'In my opinion, we should not let pass this irritating deed of bossy imperialism in resignation and silence. Least of all now, when the intervention of Great Britain and the U.S. in Japan is taking such a shamelessly selfish turn. The governments of these two nations, in their latest Notes, are concerned merely with their material interests in Manchuria and let the Devil take the moral aspect of the problem. I am sure that no one but you will open his mouth at the Council table. [. . .] You are the only Assembly delegate from whom public opinion may expect a gesture adequate for such a lamentable episode of the history of the League.'

This letter, though from a friend and countryman, did utter a general opinion then, for in the eyes of the general public I had become the champion of the League, and for many, just as generous, but less discriminating, the champion of China. I well remember one morning, as I was still staying at the Hotel Georges V, when I delivered a somewhat irate complaint by phone, because the whole staff kept bringing me Indian or Ceylon tea for my breakfast instead of China which I always took and take. It suddenly struck me as funny and I laughed aloud in my bedroom after I had laid down the telephone, for it did sound like a pro-China mania on my part. The *vox populi* of the day had decorated me with the surname 'Don Quixote of La Manchuria'.

To Plá my answer was: 'I agree with you and am doing what is necessary in the sense you mention, though bearing in mind that it would not be advisable to go forward too far from the troops that follow one's lead.' In fact, I had a talk with Cecil about it in Briand's room, and I remember exactly where, Cecil sitting on one of the golden chairs of that illustrious office, and I standing in front of him. He, again!, believed I was arguing for a Spaniard to be appointed as a member of the Commission; while I wanted a Dutchman, and had never thought of Spain. Cussedly enough, though I did notice his error, for it was plain, I did not explain my view to him in those terms, though I did mention Holland. All I said was that I never thought of Spain as a secondary power, but as a great one, at any rate a great moral power. He was always friendly and courteous with me, so he took it very well, but we were not speaking the same language.

Cecil, despite his faith in the Covenant, did remain attached to the obsolete view of the League as a co-operative of sovereignties, especially of big powers. In this, he did not differ so very much from Simon or Vansittart; for they all lived in this curious intellectual chaos that justified the big powers' privileges in the League on the ground of their armaments yet none would face its responsibilities as one of the guardians of the League; while I was trying to put forward the view that the smaller powers should be given a far bigger share in the activities of the League to emphasise the new fact: the power of public opinion; since a Commission of Enquiry composed only of big powers would look too much like a Commission of butchers sent to inaugurate a vegetarian Congress.

Well, the Commission was sent, chaired by Lord Lytton and composed of two generals, one American and one French, and two diplomats, one Italian and one German. It was not actually and fully constituted until January, and took the longest possible way in order to visit Japan first, so that April was well on when it arrived in Manchuria. It was in the nature of things that the time the Commission lost should have been precious for the warlike Japanese. A new government under the thumb of the army had taken office in Tokyo, and all pretence of dissension between the military and civilian masks worn by Japanese nationalism had been dropped. Before the Commission arrived, Manchuria was firmly in Japanese hands, and had been declared an independent State – independent, of course, from China.

This decision was taken by Japan in the teeth of the, as yet, most determined American stand against Japanese aggression. The motive

of the American Government was worth noticing. In an official Note
sent on January 7, 1932 to both China and Japan, the U.S. declared
that she would not recognise any agreement between them which
might impair American treaty rights in China, nor any situation
brought about by means contrary to the Kellogg Pact. I have deliberately lifted these words from Walters' *History of The League* (pp. 483–4)
because I crave leave to go on copying so as to define where I differ
from this most honest historian.

'Before sending it', Walters writes on, 'Stimson told the British and
French Governments of his intentions and his hope that they and others
would follow the American lead.' What lead? In this Note, the American Government reserved her own treaty rights in China, caring
nothing for anything that might happen to China so long as American
'rights' were respected; save for the reserve on the Kellogg Pact, that
everybody knew to be a mere paper tiger stuffed with pious platitudes.
Nevertheless Walters goes on to express (if with the moderation one
would expect of a well-bred Briton writing about the wrongs of his
own country): 'The sequel was unbelievable to anyone who did not
realise the spirit in which the principal Foreign Offices were dealing
with Far Eastern questions. The British reply took the form of a statement, published in the press and communicated to Washington, to the
effect that the Government were anxious that foreign commerce should
not be shut out of Manchuria; that the Japanese had given public assurances on the subject; and that it was not therefore considered necessary
to address to Japan a Note on the lines of that issued by the U.S.; not a
word about the integrity of China.'

Walters sees perhaps in the Kellogg Pact more than I am able to
discover in it. The powers, by taking the American hint, might perhaps
have been able to build up a kind of Kellogg Pact Council of Dentists
(for everybody spoke of nothing else than to put teeth into the Kellogg
Pact). Merely supplying that ghostly instrument with a more or less
artificial denture might have frightened the Japanese army. The wings
of my imagination would not fly as high or far. At any rate, the shop-
keeper answer of the Foreign Office and the silence of the Quai d'Orsay,
enabled Japan to go ahead with her warlike and imperialistic plans.

CHAPTER X

THE ISSUE GOES TO THE ASSEMBLY

W HEN the Council met again (January 25, 1932), the Japanese had made a strong and ruthless attack against Shanghai and met with stiff Chinese resistance. A stronger Council might have profited by the disconcerting effects of such a military outrage on Japanese public opinion; but the Council was weak and poorly attended by the Foreign Ministers that mattered (Simon and Laval), and public attention was being drawn away from Manchuria to the Disarmament Conference about to begin in Geneva. Stimson made a second attempt at reasserting the respect due to the territorial integrity of China, but was discouraged by Simon's indifference. Even so, on February 16, the Council (without the parties) sent a strong Note to Japan reminding her of this issue of territorial integrity; but, of course, with no effect whatever. Then, China invoked Article 15, which assured her of a procedure free from the aggressor's veto, and allowed her to pass the issue on to the Assembly, which she did. This measure brought her the backing of the general opinion of the League keenly critical of the inaction of the big powers which had emasculated the Council.

When the Assembly met (March 3, 1932) Stimson rang the bell again. Poor man. He felt he should be there himself, and he would not. It is told of Unamuno that, as he was spending a week-end in the country, his host, who slept next door to him and had left him in his room after bidding him good night, went to sleep rocked by the rhythmic steps of his illustrious guest, walking to and fro in his bedroom. The host woke up a few hours later, and still the steps beat on regularly to and fro. He knocked at the door, walked in and saw Unamuno still in his day clothes, pacing the room. 'What's the matter?' Unamuno stared hard at him. 'I am possessed by a terrific desire to cross myself!' 'Well, dear man, do so.' 'Never. My brain won't have it.'

I always felt Stimson was in the reverse situation. His brain plainly told him he should work in Geneva; his Republican prejudices stood in the way. And so, he would do everything towards it, but not it; and his actions would lack both directness and authority. This time, his contribution consisted of a letter to Senator Borah, which he meant as a hint to the Assembly to proclaim the principle of no recognition of any situation brought about in violation of the Kellogg Pact. This time, the

League took the hint because we were at the Assembly, where nearly every nation represented felt that she would be on the losing side of any aggression that might turn up; but the style revealed the crafty pen of Simon, for the most he could bring himself to say was: 'It is incumbent upon the members of the League not to recognise any situation, treaty or agreement, which may be brought about by means contrary to the Covenant of the League or to the Pact of Paris' (i.e. the Kellogg Pact).

This resolution was adopted on March 11, 1932; but the Assembly still thought of the issue as a Japanese-Chinese rather than a Japanese-League conflict. Without being dogmatic about this, particularly in view of the stand-offish attitude of the U.S. towards the League, I was always of those who preferred the matter treated as a conflict between the League and Japan.

The Assembly appointed its own Committee, in which it included all the members of the Council, and put it under the chairmanship of its own president, Hymans, a small, wiry, smiling, clever and astute Belgian of Jewish extraction. The armistice in Shanghai was negotiated (May 5th) and the rest was left to wait for the publication of the Lytton report – left, but not by the Japanese, who in utter disregard of the opinion that was to lead to the March 11th resolution, set up their Japanese Puppet State of Manchuria under the name of Manchukuo and 'recognised' it on September 15, 1932.

The Lytton report, available in September 1932, was an excellent paper, in itself sufficient to justify the procedure of the League, even if defective, as in this case it certainly was. It owed a good deal of its worth to Robert Haas, the Committee's Secretary, the same who ten years earlier had so brilliantly organised and directed the Barcelona Conference. Describing situations and events with both impartiality and moderation, it led the reader to conclude that the responsibility was on Japan though it didn't actually say so. It rejected the claim of legitimate defence and underscored the military motives and causes of the establishment of Manchukuo.

On September 22, 1932 I wrote to Zulueta, then Foreign Minister, giving him an account of a conversation I had had with Beneŝ. I foresaw that I should have to explain my strong line some day; and so I wanted to be well fortified by the stand of other delegates. None better than Beneŝ, who on this issue had taken a strong line from the first.

Beneŝ, I reported, did not trust the big powers because their traditional policy in China was too similar to that of Japan, and because their permanent services were against the League. He therefore thought we, the Eight (the three Scandinavians, the two Low Countries, Switzerland

and Spain with his own country), should keep in close touch. As for procedure, he believed that the Council should debate the Lytton Report (the debate had begun the very day I wrote, with speeches by the Japanese and Chinese delegates). This done, the Council should send the report and the Council's proceedings to the Assembly. But he opposed Drummond's plan, consisting of sending the Report first to the Committee of Nineteen, where he, Drummond, would draft the paper which would ultimately stand as the considered opinion of the Assembly under Article 15. Beneš wished the Lytton Report discussed by the plenary Assembly first; for he felt the Nineteen should not influence the Assembly, but the other way about. In his view the final resolution should include three ideas: there had been no occasion for legitimate defence; Manchukuo was not a spontaneous creation of Manchuria; and it should not be recognised. In order to raise this last conclusion above Japan's possible wrangles, Beneš wished the final report of the Assembly to be presented in two distinct pacts separated in time. The first would cover the past, and would end with the three ideas listed above; the second would consider the future.

This second phase would differ, according to whether Japan would accept or not to negotiate on the bases of chapters 9 and 10 of the Report. Beneš thought the collaboration of the U.S.A. and of Russia was necessary at that stage, and in his view possible, indeed, desired by the two nations concerned. If Japan refused conciliation and if Russian and American collaboration had been secured, he envisaged strong measures, such as a demand for evacuation, indemnisation for China and armaments boycott for Japan.

In the end, it was Beneš procedure that came to be adopted. The debate took place on December 6th, 7th and 8th. Faced with a formidable Document, the more formidable for its quiet style and attitude, Japan sent a first-rate delegate, Matsuoca, who stressed the stock argument his predecessor had repeated *ad nauseam*; namely that China was in such a chaotic state that she could hardly have been dealt with as a normal League member. There were two aspects to this argument. One was that, chaotic or not, China was a member of the League, and her internal state would not be bettered by foreign aggression; but the other aspect was more delicate, and Matsuoca was prompt in underscoring it. The big powers, France and Britain in particular, had been keeping troops and warships in China for over a century; and anyone even slightly acquainted with the history of Asia knew only too well that respect for China's sovereignty and territorial integrity had been for a long time unknown to the Europeans. This was the most serious argument of all; for not only was it well grounded in the facts of history but it revealed to the world the true cause of the passivity of the big powers: their secret sympathy for Japan and their secret conviction that it fitted their own history and attitude on the matter.

I have found in my files two sheets of paper written in pencil in Sir Eric Drummond's handwriting, bearing on the arrangements for the Council meeting on the day the Commission report was to be officially presented. Drummond's note is addressed to me. I shall copy it here because it aptly illustrates our minor difficulties, Mussolini's attitude in matters of prestige and Drummond's anxiety to defend himself against any implicit accusation that might lurk under my protest at seeing Lytton occupying a back seat during the Council meeting.

> I had naturally arranged for Lytton to come to the table, but last night he sent me a message to the effect that his Italian colleague had told him that if he (Lytton) were asked to come to the table and he (Aldobrandi) were not he (Aldobrandi) would feel obliged to leave Geneva.
>
> Lytton, who is most anxious to keep all the members of his Commission here, asked me to arrange that they should all sit together in the second row, which I have done. He is quite happy about the present position.
>
> It is intolerable that Aldobrandi should behave like this but there it is and Lytton himself would prefer not to answer questions orally but to write replies after consulting his colleagues.
>
> This does not mean that Lytton should not be asked to the table for a specific point, but I think it would be a mistake to raise the issue though I agree it is very wrong.

I must have replied to this note, insisting on 'raising the issue'; his own was already a reply to a protest of mine at seeing Lytton in a back seat ('I agree it is very wrong' must mean that Drummond felt as I did); for I have a second paper in which Drummond seems to argue with me on my suggestion to speak on the subject:

> Well, but do not forget Lytton's position. He had asked me that all the members of the Commission shall [sic] be together. If the table were bigger I would put them all there, and I would only inform the Council of Lytton's request. I have no authority to disclose the personal reasons which led to it and I only told you of them privately.

Such was the air which we had to breathe while the crucial crisis of the League was raging. For the reasons I have stated, France and

Britain were cautious and reserved when it came to condemning Japan. William Martin, always as reliable as well informed, told in the *Journal de Genève* that Matsuoca, on being asked what he thought of this speech, answered: 'Sir John has explained, in half an hour and in a magnificent English, what I have tried in vain to convey to my colleagues for hours and hours in my bad English'.

Beneš, whom I reported to Madrid as the extreme left of our endeavour, and Undén, who followed him closely in this, made powerful speeches, indeed stronger than mine was to be, because more down to earth and more concrete. Simon, indeed, did hardly more than comment on the disorder prevailing in China. That is why I dealt with an aspect of the matter no one seemed to have thought of: very good, China is weak because of internal trouble and divisions; *but so is Japan*. Her military might abroad, what is it but a military rebellion against her government and Emperor? How many public men had been murdered? We had to bow before many victims of inner strife such as the two prime ministers: Inouyé and Inoucai. Should we, while condemning Japan for an obvious act of aggression, bear in mind her internal strife and realise how difficult it was for a nation torn by internal factions, punctiliously to observe all her international obligations? When I sat down, Prof. Basdevant, then legal adviser to the Quai d'Orsay, later Judge at the Hague, came to me and cried out: '*Vous avez fait un discours terrible.*'

The Spanish delegation, in agreement with the Swedish, Czechoslovak and Irish, presented a resolution to the Assembly rejecting the (Japanese) plea of legitimate defence, the compatibility of the Japanese regime in Manchuria with Japan's international obligations and the Japanese pretence of its being really independent from Japan.

The Japanese delegate, Matsuoca, reacted with vigour and hinted at what was actually to happen later in any case – Japan's walking out: the passing of that resolution 'might entail consequences *perhaps* not intended by its authors.' The Assembly took refuge in the philosophy of the immortal Mr Pickwick and passed the text as 'draft proposals' instead of a 'draft resolution'. On such things, we are asked to believe, the peace of the world may hang.

The Assembly adopted the report and confirmed that Manchukuo could not be recognised. Japan walked out (March 27, 1933). It gave another opportunity for Stimson to endorse what we had done, and that was his swan song, for soon afterwards he handed on to Cordell Hull. Thus ended his conflict, the most sinister, in my opinion, the League had to contend with. Born under good auspices, since it pitted the League against the (then) arch-enemy of the U.S.A., it might have culminated in the vindication of the League and even the entrance of the U.S. into the League after the victory of the Convenant over Japan. But the hesitant and muddle-headed diplomacy of Hoover and Stimson and the bad conscience, habits and attitude of Britain and France in their relations with China, led to an end which was enlightened and dignified insofar as concerns the Lytton Report, yet disappointing and disheartening in that the League was let down by the U.S. and other big powers, China was defeated and humiliated and Japan left in possession of her ill-acquired gains. This outcome prepared the even worse outcome of the Ethiopian Crisis, and the piracies and banditries of Hitler and Stalin before and after the Second World War.

CHAPTER XI

OPPOSITION IN MY OWN COUNTRY

I soon began to receive warnings of a possible trend to dissent from my way of doing things in Madrid. Used as I was to the workings of envy, I had expected it. Zuloaga, who painted the portrait he was to present to me (and later to be stolen from my home as soon as the armies of the 'Law and Order' tribe entered Madrid), as he went on watching my face and drawing on his canvas, said to me: 'They will never forgive you your success.' 'They' in this case was general enough, 'on' in French, so to speak. And, indeed, it was beginning to tell. I must have received a letter from Zulueta [then Foreign Secretary] towards the beginning of December 1932, for I have in my files the text of a letter I wrote to him from Geneva on the ninth of that month; and another one, dated December 27th in Paris which I sent to Marcelino Domingo, then Minister of Trade. Why this second one? There is no clue in the text, but it is likely that I had been warned about him, for, unlike Zulueta, he was not quite the size for his post or political career, and he was going to betray at times not a little jealousy – and not only of me.

One of the promoters of the trouble was Ortega's brother, Eduardo, by no means a worthy brother of the philosopher. This good man (for after all he was not that bad, only a wee bit poorly furnished in his top storey, possibly as a compensation for nature's lavish gifts to the great brother) had spent his exile during the Primo dictatorship in Hendaye, in the company of Unamuno; and he had fancied (in the naïve way of the outs who dream themselves ins) that the Republic would grant him the Paris embassy as a reward for his years of exile. Though I had no part whatever in his discomfiture, he chose to punish me for it, and, in alliance with a disgruntled diplomat turned politician, he carried a vendetta campaign against the Foreign Office both in the Cortes and in the press in the course of which I got my full share of blows.

I left Ortega alone; but wrote to Domingo mainly on two points: one, that though we had acted on principle, and it was on principle that we were establishing Spain's good name in Geneva and in the world, it was not fair to accuse me of neglecting Spanish interests, for he should 'lend his attention to the considerable material interest towards Spain that might grow in the immense population of China on the basis of the moral interests we had created.' As a sign of it, I added: 'Among the many testimonies I have received, there is a letter full of enthusiasm for Spain emanated from all the big live forces in Shanghai.' I suggested that he might consider the sending of a commercial mission to China and the setting up of a Spanish-Chinese Bank.

But I made a second point. My association with the seven other 'neutral' States had, of course, also been criticised by the envious ones. I sent Domingo a copy of William Martin's article in the *Journal de Genève*. It was a vindication of my policy. I shall reproduce here the first, a middle, and the last paragraph.

> The most striking feature of last week's events is the growing divorce between the outlook of the small and of the big powers. Even these names do not fully apply. We are not speaking of small powers on account of their territory or population. Spain, for instance, is not a small country, and there are some of the so-called big ones, that are hardly bigger than she is.
>
> Only one country has known hegemony and has given it up fully enough to see her wisdom today in no longer being a big power. In so doing, she gives the world a great example, and one worth considering, for it is nearly unique in history. As for the other big powers, they are more or less on their way to sobriety. None is quite free yet from the fumes of glory.
>
> In today's Europe, the true great power is Law. It is not the power that rules the self-styled big nations, which are less strong than they think. It is the collective force incarnated by eight countries, penetrated by an international spirit and a peaceful will, having at their head men of the quality of Beneš, Madariaga, Motta and Undén. May their energy be such as to match the obstacles they will find on their way!

My letter to Zulueta (December 9, 1932) amounts to a defence of my policy as that of a moderate man ever ready to compromise. Its interest lies mainly in the light it sheds on the procedure that was actually followed in the Assembly and the origin of the motion presented by the group of eight small powers to which William Martin alluded. It is too long to be given in full.

It begins by pointing out that the Eight Group did not meet [on the Lytton Report] on my initiative but on that of Christian Lange, the Norwegian delegate. He was, by the way, a (morally and physically) handsome man, who led the Interparliamentary Union, and wherever he went sought to illumine the place with the light of reason and human sympathy. It was, I argued, Lange and not I that had called the Group.

There was a certain 'elasticity' in its attitude; but the 'extreme Left' of it was definitely Beneŝ, closely followed by Undén. I had sent their speeches to the minister so that he could compare. I also sent him a copy of a letter I had received from the *Bureau International de la Paix*, which must have been flattering for me for I assured him that it was for his information and appeasement and not out of vanity that I sent it. Then I transcribed the text of another letter received from 'a high French personality in the international world': 'My dear Ambassador: Allow me to tell you that your speech this morning was remarkable – the most beautiful I ever heard you pronounce – one of the most beautiful ever heard here. It was profound, moving, wise and audacious.'

Then, I went on to give him concrete examples of how I always tried to seek a conciliatory line. As a logical outcome of our speeches, Undén, Beneŝ and I had presented a motion to which Lester had later added his name. 'This led to an insolent intervention from the Japanese delegate, which made the Assembly react in our favour. I at once moved in to try to negotiate a compromise, as the Japanese demanded an immediate vote so as to intimidate the Assembly and the movers. We four met with the Secretary General, and, as we could not accept Drummond's proposal, for it meant a retreat on our part, I suggested that we would explain that our text was a mere draft resolution, which, according to the Standing Rules, had to be sent to the Committee before voting or discussing it; and that if, even then, the Japanese insisted on leaving, we should declare that their attitude was unreasonable, but that we were not ready to shoulder the responsibility of a Japanese withdrawal and so we would withdraw our text. This called forth strong protests from my three colleagues, and I, of course, sided with them.'

It was therefore evident that, though I was for firmness, I was not for intransigence, which, I felt was the reproach Madrid tended to level against me. That very morning of the day I wrote (December 8, 1932) the four 'conspirators', i.e. Beneŝ, Lester, Undén and I, had been invited to join the steering Committee of the Assembly to study the position. The President (Hymans) suggested that he might put forward that all proposals would be sent on to the Committee; but I pointed out that 'proposals' might be understood as not including our one, which was a draft resolution; that I was willing to accept the President's idea but that it should be made clear that it included our whatever-it-was, since 'draft resolution' offended the Japanese. Everybody agreed, but Motta (I don't know why) suggested that the President might act either way because my amendment was of no importance. I acquiesced in the procedure, though not in its alleged foundation; but again my endeavour at conciliation called forth a lively protest from Beneŝ who argued that it all would look like a capitulation on our part. So, I concluded in my letter to Zulueta, you will see that I am always ready to listen to other views.

Why present a proposal at all? I put the question and answered it: because 'conciliation' kept walking backwards as the Japanese advanced, and it was urgent to draw the line beyond which we would not go. And then I went on to explain how I saw our stand as Spaniards: we should be moderate but firm. What if we thus found ourselves in a forward minority? 'We were the most forward government in Europe after Russia,' wrote I, though I was already witnessing signs of the truly reactionary nature of the Soviet Regime. And I went on: 'We are in the company of nations governed by socialist governments. Beneŝ is a socialist, so is Undén. Are we, the Spanish Republic, to give up being in a minority, and forward? What can Japan do to us? While, if we become popular in China – what a market.'

I concluded with two ideas: 'To judge by the intense interest American pressmen evince in my movements, speeches and action, the American press must be following this business very assiduously. Our stand here is bound to have considerably increased the moral authority of the Republic in the eyes of American public opinion'; and then, what about disarmament? If the League does not discipline Japan, I argued, there will be no disarmament. Then Spain must arm. The Spanish Prime Minister must declare that we will set up a strong army and a formidable navy. 'We cannot carry on with our present navy in a world that will not disarm, so, either general disarmament or a navy for us. And this would mean adjourning for two or three generations our plans for cultural and economic development.'

I should be sorry, however, to leave this subject on a merely defensive note against envy. In Geneva, I had good Spanish friends who witnessed what I was doing and reported it to their acquaintances in Spain. Notable among them were Roselló, the leader of the International Institute of Education, and Plá, who had succeeded me in the Press Section of the Secretariat. I owe to Plá the text I found in my files of a letter he received from one of the prominent writers of the time in Spain, the Catalan Agustín Calvet, who wrote under the pen-name Gaziel. I shall reproduce it as a testimonial from a distinguished countryman: 'Barcelona, March 18, 1932. My dear friend: [...] I follow with as deeply-felt an interest as I have seldom felt in my life Spain's activity in Geneva and very specially that of Madariaga. I haven't the pleasure of knowing him personally but I have admired him for a long time, and more so since we both were contributors to El Sol [...]. I believe Madariaga should be our Briand. His real place is in Madrid, at the head of the Foreign Office, where for the good of us, Spaniards, he ought to remain many years, until he has been able to endow our foreign policy with shape, solidity and organisation. Supported by competent persons in Paris, London, Berlin, etc. and in particular in the capitals of the small European and American countries that possess natural affinities with our international policy, Madariaga might, in time, leave behind a substantial and admirable achievement. We lack public opinion, you say. I should, for the moment, be content with the means thereto being provided by the Spanish Government. And to that end it would suffice, for a time, to build on the work of a few men of good will endowed with a clear, cold and concrete mind.'

CHAPTER XII

AMBASSADOR IN PARIS

I presented credentials in January to President Doumer. Laval was Foreign Secretary. He looked like a gipsy, and one just kept searching behind him for the horses he was sure to be selling. But no. His were not horses on legs. He was far more clever and shrewd than intelligent; his mental eyes were far more accommodated to short than to long term events, and, if anything went wrong, their sparkling humour would vanish and they would turn sombre, threatening, and his mouth bared a cruel, sharp eye-tooth. A thin, black streak of a moustache acted as a reminder.

After the reading of the speeches and the presentation of my staff, I was accosted by Laval, who came to me smiling with mischief. '*Monsieur l'Ambassadeur*, the last time I had anything to do with the Spanish Embassy was when, after the execution of Ferrer, I joined my pals to protest in a demonstration before the Spanish Embassy.' – 'Ah, so you were there, were you?' I retorted: 'Well, *Monsieur le Président*, so was I. And I'll tell you what you had to do. The Embassy was then in the Boulevard de Courcelles, and the way was well guarded by police. So, you went to the Place Clichy, took the tram, your pockets well stuffed with stones, and when you passed the Embassy building, the driver (who was in the conspiracy) slowed down, and you threw your stones at the windows. The pavement sparkled with broken glass.' Laval enjoyed this thoroughly. 'Ah, that was a time! We were all young.' 'Twenty years younger.' We became good – no, not friends, that was not in his style – but good companions.

Not very long after I had occasion to test it. Laval was mayor of Aubervilliers, a *commune* close to Paris, in whose factories many Spanish workers were employed. One morning, my staff reported to me that the municipality of Aubervilliers, in financial difficulties, had simply abolished all official unemployment and illness benefits in the case of its Spanish population. To the astonishment of my orthodox, diplomatic advisers, I reached for the telephone and got hold of Laval. I reported the case to him as if he knew nothing about it, though I felt pretty certain the measure was in his draconic style; and, sure enough, he replied that it was his doing, that the money was not there, and that it was only natural that the foreigner should be the first struck. 'That won't do,' I retorted. 'By the treaty of Establishment, which dates from

1853, Spaniards in France and Frenchmen in Spain enjoy the same rights as the nationals, so, if you don't relent, we shall retaliate, and, of course, we shan't bother about French workers in Spain. We shall go for technicians, teachers and bankers.' He thought it over, and after a silence, spoke again: 'Very good – you've won.'

That was in the morning. In the evening, the Minister of Foreign Affairs, a socialist, rang up from Madrid, informed me of the case and urged me to act. I told him the matter had been settled to our satisfaction. He could not believe it. I told him I just had settled it by telephone. While this way of doing things was spontaneous in me, I was no doubt encouraged to use it because it was also Laval's own way. It was Laval himself who had revealed me the trick. I remember he once told me how, at a delicate moment in the relations between France and Germany, he had called Berlin on the phone to talk to the Chancellor, Dr Brüning. He got him soon enough but couldn't hear a word the German Chancellor said. He was too shrewd to wonder why; so he roared down the line: 'If I cannot hear Dr Brüning's next sentence as if he were in my room, there will be many expulsions from the service to-morrow morning in the *Official Journal*.' He heard him. Perfectly.

The traditional round of visits to my colleagues soon revealed that whatever sympathies we might expect from the peoples of Europe, and even from a number of governments, diplomats were not on our side. I got the first inkling of this situation when, before leaving for my first post abroad, Washington, I called on my opposite number, the American Ambassador in Madrid. What an unlucky man! He was Ambassador in Athens when, led by his irresistible snobbery, he asked for and obtained the Embassy in Spain. Fancy, this great historical monarchy, all gold, lace, glass and ebony coaches, glory! He arrived in Madrid, and hardly had he begun to live his dream, when all crashed down and he found himself in as vulgar a Republic as (he must have thought) his own native land! As I listened to him, I scented all his bitter disappointment beyond his professional courtesy.

I was already in Washington when news came through of his misadventure. He had called a press conference to give his off-the-record views on what was going on; of course, strictly limited to American journalists. Unfortunately for him, there was one man there who, technically, was within his rights to be present, yet did not really belong to the herd: he was a Frenchman by birth, an acute mind, a shrewd observer and, I do believe, a bit of a mischief-maker. He leaked, if not to his paper, at least to a number of his friends, that the American Ambassador, asked what he thought of the new government, had answered: 'I never saw such a pack of jailbirds in my life.' He had to be removed.

My own experiences in Paris were nothing like as unhappy. No one called me a jailbird. But I do remember at least three cases of a definitely unfriendly attitude. The first was that of the Belgian Ambassador. He was a very 'hoity-toity' person, suffering from high aristocratic-blood pressure, who was determined to make me feel that, no matter how many good friends I, as a person, might have in his country, the Ambassador of a plebeian Republic would not be considered good company in such an exalted mansion as his embassy was, at any rate while he was in command. I never crossed his gate again.

The second case was that of Tyrrell, the British Ambassador. Now, I liked Tyrrell very much indeed. I found him a most attractive kind of Englishman, although he was a Roman Catholic. By 'although' I mean that a British Roman Catholic is apt to appeal to me as an oddity not very easy to case, something that should not be there, nearly as odd and awkward as a Spanish Protestant. Tyrrell, whom I knew already fairly well, was, of course, his all polite and graceful self. But much to my surprise, and regret, he did not come forward at all after our first, official talk in his embassy; while I noticed that he gave a good deal of well publicised hospitality to my monarchist predecessor, Quiñones de León. Whether this odd behaviour was due to the Queen of Spain being British or to other causes, I don't know.

My third case was the Polish Ambassador. He hailed from that part of Poland which in her last partition had been Prussian; and he had even been a member of the Reichstag. He combined the less attractive features of both nations: the impertinence of the Polish estate-owner and the arrogance of the Prussian Junker. While Tyrrell's attitude pained me, because I wanted to like him, the Pole's attitude pleased me because I wanted to detest him. I have known Poles before and after for whom I felt great attraction and sympathy. Witness Raszynski, the last free Polish Ambassador in London. But this specimen in Paris, I thoroughly disliked.

The feeling, which grew from my first official call, betrayed me into almost a diplomatic gaffe. His wife sent me a request for money for her charities to the Polish colony. It drew in my screw the wrong way. It seemed to me senseless, and still does, that heads of missions should bleed each other for their charities. I sent her one thousand francs, warning her soon to expect a similar request from my wife. They might have laughed it off. He sent me back the money. I made them accept the money and a bouquet of roses as thorny as I could find at the florist. I think I was wrong. That is why I tell the story.

My memories of President Doumer went back to my school days. The third centenary of the publication of Don Quixote was celebrated at the Sorbonne in 1905, and it was Paul Doumer, then President of the Chamber of Deputies, who presided. I was nineteen. The big hall was crowded; and the ceremony – speeches, no music – was dull. Two incongruous details have stuck in my memory: in his opening speech, Doumer got mixed up and instead of *civilisation* he said *siphilisation*, which was just unmeant satire, I thought; then, or later, the legal adviser of the Spanish Embassy spoke. He answered to a name that began well but ended less well: Cristóbal Botella; and I rejoiced in hearing Doumer call him: *La parole est à Monsieur Cristobál Botellá*. He was, I do believe, the ugliest man I have ever seen, but his face was full of fun which beamed from his toad's eyes and twisted his very long, red-worm sort of a mouth into all kinds of unexpected shapes, now a saucer, now a letter-box-slit, now a slice of a steak. . . . He was speaking (in Spanish) on an idyllic subject: 'My uncle's library', a garden, trees, birds, quiet, a blue sky . . . but with the utmost emphasis and energy, so much indeed, that I overheard a girl behind me ask her mother: why is he so angry?

And those far distant thoughts, images, memories, floated in my mind when twenty-seven years later, I presented credentials to the same Doumer, now President, no longer of the Chamber but of the Republic; smaller, I thought, and less stand-offish, indeed friendly and debonair; and the same memories and thoughts floated back in a melancholy mist when, a few months later, I paid my official respects to his remains at the Elysée, the day after he was murdered.

Madame Doumer was there, very quiet and dignified, silent, a sad smile on her face, the face of a simple, modest, old French provincial bourgeoise, miles away from any Parisian elegance, brilliance, show. A perfect couple, united even in death, made one by their harmony on essentials. And when I went to see Tardieu, then Prime Minister, he uttered what I had been thinking: 'Jouvenel came to see me and I told him: you know, you and I, in different ways, have known many women. You know what I mean. But when you see an old couple like that, well, *ça vous a tout de même une autre allure*.'

CHAPTER XIII

AMBASSADOR IN PARIS (CONTINUED)

QUIÑONES had a keen sense of the duties of the man of the world, and therefore knew that in France an Ambassador could not receive and entertain without a certain amount of pleasure offered to the better sort, or as the uncouth Anglo-Saxon expression will have it, the highbrow. So there would be ballet, and even some show borrowed from one of the French subsidised theatres, preferably the Opéra Comique. As for the world of arts and letters I don't think he had ever troubled to venture beyond the 'how d'you do' of cocktails.

I had, from the very first, thought of establishing the Republic in that no-man's-land; so that at an early stage I got the Government to grant titles of Commander of Spanish Orders to Paul Valéry, André Maurois, and Maurice Ravel. We gave them a lunch at the embassy and the *cravates* were hung round their necks by C.H.M.A. and our two daughters.

In no other European nation are intellectuals expected to take sides in as responsible and exacting a way as in France, while in Britain if a politician is too clever and not shrewd enough to hide the fact, he is sure to fail; and in Spain one might be tempted to think that a politician is expected to be stupid. Intellectual power, though, is in France a help rather than a hindrance to political prestige; but I am straying, though slightly, in that my theme is not how much of an intellectual a politician can or should be, but how much of politician an intellectual must be. To be sure, he is not expected to go right for a seat in Parliament and a ministry in the Cabinet; but he is expected to give his opinion on every matter that counts, and in no uncertain terms.

Had I remained for a longer time at the embassy, I should certainly have opened it widely to the world of the French intellectuals; and my modest fête for three of them was meant as the opening for such a perspective. Meanwhile, I did my best to associate the embassy with every Spanish cultural activity that happened to occur, and in particular, recitals by Spanish artists. They knew that they were welcome and that nearly always the prelude to or the epilogue of their recitals, or both, was a family reunion at the embassy with their friends.

Chief among them was the great Andrés Segovia, known to me from the days when he had risen on our horizon in Spain, before he became a musical star of the first magnitude for the whole world. He has achieved perhaps for the guitar what Casals has for the cello, a near-revolution in the way of playing it and of drawing out of it the potential wealth of beauty it had so far concealed; but in at least one way Segovia's achievement was wider and more complex, not merely musical but sociological and psychological as well; for he received from tradition a popular instrument, fallen from the status the *vihuela* had enjoyed in centuries gone by, to conquer the taste and imagination of the people of Spain, who do wonders with it but in a different, so to speak, sociological key; and this instrument it was which by faith, science and will power, Segovia raised to the sovereign status it enjoys today among the best musicians.

As luck or ill-luck would have it, though, we never coincided in Paris while I was at the embassy; but we met now and then in Geneva; and I remember one day – or rather night – when after some persuasion, and with a borrowed guitar, for he would not expose his instrument to the damp vapours of the lake, we took a boat, rowed out in the light of the moon and listened to him playing, it seemed to us, lighter and more liquid and luminous than ever, lapped by gentle waves.

Among the many jobs I had to perform at the embassy was to organise the transportation of Blasco Ibáñez's remains from the Côte d'Azur, where he had died in 1928, to his native Valencia. He had all his life been a fervent republican, so the occasion was seized by the two republics, now sisters in the democratic faith, to assert their common tenets and heroes. A French cruiser was to convey the ashes of the great Spanish novelist. I had to propose the list of guests and, after approval in Madrid, to extend the official invitations.

I recall this episode because it led to a remarkable observation. My list of guests was of course established on official grounds: the presidents and secretaries of political and cultural organisms whom, either on general grounds or because of their relation to Spain, we had to invite. There was not, I believe, a single case in which a man was invited on purely personal grounds. Nevertheless, in spite of this absolute objectivity, I discovered on reading the list that the majority, nearly three quarters of these Frenchmen, were Jews.

What a remarkable pointer to the outstanding ability of the Hebrew people! On this occasion, I received the visit of one of them, a member of the Chamber of Deputies who occupied a strong position in French political life, though he was not a Cabinet minister. A ʿʒchnician, yet, like most Frenchmen, a man with a keen eye for the arts, he went straight to a small picture hanging on the wall opposite my desk, a landing plank, a wooden post half in half above the level of the lake, and the rest a grey-blue dream in which sky, water and air melted as parallel lines meet in infinity. 'Ah, *Monsieur l'Ambassadeur*, that is a fine de Segonzac, you have.' I said nothing. It went with my mood. Every visitor made a similar observation, and if I was in a sincere mood, I used to answer: 'It is a picture by my daughter Nieves who is fourteen and never heard of de Segonzac.'

However, this time I didn't let go, and bade my visitor sit down with a merely cryptic smile. He was a graduate of both the Ecole Polytechnique and the Paris School of Mines – just as I was; and in the course of our conversation, he wondered whether we hadn't something else in common; by which I understood him to mean that he supposed or surmised that I was also a Jew. I had to disappoint him. It may be that he mistook for something stronger or deeper the cordiality wherewith I usually receive strangers, no matter their nation or colour. This cordiality overwhelmed him so much that he invited us to go and stay at his Château (for this socialist lived in a Château) and on taking leave, he begged me to present his respects 'to Madame l'Impératrice', a rather unexpected promotion for my *ambassadrice* on the part of a republican and one that would have enchanted Freud.

CHAPTER XIV

ALEXIS LÉGER

THE Quai d'Orsay was in those days led by Alexis Léger. Under the pen-name of St John Perse, he is now a Nobel Prize Winner for Literature, and a world renowned, rather than world-read, poet. A truly great one, whose very originality may, at times, work against his renown. He has himself written (and, of course, I quote from memory) *On m'appelle l'obscur et j'habite l'éclat*; but it may be that both '*on*' and he are right, for thought is at times like that kind of cloth that is luminous on one side and dark on the other. We soon became good friends. His first-rate mind was just as masterly in the political as in the poetical world. Much later, in 1960, I was asked by the *Nouvelle Revue Française* to write a page for a book in his honour. This is a translation of my contribution: 'Much of a marginal, singular man though he is, a comet in the firmament of the mind, Léger appears in the diplomatic sky as a star of the new constellation, a portent of the times that followed the First World War.'

I felt it definitely from our very first meetings, when 'the Quai' lived under the aegis of Philippe Berthelot. 'This will kill that' thought I, while I eyed them both, standing, as fluke would have it, like two caryatides on either side of a long mantlepiece, in one of the rooms at 'the Quai'. On the right, Berthelot, his forehead narrow and lofty, his face widening downwards, his eyes lively and mischievous, a heavy nose, an even heavier but a powerful chin, disenchanted lips letting fall subtle abuse. For him, diplomacy was but a polite way of handling the French army. He was immersed in the tradition of that nineteenth century which had prevented the great States from assimilating the consequences for international politics of the social revolution we were all witnessing. These great masters of the declining diplomacy, von Bülow, Eyre Crowe, Berthelot, still wore their nationalism like the Crusaders their armour.

At the other end of the wide chimney piece stood the young, svelt figure of Léger. Hazard, not always mistaken, had made of him the favourite assistant, the hope, perhaps the heir of Berthelot. But the follower-up? That was the question I asked myself; and looking at them both, I felt: this will kill that.

Everything moved down towards the ground in Berthelot; even the skirts of his coat, his shoulders, his jaws, his cheeks, the bags under his

237

eyes, his lip-corners. Everything moved up in Léger, whose foot seemed just poised on the ground to draw from the earth its natural urge, as a geyser of energy, towards the strong chest. The shoulders held back, the straight, grave face, dominated by a large, straight forehead and lit by unforgettable eyes. I dreamt of the luminous Vulcan in Velázquez's *The Forge*. My eyes wandered from the one to the other. No. The difference that separated them was not merely one of age but one of epoch, like that black empty chimney that yawned between them.

And I said to myself, while listening to them, mostly to the elder one (who spoke willingly), that I had under my eyes a striking contrast between art and nature; for Berthelot was all art, polished, finished (in every sense of the term), back from everything, having seen all there was to see at the most refined salons in Paris, and of the most exquisite porcelain pieces of Peking so that his spirit, having gone beyond the contrary poles of good and evil, seemed to have collapsed within itself, like a Buddha all quiet, falling curves; while Léger was all nature, so that at his mere aspect and presence one felt that his experience came straight from the earth, rocks, trees and waters; and while I knew nothing yet about his love of the sea, I was haunted by I don't know what sense of fluidity in his motions that reminded me of the rhythm of the waves.

That is perhaps why their contrast remained just as strong in the intellectual field. Berthelot had a dazzling intellect which fused at every one of his words in or out of season: not in the least the vivacity of a mere conversation-master, but the force of a mind whose ideas, under their scintillating surface, revealed a substantial thought that had to be respected; while Léger never said anything striking, nothing that would draw one astray from the subject so as to admire the depth of the thought or the art with which it was said. He smiled at his senior's words, perhaps with more affection than admiration, but would offer to the debate nothing but thoughts of a current-looking gait which seemed to fit into it without effort.

I was no longer young enough to be taken in. I felt that this refusal to dazzle sprang from a solid intellect, and I endeavoured to fathom its sense and quality in the depth of the two wide windows from which it was watching me. Grave, I thought, these eyes are grave. And that was, I do believe, the essence of this choice soul: a kind of gravity in depth, not in the least put out by witty words, that accepts and even enjoys humour, yet remains proudly aloof from it. An earnest mind. Of course, by no means naïve. Too penetrating for naïvety, too earnest to allow itself to be rocked, too interested to let go when precious things are exposed to the hazards of an error of judgement or of a too trusting heedlessness. Too grave a spirit, in one word, to dodge the insistence of a real case through mere playfulness.

How often, later, when the flow of events brought us together, he as Secretary General at the Quai, I as Spanish Ambassador in Paris, how often have I remembered this contrast I had once guessed, between art and nature. We were no longer playing a subtle game of chess, but dealing with floods, deluges and earthquakes; henceforth, events would demand that the men who would have to affront them should possess eyes, brains, hearts fit no longer for the mere study but for the seas and the continents.

These vast perspectives, though, that were to open wide for the world the marvels of his poems, the young diplomat never mentioned them; nor did he even betray his care for them in the serenity of his day to day work. In his positive, clear, definite style, as expressed from his haircut to the shape of his shoes, Léger remained the Secretary General of the Ministry of Foreign Affairs. Correctness, exactitude, competence, those were his virtues, which he would not advertise but live, well, yes, he did one day talk to me in his official room, at his desk, of the prosodic shortenings due to a lack of feeling for vowels in the poems of a famous novelist who believed himself to be a poet; but we had by then completed our survey of the interpretation Spain gave to Article 16 of the Covenant.

One man, though, realised all that the young diplomat could contribute to the bureaucratic craft of the past from his sense of greatness, of nature, of the sea; who saw that Léger understood, better still, felt, lived the anguish of an international community in travail. Aristide Briand was the ideal minister for Léger, just as Léger was the ideal Secretary General for Briand. They felt at one as soon as they saw each other. This happened, in fact, on board a ship on the Potomac. Briand was also an artist, as every true statesman is, a poet of politics, a sculptor of peoples, a mind capable of seizing irrationality. And had fate caused him to be born ten years later, Europe might have been spared Hitler, and Léger, exile.

Our relations were always cordial, indeed, a true comradeship. The only incident between us was caused by what I considered an official duty on my part. I had an appointment with him at the Quai, and he made me wait an hour. On the dot of the sixtieth minute, I wrote a note: 'S. de M. would wait for you for years; but the Spanish Ambassador cannot wait for more than an hour.' And I left. He was a master at solving these situations, less because of his diplomacy than because of his personal gifts.

We could see the comic side of things in very much the same way; and

I remember one day when I was in the Chair at the Council and he sat not at the Council but close to me and to his chief: we had been for hours engaged in a tedious debate leading nowhere; and I scribbled for him a Spanish proverb, rather obscene, I am afraid, on patience, an elephant and an ant. He suggested that I pass it on to Eden. I frowned hard. As we went out, I told him that at the Paris Conference, as I knew from a first hand witness, Orlando ruined his relationship with Lloyd George by depositing in his hand a beautifully carved coral, carved in the shape of a phallus. The exquisite perfection of the carving was powerless to moderate the indignation of the Welshman's puritanism, and what Orlando had meant as a gift (English sense) turned into a gift (German sense) and poisoned his relation with the Italian chief delegate.

We did not always see eye to eye. Browsing in my old files, I have come across a paper I sent to Madrid on an interview I had with him (August 27, 1932) when he was still Director of Political and Commercial Affairs, mostly on our plan for a visit of Herriot to Spain, on which I shall return later. We talked of a number of things that day, and in particular of one he felt very strongly about: his point of departure was the need for a coalition of Western democratic nations, namely, Britain, France, Spain and the U.S. to oppose to the Italo-German coalition, since this group sought to rearm and possibly go to war.

From this basis, Léger went on to propound the doctrine that Spain should henceforth take on a big power rôle in Europe, sharing the responsibilities of international power, which, in his view, were the true basis of the political, moral and even financial credit of a country. I could not agree with him on this view, for more than one reason, though I did not think I was called upon to say so either to him or to my Government. I was persuaded that Spain did not possess the where-withal to play the part of a great power; nor did I believe that the great powers could be trusted to act for world peace without a close watch on their deeds and misdeeds. I did, though, point out to Léger that in a wholly spontaneous and natural way, Spain had struck up comradeship and solidarity with the Scandinavians, the Dutch and the Swiss; and in the course of time, it was with this group (adding to it the Belgians and the Czechs) that we worked in Geneva until I ceased to be Spanish Delegate.

CHAPTER XV

BETWEEN FASCISTS AND COMMUNISTS

LENIN'S and Mussolini's apparent success in stabilising their regimes had been achieved in spite and possibly because of their contempt for liberal-democratic institutions, chief of all, parliament. Their success brought about a rash of anti-liberal movements in France, whose positive ideals or ideas were apt to be vague and woolly but whose manner was uniformly and monotonously violent. Finding by experience that their heads were not much use to them, they assumed that those of their adversaries were equally expendable. In France they took sonorous names such as *Solidarité Française, Jeunesses Patriotes, Francistes*, all outdone by the *Croix de Feu*, a name which tried to bring back the attention of public opinion to the dead of the First World War. It is never pleasant, though it may be sweet and honourable, to die for one's country; but one of the most unsavoury aspects of this is to have your name exploited by the bounders of the next generation. Honour to the Englishman (who was he?) who wrote: 'Patriotism is the last refuge of scoundrels.'

It was from this magma of opinion fermenting under the influence of fascist communism and communist fascism, that the heroes of the battle of the Trocadero had sprung and had drawn their fighting spirit; and, while ready to counterattack (as described above) with more spirit than wisdom, I felt in my passion for objectivity, that there must have been something the matter with liberal democracy when so many sectors of opinion, right and left, rose against it, and some even succeeded, as in Russia and in Italy. In short, I put a minus sign to the Spanish proverb ('There must be something in water since priests do bless it'): there must be something wrong in liberal democracy when so many people curse it.

A critical look at our political faith was imperative. I have been at it since then, and have even written two of my books on this theme on which I still have the text of two speeches I delivered in 1933. I found that our way of talking about liberal democracy was misleading, for liberty is the very core of our faith, while democracy is a mere method; and this led me to a firm conviction: we would have to struggle against both the right and the left.

In my inquiry, I avoided books and sought my thoughts in experience and meditation. 'You write your books out of your own head!' a well-

known socialist intellectual cried out to me once. He got most of his out
of books. I do not – how could I? – disdain what a good head (his was)
can get out of other heads through books; but that is not, and never
was, my way; for in the picturesque words of Ortega, Spaniards are apt
to be 'adamic', i.e. they look at the world direct, just as Adam did,
before any learning began. You may like it or not. It yields considerable
advantages. Adamic thought is fresh, spontaneous, new, untrammelled
by previous notions. The practice of it, though, is also dangerous. It
may lead, and it does now and then, to what we call in Spain 'discovering the Mediterranean'. On the other hand, the way of the scholar does
now and then induce an erudite mind to place the Mediterranean at the
North Sea. If err I must, I prefer my own errors to those of others.

Political philosophy cannot claim to be a science leading to permanent conclusions unless these conclusions are rediscovered after an
analysis of the *present* form of life. It is this rediscovery at every epoch
that bestows on them their permanent character. Furthermore, such
words as 'freedom' or 'democracy' did not mean the same to Aristotle,
St Thomas Aquinas, Montesquieu or Herbert Spencer, still less to us.
Not to speak of Lenin or Mao. Such are the reasons whereby, after the
event, I justify that my inquiry into liberty and democracy was live and
not bookish. For as to its being so, well, it was so.

The first of these two speeches was addressed in Madrid to a gathering of intellectuals of many countries. It had been organised by the
Committee of Arts and Letters of the League of Nations, of which I was
a member, and it was presided over by Madame Curie. We sat in an elegant hall the Students' Residence of Madrid had built as a theatre for
their shows, concerts, lectures; since then transmogrified into a chapel.
It had been beautifully decorated by the simple addition of a superb
Flemish style tapestry from the Spanish Manufactures. And under that
wonderful witness of the permanent and universal value of beauty, we
argued, irritated and provoked by the presence of two Fascists and
two Nazis, forced down our throats by their respective governments
(though, in theory, governments had nothing to do with the selection of
the persons who came to our meetings).

It was to this gathering of minds, all but the Italian and German contingents, first-rate European minds, that I developed my criticisms of
our liberal democracy, and the reasons why I felt it necessary to insist
on the essential – and not merely functional – value of liberty. Opposite
me, across the narrow table, I could see and feel the barrage of the two
Nazis and the two Fascists: and the Devil tempted me to add a quip
(which I confess I have often re-stated since): 'The dictator' I was going

to say . . . I remembered I was an Ambassador, and I said: 'The tyrant is not necessarily a foe to liberty. On the contrary, the tyrant is so ardent a friend of liberty that, not content with his own, he grabs that of everybody else. He is the man who loves liberty above everything else. He is a kind of Don Juan of liberty, and once this idea has been grasped, many a political phenomenon becomes clear.'

While I spoke, I could see the two Nazi and the two Fascist faces grow more and more sombre; and while I spoke further, (for the remark I have quoted turned up before I was half way through) I could see, indeed hear, that our four totalitarian guests were definitely worried. It was obvious to me, as it was obvious to everyone else, that what worried them was what would be the reaction at home; not precisely of the two dictators, who probably would not even hear of the incident and if they did would not care a farthing what I said; but of the chums with more gold braid, who would, of course, be waiting for them round the corner, if only to make them pay for a pleasant trip to a pleasant land well known for its hospitality; and sure enough, on the next day, one each, a Nazi and a Fascist, asked to speak before the day's agenda began, and explained (without mentioning me) that they had understood the reference to 'a tyrant' made in a speech the previous day not to refer at all to any Chief of State or of Government actually in office at the time. I was, of course, in my seat, less than three feet away from them and facing them; I did not ask to speak.

About half a year went by, and I had to face another somewhat similar situation. I had been booked by the Centre d'Etudes de la Révolution Française to speak for them on November 25th of that year (1933); and when I arrived at the Sorbonne, where my lecture was to take place, I found it in a hubbub. It was obvious that there was considerable interest in the lecture, both among the 'progressives', who wished to manifest their goodwill towards our Republic, and among the fascists, whose aim was exactly the reverse. Amidst the officials who received me at the street entrance, I detected members of the police, not all in uniform. The proceedings, though, despite one or two attempts at disorder, were peaceful enough, possibly because the way I dealt with the subject kept the brains of both sides too busy for mischief; for I tried to analyse the century and a half gone since the French Revolution precisely from the only point of view common to both sides – what was wrong with the result?

First the confusion between democracy as an end and democracy as a means. 'The citizen disposes neither of the intellect nor of the information he needs to tackle the problems of collective life'; then the growing power of the technician, and therefore, of the permanent heads of the departments of the State. I then pointed out that Lenin had bestowed a leftish prestige to tyranny, which until then had always come from the extreme right, so that since Lenin, every dictator, no matter whence he came, had tried to 'cover' himself by assuming socialist views. Their relative popularity was due mostly to the inability of liberal-democratic governments to deal with economic problems beyond their means to solve.

Then, why not follow the countries that have abjured from the conquests of the French Revolution, notably individual freedom? Precisely because of the unique value of freedom. 'All these new regimes condemn democracy, condemn the parliamentary system – but it is freedom they execute.' And I went on to conclude that we had to seek a remedy to our collective ills not in mechanics, for our societies could not be machines, but in biology.

Strangely enough, those fascists who listened to me, had they been sincere, would have grasped this possibility for at least a dialogue. But they lacked the sincerity – and I suspect, also the ability – to fathom what I was driving at; and all they wanted was to bray some slogans and exercise their muscles. So, when the lecture was over, the police quietly advised me to leave by a back door. I didn't like this very much. We left by the front door. Aguinaga, my Counsellor, told his wife to go home in their car, and came with me in the embassy car. Nothing happened.

While I thus argued with the fascists now in public now in private, I was carrying on an off-and-on argument with the most authoritative exponent of Communism I could find: Rosenberg, who for a long time led the Russian Embassy though only as its *chargé d'affaires*. This man's charm was all concentrated in his face, which was luminous, open, friendly and, I thought, sincere. Otherwise, his body was small and misshapen. He was supremely intelligent and always as ready for an argument as if he were a true Scot, instead of a Russian Jew. We had innumerable discussions on Marxism.

But we had another argument. I wanted a fur coat. He heard me or somebody else say something about it and offered to get the skins for it in Russia. I accepted. The skins came and they were so good I still possess the second of the two coats I had successively made from them; but, in straight infringement of the explicit condition I had laid down for allowing him to offer his services in this matter, he would not accept payment. I had to tell him in all earnestness that unless he took a cheque for the normal trade cost, I should send back the stuff to the embassy; and he then agreed.

So, though we were on excellent terms and I even enjoyed his company, this incident made me test his cunning and his stubbornness; and I was the less surprised when, during our civil war, I was told that Rosenberg, appointed Ambassador to Spain, had incurred the anger of Largo Caballero to such a fiery intensity that he very nearly perished when Largo threatened to throw him out of the window.

CHAPTER XVI

THE TRAGI-COMEDY OF DISARMAMENT

'I am wearing off the steel of the rails between Paris and Geneva with the weight of my body', I wrote to one of my successive Foreign Secretaries during those days when I had to be both *de facto* Chief Delegate in Geneva and in fact Ambassador in Paris. It happened to me to leave a Commission in the middle of a discussion on the reduction of armaments in order to battle by telephone on a reduction of the quota for Spanish new potatoes in France; and if the phone pow-wow failed, I had to go in for a night of sleep in the train to fight it out in Paris. This was always bad, but never worse than during the Disarmament Conference which began in February 1932 and outlasted my stint at the Paris embassy.

I had got busy preparing our delegation as soon as I knew the Conference had been fixed for good. I was determined to have Azaña himself (then Prime Minister) as our chief Delegate. I was certain he would be a great success; I thought this success would be beneficial for the Republic in more ways than one. It was by no means easy to win him over, but in the end, he did take it on. Unfortunately, he was not able to come. Considering my record in such matters, I had to take upon myself to head the delegation.

I did, however, take care to choose for it the best men I could find in as many fields as possible; not merely because that Conference would call on the services of many good men in the country, but because I felt I had to dispel any idea that I wished to keep League affairs for myself; and so I got the ministry to appoint among other lesser-known names Luis Araquistain and Américo Castro, two men of letters both ex-Ambassadors. In agreement with the opinion of other delegations, ours (for practical purposes, Oliván and I) thought that the Conference would be long and would split into numerous committees needing a number of delegates. I will say at once, to get this subject out of the way, that most of my nominees deserted us, finding the work too exacting or too boring or both.

Paul-Boncour (and intermittently Tardieu) came for France and Simon for Britain. Henderson presided. A nicer, kinder, better-meaning man it would have been hard to find. One less apt for the job, either. A socialist leader who read the lesson at Sunday services of his particular brand of religion (which I forget) to pit against a socialist atheist like Paul-Boncour or an over-super-developed cynic like Grandi or Scialoja, was delightful for the dramatist or the psychologist, less so for the politician or the Europeist. However, such are the vagaries of political life.

My old friend Litvinov came for the Soviet Union. His game was not then very clear, not even, perhaps, for him. He had to prove to his master, the formidable Stalin, that his policy would deliver the goods. His policy was to keep on good terms with Britain, France and the United States, and, therefore, to back the League, in order to prevent a German aggression to the Soviet Union; and he knew that, if the goods were not delivered, i.e. if a German aggression remained a possibility, his, Litvinov's, political life would be at an end – and his actual life perhaps also.

Litvinov was a pre-Stalin bolshevik. There was a sincerity in him no longer to be found in later generations – that of the infamous Vishinsky or the hypocritical Kossygin or the brutal Brezhnev. When he was worried he showed it, and he was very worried indeed at the time of the Saar Plebiscite. He hoped against hope that the plebiscite would be won by the French; and he kept asking the opinion of his circle of Western acquaintances on what the outcome would be. I told him I felt certain that the Germans would win by an almost unanimous vote.

Why shouldn't they? There was no reason whatever why the Saarlanders should feel less German than the Ruhrlanders or the men of any other valley. Indeed, if one compared them to the men of Alsace and Lorraine, the contrast was striking. These latter, so often transferred from Germany to France and vice versa, were Germans who wanted to be French. Force was the agent that altered their official nationality in both directions; but in one case, westwards, force liberated them, while in the other, eastwards, it enslaved them just because they felt it so; while in the Saar case, everybody knew that France did not want the land for its men but for its coal. Why should the men of the Saar want to remain French? The more logical the argument, the more it worried Litvinov; and he often aired his concern by discussing the German menace in that steel and glass Peace factory that the League architects had erected next door to the old building, walking to and fro in the spacious hall so aptly known in French as *La Salle des Pas Perdus*.

Most of us knew that nearly all our steps there would be lost. Litvinov could have no illusion as to his own sensational step at the very beginning of the Conference. This was no less than a proposal for a total and immediate disarmament by everybody. He was, of course, far too shrewd not to see through his own plan; and the embarrassed silence of the big power delegates must have proved to him that the passion of the Soviet Union for propaganda stunts had this time put her and him in a somewhat ridiculous position. Since none of the stars of first magnitude would ask to speak, I did so, but Politis, an older man, had put his name down first.

He was superb as usual. With steel-like clarity, he showed that the Soviet proposal was impracticable. He made an unanswerable refutation of the plan. But what I had in mind was quite different. I felt the situation would not be met by a merely intellectual debate, for such a debate would lose most of its impact on leaving that hall towards the wider spaces outside. Something alive and dramatic was necessary, an apologue and a gesture. And it was thus to an apologue and a gesture that I devoted my speech.

I acknowledged the apologue 'to a distinguished British Statesman' meaning Churchill, (though I was many years later told that it turns up in the eighteenth century) and told it thus: the animals decided to disarm and so they met in conference. The bull, eyeing the eagle, advocated the clipping of wings to a minimum size; the eagle, fixing the lion, proposed that all claws should be cut down; the lion staring at the elephant, demanded that all tusks should be filed off or extracted; and the elephant, winking at the bull, said something about horns; whereupon the bear came forward and demanded that all weapons of every kind whatever should be done away with, so that nothing remained but a fraternal hug.

The effect was electric. The hall was shaken by a storm of laughter. '*La salle est dans la joie*' wrote a Parisian journalist to his paper. Litvinov himself laughed heartily, but I stood waiting, for after the apologue, the gesture was still to come. So I went on to make it quite clear that armaments were a costly nuisance, that nations kept armed because they feared war; that it was no use whatever to try to make them give them up while their fear persisted; and that, therefore, the true way to disarm was to organise a world government. 'So, my friend,' I added turning to Litvinov, 'stop talking disarmament and begin talking about the Soviet Union joining the League.'

When Litvinov rose to speak the effect of his sensational offer had evaporated, and he knew it; so he pointed out how surprised he was that the Spanish Delegate invited the Soviet Union to join the League when the Spanish Republic had not yet recognised the Soviet Union. In a brief retort, I put it to Litvinov that one begins by inviting new acquaintances to one's club before asking them for a meal at home. This was readily and joyously accepted by the audience; but it really was a poor answer, as Araquistain rightly pointed out to me; for my retort should have been that it was for the Soviet Union, being the older regime of the two, to recognise the Spanish Republic, and not the other way about.

Now that I recall the event, Litvinov's mistake strikes me as odd. It was so obvious that the initiative for recognition should have come from Moscow and not from Madrid that the case seems to require some attention. Litvinov was shrewd as well as intelligent. Two circumstances may have influenced him: one is that the Soviet Union had not been recognised by the Spanish Monarchy; the other, that the Soviet Union had not been recognised yet by a number of nations. It is idle to speculate on what would have happened if the Soviet Union had unilaterally declared that it recognised the Spanish Republic. My guess is that the Spanish Republic would have taken it as a compliment. Furthermore, it is worth recalling that recognition of the Soviet Union by the League preceded recognition by quite a number of League members; so that my quip about 'lunching at the Club' was well founded on League facts.

The Conference might laugh but the occasion was by no means to be faced lightheartedly. Nothing sums it up better than this fact: the opening meeting had to be postponed for an hour because the Council were meeting on the grave China crisis then at its worst in Shanghai. Britain was confronted with one of her worst financial and monetary crises; Germany was beginning to feel the effect of her worst fever of insane nationalism; and Japan was defying the League under the unsympathetic and distant eyes of the U.S.; while France, ill at ease because of the growing German threat, was in the throes of the Stavisky financial scandal.

The long years – seven at least – during which we had been hard at work discovering how not to disarm, when subjects such as 'how many angels could be poised on the point of a bayonet' very nearly came within our competence, all that castle of paper collapsed; and the nations, which until then found nothing but ifs and buts in every plan put forward, faced now with a Conference of sixty States, hurried to prepare plans, yes, plans, for disarmament. Even Litvinov, after his sword stroke on the water of the lake, would have produced something less nonsensical. He didn't. Perhaps he remembered what had happened in 1928 at the Preparatory commission when he presented his proposal: 'What do you think', he asked me. 'Will they reject it?' – 'Oh no!' I answered. 'They'll do much worse. They will consider it very carefully.'

That is exactly what they did with the plan presented by Tardieu, then first delegate as Minister of War (and later as Prime Minister). The chief trouble was, of course, political. The Germans wanted their *gleichberechtigung*. They felt they had been pariahs long enough; the French stood on the letter of the Treaty of Versailles and insisted on the

Germans being kept locked into it. Tardieu's plan was, *à la française*, as strong on security as on disarmament. Simon was keen on discriminating between defensive and offensive weapons, to which I objected that the very paragon of defensive weapons, a shield, could be used as an offensive weapon and even to kill a man with; while a rifle could be used as a defensive weapon and to parry a thrust with. 'Tanks should not be too big,' the British insisted. 'What is too big?' someone asked. And Simon: 'Let's not define and be theoretical. I can't define an elephant but I can tell one if I see it.' 'Can you tell a whale?' I asked. This was no mere banter. The British and American delegations held that a battleship was a defensive, a submarine an offensive weapon; while the French delegation held that both were defensive, which was even more objective and impartial. Everyone came determined to leave stronger than he had arrived, *relatively to his adversary*. Brüning, always cautious and conciliatory, insisted on German equality, but he declared himself ready to attain it by others coming down to the German level – which was precisely the French view; only he meant business. 'All you need do', he preached, 'is freely to adopt the limitations, in number and size, that you have laid down for us at Versailles.' Grandi, for Italy, backed this plan, which proves that he or his government considered it a good idea in order to make Italy relatively stronger than it was then.

CHAPTER XVII

THE HARD REALITIES OF DISARMAMENT

BY February 24th, when the general debate was closed, some of the more optimistic observers were beginning to wonder whether, at last, something might happen – which in fact meant less disarmament than satisfaction of the German claim. This, again, was inevitable, since it amounted to a natural transformation of disarmament issues into political issues; just as a knock on the eye gets transfigured into light. It was doubtful, though, that even if Japan's bellicose policy and Hitler's threat had not been in the way, such an achievement could have been within our reach. At any rate, we had to adjourn, for the special sitting of the Assembly to deal with Japan had been called for March 3rd. The Conference went into Committees.

When this work began I found that the Secretariat had reserved for me the chairmanship of the Budget Committee. I talked to Aghnides, my predecessor and successor as head of the Disarmament Section, and made it clear: 1, that I was not asking for any presidency; 2, that if I was to take one I could only accept that of the Air Committee. He was surprised at my choice. I was surprised at his surprise. It seemed to me evident that the true battles of the future would be air battles; while I was not good at budgets and budgets were nothing but lies anyhow.

Even for Air affairs, though, the work was, of course, tedious because it was hopeless. If we were to go anywhere worth the trip, it should have meant total abolition of air warfare; but this aim, in its turn, demanded that for which I worked for years in vain: a world civil flying administration, or, in other words, only one air line for the whole world. My argument was that supervision was openly based on mistrust, while peace could only rest on trust: so that, if we developed a team of 40 to 50,000 pilots and mechanics of all nations, all working for the same line, their brotherhood would have been sufficient to ensure that not a single plane could be diverted to nefarious deeds. I still think that nothing in this plan would have been beyond the reach of men of common sense. The air was a new element, common to all, and we ought to have kept it clean from our murderous ways.

I was later to discover that one of the chief obstacles in the way was the belief held by the powers that be in the U.S. that world air traffic would bring them more profit if left in private hands. The story will be told in due time, but meanwhile, the point deserves some attention.

As a liberal, I believe that a wide sector of economic (as well as of every other kind of) activity must be left in private hands; but I also believe that, for this private initiative to yield its best results, it must move within a framework of collective ownership, power and responsibility. For over forty years, this has been my stand, in not only national but also international affairs.

There are economic activities that should no longer be left in private or even in national hands. One of them is oil; another one is armaments; the third one is air-navigation. I can think of a longer list; but I should be content with having this passed. The incidence of private ownership, on oil production, transport and trade on world affairs has been disastrous throughout our century; the history of the manufacture of and traffic in armaments is a shame on all of us; and, while in the days I was busy with these matters, nations were shamefaced about it, they have now-a-days grown utterly shameless, and openly vie with each other in the arming of nations that should be spending their money on bread. As for aviation, I feel certain that the untold misery mankind – and in particular, Europe – has suffered in the Second World War could have been spared us, and even that war itself, if an Air Convention such as I suggested in 1932, had been achieved, outlawing air warfare and organising a single world air line – two faces of the same plan.

The political conjuncture was not favourable and the men in power in the big countries were not big enough. The inexorable law of all disarmament activity, that it automatically turns into an armament activity, held full sway over our Conference. The smaller powers were left to stand and watch as a chorus, often inactive and dumb, while the big powers pow-wowed in secret over their guns, aircraft and navies. These secret talks were not remarkable for statesmanship. It was obvious that in Germany the only alternative to a Nazi regime was the mild, moderate yet firm regime offered by Chancellor Brüning. He seized the opportunity afforded him by Stimson and Ramsay Mac-Donald in April 1932 to put to them plans which the two Anglo-Saxon statesmen were able to accept. But Tardieu pleaded illness and an election campaign; and this defeat abroad sealed Brüning's fate at home. On May 30th, President Hindenburg dismissed him and brought in Von Papen, who turned out to be but Hitler's usher.

Herriot who succeeded Tardieu would have been more amenable; but by then, the German case was in not only harder but less trustworthy hands. Secret talks went on between Herriot, MacDonald and Gibson, with Simon and Paul-Boncour thrown in. Progress was slow, if any. Suddenly, on June 22nd, Henderson received what amounted to an order to call a plenary meeting: the U.S. had had an idea. All offensive weapons to be scrapped and the rest reduced by a third. Air bombing was to be forbidden.

Grandi dramatically accepted the plan in a sensational speech. This of course started people thinking, even those, and they were many, who had accepted the idea at its face value. The Germans were pleased. The French pointed out that it would force them to disarm just when Germany was becoming dangerous. Japan rejected the idea. This idea, though well meant, was too elementary; and in any case, it overlooked the primacy of politics over armaments. What was then necessary was not physically to disarm the French but morally to disarm the Germans. After so many weeks, the quintet of mountains had given birth to a *ridiculus mus*; and the lesser powers were getting restive. If at least the big ones had delivered the goods, their arrogance and bad manners – even towards our President Henderson – would have been forgiven; but failure can hardly be allowed any claims.

I must quote Walters: 'The smaller powers were indignant, not only at having had to wait so long without a public meeting, but also at realising that an initiative from which they had hoped so much, had been frustrated before they had been able to say a word in its support. They found a spokesman in Salvador de Madariaga, who had been head of the Disarmament Section of the Secretariat during the first six years of its existence, and had written a wise and brilliant book on the subject. As Spanish delegate both to the Council and the Conference, Madariaga was allowed an unusually free hand and effectively laid bare the shortcomings of Britain, France, and even the United States on many occasions when others who agreed with him did not venture to speak. A number of European States – Belgium, Czechoslovakia, Denmark, Norway, Sweden, the Netherlands, and Switzerland – joined with Spain in forming a group based on the common conviction that the Conference could only succeed by keeping affairs in its own hands, and that it would be fatal to leave disarmament once more to be discussed in secret conversations among the great powers. But they could do nothing to restart the machine: and they had no intention of creating a crisis by pushing their protests too far.'

A wishy-washy resolution was hammered out by the joint efforts of Simon and Beneŝ. It pleased no one, though it settled nothing and cleared nothing. It was voted (July 23, 1932) by forty-one States, most of them disgruntled and depressed. Litvinov declared that he 'voted for disarmament but against the resolution'. Why 'but' I asked him later. Why not 'and therefore'? That 'but' gave him away as the showman he was or rather was made to be, for, though a communist, Litvinov was sincere enough. Italy had withdrawn Grandi, too intelligent for fascism, and sent Balbo, who made up with arrogance what he lacked in brains. He made a defiant speech to explain that he would not vote – rather a blunt point for so heavy a sword. As for Germany, she declared through Nadolny that, since equality was not conceded by her ex-victors she would not come again. The hardest that can be said, and it can be said, of the ex-victors of the First World War is that they had managed to put Germany in the right.

The Conference then went underground. The big powers began a phase of negotiations devoted to the problem that worried them most: Germany's demand for equality in armaments. The Treaty of Versailles had lost its magic for Germany, i.e. she simply would not hear about it; and that was that. Mussolini, now Foreign Secretary as well as everything else, backed the Germans. The French, under Herriot, were no longer convinced of their own ability to keep it alive, though of course they went on invoking it; the British under MacDonald and Simon, much to Vansittart's disgust, were inclined to bow to the inevitable rise of German force; and the Americans were very far away and, in any case, busy with choosing a new President who turned out to be Franklin Roosevelt. This meant Norman Davis, a debonair chatterbox and little more.

These were the pundits who drove the Conference underground, and they were churlish enough to keep Henderson out of their tractations. These tractations were laborious, and futile. For by then Germany was no longer ready to talk in earnest, but only so as to erect a screen of words for her warlike designs. There was, of course, agreement on a form of words (December 11, 1932) meant to brush aside the Treaty of Versailles and its smaller brothers; Germany got her equality and everybody was, or professed to be, satisfied. In the usual fashion, the League members other than the Powers were asked to ratify what had been done without them, and a plenary session of the Conference (December 14, 1932) did so not without grumbling, and a demand that any future negotiations would include the President of the Conference. This done, we adjourned to January 31, 1933. The League was sinking and the river of events was rising around its fragile structure.

CHAPTER XVIII

SOUTH AMERICAN CONFLICTS

A S if the duties of my Paris embassy, the Manchurian Crisis and the Disarmament Conference were not enough to break a man's back, I had to take a prominent share in the troubles caused by two conflicts within our own Hispanic kith and kin; one that led to the Chaco war between Bolivia and Paraguay (1932–35) and the other between Peru and Colombia over Leticia (1932–34). It is one of the mysteries of human nature that countries that share a common language, culture and history, such as those of Spanish America, should be able to find motives for dissension and even war, which they have to seek in territorial issues, although territory is for all of them the widest, cheapest and often most useless of their assets.

In this, as in every other aspect of their lives, the countries of Spanish America are too proud to shake off their responsibility on the foreigner. Sovereignty and responsibility for one's actions are but two sides of the same coin. But a detailed and concrete study of the finances of the Spanish American states would reveal that a good deal of the responsibility for this state of affairs weighs on the shoulders of the armament industry, actively aided and abetted by the national authorities of the manufacturing nations concerned.

One of the most scandalous facts soon revealed as the Chaco conflict drew the attention of public opinion to the two contending parties was that, while neither Bolivia nor Paraguay could devote nearly enough money to education and welfare, nor even, indeed, to paying their League subscriptions, they lavished millions to acquire armaments, precisely during the period that elapsed between the first flare up of the conflict in 1928 and the second crisis in 1932, that led to the war between them. Now, this period had been, so to speak, 'administered' by a so-called Neutral Commission, composed of the heads of missions in Washington, of Colombia, Cuba, Mexico and Uruguay, with Mr Francis White, of the State Department, in the chair; and this Mr White proved such an excellent Christian that his right hand, busy blessing peace efforts in South America, never knew how busy his left hand was pushing the selling of American weapons to the two future belligerents. (I am by no means suggesting that Mr White personally profited by this game, but I do say that he certainly knew it was going on.) That the British, the French, the Swiss and a bunch of other peoples were doing just the same only shows how much admired and imitated the U.S. are in the world; but then, these other States had not bethought themselves of the Monroe Doctrine as the way to lead the New World to peace, freedom and the pursuit of happiness.

President Wilson had. And he saw to it that this famous instrument of American Policy got its safe shrine in the temple of the Covenant, to wit: 'Article 21. Nothing in the Covenant shall be deemed to affect the validity of international engagements, such as treaties of arbitration or regional understandings like the Monroe Doctrine for securing the maintenance of peace.' Now, that wording was rather neat for it was tantamount to saying: 'No vegetarian shall be deemed to be bound to reject as proper food such well known vegetables as ham or chicken.' Who had told President Wilson that the Monroe Doctrine was a 'regional understanding'? It had never been negotiated or discussed with, still less by the Spanish American nations. It was laid down by the U.S. as the Law of the Continent on a take it or leave it basis. All President Wilson could have meant by 'understanding' was that every South American nation understood quite well what was afoot, and knew how to swallow its saliva when unable to spit.

At any rate, there is little doubt that the Chaco conflict owed most of its intractability to the Monroe Doctrine. Much, no doubt, was also contributed by its two protagonists, ever ready to fly at each other's throats, and by the peculiar character of their respective delegates in Geneva. One of them, Caballero de Bedoya, who spoke for Paraguay, was stiff and unyielding, and tried to play the U.S. against the League, by keeping aloof and away from Geneva when not officially wanted; while the other one, the Bolivian, Costa du Rels, was a thorough European, who spoke French like a *boulevardier*, and had an unconquerable passion for the somewhat unusual and bookish word *derechef* (once again), to which he owed his nickname of *Monsieur Derechef*. He would have fully deserved it if only because of the number of occasions when, clever and witty though he could be, he made us all begin all over again.

The question whether possession of the vast territory in dispute would have been of any use or profit to either country, neither of which had as yet fully occupied its own territory by a very long length, had better be left as unexplored as the territory itself. It was again a case of the ill-humour causing the quarrel and not the quarrel the ill-humour. By June, the tension between the two trigger-happy forces had grown to such dangerous proportions that both governments wrote letters to the League, and then the conflict of competence and jurisdiction between Geneva and Washington grafted itself on that of territory and prestige between Bolivia and Paraguay.

When the Council met (the Irish Prime Minister Eamon de Valera in the chair) it had to debate both conflicts simultaneously which made matters more complicated; because on the first (Washington versus Geneva) Britain (under Simon) was apt to be cautious and to care far more for the U.S. than for either the League or peace (that local peace at any rate). This attitude went as far as to amount to an actual boycott of the Council by Simon. I argued that the Neutral Commission, the U.S., Argentina and other well-meaning meddlers were but amateurs; for they were not bound to intervene; while the League was the one and only agency bound by law to try to solve the trouble. President de Valera concurred.

The Secretary General (Eric Drummond) as the loyal Englishman he was (being a Scot) found a Pickwickian solution: the League would take the matter up and would prove it by handing it over to the (Washington) Neutral Commission to solve it for us. We, in exchange, would be kept informed by the Commission. We weren't. In matters of procedure, the State Department was as determined to resist the League as Japan was in matters of war or peace. And as successful. By the end of the year, the problem *was* bogged in a morass of well-meaning meddlesomeness, now the Commission, now Argentina, now Brazil. It soon dawned upon me that the preliminary measure for putting things back on the rails of the Covenant might well be a motion requesting the abolition of the Nobel Peace Prize – for that was what more than a Peace-Doctor was after when offering his paper pills.

We had already proposed in the summer the sending of a Commission of Enquiry, but the Neutral Commission had objected. We revived the proposal, strengthened by a Franco-British plan for an embargo on arms. How sincere? The idea was forgotten when a similar plan proposed to the American Senate by President Hoover was rejected by that august chamber – a fresh illustration of the deadly harm done to the League by the separatism of the U.S. Then came the turn of Argentina and Chile to have a go at peace-making; it failed after wasting yet another four months. Bolivia, elated by some military successes, asked for the matter to be sent back to the Neutral Commission, but this time, the Commission, tired of its fruitless efforts, sent it back to us. I felt like retorting in the words of the lover of one of the girls abused by Don Juan:

> You have left the girl impossible
> Both for yourself and for me.

Paraguay then declared war (May 10, 1933), whereupon Bolivia demanded that Article 16 (sanctions) should be applied to the aggressor! This was a new danger: the turning of the Covenant into a comedy for tears or a tragedy for laughter. We of the Council insisted (May 10, 1933) that a Commission should be sent at once to impose an armistice and to draw a frontier.

Though with much quibbling and disputing, both parties agreed, Bolivia all the while preparing an offensive. Hence her refusal to accept the condition, wished by Paraguay, that hostilities should cease – which was pure Covenant doctrine. In the end, the Commission was set up, composed of citizens of Britain, France, Italy and Mexico, and presided over by Alvarez del Vayo. This last had been my choice. As I had led the work of the Council with my friend Seán Lester (a wise and shrewd man and a loyal friend) the Council had readily agreed both to my proposal that the Spaniard should be President, and that this President should be Vayo. I held him then as a good left-wing socialist, honest and intelligent enough. He was later to show an unfortunate trend to follow the Moscow line. This may already have been the case in 1933. If so, I had not noticed it.

Was this appointment wise? I, now, incline to believe that it wasn't. Vayo was good enough for the job. He was a good journalist, a well travelled man and, as a person, thoroughly honest; but brushing aside for the moment his leanings towards communism, he was a Spaniard. Now, we in Geneva knew perfectly well that there was a hard core of men in the State Department who considered the whole Continent as a preserve for the U.S. and that the Monroe Doctrine was meant to act as a poster: PRIVATE – TRESPASSERS WILL BE PROSECUTED. In the circumstances therefore, it might have been more tactful to have selected a president from another nation.

These considerations might well explain the eleventh-hour manoeuvre that was sprung on us that summer, when the Commission was at last ready to start. The two belligerents, at the same time and in the same words, requested the Council to hand the conflict back to the four South American powers, and that, meanwhile, the Commission should wait. Walters writes: 'It was never clear who had induced the two belligerents to agree on this strange course of action. The Council could not refuse a request which they put forward in concert. Yet the neighbouring powers seemed far from willing to accept the new mandate and on September 30th, after some exchanges of correspondence between themselves and Bolivia and Paraguay, informed the Council that they must decline it.'

Now this is very much like the opacity of an opal or mother-o'-pearl, in that it beams with side-lights. Who could have provided the initial impulse for such a joint and simultaneous move on the part of the belligerents? Not they, for they were not all that agreed to produce the same plan at the same time; not, of course, the Council; not the four

South American powers, for they rejected it. Therefore, the move came from the State Department. Which floor, which desk? That is another matter. But it is practically certain that some sexton or priest or acolyte or bishop or cardinal of the Monroe Doctrine thought of this eleventh-hour operation to rescue the sacred text. And this episode may well have been fused by the appointment of a Spaniard to head the Commission.

The net of doctors' rivalries round the patient's bed delayed the departure of the Commission until November 1933. Beyond the difficulty of the task itself, the Commission had to struggle with a change in the military situation in favour of Paraguay, and a meeting of the Pan-american Conference in Montevideo. Though feared by many observers in view of the cool attitude of the U.S.A. and of Brazil, the Conference behaved correctly, adopted a unanimous resolution favourable to the League (December 15, 1933) and received the members of the 'League Commission' with an ovation. This time, however, the League's good work was frustrated by Paraguay, which, elated by military success, rejected the Commission's plan for peace.

The prominent feature of the Commission Report was a courageous denunciation of the traffic in arms which was feeding the war. It is practically certain that this, its healthiest effect, was mostly due to Vayo, for which he deserved full credit. The trouble was that no nation would vote the embargo unless its commercial rivals would also; and this took time. Nor would it have led very far, even with time, if Eden, then in charge of League of Nations affairs, had not taken up the matter. Britain had already proposed such an embargo on February 25, 1933, but 'the Trade' had proved stronger. This time, Eden's resolve, backed by the new President of the Commission of Three, Castillo Nájera (of Mexico), was at last successful, and Roosevelt at last took the plunge, though not without a good deal of splashing. What with 'the Trade' and the laggards, such as Germany and Japan, it was August (1934) before the flow of armaments showed signs of drying up for two belligerents who had begun to fight in 1928, and then had adjourned until 1932 so as to give time to the U.S. and a number of League members to flout the League and make paper-birds with the pages of the Covenant.

The matter went over to the Assembly on Bolivia invoking Article 15. The bigger Spanish American nations were by now coming into line, but the U.S.A. and Brazil were unco-operative. A draft treaty was prepared in Geneva and adopted by the Assembly (November 24, 1934) as a basis for peace. Bolivia agreed. Paraguay carried on the fight. The Assembly voted to lift the arms embargo for Bolivia and not for Paraguay. Then,

Paraguay left the League. The military situation deteriorated for Paraguay, but it was not until the summer of 1935 that the two parties, now
bled and ruined, agreed to talk on the basis of the treaty approved by
the Assembly. The peace Conference, however, met in Buenos Aires
and the Monroe Doctrine was saved.

The conflict between Colombia and Peru (1932–34) is a model of its
kind. It seems to bring together most of the elements that would go
to the making of a theoretically contrived quarrel between nations.

Peru was ruled by a military dictator, a Colonel Sánchez Cerro, endowed with more blood than judgement to a degree unusual even for
dictators. As such, he was prone to see in a conflict outside the borders
of his country a diversion from the all too numerous troubles which
his rule, more energetic than intelligent, was bound to provoke. He
therefore found convenient an incident that just happened at an outlying post of the Peruvian nation on the eastern side of the country, the
port of Iquitos, on the Amazon. By a treaty signed in 1922 and ratified in
1923, Peru had ceded to Colombia the Leticia district, whose importance for Colombia consisted in its possibilities as a port on the Amazon.
The Peruvians of Iquitos, disliking the idea, though Leticia stood 200
miles down the river, sent an armed force, expelled the few (unarmed)
Colombians and took over Leticia. Whether this outrage was committed with or without the connivance of Sánchez Cerro, is not clear;
but, once committed, the dictator found it a good idea: something to
talk about, and a call for sacred unity within.

Lester, who with a Guatemalan delegate and me, was also entrusted
with this issue, while we were already busy with the Chaco affair, sent
cables to the parties, demanding respect for the Covenant (January 14,
1933); but there was no parity between them. The aggressor was Peru;
and Colombia, then under a liberal President, was sending a military
force to occupy a territory which was hers. Peru, however, declared that
Leticia would be defended until a negotiation had settled the issue. This
was the absurd claim of a malevolent and blunt mind.

The difference between the two attitudes was reflected in their delegates. They were equally able, both very able indeed; but Dr Eduardo
Santos, who spoke for Colombia, was a man of outstanding integrity,
whose leadership as President of his country (1938–42) was later to confirm his moral authority over the whole continent, while Francisco
García Calderón, a publicist of note, an intellectual diplomat, was a
cosmopolitan sceptic who resided in France and found no inner
obstacle in serving a rough-hewn dictator such as Cerro, or in defending
such a poor case as that of Leticia. Too clever not to realise that he was

wrong, too honest not to be worried by his own rôle, he should have resigned, but he didn't. He did his best to make Cerro see the light. But Cerro was mentally blind.

The conflict of procedure took a course similar to that which had dogged the Chaco affair. Brazil and the U.S. wanted to mediate. It took some time before they gave up their endeavours and the League Council was able to act unmolested. The Peruvian dictator pushed his country to an aggressive policy, and his aircraft forced the Colombian ships sent to free Leticia from the river to give up their task. Colombia asked for the conflict to be passed on to the Assembly under Article 15. On March 13, 1933, the Council voted that Peru evacuate the Colombian territory she had occupied, as a preliminary to a negotiation on any counter claims. The Assembly adopted this report, against the vote of Peru, and so as to ensure its application, set up a Committee in which the U.S. and Brazil were represented. In open violation of the Covenant, Peru sent a naval squadron through the Panama Canal to sail to Iquitos up the Amazon.

This move could not be tolerated; and the Committee formally requested League members to lend no aid whatsoever to the aggressive squadron. Both Holland (in Curaçao) and Britain (in Jamaica) chose not to comply with this request, alleging various quite valueless pretexts. The Committee was non-plussed; but the Secretary General, Sir Eric Drummond, rose to the full stature of his rôle and wrote a strong letter of rebuke to the two governments concerned. While due credit should be recorded for his exemplary behaviour in this case, the query is obvious: why did he not act with equal energy in other cases such as, for instance, the Chaco one, in which the supply of arms by League members to both parties had been scandalous?

It is, of course, a fact that no two cases are identical; and we must accept the possibility that Drummond felt he could act in the Leticia case as he could not in the Chaco one. He was wisely averse to empty gestures. But the fact remains that if he had felt oftener in that mood, as the World Chancellor so to speak, our history might have been different.

Meanwhile, a League Committee had been sent to Leticia, led by a Spaniard, Major Iglesias, who had explored the region in years past. It was to hold the disputed territory in trust for a time before returning it to Colombia. And so it did, and with the satisfaction of being able to report a year of peace, and enlightened activity under its leadership. As for Peru's acquiescence, it was due to an act of God (if one dares say so without blasphemy): Sánchez Cerro had been murdered (April 30, 1933) and the Peruvian nation returned at once to sanity, so that the League compromise had been agreed upon on May 25, 1933.

CHAPTER XIX

TARDIEU AND HERRIOT

THERE was one line of criticism, among those who disliked my work or me or both, which rested on fact. The Republican Government had landed itself in the same awkward situation the Monarchical Government had contrived: the chief delegate in Geneva and the Ambassador in Paris were one and the same person. The difference between Quiñones de León's way and my way was that he subordinated Geneva to Paris, while I kept the two jobs mutually independent, which in fact worked against the embassy; for big powers demand absolute allegiance from smaller or less powerful ones. I believe I can say with some confidence that I, nevertheless, managed to carry on in Paris with no trouble whatever, mostly for two reasons: my objectivity in substance, and my good personal relations with the leading men in French political life.

I had struck up excellent relations with Tardieu, a man generally considered as aggressive to the edge of violence. Long before I met him as Prime Minister, I had admired his articles in *Le Temps*. This newspaper occupied in France a place not unlike that of *The Times* in London; for it was so eminently identified with the country's interests that its views were often given an official value or significance beyond what actually was the case. This was so more especially in foreign affairs, a subject usually covered in the first column of the first page by a first-class writer. For years, this column had been signed François de Pressensé whose articles I never missed while a student in Paris; his successor had been André Tardieu.

When I had to deal with him as Prime Minister, I knew his mind well because I had missed very few of his remarkable articles; and I found he knew my mind just as well, because he had read my books, notably *Englishmen, Frenchmen, Spaniards*; and, though he knew I did not see quite eye to eye with him, we got on very well. Sometimes, though, I played big stakes; and I will remember his wry face when I told him, in his official room, that I was going to deliver a speech at a gathering of the Federation of French Societies for Peace. His eyebrows went up. 'Well, you see,' I explained, 'I am the President of their Permanent Delegation.' That didn't bring down his eyebrows at all. 'And what are you doing in that galley?' he asked, quoting Molière. We argued a bit, then I concluded: 'My dear President, here is my bet: I shall make a speech they will like and you will also like.' He smiled incredulously.

What I did not tell him was that my own embassy councillor, honest, straight, loyal Aguinaga, had felt exactly the same misgivings on learning of my plan. I did tell Aguinaga of my talk with Tardieu, and so I prepared my speech on the basis of my wager. I had never doubted that I should win; because I knew my Frenchmen. I began by thanking my peace-minded friends for having asked me to speak as an understudy for Briand whom we had recently lost. I then pointed out that the often-mentioned case of the long, undefended frontier between the U.S.A. and Canada was after all but natural since both countries spoke the same language and shared the same civilisation and culture; but a far more remarkable case of an unguarded frontier was that between France and Spain.

And from this I went on to affirm that peace was the ideal of all Frenchmen. The French were a great military people, but not a warlike one. The difference? The warrior wages war on his own; the military submit to a discipline. France, moreover, was an intellectual nation, and the intellectual category *par excellence* was order. Order and peace were therefore typically French categories. The best example: Napoleon. We heard much about Napoleon's conquest of France; not enough about France's conquest of Napoleon. He began as a warrior, making war for the sake of war, he ended declaring: '*War is an anachronism. I had wished to set up a European Union.*'

The problem, then, I went on, was to raise the fact of unity to the awareness of unity; and this was a task for French statesmanship. I paid tribute to Tardieu's own disarmament plan, then being considered in Geneva, and went on to point out that the military genius of France would inevitably lead to the organisation of peace. I described Paris as a city that 'catches the free landscape by means of a net of perspectives'; hence, the hope that France might catch the whole world into a net of new perspectives that would bring out its unity. I described the perspectives north, south, east and west of Cleopatra's needle, the buildings in military order, their 'columns' ready to march, and yet, the name of the meeting point: *Place de la Concorde*; and I ended: 'There is France, mother of ideas, France with her clear eyes and luminous forehead. Her helmet is no longer that of Mars, but that of Minerva. *Là tout n'est qu'ordre et beauté.*'

My peace-minded audience were enthusiastic. I sent a copy to Tardieu. He rang me up: he was very pleased.

During the late spring or early summer of 1932, I happened to be in Geneva, dining with Herriot, no one else present. In one of those outbursts of spontaneity which no diplomatic discipline in me was ever strong enough to repress, I asked him: 'When are you going to Madrid to decorate the President of the Republic with the Legion of Honour?' True, I had more than once mused on this move in which I saw an obvious advantage for our still young republic; but true also, I had never mentioned the matter either in France or in Spain. Herriot was just as spontaneous. 'As soon as we can. And with great pleasure.'

In a letter to Zulueta, then Foreign Secretary (May 27, 1932), I find that Herriot had requested to see me when he was trying to form his Cabinet as Prime Minister designate. He asked me to give him my opinion as to what should be the foreign policy of France, to which I answered that France might envisage a number of tasks: to lead a movement towards world order, since neither of the two Anglo-Saxon nations seemed disposed to do so themselves; to set up during the summer a technical study to endeavour to persuade the world of the failure of acute economic nationalism, thus preparing world opinion for a plan to co-ordinate international economy and finance which he, Herriot, might present to the Assembly in September; to stress the need to strengthen the faith of the political world in the Covenant and in the sincerity of France on disarmament, by changing France's attitude in the Japanese conflict and by backing the Spanish proposal on prohibition of arms manufacture. He asked if, for the carrying out of such a programme, he could count on Spain, and I gave him that assurance.

In the same letter, I reported to Zulueta my talk with the acting Premier Tardieu. I had requested to see him, and the talk was full of interest on a number of points, for Tardieu was a lively man; but I shall only retain here the two points for which I had requested the meeting, a decree already out, whereby our fish preserve imports were to be subject to a special licence and a similar decree being prepared for our imports of bananas. These petty measures were in my way; for it was my hope to bring in a closer connection between the two republics, with a view to consolidating the internal situation of Spain and the European situation of France; and I was aware of the forces that were at work in Spain against such a development.

On August 27, 1932, I had a long talk with Léger. We wasted some time on whether a number of prominent monarchist 'conspirators', led by General Barrera, should be allowed to remain south of the Loire or should be made to live north of it. And I cannot resist the temptation of telling a story about this General Barrera, who was later to be one of the men who solicited Mussolini's help to start the Spanish civil war. While he was still a colonel, he used to live in Tetuan in the same house with a number of other officers one of whom was my father, then also a colonel; and they often argued on the probable outcome of the (first world) war. My father, at a table of about twelve, was the only one who was sure the allies would win; the other eleven, led by Barrera, were sure the German and Austrian empires would win. Then my father sprang a proposal. He and Barrera would exchange papers duly signed and witnessed, allowing the other one to call him a bloody fool if his view turned out to be wrong. We found in my father's papers the sheet signed by Barrera which thus gave him power to call Barrera a bloody fool – which he was – quite apart from my hereditary right to say so.

But to come back to Léger, we were soon discussing Herriot's visit to Madrid. I proposed 5th to 10th September, but Léger assured me that by then Herriot would be sunk deep in the problem of German rearmament, which the German government defined as 'equality in armaments'. Much to my concern, I had to accept an adjournment until October. This point settled, Léger volunteered a limitation of the meaning of the event to two points: an assertion of the mutual cordiality between two countries under similar regimes; and an affirmation of our common way of understanding world problems as the extension to world affairs of our republican principles: open policy; order; peace. I felt all this a little too abstract, so I asked Léger how it would work in a concrete case, whereupon he launched forth into one of those vast pictures he loved (and still loves) to paint, with Germany in the centre, insisting on demolishing the (German) disarmament clauses of the treaty of Versailles using equality as her tool in order to rearm, while France maintained that the right policy was for France and the rest of Germany's ex-enemies to disarm *down to the German level* rather than that Germany should rearm up to theirs. *Only*, who could disarm in view of the state of politics and opinion within Germany?

How about Britain and U.S.A. I asked. He thought the British were just spending the summer away from worries, and in any case, 'waiting and seeing', but that in Washington there was a strong anti-German feeling. My impression was that Léger sought to create a kind of coalition of Britain, France, Spain and U.S.A. to oppose the Italo-German alliance in the matter of armaments, possibly for war. I perceived here the root of Léger's desire to raise Spain to a big power eminence, especially when he put it to me that Mussolini was unable to see international life as it is because he was unable (for security reasons) to leave his country, so 'he saw the world only through a periscope'. This revealed to me that, contrary to Italy's complaint that France paid no attention to her, what really must have been happening was that France solicited Italy's help and Italy didn't 'hear'. Léger did, however, make a point that seemed to me well-founded. Franco-British friendship was not based on the actual texture of Franco-British problems, which, in themselves, were rather an obstacle than a help to their *entente*; but on a common concern for matters of international power.

Léger knew well that I was by no means enamoured of his image of

Spain as a big power, for I preferred to see her inserted in the Scandina-
vian-Dutch-Swiss group, to which, he thought, our country did not
belong. I, nevertheless, kept thinking of my 'tag': 'Spain is an Empire-
builder retired from business.' As I put it to my Foreign Secretary in my
letter, I thought it the more necessary to ascertain Léger's thoughts
on Herriot's visit to Madrid; and I put my conclusions thus:

1. As for concrete responsibilities, France was expecting from Spain
nothing but the fulfilment of the Covenant. For us therefore, this was
less a risk than a limitation of risk.

2. There was no explicit expectation of a direct or indirect military
aid, such as naval protection on passing of troops through Spanish
territory – though it might come to that if the Covenant was fully applied with France on the 'good' side.

3. France expected a moral backing from Spain so as eventually to be
able to oppose the moral authority of the united west to the Fascist-
Nazi cluster.

4. The French were expecting no concrete agreement, joint declaration
or even *communiqué*; but the usual cordial effusions and no more.

CHAPTER XX

SPAIN, A GREAT POWER?

T HIS situation was, on the whole, rather more modest than I should have wished, and risked failure through being too anodine. In Spain, we had to move against a twofold opposition: the more reactionary conservatives would have no dealings with France, first because France was the left, i.e. the Devil incarnate, freemasons and all that; and then because any consolidation of our Republic was anathema to our right; but we had also to struggle against a far more objective statesmanlike and intelligent opposition: that of Azaña and his friends, who, owing to the dismal state of unpreparedness of our forces, saw in every foreign commitment, even under and within the League, a danger to the country.

After all, Azaña, who had never owned or used a weapon in his life, had chosen for himself the Ministry of War. He was an earnest man. He had studied the subject, and found that, under the monarchy, the army had become a noisy, exacting and domineering, but thoroughly inefficient, bureaucracy in uniform. When we spoke of Spain assuming the rôle due to her in world affairs, he remained cold, negative and silent. I now believe that this was the reason why he did not give me the Foreign Office when he became Prime Minister in January 1932; and, for all I know, he may have been right.

Being of a different temperament, I reacted in a different way. I felt that the way to save Spain from her stultified political life, the way to thaw her icebound state, was to force the country to plunge into the *world's debate*. Once we had agreed to help the French through and through, the French themselves would see to it that our army and navy became efficient. But this was and still is my opinion; while Azaña was entitled to his.

Seen in this light, the 'modesty' of the French expectations, as put to me by Léger, was on the whole wise, though bound to destroy my plan, insofar as I had a plan. The Italo-Germans were by no means inactive, and they had their friends well entrenched, notably in our Foreign Office. Whether inspired by them or not, a rumour got going in Madrid, to the effect that Herriot was visiting Spain to wrench from us the right of passage through our territory for the French troops in Northern Africa. And, sure enough, on September 30, 1932 while in Geneva, I received a letter from my Embassy Counsellor in Paris to the effect that Herr Hans E. Riesser, the live-wire first secretary of the German Embassy had called to ask whether there was any truth in the news that Herriot was coming to Spain on November 6th. The answer was that if, as it seemed likely, the President went to Spain, it would be soon; whereupon Herr Riesser asked whether the President intended to ask Spain to let France's African native troops pass through her territory, which would amount to an alliance. He was told there was nothing of the kind.

This was true, but not so very true. For by then I had had a conversation with Herriot, the report of which I must reproduce here verbatim:

Confidential Note on a conversation with M. Herriot to-day, August 13, 1932.

The President, who put off his departure so as to receive me, did so with his usual cordial simplicity.

1. He uttered his satisfaction at the success of the Republic through the events on the 12th* and asked me what we would do with the generals. I answered that the law would be applied to them by Civilian Courts. He pointed out that, in such cases, the Republic had the right to shoot. 'A general who causes disorder and leads men to death must face the consequences.'

2. *Without my having mentioned the subject*, he asked me what were we doing in the matter of the President's decoration. I told him we were very pleased about it. With a certain impatience in his voice, he then asked me whether the moment had come for him to put the matter before the [French] Council of Ministers (end of the month). I answered yes. He reminded me that he had been ready for some time to visit Spain but that it was I who had begged him to adjourn his visit. 'Now, are you ready?' I reminded him that it had been my wish not to mix the good effect of the Grand Cross with the bad effect of the French quotas restricting our fruit imports. He did express his wish to separate such things, but also his firm conviction that in trade matters Spain was harder on France than France on Spain.

Journey to Spain: He explained:

a. That he would go to Spain with pleasure, as soon as we wished it.

---

*Sanjurjo's rise in arms against the Republic, which ended in failure.

b. That he had rather go to Madrid than to San Sebastián for he feels that he should go and hand over the Grand Cross to the head of State in the State Capital.

c. That he should like to see the Prado and Toledo.

I suggested between 13th and 18th September and he said he was content, but he thought he ought to adapt himself to our President's dates, which he would do, if he were told in time. We agreed that a plan for his journey would be prepared in Madrid *in strict secrecy* to be submitted to him here as soon as possible.

3. He then spoke to me about European politics. Very much worried over Germany and Italy. He showed me and let me read a long confidential report from his Chargé d'Affaires in Berlin, followed by a copious Appendix by their Military Attaché, in which, by the way, a special weight and length are granted to the opinions of our own Military Attaché, Beigbeder, in flattering terms for our contryman. According to these documents, Germany will reduce her military service from 12 to 4 years, increase her air and tank armaments, and apply a 'state of exception' and even a 'special state of exception' to the Rhine region – all of it in violation of the Treaty of Versailles. I asked him what England thought about it: and he answered he had asked his legal advisers to study it. The President [Herriot] seems sceptical as to how to avoid the final tearing up of the Treaty, and thinks that in September the gleichberechtigung will give rise to unpleasant debates in Geneva. He added that the French Legal Authorities had strong hints to the effect that the Rennes bombs that destroyed the monument commemorating the union between Brittany and France and the bombs in Vannes (aimed at killing him) could be traced back to Hitler.

He then talked about Italy. Deeply hurt by the theme of the Italian air-sea manoeuvres which he considers as a provocation, he stated that he was convinced that a collusion existed between the two dictatorships, the German and the Italian. He gave vent to his profound mistrust of the Italian character, which he knows well as mayor of Lyon.

4. 'We are closer to war than to peace.' 'Peace is an ideal for democracies, which dictatorships do not share.'

On this background he developed to me his idea of a close collaboration with and trust in Spain. 'That would allow me to drop the Italians and to direct towards Spain my exclusive preferences, commercial, economic, etc..' 'I am already in

agreement with England. I need Spain.' 'The Western World,
the three nations of the Occident, must save Europe' etc. 'All
I ask of Spain is: if a combination of dictatorships were to
try to murder the French Republic, will Spain let me defend
myself?'

I felt my duty was to feign to understand less than I did and
answered: 'Your question offers two aspects. Legally, Spain,
like France, is a member of the League of Nations. She will
act as the Covenant demands. Politically, it will be necessary
that Spanish public opinion allows the Government to work
in favour of France. Here, two obstacles: the policy of France
towards Spain in trade matters, in schools [for Spanish children in Algeria] etc. and the fact that, for the first time since
the eighteenth century, she is expected to return to active
European politics. We must think it over.'

To this, he reacted is a somewhat lively way: '*I don't want
an alliance of any kind, least of all, a military one.* My military
men want our Franco-British pact to lead to General Staff
talks. I am against. That is not the way politics is made nowadays. I don't even want a policy of balance of power. I want
the Covenant and nothing but the Covenant. If we are attacked, will Spain let us be murdered? More concretely, I
want my troops to pass, if not through Spanish territory,
through Spanish territorial waters, so that I do not get my
passage blocked.'

I answered that Republican Spain felt closer to France
than to any other nation in the world; that the men in office
now were those that had backed her in 1914–18; that a
blameless France if attacked would call forth a considerable
pro-French emotion in Spain; but that the matter demanded
much meditation. And we left off in this mood of sympathy,
earnestness and gravity.

CONCLUSIONS. I wish to put forward the following:
1. It would be a mistake to connect the granting of the Grand
Cross and Herriot's visit on the one hand and the proposals
and ideas mentioned above under no. 4. Herriot gave me the
Grand Cross [for the President] and the trip to Madrid without – I should not say having the other ideas in mind – but
without laying down conditions. I believe therefore, that it
is advisable to cash in on the concession of the Grand Cross
and the visit without letting the other affair turn up at this
stage and complicate the issue.
2. But, inevitably Herriot will speak about this in Madrid.

Therefore, it is *advisable to be prepared* for such a conversation. I think it necessary to prepare:

a. A legal study of our obligations such as they are: Covenant, Convention for the prevention of war, etc.

b. A political study to find out how far we can go, and how advisable it would be to put forward counterclaims for French goodwill towards us (Morocco? Tangiers? Spanish Schools in Algeria and Tunisia, trade matters etc.)

c. A legal military study of what France could expect from us in the case of a war, and of the consequences which might flow for us from a complaisant attitude in such a case.

Note. In case I have not put it clearly enough, I insist that what the President [Herriot] asks for is a 'benevolent neutrality *within* the Covenant. A juridical monster, no doubt, since, when combined with the Kellogg Pact, the Covenant destroys neutrality: nevertheless, this idea deserves to be studied for its empirical possibilities.'

Read in conjunction with Léger's ideas on the rôle of Spain as a great power, this note shows that France had long views on Spain, and that her modesty with regard to the first visit was but a prudent approach so as not to frighten a nation taught by adversity to keep out of European trouble. My own cautious attitude towards Herriot's suggestions was also due to prudence, in view of the somewhat reserved stand of Azaña; let alone the determined opposition of the anti-French Right.

The outcome of all this caution was a subdued reception for our guest in Madrid. What was happening soon became clear to me. Azaña was sheltering behind the opposition of the Right to France in order to cover his own opposition to European adventures. Let me give here a translation of Herriot's own story: 'I went there [to Toulouse] on my way back from Spain, when I had gone to present the Grand Cross of the Legion of Honour to the President of the Spanish Republic. In truth, as I arrived in Madrid, I had been not a little astonished to see the amount of police deployed to protect me during my drive to the Embassy. Towards midday, I heard that my visit had provoked scuffles between students. I even noted on a wall threats of death against me*. Evidently my presence gave rise to certain complications. I realised it on noticing how carefully the Spanish government organised in my honour picturesque archeological excursions to Toledo, Alcalá and other places. My friend the Ambassador Madariaga seemed worried. I under-

---

*This is most doubtful. How could he from his car?

stood that a certain propaganda, in fact from abroad, had misrepresented my visit as a manoeuvre to drag Spain into a military alliance with France.' All this was based on facts, which the papers quoted in these pages will perhaps contribute to clarify. But the pro-French, Republican, left-of-centre section of opinion, by far the most numerous and vigorous in the country, had in the end its say. Thus Herriot writes on: 'A noisy compensation awaited me. On the evening of my departure, I saw the demonstrations converge towards the station, headed by flags, banners and bands. The railway coaches were besieged. We were flooded with presents and flowers, and as the train began to move, a formidable *Marseillaise* shook the glass roof of the station hall.'

During the three days of his stay in Madrid, Herriot was not able to see Azaña by himself. The Spanish Prime Minister was game for everything, luncheons, dinners, theatre shows, excursions to Toledo (with a brilliant midday meal at Marañón's country house) – everything but a square talk with his guest. Much as I admire Azaña, I believe his attitude then cannot be justified. He had a good case – though it was by no means my case, I think it is fair to say this – and he should have put his views on Franco-Spanish relations squarely and frankly before Herriot. As it was, Herriot had to leave Spain not only empty-handed but frustrated and even humiliated. These results were not inevitable. They did Spain no good and the Republic much harm. As for Herriot, we parted company at the Spanish frontier, for I travelled on to Paris and he sped to Toulouse, to attend the Radical Congress. He then, dispite his August confidences to me, was driven by his bitter Spanish experiences to offer a hand to Mussolini; which Mussolini did not grasp.

CHAPTER XXI

ENTER EDEN

B Y the end of 1932, Eden began to assert his personality in Geneva, even though he was to be a mere Under-secretary until January 1 1934 when he was put more explicitly in charge of League affairs under Simon first and Hoare afterwards, before he at last became Foreign Secretary. In 1933, he was thirty-six. His arrival in Geneva was soon felt. What an improvement, what a novelty! After the Madame Tussaud wax works which was Austen Chamberlain, after the insular, enigmatic and arrogant Simon, there was at last a man alive who spoke to all comers as man to man and who needed by no means to smile in order to be open and friendly.

And he knew his job too. We all felt it in the modest way he administered his knowledge – for there are also *nouveaux riches* in knowledge as there are in wealth, who, unable to get over the lot they know, exhibit it as a *parvenu* does his diamond rings and Havana cigars. None of that stuff with Eden. Clear, definite, efficient, he was always moderate, not merely 'willing to listen' but an excellent and intelligent listener of what was said, no matter who said it.

The Penelopean tapestry-weaving of the Disarmament Conference went on, the warp of the big powers trying to keep Germany out of mischief, which in fact meant out of power, and the woof of the smaller powers, trying either to ensure a permanent peace or to retain each whatever armaments he already possessed. MacDonald, Simon and Herriot were busy trying to 'warp' out von Papen, represented by an impressive façade of diplomacy named von Neurath. By December 11, 1932, the big powers had papered over their discords enough to let it be known that Germany would return to the Conference. The news was soon damped by the fact that in January 1933 Hitler in person had laid on the helm his firm yet insane hands.

The Conference itself had set its hopes on the complete air disarmament scheme that I had been advocating, and on which the Spanish delegation had officially presented a draft scheme. Curiously enough, despite its radicalism and boldness, this idea seemed to appeal to at least some of the official leaders of France and of England. In late September 1932 I had had a talk with Tom Jones in Geneva, where he had come for the day from Aix-les-Bains where Stanley Baldwin was then staying. I knew that Baldwin liked the idea, and also that Eden was in favour of such a plan; and I cannot resist the temptation to point out that at least in Eden's mind, even this plan followed the law that all disarmament aims at rearmament: 'I had written to Baldwin in the same sense nine months earlier, pointing out that since we were so weak in air power, any international limitations were bound to be to our advantage.'*

I still think, however, that the true revolutionary aspect of my plan was the World Air Authority for traffic, and this mostly because its working implied the weaving together of the tens of thousands of professional pilots of the world into a confraternity that would almost certainly have blocked all attempts at any form of air warfare.

The issue did not reach the level of positive politics; for though men like Baldwin, Eden, Paul-Boncour and Herriot would have been ready to consider it the services were hostile in every big power, and the plan was lost – even after it had been later revived by Pierre Cot with the addition (in my opinion idle) of an air world police.

Much to Eden's annoyance, the British delegation often took a negative and even an obstructive attitude; and at one stage, were insisting on freedom to use bombs for 'police purposes'. This was another of those conundrums that flourish in muddled heads, whether brass-hatted or not. We had it more than once, coming always from London. When Paul-Boncour had proposed that there should be no bombing beyond fifty kilometers behind the fighting line (incidentally, an unworkable and unrealistic proposal) the British had insisted on freedom to bomb 'in outlying regions' – whereupon a Japanese expert had enquired whether that gave Japan the right to bomb London which, for Tokyo, was an outlying region. The whole conundrum had arisen out of the fog accumulated under some British brass hat obsessed by the Indian Northwestern frontier.

There were two Britons in Geneva who were too shrewd and clear-brained for such stuff: Eden and Cadogan. Eden had a fine face, and eyes, if anything, too beautiful for a human creature of the male sex. Cadogan's eyes were, as it often happens with upper-class Britons, two glass beads that street urchins would have coveted for a game of marbles; and his nose, raised in an adenoidal effort to breathe, completed the impression of slow-witted, conventional snobbery which his diplomatically correct figure suggested. How misleading it all was! Behind that façade of intellectual mediocrity, a sharp, ever-present wit stood ready to see all and weigh all with faultless accuracy, and his mind was never more acutely on the spot than when his glass-bead eyes looked absent-minded.

*Memoirs. Facing the Dictators, p. 29.

It was to Eden and Cadogan that the Conference owed its return
to life when, after Herriot's fall, the French trio Paul-Boncour, Pierre
Cot and Massigli had to give up all hope of squaring the Germans
on the basis of the December 11th agreement. This Eden and Cadogan
did by actually drafting a Convention remarkable in that it was concrete, precise and built on the balanced inclusion of every one of the
sine qua non requirements of each of the important powers. It was as
good a racehorse as ever had run the Disarmament stakes; but it had
started twelve months too late.

Once again, I thought of Geneva as an orchestra that took a dreadfully long time to rehearse; and when at long last, the conductor was
ready to raise his baton and begin the actual concert, a voice at the back
of the hall would call the first violin: 'Come at once. Your wife is having
her baby' – and we all had to begin our rehearsals again. It was no longer
Brüning who ruled in Berlin, and who would have lapped up Eden's
idea, thus, by the way, saving his political life; but Hitler who wanted
to damn and be damned.

And then, there was Mussolini. Now, in politics, as in grammar, one
should be able to tell substantives from adjectives. Hitler was a sub-
stantive; Mussolini only an adjective. Hitler was a nuisance; Mussolini
was bloody. Together, a bloody nuisance. This can now be clearly
seen; it was not yet so in those days. One day, I was presiding at my
Air Committee when Eden came up the steps, bent over and whispered
in my ear: 'MacDonald and Simon are going to Rome.' I turned round
more sharply than a born diplomat would have done: "What!' – 'Yes,
to see Musso. What's wrong?' (I could see Eden was on the whole
pleased that I was shocked) 'Wrong?' Well. Everything. To begin with,
the British Prime Minister does not go to Rome to see Mussolini. That's
the way I see it.'

It was again big power warp versus conference woof. Even as Mac-
Donald and Simon were in Geneva preparing the presentation of Eden's
British draft Convention to the Conference, Aloisi was working for an
adjournment of the whole thing so as to brush aside the British idea
and push forward an Italian delusion. Once again, the disarmament
bottle thoroughly shaken, produced a precipitate of politics.

This is no mere fancy. Eden has revealed that MacDonald, drawn to
Rome by the lure of Mussolini's plan, would not tarry in Geneva even
to present the officially British draft Convention until he was made to
stay and do so on grounds of sheer decency. (Vol. II. p. 34.) Even so,
the Prime Minister and his Foreign Secretary left within two days,
which was by no means the best way to recommend their own wares.
What had drawn them to Rome was a draft treaty to be signed by

Britain, France, Germany and Italy. It was therefore again an idea essentially contrary to the Covenant, a league of physical power versus moral power, and therefore the very reverse of the spirit of disarmament. Eden was then right. He stood for the Convention he and Cadogan had drafted to seek to structure the powers, big and small, into a political system that (in the perspective of those days) might eventually lead to some reduction in armaments; Simon who felt no sympathy for the League and was steeped in big power political philosophy and outlook, a man politely contemptuous of smaller nations, was in Rome in his element; but Ramsay MacDonald, a pacifist, democratic Labour intellectual, what was he doing there?

The whole thing was an exercise in futility on the part of the Western powers; and on that of the two dictators, a new endeavour to disintegrate the European structure. What were its professed aims? To co-operate in the maintenance of peace – a consummation for which neither Hitler nor Mussolini felt the slightest interest; to carry out treaty revision within the framework of the League – which Hitler would never consent to do, for it was his wish to impose his plans, and not to have his views just 'accepted'; to promote general co-operation in both economic and political European activities – which again was a matter of complete indifference to Hitler. Yet, the Four Power Pact, as it came to be called, was signed in Rome on June 8, 1933.

Why? Because Hitler lost nothing thereby, since he did not mean to honour any of his engagements anyhow, but got France embroiled with all her allies as a consequence of it; and Poland in particular lost all trust in France, which suited Beck perfectly. These sideshows of history can be weighty. Beck, Poland's Foreign Secretary, Kánya, Hungary's Foreign Secretary, and Fey, Austria's Minister of the Interior, had been colleagues in the same Secret Service Bureau of the Austro-Hungarian Empire. Beck had no idea or feeling for peace, or democracy, or the League; he was as convinced a *Realpolitiker* and a believer in sheer force as Simon or for that matter, Lloyd George, but he was more cynical about it.

Though, for the sake of clarity, every strand in a narrative has to be followed by itself, the rope of events is but one, so that, while the big powers were trying to settle the problem of disarmament by themselves, Japan was leaving the League (March 27, 1933) so as to be freer to play truant in her hunting ground. The Western powers had to envisage the likelihood of similar behaviour on the part of Nazi Germany. A man worlds away from Hoover was now at the helm in Washington; and on May 16, 1933, Franklin Roosevelt, prompted by Ramsay MacDonald, sent a message to the States represented at the Disarmament Conference recommending the British Draft Convention to them. This message might have been described as a pill to prevent an earthquake; but the world is so subtle that this well-meant admonition from Roosevelt may well have contributed to the earthquake it meant to conjure away, for it seems to have tempted Hitler to don a white mantle of peace over his Lohengrinesque armour. At any rate, precisely then, when he was maturing his plans for aggression, he began to lure world public opinion with beautifully conciliatory and peaceful speeches, and he even seemed willing to approve the British Draft Convention. Behind this screen of sedatives, though, the positions of the big protagonists remained the same, and the Conference was in the doldrums.

Now that Mussolini's Four Power Pact was signed and dead, the unlucky British Draft Convention had met with another rival, a World Economic Conference met in London. It proved far more efficient than our Disarmament Conference for it took fewer weeks to fail than ours took years. Piqued, our own Conference decided to adjourn until September; and the big powers felt the freer to devote the summer to their favourite sport – negotiating behind the back of the League and without results.

There was no lack of men of good will to urge them thereto. Norman Davis, the American Ambassador at large, gathered Daladier, Paul-Boncour, Eden and Londonderry in Paris (June 8, 1933). Why Londonderry? Because he was Air Minister and the British Cabinet did not think Eden sound on the principle of 'bombing for political purposes in outlying regions' on which they remained adamant. Then there was Henderson, the President of the Conference, an honest-to-God man, closed in, though he was, into his native English, and though able enough to tell right from wrong, not subtle enough for the many shades of grey in between which are the true colours of human actions. He was busy all July, in London, Paris, Rome, Berlin and Prague, where he found that the musicians of the orchestra insisted on playing each his own tune, no matter how the other ones were reading the score. The French wanted a Convention in two phases: consolidation then disarmament; the Germans insisted on equality while working for it by simply rearming for all they were worth.

Attempts by the French to stiffen the Convention by prolonging to eight the period of five years stipulated for the trial period gave the Germans an opportunity to ripen their pre-determined decision – to break. The convention, with its French amendment, was presented to the Conference by Simon (October 14, 1933). He had hardly sat down when Henderson received a telegram from von Neurath announcing Germany's withdrawal from the Conference. That evening, in a broadcast to the nation, Hitler announced that Germany was also withdrawing from the League.

CHAPTER XXII

THE SECRETARIAT AND ITS SHORTCOMINGS

WHEN, after a spell of three short years in academic seclusion, I returned to Geneva at a higher level of official authority, my memories of the most flagrant shortcomings of the Secretariat were still fresh in my mind; indeed, most of my erstwhile colleagues with whom I had discussed them were still at their posts where I had left them when I had gone to Oxford. I was determined to do my best to improve the house.

Precisely, though, because it was so good. For it was unfortunately true that the Secretariat was not what some of the more exacting of us wanted it to be; but it was nevertheless an admirable institution; and I wish to repeat that it owed its excellence mostly to the traditions of the British civil service incarnated in Sir Eric Drummond and to the ability of the French intellect, incarnated in Jean Monnet.

Nevertheless, shortcomings there were; and they had been allowed to grow owing to an unfortunate combination of circumstances such as Drummond's pragmatical trend towards compromise and Jean Monnet's departure in 1923. For Monnet would have effectively resisted Drummond's defeatism, an attitude Avenol was not in a position to take, for lack both of ability and of conviction.

The trouble was a growing tendency to gain control of the house on the part of the big powers. They had secured exorbitant privileges: the Secretary General, his deputy and all the Under-secretaries General were supposed to be nationals of big powers, which also got a good share of directors as well; but as time went by and as the League asserted itself as a centre of calm and common sense in the entangled net of international tensions, the powers, and in particular, their diplomatic offices, put more and more pressure on the Secretariat and endeavoured to infiltrate into it.

Drummond had chosen his men with the utmost care, avoiding, in particular, members of the national civil services, which in practice, would have meant diplomats. Gradually, however, the national civil services secured a foothold in the house and this was a predictable result from the 'right' of near ownership of the highest posts of the Secretariat recognised to the powers. This happened when, on Dionisio Anzilotti, being appointed a Hague Judge, he was succeeded as 'Italian' Under-secretary General by Bernardo Attolico; for, though neither of them was a civil servant, the fact set up the precedent for Joseph Avenol, an Inspecteur des Finances, to succeed Jean Monnet as Deputy Secretary General.

When Inazo Nitobe – no civil servant – left, he was succeeded by Yotaro Sugimura, a diplomat. And this evolution went from bad to worse. When Mussolini stole Italy's government, Attolico began to feel the squeeze. He himself told me that at the Foreign Office in Rome he had been asked whom he obeyed, the Duce or Drummond; to which he made answer: 'When I am in Rome, the Duce; when I am in Geneva, Drummond.' This was more ingenious than either possible or in harmony with his obligations as a League official.

And yet, it was not good enough for the Duce, who sacked Attolico and got Drummond to appoint his own chief assistant Paulucci di Calvoli Barone in his stead. Here began the downfall of the Secretariat. The Fascist Under-secretary's room became a kind of Italian Embassy at the League (save that the Ambassador's salary was paid by the League), linked directly with Mussolini and openly accepting orders and instructions from him. Paulucci, in himself an attractive and friendly person, was nevertheless zealous enough to go about even during official League gatherings sporting the Fascist badge on his lapel.

Drummond was no longer the strong internationalist he had been in his earlier days. He had had a meeting with the Duce and had seen himself in the delicate situation of having to decide whether it was best to turn a blind eye to such pranks or to engage in a fight he might eventually lose. He tolerated what he felt unable to repress. I tried to apply homeopathy by inducing the Soviet Under-secretary to wear a Bolshevik badge, but for once met with a discreet communist. Germany, explicitly admitted as a great power, demanded her pound of flesh of privileges; not only an Under-secretary, but heads of Departments and what not; and objected to Comert as head of the Press Section because he was a Frenchman.

I thought the time had come to recall that the Secretariat had been founded on a document known as the Balfour report, in which the principle was laid down that its members took their orders from the Secretary General but not from their governments; and I insisted on making this principle work by having it enacted that League civil servants would swear on oath allegiance to the League and not to their governments. I got my point acknowledged, and everybody, including the Secretary General had to take an oath of sole allegiance to the League and its institutions. I was under no delusions as to the actual strength of this oath in cases such as the Fascist or Communist States, indeed even of other nations: but I felt that even if its efficiency were not total, it would be a useful moral force.

In this as in other campaigns for the improvement of the Secretariat, my chief standby was a group of small power delegates, led by Carl Hambro, of Norway; and William Rappard, of Switzerland, who like me (as we say in Spain) had been a cook before he had become a friar. Hambro had for years led the van in this endeavour to keep the Secretariat on an even keel of world objectivity; and Rappard had closely watched how things were actually done. Hambro had as far back as 1929 suggested that three members of every delegation should have their expenses paid by the League budget, so as to get rid of the monopoly of diplomats and allow the voice of the people at home to be heard. It is one of life's little ironies that this evidently sound plan failed because of the opposition – by no means of the great powers – but of the Latin Americans. I do not say the Latin American *States*, because, in fact, it was killed by Latin American diplomats many of whom would have lost their yearly trips to Geneva and the publicity it brought them, if with money available, the politicians and officials in their far off capitals had felt able to oust them. I note the fact lest my general trend would appear to suggest that the big nations are of a human species inferior to that of the small ones. The only reason why, in general, the big nations do more harm than the small ones is just because the small ones haven't as much power as they have.

I had always stood for the principle of competence above nationality in the choice of the League officials; and I was displeased when Avenol was appointed to succeed Monnet, merely because he was a Frenchman, though I should not have favoured Attolico either, who came to see me in my room, although he was my chief, to protest furiously against the move, obviously considering himself as a fitter choice; for, though there wasn't much to choose between him and Avenol on the score of either ability or devotion to the 'spirit of Geneva', (for both were *Realpolitiker* with possibly a slightly lighter dose of world spirit in Attolico) the underlying attitude was for both the special rights of the nationals of big powers. This idea used to be advocated on the ground that it was good for the League to keep in powerful positions men who were apt, indeed bound, to act as liaison officers with the governments and bureaucracies of the great; but too much should not be made of this argument; rather should we prefer (though I did not go so far) to exclude the big powers from the League's strongest posts, if only as a guarantee against too much interference in the proper work of the Secretariat, as the protagonist of world versus national interests.

This interference was real and objectionable. I disliked the idea that while Salter was kept away by British official duties, his post as head of the economic section should be entrusted to our good private friend Hugh Mackinnon Wood, just because he was British though no economist at all, but a lawyer. And I was therefore the more opposed to the habit of appointing Under-secretaries General exclusively among nationals of the big powers. I therefore campaigned for the modest proposal that at least one Under-secretary General should be a citizen of a small power. I even had my candidate *in pectore*: Seán Lester, my Irish colleague and companion in more than one Council Committee. But here I met on the part of Drummond with a counter-move which puzzled me at first, and saddened me later, when I saw through it. With lightning rapidity, as soon as the principle had been accepted by the League, Drummond appointed Pablo de Azcárate.

Now in a general and abstract way I had nothing to object to in this appointment on grounds of competence although it would never have been my choice; but it seemed to me that it ran counter to my intention and endeavour, since Spain, though not a big power, was not a small power either, being a *de facto* permanent member of the Council; so that, both from the personal and from the national point of view, Lester seemed to me by far the better candidate; and that was, no doubt, why the last person I should have thought of for the job was the man who actually got it.

But this was not to be the end of the story. Why such a rush to get the post filled? The answer to this conundrum revealed the saddest aspect of the whole story: because Drummond was persuaded that my ardour in advocating the reform was due to my desire to get the job myself. This revelation was most painful to me. Again my own objective eagerness was misinterpreted as due to a subjective passion for power. Furthermore, the idea that I should wish to re-enter the yoke of civil service when I had shaken it off in 1928 and the much lighter bond of the Oxford Chair in 1931, appealed to me as just dreadful. Drummond, however, seemed incapable of seeing me as I was and am. On the other hand, now, after so many years, I do not exclude the possibility that he may have been ably led towards an error that he was only too prone to make.

All these changes acted as a kind of prelude to Drummond's own departure, which though known to come for many months before, actually took place in June 1933. The decision was entirely his, and it was sincerely and generally regretted. I took upon myself to initiate and negotiate a presentation by all my colleagues of the Council, for, though we seemed unable to understand each other, I held him in high esteem and was sorry when he left.

My candidate as his successor would have been Albert Thomas, by far the ablest, strongest and most spirited of world leaders of those days; but Albert Thomas had died in 1932, and then there was no hesitation in my mind that the best man available was Arthur Salter. Whenever I suggested his name, I got the same reaction: 'What, another Englishman?' My retort was: 'Not because but in spite of. He *is* the best man.' There was nothing doing. If at least the principle had acted positively as well as negatively, if it had led to a good Swiss (Rappard, for instance) or Dutchman – but no. After Britain, France, even if, instead of Albert Thomas we had to put up with Avenol.

Now Joseph Avenol was an Inspecteur des Finances, and no man ever got that diploma who did not possess a good brain. So, a good brain he certainly had. But very little else. No grace, not even of that awkward, charmless kind Drummond managed to turn on when he wished; nor was he, in fact, lit up inwardly by any *feu sacré*. What on earth he was doing in that *galère* of the League, God only knows, for, though he was correct and never trod on the toes of the Covenant, he was as hard-boiled a *Realpolitiker* as one could find at the time. And one thing he did utterly lack – a sense of humour.

His two deputies were Massimo Pilotti, an Italian jurist who was an immense improvement on Paulucci though he always gave the impression of funereal sadness, perhaps for his attachment to black clothes; and Azcárate who by no flight of imagination could be described as hilarious. This trio of undertakers excited the humour of Plá, who assured me that when the three of them got together, one could hear the peals of laughter out on the lake. Humour or no humour, the fact is that by our insistence, we had succeeded in liberating the Secretariat from the stifling domination of the big powers.

CHAPTER XXIII

A POLITICAL CO-OPERATIVE OR A SUPER-STATE?

THE struggle for a better and a more independent Secretariat was part of a more general battle which lasts to this day within the United Nations and the European Community. A co-operative of sovereignties or a Super-state? The line that separated these two conceptions did not necessarily leave on one side the big and on the other the small powers, but it did leave all the big powers on the side of national sovereignty. This division was apt to be complicated by another clash of opinions. The partisans of full national sovereignty were apt to emphasise the maintenance of peace as the chief, indeed, the only work for the League; and this limitation was so rigidly conceived by most of them that, in case of a conflict, they would have the League do nothing until the conflict imperilled the peace of the world.

On the other hand, those of us who favoured a certain degree of sovereignty for the League were also in favour of the widest possible extension of its competence; and we based our conviction precisely on the very patch on which our adversaries had dug their toes: peace and disarmament. I had elaborated this line of thought during my years as summer teacher in Geneva and winter peace-preacher in the U.S., and I would put it now to my colleagues in the League Assembly whenever I thought it necessary.

My line of argument could not be clearer: you want to disarm. You must drive out the cause of armaments: fear of conflicts. What is a conflict? It is a problem that has become poisonous. What is a problem? It is a question that has been neglected. What is a question? It is an everyday matter that needs our attention. If therefore we want to avoid wars, it is very little use waiting to tackle our ordinary, humdrum matters until, unattended, neglected, poisoned, they have become conflicts. That is why we must allow the League to develop so as to catch differences when they are still in the bud.

That was my political argument. I had another argument for the Hague Court. There are a number of differences between nations which can fortunately be formulated in clear legal terms, and they should, therefore, be submitted to the Hague Court. The ingenious method evolved for the appointment of the judges of this Court had resulted in a judiciary of considerable prestige and moral authority. But a Supreme Court, such as the Hague Court was, had to render justice in the name of an authority. In a monarchy such as Britain, justice is awarded in the name of the King; in a Republic, like France, in the name of the State. The Hague Court had no central authority in whose name to pronounce its findings and awards. We had to set up a sovereign commonwealth that would stand behind our judges and their sentences.

This was a new language in Geneva, where professions of faith in the League were often apt to be regarded by their utterers as mere matters of politeness and salutation towards the small fry that believed in such things. Reasoning out the League as a necessity logically deducible from the premises uttered by conservatives, cynics and *Realpolitikers*, was a form of *propaganda fidei* which many found awkward but many more found overdue.

As, owing to the freedom my government allowed me, I was in a position both to present these ideas freely and to stand by them in my official activity, my following among the crowds that used to gather in Geneva grew day by day, and it was a remarkable fact that it grew most speedily among Britons and Americans, though they were the citizens of the two countries whose States were most determined to resist everything I stood for.

This enviable freedom led me, at times, to allow the impression to be formed that my own personal opinions were the official stand of Spain. I fully realise that there may have been on my part a certain amount of subjectivity and even of exploitation of my official position in favour of my private views; if such was the case, I was not aware of it at the time; nor do I see how it can be avoided by any public man with ideas of his own. Thus, for instance, Briand's policy differed from Tardieu's precisely because their private thoughts and attitudes were different; and the same goes for Simon and Eden. I should add that it was the easier for me in that the Republic had not evolved yet, nor did it look at all like evolving, a reasoned-out foreign policy of her own.

I was therefore able to make a statement of my views in the form of an official speech which I delivered as the Spanish chief delegate at the fourteenth ordinary session of the Assembly of the League of Nations (October 2, 1933). I first described the crisis through which the League was struggling as 'an anarchy of anarchies', and I successively dealt with anarchy in the facts, in the minds and in the methods. On the first, facts, I pointed out how the world had given up the wise old system of arbitrating differences in trade, in order to adopt a disastrous autarchy tempered by an unattainable set of bilateral balances of payments; how in politics, though we saw the Colombia-Peru conflict moving towards a peaceful settlement, the Chaco war was still intractable; and here, I insisted on the scandal of the traffic in arms on which I gave facts and figures, including the following concrete fact: 'In 1932 one single exporting country has supplied two countries in conflict with the League of Nations – I insist, two countries and one single year – four times as much ammunition as it had sold to the whole world in 1930, and this happened while we were trying to lead those two countries to peace. Furthermore, on the basis of the figures published by the League, the sum total of all the exports of all the countries between 1920 and 1930, was 616 million dollars. Now the total of imports accounts only for 478 million. There remains therefore a difference of 138 million dollars of armaments whose destination was unknown. "Can a civilised society, organised and ruled by a system such as ours, allow 178 million dollars of armaments to vanish every ten years, no one knowing where they go?"'

I then analysed the anarchy in our minds. I first insisted on the fact that it was becoming harder and harder for any nation to draw the line between internal and foreign policy and that such an attempt mattered less than that to draw the line between peace and war. It was also harder because in the days of old, the gamut of politics spread on a straight line between extreme right and extreme left, while of late, dictatorship having acquired the dignity of a left status thanks to Lenin, the map of internal politics had become much more complex, and political systems gravitated towards either the pole of liberty or that of authority; and it was bewildering that a system claiming to be progressive should declare itself against freedom of discussion and liberty, two basic principles for Geneva.

As for the anarchy in our methods, I defined confidence or mutual trust between nations as the gold of the political international bank, and pacts as its paper money; – which, at this distance, seems to me one of my best finds. I went on to argue that since our stock of 'gold', i.e. trust, had not increased while pacts went on multiplying, we were facing a state of political inflation, the most dangerous of all. Nations had so far proved unable fully to organise the League – hence their tendency to return to national and even nationalistic ways. We should not conclude that the League had failed. We hadn't tried it.

I then reminded the Assembly of the famous speech of Charles V before the Pope, 'a speech that Aristide Briand might have delivered before this Assembly in Geneva'; his effort failed because it was too narrowly confined to Christendom, in itself a slight on two great cultures, Islam and Jewry. And as we were already (October 1933) witnessing the menacing beginnings of what was to become a sinister outburst of anti-semitism, I went on to say: 'In our day, when the Jews are on the agenda, the Spanish Republic wishes to turn to this fine race of men to which she owes illustrious men of letters, jurists, mystics, physicians, statesmen. Spain believes that the endeavour of the twentieth century must cover the whole earth and nothing but the earth, and comprise all men, all races, all religions and all nations.'

This was the spirit I wished to serve in Geneva; and while I was aware that there was a whole sector in Spain out of sympathy with it, I also felt certain that it was in harmony with the best of the country. This speech contributed to establish my public image, as we now say, with the liberal left; and as, in any case, I was often involved in committees and negotiations, I reached the supreme height to which a public man can aspire: I became a frequent subject for cartoons.

Visitors to Geneva can still enjoy some of the best of them, for they decorate the walls of the *brasserie* Bavaria there. I owe to the cartoonists (for they were two working together) a revelation of what I really am. With an intuition I have always admired since, they pictured me as a bird. It is a fact that, in spirit, I am one. Every human being carries in his or her inner essence the essence of one or more animals. We all have seen and guessed the hare, the lion, the tiger, the serpent, the rat and the mouse (so different!), the fox, the rabbit and the parrot.

I left the parrot for the last so as to put a brake on any tendency I might let loose to exalt the qualities of the bird, since I think I am, in spirit, one of them. But the parrot is not an ordinary bird. It is a bird that talks instead of singing, and not what it thinks but what it hears. Of the birds I believe I have the idea for essentials (bird's eye), the need for swiftness, the impatience and horror of plodding and trudging, the urge to go from one point to another in a straight flight, all features to which I owe the best and the worst of my literary work.

CHAPTER XXIV

SHOT IN THE BACK

O *H mon Dieu, délivrez-moi de mes amis, car de mes ennemis, je me charge.* How often, during those days, I had in mind that prayer of Voltaire! As the active man that I was, in realms in which vested interests were powerful, I had always taken for granted that I should not lack critics, adversaries and even enemies. There were no lack of them in Geneva, chiefly among Nazis and Fascists, though the more touchy among French nationalists were not idle either. These people could always count on envious Spanish journalists, unemployed politicians who detested the Republic and disgruntled diplomats to pinprick and embitter my life. But the worst and hardest to bear was the hostility, the meddling or the lack of true cordiality of my own friends, those who served the Republic, or thought they did, with a sincere desire to do well.

From the very beginning, I tried to impress the seal of objectivity on all I did and wrote. As early as May 9, 1932, I had sent to the Foreign Secretary (Zulueta) a note on the organisation and working of the special attachés of all kinds that peopled the embassies. I insisted on the chaos, overlapping, and waste of man-power and money caused by the tendency of every department at home to consider its man abroad as a separate Ambassador, so that Spain presented in every foreign capital the image of five or six Spains, one military, one naval, one aerial, one financial, one labour and so forth. These attachés wrote direct to their respective ministries, and received their answers direct. I recommended that there should be one single channel of communication – that linking the Ambassador with the Foreign Secretary. The idea is too obvious to be elaborated. It was not acted upon, less, probably, because it was thought inadequate than just because it was not 'thought' at all.

I soon had to write another letter to the Foreign Secretary because an able man recently sent to work with me had received a cable from the 'jury' that was supposed to select Commercial Attachés suggesting to him one or other of two or three posts in the wide world. I pointed out that our diplomats were already far too mobile, and that the Jury should have first got in touch with me. I added that the man in question had turned down the offer, so I was merely protesting out of principle. This was on June 3, 1932.

Yet, by July 19th I was already in the thick of the J.L.L. business.

This showed the weakest side of Zulueta – an excellent man, a keen mind, almost a puritan, indeed so much so that his Madrid staff told me he would have nothing to do with secret funds; yet, a weak character, and, out of weakness capable of things he knew he should spurn. This J.L.L. was a good-for-nothing who, in order to live and keep his family, hung on the coat tails of powerful freemasons. He was sent to me by Zulueta 'to work at the Embassy', for which he had no qualifications whatsoever. He knew nothing about anything, was no linguist and didn't even have the physique for the job, for he was a ridiculous, chubby, little man, all pink cheeks and blond hairlocks, with a lorgnon like a toy bicycle riding his ball-pointed nose. He had secured for himself 1500 francs a month from which the Embassy budget had to provide a thousand while the rest, Zulueta assured me, would be sent from Madrid; but for doing what? No one knew, not even the Minister.

I soon found that his favourite activities were peeping into the papers, official or private, of my diplomatic staff and pleading to me that his 'little sister-in-law' who knew nothing and no language but Spanish be given a job as typist at the embassy. Things went from bad to worse until the Embassy Counsellor, a man whose Republican sympathies no one could doubt either at the embassy or in Madrid, told me the staff would no longer tolerate his presence. I sent him back to Madrid, his expenses paid and a generous margin of prepaid salary in his pocket.

J.L.L. was not pleased. Zulueta, having got chapter and verse on the misdemeanours of his *protégé*, thought it better to keep altogether out of it all; and, as I was soon to discover, J.L.L. began forthwith a whispering campaign against me. His field of action was two-fold: freemasonry and left wing socialism. His line of attack was best defined by a letter I received (January 13, 1933) from Augusto Barcía, then one of the top men in Spanish freemasonry. Barcía was a straight person, a good friend, and a man to be trusted; but he was not wholly free from gullibility.

I had complained to him about intrigues by one Geo Meye in Paris. He answered that he was certain I had been misled; then he proceeded to describe the trouble as he saw it: 'What happens is that the nets woven around you, if they have not altogether caught you within, have isolated you from those who, possibly with some passion, but always with rectitude and enthusiasm, would have served you. I know well, and you know it better, that in that house (the embassy) people who do not hesitate to campaign against the Republic in a public and solemn way, find access, keep in touch and have not lost their old influence. Why? How? That, I do not know but that the fact is correct, I do know and I maintain it. On the other hand I hold proof of the fact that essentially liberal people, impeccably Republican, who without vehemence or rancour would have wished to help you in the work of gradually correcting the traditional atmosphere and ways of that house have found themselves bound to give up their task so as not to get mixed up with some of the elements that surround you. Causes? Motives? As I don't know them exactly, I just record the reality and register the facts.'

Since there was not one word of truth in all Barcía said, and since I knew him to be far better provided by nature with honesty than with acumen, I soon saw that this letter was the outcome of a conversation with J.L.L. The verbose and nebulous description of the situation, with its vague plurals 'people', 'elements', concealing the single character of the person concerned, described accurately enough the opposition between J.L.L. and my diplomatic staff, translated from what it actually was – a clash between decent men and an undesirable adventurer resolved on climbing by crooked ways – into a struggle between the Republic and a pack of monarchists.

When he found that Zulueta had seen through him, J.L.L. sought to enlist the help of Luis Araquistain, and was only too successful. Araquistain was then veering to the left wing of the party; though by no means to communism, for which he never had much sympathy, but rather to an extremist form of socialism, at bottom less inspired in doctrine and ideology than in the fissiparous tendency of all Spanish parties. In those days, the Spanish Socialist Party was split into left, led by Largo Caballero, centre, led by Indalecio Prieto, and right, led by Julián Besteiro.

So Araquistain was a left socialist or 'caballerist'; and as such, he had founded a daily, *Claridad*, which the official party paper, *El Socialista* (centre) attacked on the ground that there was not too much *clarity* as to the origin of the money. In *Claridad*, J.L.L. began to publish articles in which all sorts of fairy tales were told about me, including that I had secret meetings with Quiñones de León – whom, since I had taken over the Embassay, I had seen only once, in Briand's death chamber, and even then did not speak to him for more than the three-minute whispers the occasion allowed. I warned Araquistain, told him the story, showed him J.L.L.'s receipts proving him to be a parasite living on the embassy; all to no avail. Araquistain went on publishing the stuff.

Unfortunately, I was still a Member of Parliament; and Zulueta who should have shielded me, preferred that I should come to Madrid and stand up for myself and for my staff, and I, very foolishly as I now see it, agreed. I faced my critics in Parliament, I left them totally devoid of any grounds for criticising either me or any of my collaborators, but since they did not rely on arguments but merely on prejudice, my ordeal was of little avail, save perhaps that it increased my pessimism as to the future of the Republic.

CHAPTER XXV

A PROGRAMME FOR SPAIN

THIS feeling was by no means soothed by my official relations with Zulueta's successor. Sánchez Albornoz is a first-rate scholar and masterly historian of medieval Spain, but he was less admirable as a Minister of Foreign Affairs. His appointment was again one of those utterly arbitrary choices that Azaña seemed to favour. The first time I noticed this foible in him was when he offered me the Finance Ministry in December 1932; perhaps the most scandalous was his appointment of an inexperienced, light-weight journalist as Secretary General of the Agrarian Reform Institute*. This was the institution in charge of the key measure the country expected from the Republic. The appointment of Sánchez Albornoz for the Foreign Office was on a par with the other two. The new Minister, who was at the time in Buenos Aires, had to be waited for in those aviation-less days, knew next to nothing about Foreign Affairs and still less about Geneva and gave me tons of courtesy but little understanding or sympathy.

In my desire to make Spain's presence felt in League affairs, I had asked and obtained that a League Committee to deal with the situation of the Jews threatened by the Nazi persecution should comprise a Spaniard, since a considerable part of the persecuted Jews were Sephardites who still spoke and wrote Spanish. The new Foreign Secretary arrived, and, without consulting me, wrote to Geneva that Spain was not interested in the problem. This, though, was but a prelude. More trouble was coming. I had always worried about my very freedom in Geneva, and more than once had spoken in and written to Madrid urging the ministry to endow the Delegation with some substance and continuity, in fact, to make of it an institution instead of a free run for any one who might happen to be a delegate; for this situation, agreeable though at first sight it might be for me, could eventually lead to capital mistakes or – what would have been far more likely – to complete apathy on the part of 'Spain' even in matters where her interests were at stake.

On May 27, 1932 I had sent to the Ministry a note eighteen foolscap pages long on what in my opinion the foreign policy of the Republic should be. I started from the view that there was no reason for Spain

---

* This man became a Franco-ite and served as Franco's Ambassador somewhere.

to adopt an offensive policy but there were a number of them to force us to watch over our defence. On this basis, I defined our first aim as 'the reduction of the technical and financial collaboration of foreigners (in our affairs) to bounds that allow the State a full exercise of its sovereignty.'

I then drew the picture of the tensions between Spain and France, Britain and Italy, as well as the U.S. owing to the situation of Spain on the one hand at the back of a France whose eyes were on the Rhine, and on the other, right on the Straits of Gibraltar; as well as to the strength of Spanish culture in the New World. The outcome of it all was that the subjects of our concern should be (in an order from the innermost outwards): economic liberation; the Straits and Portugal; Tangiers-Morocco; relations with France and with Britain; relations with Spanish America and with the U.S.; obligations under the Covenant.

I then discussed our moral force, the first asset of which was our culture. Spain was morally a great power, and in their imperial creativeness, the Spaniards were only comparable to the Britons and the Romans. I warned against any undue extension of our Republican zeal for rationalism leading to an unfair criticism of our monarchical and colonial institutions of the past. This led me to define our position towards Spanish America: 'If and when Spain happens to be wrong, it is extremely unlikely that Spanish American states will back her; but if and when she is right, this backing is practically certain.' Nor was Spanish Americanism as such a mere source of strength for Spain, since it might lead her to show solidarity in circumstances not favourable for her prestige.

On other moral forces: I referred first to the fear felt by the middle class abroad about the possibility of a social revolution in Spain. The second was the perspective of a considerable prestige for Spain in the Hebrew and Islamic world on the day we should be ready to open up the possibilities of Andalusia as a centre of Semitic culture. The third was the opportunity afforded us by Geneva to develop a policy of international justice free from political ties.

I then dealt with the economic forces that determined or limited our policy, particularly with regard to the most important members of our economic family, France and Britain. And from these premises I went on to state our programme and orientation. The first aim should be to build up a strong State, conscious of itself and capable of continuity – an aim in itself, but also an indispensable means towards reaching the aims of our foreign policy. Hence, it seemed to me necessary to create a Ministry of State* capable of conceiving and carrying out a coherent,

* Our traditional name for the F.O. from which the American State Department derives its name.

organic and continuous policy, subject to a periodical revision by parliament and the press. This, I advocated, implied the formation of a panel of competent foreign policy publicists and journalists. I advocated:

> A rise in the technical ability of Spanish financiers, through co-operation between the Finance Ministry and private banks in order to send young economists abroad;
> The development of faculties of modern humanities in our universities so as to foster a European culture by the study of the language, the literature and the history of every important European people, and the setting up of a school of Oriental languages, from those of the Slav group to the Chinese;
> An improvement of the level of the Spanish Civil Service and its rationalisation;
> A centre for the spreading of Spanish culture abroad on the lines of *l'Alliance Française*;
> A vigorous development of the Bank of Foreign Trade;
> The repatriation (though not necessarily nationalisation) of the metal and mining industries, especially those of lead, copper and silver;
> On the basis of Spain's wealth in pyrites, sunlight, water power and potash, the development of a strong chemical industry;
> A reorganisation of the merchant marine;
> An original foreign policy based on the principles of the Covenant. This was not merely advisable but necessary since we had to bow to destiny, which made of Spain the present or potential adversary of all the big powers. Our aims should be to back every plan for preventing war and thus to lead to as complete a reduction of armaments as possible. Spain should also take part in every form of international co-operation that would tend to separate financial from political power, and in particular to back every institution likely to uphold the national integrity of countries having to apply abroad for credit.

As for Portugal, I suggested that, without giving up all hope of an Iberian Federation, we should leave it to the Portuguese to take any initiative towards coming together. We should promote Iberian arbitration courts and a close financial co-operation.

On Gibraltar, I suggested a study of the railway under the sea, to enable us to decide whether to give it up altogether or to build it ourselves, if workable.

On the Covenant, I drew attention to the possibility of our having to take peace or war decisions on the strength of Article 16, so I recommended a study of that question by the Government itself. I pointed out that it was in Spain's interest not to go beyond or fall short of the strict obligation defined by the Covenant.

On Spanish America I recommended an agreement with the U.S.A. to back every move favourable to both North and South, on condition that the anti-Spanish bias observable in American policy should be eliminated.

I concluded that Spain should develop closer ties with the European Protestant nations such as Switzerland, Holland and the Scandinavians as well as with progressive countries such as Czechoslovakia or Ireland. And as for the Soviets, I recommended an empirical policy mindful of the possible effects of a Soviet diplomatic mission in Madrid on our inflammable working class.

I was myself to open this gate, for after the Soviet Union was admitted to the League of Nations our Government thought it wise to discuss with her the matter of mutual recognition. It was no easy matter. There was first an agreement negotiated by Azaña's administration in 1933, and things went so lustily on that the Russians appointed Lunacharsky as Ambassador. He came, with his wife, to lunch with me in Paris and struck me as the most 'intellectual' bolshevik I had so far come across, even more so than Rosenberg; for Rosenberg hardly ever strayed aside from the issue of capitalism versus communism, while Lunacharsky preferred every other possible subject on earth, and was lively and interesting on all, especially on that of Don Quixote.

He had been Commissar for Education and was definitely a bookish man, a fact he betrayed even in the usual direction of his glance, which kept at the reading rather than at the seeing angle. His *pince-nez* and his *barbiche* were definitely nineteenth-century French. His wife, an actress, carried with distinction the elegance of her profession, though her conversation was just discreet, probably through linguistic fetters. I teased him on my *Sacred Giraffe*, a fantasy on which more will have to be written anon. This futuristic novel must have appealed to some exalted inkpot in Moscow (if for other than literary motives), for I suddenly got a request for a biographical note to be printed with a Russian translation that was to appear in the Union. No mention, of course, of permission, agreement, or anything as materialistic as fees. Eventually I did receive two copies.

I began by requesting that a few more copies be sent to me, then I enquired about whether I was to be content with having my author's rights just cashed by the Soviet Union. Lunacharsky countered that the book had not sold at all and was a dead loss. It did not seem to me correct to point out to him my conviction to the effect that, had I proved myself an obedient fellow-traveller, the book would have brought me substantial fees whether it sold or not; certain as I was that such and no other had been the purpose of the eminent Inkpot in the Soviet administration.

Nevertheless, everything went on in the best of moods, and the Lunacharskys left wreathed in smiles to spend a short holiday at the Côte d'Azur before leaving for Spain; but I soon heard that Lunacharsky had died there of a heart attack.

Meanwhile Azaña's Cabinet had died also, and Lerroux's man at the F.O. thought that the agreement signed by his predecessor was not cautious enough. I was instructed to reopen the question on the basis of no recognition before the number of diplomatic and consular agents had been fixed, for Spain feared (in my opinion rightly) that the Soviet Union would exploit her extra-territorial rights in order to organise propaganda and even subversion in a big way. Lenin and Trotsky had always seen Spain as the most promising land for communism to spread to.

Litvinov was adamant. First, recognition, then discussion on numbers of diplomats and consuls. This cat-and-mouse business did not last very long. I proposed to Litvinov that we drafted a paper stating simultaneously the recognition and the limitation, to be 'initialled' by both of us; and on the basis of this paper, to appoint our Ambassadors, it being understood that the limitations would be binding. He agreed, and thereupon spent some time trying to persuade me to go to Moscow as Spanish Ambassador; which tempted me very much indeed but did not seem favourable for my family. I left the matter undecided. I was three or four steps down on my way to the street (having all my life felt an objection to taking *lifts* downwards) when he, from the landing, asked: 'Whom should we send to Madrid?' And I answered: 'Any one you like except Kaganovich.'*

Yet, it was not to be. In Lerroux's circles there were many candidates for Moscow, some, I am afraid, tempted by a vague idea that there was good business in Russian oil. This was a two-fold error. Dealing with

* My exclusion had of course nothing to do with Kaganovich's being a Jew. So was Litvinov.

Russia leaves little if any margin for 'business'; and, in those days, Russia had no oil to spare, mostly because, scared by Hitler, she was building up her reserves. But all these calculations, hopes and ambitions came to nothing; because on October 4, 1934 there was a rising of some of the forces of the left, and the Government thought it better to file the whole affair for the time being.

My memorandum, written in 1933, witnesses to the earnestness of my concern for the actual facts and circumstances that determined our foreign policy, and therefore, of my endeavour to endow it with an objectivity it was bound to lack while the titular head of the Foreign Office changed every three months, and I was allowed a free hand. The obvious corollary of this attitude of mine was a request for permanency, stability and competence in the Spanish Delegation to the League of Nations. I had repeatedly put this issue to my string of chiefs, without success. I seized the opportunity of some vacancies and changes of staff to request that the two most competent men for League affairs in the Spanish diplomatic service were assigned to the delegation: Oliván, by being transferred to Bern, as Minister Plenipotentiary, and Teixidor, (who had been for years a member of the political section of the Secretariat) to be appointed Consul General in Geneva.

I do not propose to load these pages with my correspondence on this subject with Sánchez Albornoz; all I shall say is that, rather than give up his rights as Cabinet Minister to appoint whom he pleased to wherever he pleased, Albornoz was ready to let me resign both the Paris embassy and my Geneva post. The embassy did not matter; as for Geneva, he had not the slightest idea of what the loss would have been for Spain. I had: that is why I did not insist on my resignation which, on the other hand, I should not have tendered at all.

CHAPTER XXVI

A SOUTH AMERICAN PEACE PACT

A new President, General Justo, took charge of Argentine affairs in 1931. His name, at any rate, was a good omen. He had, moreover, though a general, reached the top by strictly constitutional means, thanks to a good reputation, which his wise government was to vindicate. In foreign affairs, his government was to assume a number of initiatives due to the ambitious personality of his Minister of Foreign Affairs, Dr Carlos Saavedra Lamas.

By 1932, Saavedra Lamas had presented an anti-war Pact to an Assembly of American nations, meeting in Río de Janeiro, and sent to Europe no less a person than Roberto Levillier as a roving Ambassador to 'sell' his Pact to the Europeans. Now Levillier was not merely an Argentine diplomat. He was a good man of letters and a historian who was in later years to publish an outstanding work on Amerigo Vespuccio. It soon became common knowledge in Europe, and more especially in Geneva, that Levillier would, whenever possible, blend his advocacy of the Saavedra Lamas Pact with that of the merits of its author and contriver as a candidate for the Nobel Peace Prize; and thereby hangs a tale which will presently be told.

By then I had become saturated with Pacts; for there was hardly a statesman, real or imaginary, who did not fancy himself as the author of the pact of the century; and the halls and corridors of the World Parliament were then enlivened by two quips for which this time, I am afraid I was responsible. 'The state of the world is pactological'; and 'the international hell is paved with good conventions.' Indeed, good conventions or bad were not considered indispensable. I once received the visit of Max Henriquez Ureña, then Minister of Foreign Affairs of the Dominican Republic. Max was one of a trio of outstanding literary persons in their country (two brothers and a sister), but he, the eldest, had strayed into politics. He came to enlist my support for a Nobel Peace Prize for the two presidents of the two nations in the Island, Haiti and Santo Domingo, because instead of cutting each other's throats, they had signed a pact of peace and amity.

There is no doubt that Saavedra Lamas's contrivance was theoretically a good convention. Whether its utility went further than that of paving a square foot of our hell is another matter. Its author, however, lost no time in realising that a good certificate from me was, in the circumstances, indispensable for the success of his venture, and this was put to me by Levillier with his usual charm and ability. My colleague at the Council table and Argentine Minister in Berne, Ruiz Guiñazú, wrote to me from Berne on July 12th reminding me of the fact that his chief expected me to do something about it. 'I have already expressed to you the pleasure with which the author will receive your authoritative opinion. Should your many occupations have prevented you from doing anything in the matter, I take the liberty to beg you not to lift your hand from my request.'

These hopes were very nearly ruined by a motor accident I underwent then – all due to the extreme legalistic mind of my driver. He was a Navarrese, and as for fastness of ideas, his brain seemed to be built of granite, nay, basalt. In case of doubt, his decision would never be dictated by the miserably utilitarian consideration of saving human lives including his own, but by a loftier one: the answer to this noble question: who is right? One night, at midnight, returning from a dinner with my old comrades at the *Ecole Polytechnique*, as he ran at a good speed along the Cours Albert Ier, a taxi, crossing from the other side through the double row of trees between the two lanes, protruded and stood in his way. Who was right? My driver, of course. So, on he went, and after some sinister billiards, we were stopped dead by a neutral tree. My head went through the glass screen between me and my driver, and I was not beheaded by the glass because Providence had made up Its mind that I should live and these memoirs should be written. I got a ring of small wounds round my face: corner of an eye, a side of the nose, lip, under the chin; everything was threatened and nothing endangered – no doubt because of our respect for the law.

But the blood! These head wounds seem to let out blood by the gallon. When I arrived at the embassy warning all and sundry to be quiet so as not to wake up the family, our housekeeper helped me to doff my summer light black coat: it stood on the floor, heavy and stiff with the cold blood it had imbibed. The consequences for my body were very slight and soon repaired – but alas for Saavedra Lamas's Pact: it had to wait for three months.

My comment on it took the form of a speech delivered at the *Académie Diplomatique Internationale* on October 20, 1933. This institution was a kind of unofficial forum for the less active members of the diplomatic profession, and it had been founded in Paris by an equally unofficial but very industrious Greek. My speech was to be the *pièce de résistance* in the presentation of Dr Saavedra Lamas's creation. It was no easy task for me; for, on the one hand, my enthusiasm for the Pact in question was by no means uncontrollable, while on the other hand, I could not forget for a moment that I was no mere private person uttering his private views, but the Spanish Ambassador in Paris and Chief Delegate to Geneva discussing an official initiative of the Foreign Secretary of the Argentine Republic. I managed, I do believe, to conciliate sincerity with diplomacy, but not without a considerable outlay in epithets. Saavedra Lamas had taken the precaution of cabling his thanks in advance. This enabled me to thank him for his cable expressing my satisfaction at having 'shared in the task of spreading the knowledge of your noble initiative in a sitting devoted to your work so worthy of the incomparable tradition of Argentina.'

Most speeches are sterile. This one wasn't. It yielded results, not altogether unexpected yet somewhat unorthodox. Less than a year later, I was in Argentina, addressing all kinds of audiences on peace, war, the League and Pacts more or less useful. Nor did the fecundity of that speech end there. But the story of its after-effects is complex and woven of many strands to some of which we must now turn our attention.

CHAPTER XXVII

I LEAVE PARIS

THE visit of Mohammed V ben Yussuf to Paris was, of course, the occasion for a festival in his honour at the Spanish Embassy, Spain being the 'Protector' State for a part of Northern Morocco that, despite the several nibblings it had undergone at the tooth of French diplomacy, was still far from negligible. The Sultan was then youthful, and his eyes were intelligent, yet curiously tired for his age. This feeling of tiredness could also be observed in his legs. Well-built and handsome though he was, he would not stand for long without his glance searching around evidently for a seat. Someone explained to me that this feature of the youthful yet worn-out monarch was due to the generous supply of young, irresistible women the chief Protector State provided for him, precisely so as to keep him in no state to waste his energies on political pursuits.

Yet, Mohammed V was to outgrow this erotic period and become one of the most virile Sultans of Morocco, and the leader of the movement for independence. In those days, when few as yet were those who thought of such things at all, I remember I had a conversation with Monsieur Ponsot (who had filled many a high post in the 'colonial' administration of his country), during which I put it to him that the subordinate status of the Northern African nations would not last fifty years. 'Fifty?' he asked. 'Not twenty.' And yet – as I am about to illustrate it – how assiduous, clever, 'patriotic' was the endeavour of the governments and upper bureaucracies of the European powers to secure illusory advantages in that land of imaginary conquests Africa still was or seemed to them.

Such things as the party for the Sultan of Morocco could, if necessary, be financed in whole or in part by an *ad hoc* subsidy from the ministry; but, in general, the Paris embassy kept the Ambassador under a constant threat, if not of bankruptcy, at least of loss and debt. This was a situation by no means enviable for a man who had to earn his living; and though I enjoyed the opportunity for doing things that the embassy afforded me, the financial exposure, implicit in my function, made me more than once think of giving it up. This feeling was strengthened by the fact that the cumulation of the embassy and the Geneva delegation was too much for one man.

Nevertheless, I had let go two opportunities to leave Paris. The first, when our Parliament declared Ambassadors incompatible with parliamentary mandates. It was, of course, plain common sense. I resigned the embassy, wishing to remain in Parliament; but the Government put strong pressure on me to force me to remain in Paris. The second was when Lerroux in one of his Cabinet-making endeavours (September 1933) asked me to come to Madrid and take charge of the Foreign Office. I asked the opinion of my party (the Home-Rule Gallegan Party) and they frowned at it, for Lerroux was anathema to them, since the Gallegan Home-Rulers considered themselves as allies of Azaña; so I turned down the offer, whereupon Lerroux achieved his Cabinet-making including in it a member of my own party.

Then, one day, at the beginning of March 1934, the phone rang and it was again Lerroux, again Cabinet-making. 'I need you here, this time for the Ministry of Education. The right and the left are at logger-heads about it. Both will trust you.' I asked for reflection, I did reflect and wrote him a letter, the gist of which was that I would come on two conditions: the Government would make a sincere and sustained effort to get on with the socialists; and there would be no amnesty for Sanjurjo. I own that I sinned on the side of naïvety when I assumed that Lerroux would conform to the Spanish proverb: 'he who keeps silent, grants', and taking his silence for an acquiescence, I left Paris and took office as Minister of Education.

My French friends did not cherish my decision. By then, the Minister of Foreign Affairs was Louis Barthou, with whom I had struck up a good relationship, as I shall relate presently. Léger, the Secretary General of the Quai d'Orsay, was a friend. Both made long faces. However, longer still was the face of President Lebrun when I paid him my official farewell visit; but this time the fact was due less to sadness than to solemnity. He stood up, looked solemn and conferred upon me the Grand Cross of the Legion of Honour, a rare distinction for an Ambassador. I have remained ever since in admiration for that noble gesture, for I never was anything but a difficult Ambassador, stubbornly sticking to my own line in striking contrast with the pliant policy of my predecessors; and I interpreted the distinction to the fact that Barthou and Léger, both men of letters, appreciated my keen interest in French culture and the fact that I also sat, though on a modest stool, at the French Parnassus.

As an amateur mathematician and *polytechnicien*, I am always fascinated by cases in which events run riot over the calculus of probabilities. In 1909, as I took my final examinations at the *Ecole Polytechnique* and wished to enter the School of Mines, I wrote a request to the Minister of Public Works in Paris, explaining that, since in 1907 I had passed the entrance examinations for both Schools and had chosen the *Ecole Polytechnique*, I might be now exempted from passing a second time the entrance examinations for the School of Mines. A decree to that effect signed by the Minister appeared in the *Journal Officiel*. In 1934, another decree, signed by the Minister of Foreign Affairs, granted me the Grand Cross of the Legion of Honour. These two decrees separated by a lapse of twenty-five years, the only ones devoted to me and only to me, in the French State Newspaper, were signed by the same man: Louis Barthou.

I was not happy about leaving Paris, and I felt that my stint at the embassy, though generously appreciated by my French friends, could and should have been more fertile. The trouble was the rival work at Geneva, in itself also fascinating for me, in part through conviction, in part through the feeling that I was the very man for it, a point on which I may have to return. There was a small group of sour critics in Spain who argued that the cumulation of the two posts was good for neither, and the curious fact was that what they said would have been right had they said it 'with good intent'; but, as it was, it led them to argue it on the wrong 'facts'; i.e. that my work as a delegate was bound to suffer from my work as an Ambassador and vice versa, which was certainly not the case, while the trouble came from the sheer excess of work the situation heaped on my back.

It was a fact, though, that I was a somewhat unorthodox Ambassador; I have already set down a few instances. Here is one more. There was a brilliant gathering of European intellectuals at dinner on some occasion or other, at the Claridge Hotel in Paris, and I was asked to preside (October 18, 1933). When the time came for me to speak, I drew a picture of Europe in which I endeavoured to express the vital union of her geography, her history and her character; and in a paragraph of some eloquence and drive, I described the city predestined by these three factors to be the capital of Europe, in terms that must have led many of my listeners to expect 'Paris' at the end of my drive; but it was not Paris but Vienna. I knew it was a heretical thing to do, and far away on the left in the big glittering hall I could see the sardonic smile of Aldous Huxley celebrating it; yet I also knew that the best of the excellent minds of France who were listening would agree, and I dared it and I do believe that some good came out of it.

CHAPTER XXVIII

A CABINET MINISTER FOR FIVE WEEKS

MANY years have gone by since I left the embassy to accept a ministerial post that I could on no account expect to last, since I was not a Member of Parliament; and I have not yet made up my mind as to whether I was right or wrong. It is, in any case, a question hard to decide, since it amounts to a comparison between an 'is' or 'was' and a 'might have been.' Furthermore, we do not usually make up our minds on the criterion whether this or that is better for us and for the world; but on some complex set of forces one of which is curiosity for the unknown. The life of an Ambassador was known to me. Political life in Spain wasn't. I felt perhaps that it was worth while to get to know it.

Well, it wasn't. I soon began to feel ill at ease. With the distance of the years, I think I can discern the chief cause of my *malaise*: I had passed from a world in which things weighed more than men to a world the other way about; from a world on the whole governed by a formidable 'IT' to one misruled by a crowd of I's, by no means each formidable in himself, yet as a crowd a most formidable obstacle for anyone impelled by an impetus to get on with the job.

The situation was the more irritating for the purely personal advantages it entailed for me as, for the moment, one of those I's. At Irún, the lordly car of the Minister of Education was awaiting me and my younger daughter Lol who came with me. It was driven by a smart man in uniform with a wide stripe of gold on his cap and a spare driver who in fact was but the nationalised heir to the 'lackey' without whom the carriages of the V.I.P.s in the Spain of bygone days would have been unthinkable.

Off we went driven with the utmost skill, vigour and brio at vertiginous speed. At Burgos, the Governor and his wife were awaiting us for lunch and, after lunch, as I suggested having coffee in another place than that hotel, we were driven to the local Club, where ladies were not admitted, but where the rule was broken in my daughter's honour. It was well meant, but it rubbed me the wrong way. In a Republic, too!

In Madrid, I found I had to be guarded. I had never known such a thing so far, not even in my official life, for neither in Geneva nor in Washington nor in Paris had I as much as thought of it. It simply did not enter my mind. Three persons devoted to my safety: a car with its driver and two secret service men. I found it a heavy drag on my freedom. I had left Lol with relatives in Madrid and settled for a time in a hotel. Every morning I went for a longish walk in a park close by, but not so close by. In the evening my escort would ask at what time I wanted them the next morning. I answered ten o'clock, for I meant to leave for my walk at nine. One day, having grown suspicious, they turned up as I had just left the hotel. I saw them and hid behind a tree until they were in, then gave them the slip. No doubt betrayed by the hotel staff, my escort appealed to me against me. 'You see, Sir, it is our bread and butter that is at stake.' I had to surrender, and take my morning walk with my police tail dragging behind. When, as I shall tell presently, I accumulated two portfolios for a fortnight, I called together my six escort men and explained to them that if they saw a man stealing along or rushing to murder me, they were to ask him first whom he wanted Spain rid of: the Minister of Education or the Minister of Justice; if the first, 'you' deal with him; if the latter, 'you' must take over the job. They thought I was a bit unorthodox for a cabinet minister. I felt the whole thing was a waste of money, for I don't gather that such so-called security arrangements have ever been effective in normal times, and I was soon to be confirmed in this opinion by the tragic end of my friend Louis Barthou.

My kingdom was to be the Ministry of Education. When it was built, Azaña wryly wrote in his weekly: 'As the budget for it is but half that once voted for the General Post Office, they will only be able to make it half as ugly.' For once, he was wrong. It was far uglier, so that its ugliness turned out to have been relatively cheap. It was also inconvenient and, as a building, inefficient.

But, if only as a building! I soon discovered that our primary education, the pride of the Republic, was in a chaotic state. I summoned the Director General. Puncturing his circumvolutions, I found there were about 11,500 schools that lacked schoolmasters and that there were about 11,500 schoolmasters that lacked schools, though they were being paid. I was not surprised for I remembered that when I landed in La Coruña in the first days of the new regime I had been shown a fine brand new building for a big primary school and I was told that it had been ready for months but there was no teaching, there were no classes, no children. Why? Because the state and the city each held that the other was to pay for the fuel.

I told this story to my civil servant, then asked to see the list of these truant schoolmasters. Putting my finger on one chosen at random, I asked: 'Why is this man away?' – 'Because he is studying pedagogy in Louvain.' – 'But meanwhile?' – 'Meanwhile we cannot put another man there because it is HIS school.' – 'And this one?' – 'He is a Member of Parliament on permanent leave.' – 'So, while he is in Parliament, the

children?' – 'Well, Sir, it is HIS school.' – And so on all 11,500. 'Very
good.' I said; 'this is March 15th. If by August 15th you have not reduced this scandal from 11,500 to 500, you will resign.' – It was I who
was 'resigned' and within five weeks.

It made me despair not of the Government nor of the Republic but of
the country, for the form of government had nothing to do with it. I recollect another case when a secondary school teacher who was supposed to teach in Barcelona lived in Madrid. He came to Barcelona at
the start of term and when he had sold a copy of his own textbook to
every student, reported sick and sped to Madrid. At the end of term,
he went back to Barcelona, to preside over exams, which meant fees
and also a personal control enabling him to ensure that his victims (you
could hardly call them his students) had learnt his own and no other
text book. He had an accomplice at the ministry.

I called a meeting of the Council of Education of which, as the
Minister, I was the *ex-officio* President. It was one of those cases in
which I allowed myself far too much freedom to tell the truth. And the
truth was awful. For under the general mantle of tolerance woven by
bad conscience over low salaries, a trade in textbooks was allowed if
not fostered – a sheer waste of paper, print and youngsters' energy;
for in order to exact a higher price their authors saw to it that their
textbooks were big and heavy. I unloaded my packet on those men,
most of whom were the representatives of the sinners and sinners themselves. That speech was the prelude to my exit from the Spanish scene
as a politician.

I must recount yet another story related to this period, for it spreads
the absurdity of things and people in a more even and fair manner. I
received from a young Catalan doctor a complaint to the effect that
he was the son of a Catalan mother and a Venezuelan father, who, led
by his love of France, had volunteered and been killed in the First World
War, leaving a baby and a widow in Barcelona. This 'baby' had never
travelled abroad, never known his Venezuelan father, grown up as a
Catalan boy all his life and become a doctor of medicine at the University of Barcelona. On the day he applied for a licence to carry on his
profession, his colleagues barred the way. As a Venezuelan, he could
not carry on his profession in Spain.

The idea that he was a Venezuelan had never crossed his mind nor the
mind of his mother; yet, it was so. I called the official in charge and told
him no matter the letter of the law, he must be allowed to practise.
The official was adamant. There was one way and one only: he had to
take Spanish nationality and begin all over again the whole of his
studies of medicine as a Spaniard. This seemed to me monstrous, for
the reason why a foreign doctor cannot be allowed to practise is purely

due to the need to guarantee that his training is up to the level required
in the country, and this level the young doctor had already reached
by passing his exams in Barcelona. No matter the letter of the law, I
was not going to tolerate that it be invoked for an act of outrageous
protectionism. I told my official so, and explained that either the
medical union (for so it was in fact) behaved itself or I should have a
bill rushed through Parliament to get the young doctor free to practise
that very year with a gong of publicity that would not help the profession. The Doctors' Union proved wise and all ended well.

In later years I was to observe other cases of medical protectionism.
I shall limit my examples to one. Gustavo Pittaluga, Italian born,
naturalised Spaniard, was one of our most eminent doctors and a member of the Academy of Medicine. He was elected to the constituent
assembly and during the civil war settled in Havana. Practically every
physician there who stood above the common crowd of medical men
had been a student of his in Madrid. When he made it known that he
had come to stay, his ex-students offered him a degree h.c. for the University of Havana. He retorted: 'No, thanks. I want a real degree, so
that I can practise.' This they refused. He had to pass his exams all
over again from the beginning before juries nearly always composed
of old students of his.

On taking office, I found the Under-secretary was a politician belonging to Lerroux's party. I sought another man and made enquiries, for I
had no candidate in view. A professor of Law at Oviedo University
emerged as the most desirable choice. I rang him up, and when he
recovered from the surprise, he accepted. He was a first-rate collabor-
ator, competent and hard working. But again I had behaved as an
intellectual who makes a bee line for the best (theoretical) solution,
with a typical disregard for the demands of mere politics, and by choosing Prieto Bances as my Under-secretary, I had left the ministry with
no other liaison with Parliament than what I could ensure, for as a
Cabinet Minister, even though not an M.P., I could sit in Parliament,
though I could not vote.

One day a draft decree was sent to me for me to present to the
Cabinet so that, if approved, it could be signed by the President of the
Republic and countersigned by me. It came already in its spick and
span garb, on fine thick paper duly gilt-edged. After reading it, I wrote
in the margin: *Back to the service concerned with a request that it be
written in Spanish.* It went back again, and yet again. The fourth time,
Prieto Bances himself brought the last draft. He had seen the flaw. I
thanked him. Henceforth, I got better-drafted decrees, but also I dare-

say a reputation for being something of a bore. Let my excuse be that the Spanish of official documents is even worse than the English of British documents; and I assure my English readers that I am not boasting at all.

All these disappointments seemed to me to flow from a low spiritual level of our collective sense. Yet, despite the shortcomings of our universities as teaching institutions, I still hold the view that, even so, the university is the best thing we have; just as I think that, on the whole, the barristers of Spain are our best political asset. Nevertheless, the standards of our universities are not good; and the professors take far too many liberties with their duties as teachers – though there are many honourable exceptions.

Meanwhile, I was growing more and more uneasy about the consequences of my resignation in Geneva. I had only resigned from the embassy. I had not resigned as the Spanish Delegate in Geneva simply because, though I had acted as such for three years if an occasion arose, no such person existed officially. Of course, the Government could have sent me to Geneva all the same; but then, what became of the Minister of Foreign Affairs? Pita Romero was a clever lawyer born in La Coruña; but his appointment to that ministry could only be due to President Alcalá Zamora's wish to be his own minister of Foreign Affairs. Lerroux gave me to understand that Pita Romero would be sent as Ambassador to the Vatican and then I should be transferred to the Foreign Office. But something no one could have foreseen happened then: Pita Romera was appointed Ambassador to the Vatican and retained his post as Minister of Foreign Affairs.

This absurdity was swallowed by a public opinion that seemed unable to assimilate the notion that Spain is in the world of nations. It bore the extravagant style of that Baroque masterpiece, Alcalá Zamora, intent on ruling over foreign affairs, but, indirectly, it revealed the weakness of Lerroux himself, for he should obviously have stood against such patent nonsense. His weakness came from his excessive dependence on the President of the Republic, whose policy towards political figures owed so much to that of Alfonso XIII that he soon became known as Alfonso XIII 'unbound', in which the stress is on the twofold meaning of 'unbound' in Spanish: *en rústica.*

Meanwhile, since Pita Romero knew no foreign language and was by no means well-versed in Geneva affairs, my place at the League was occupied by underlings, one of whom, thoroughly anti-French, took the opportunity to try to eliminate from our neutral group the two nations closest to French policy: Belgium and Czechoslovakia. I was worried, but not too much, for it was becoming clearer every day that the Lerroux Cabinet would not last.

I was soon to find my surmise confirmed by an indirect confession to that effect from the Prime Minister himself. It all happened, as is so often the case in politics, through a somewhat irrelevant blunder that raised a dust of indignation, some of it sincere. Our Minister of Justice, one Valdés, inherited by the Republic from the *reformists*, a party of liberals that had come as close to the monarchy as republicans could, was not a man any one would consider as of the left. In the course of some unimportant answer during an unimportant debate, he made a tactless remark on Captain Galán, an extreme left officer who had tried to steal a march on the republicans and proclaim the Republic too soon. The left in the House rose like a man to protest; and Lerroux felt Valdés had to be thrown to the lions.

But who was to be his successor?

CHAPTER XXIX

A DOUBLE CABINET MINISTER

L ERROUX asked me to come and see him. Every member of the cabinet but two was a lawyer. If any of them took the job, even on a temporary basis, he would be bound by law to suspend the practice of his legal profession for a year. The other man, a doctor of medicine, was not suitable. Lerroux begged me to take the job on top of mine, for he did not think it worth while to appoint a new man as the life of the Cabinet was limited. I proved again my inability to grasp the peculiar style of political life by agreeing. Now I feel that his reason was not genuine. He knew the amnesty bill aiming at freeing Sanjurjo from jail was on the stocks; and did not want to jeopardise any of his colleagues with the responsibility for it.

Now, I had made it clear to him on joining his Cabinet (being neither an M.P. nor a member of his party) that one of my conditions was that Sanjurjo was not to be amnestied; therefore, Lerroux was not behaving with any particular regard for my wishes or opinions. Should I resign? I shrank from this solution; for it cast me in the unwelcome part of a wrecker of a Cabinet that was not yet one month old; and it seemed to me that my resignation would be an empty gesture. When the amnesty bill was at last presented to the Cabinet, I felt that I had not been treated as I had expected and assumed, and that my own views had not been respected. This fact and the general scepticism about the duration of Lerroux's Cabinet allowed me to take my own line in the matter of the amnesty bill itself. Since the freeing of Sanjurjo conferred on it a marked rightist tendency, I accepted practically every amendment offered by the left aiming at extending the bounty to those of their hotheads who happened to be in jail. The majority behind me were furious, but had to accept my decision or else take upon themselves the responsibility of killing the whole Cabinet.

The resignation of Valdés had another unfortunate result, the responsibility for which was shared by his son and by me. I had asked his son to carry on for the duration as my private secretary as Minister of Justice, as he had been for his father. Valdés junior could have refused. He accepted and I believed him. This was my part in the responsibility for what happened then. I read one morning an intemperate attack on me from the pen of Zugazagoitia, a middle-of-the-road socialist M.P. who was then editing the socialist daily. He protested against my refusal to answer a letter he had sent me, drawing my attention to the fact that two socialist militants in jail were being kept handcuffed. I then realised that I had not yet seen any letter addressed to me as Minister of Justice; and late in the morning, I received a packet of them from my other office, including Zugazagoitia's old and, of course, unanswered letter. Valdés junior had not taken the trouble to call at the office and look through my mail, until he had read the fierce attack against me in the morning *Socialista.* Nothing that I did to convince Zugazagoitia of my innocence had any effect. He refused to apologise.

There was no doubt in his stubbornness a certain element due to personal idiosyncrasies; but certainly also the civil war spirit that was already beginning to raise its ugly head; for the socialists had made up their minds and hearts against Lerroux, and though I gave them daily proofs of the independence of my political attitude, they would not forgive me for serving under Lerroux; while I thought that if we did not succeed in forming a strong centre, a civil war might destroy all of us.

One of the ways whereby I thought to bring about this 'de-electrification' of our political atmosphere was by means of institutions that would bridge the gap between the right and the left, provided they were both liberal-democratic, in fact, parliamentary. I tried my hand at several. One of them whose creation I advocated was the 'Council of State' to be composed of the Prime Minister and the Secretary of State, plus all the men who had served in either of those two capacities; its powers being to examine all questions of foreign affairs and advise the government on them. The plan failed because the socialist party demanded that its men sitting on the Council should report to the party on all its debates. Oddly enough, when I attributed to Fernando de los Ríos the invention of this institution (in the hope of bridging over our difficulties and of making the scheme more acceptable), Diego Martínez Barrio raised his claim to authorship.

Another of my ideas was the creation of a citizenship of honour. There was to be one man or woman raised to this honour every year, on the day of the anniversary of the proclamation of the Republic (April 14th). The person chosen would receive a diploma and a gold medal, no money; but a very high rank in the scale of precedence. My plan was to award it first to Unamuno, the next year to don Bartolomé Cossío, the patriarch of Spanish education, and when its rank was well established, to find a humble, obscure man who would really deserve the honour for a lifetime of public service. There seemed to me no reason why this institution should not have taken root; but it was not to be. As soon as the Azaña-socialist tribe took over from the Lerroux tribe, they let it fall. I also took the opportunity offered me by the fact that I was Minister of Education on the 12th of April (anniversary of the birth of the Republic) to direct the festivities in the same sense of union in freedom. Of the programme I devised and led I shall recollect three items: I organised a gathering in a big theatre, of which I reserved the two upper storeys for the primary school children of Madrid, and I arranged that the programme should be heard by radio for the benefit of similar gatherings in every city of the land. The festival opened with an oration by the President of the Republic. Alcalá Zamora; and it really was an excellent speech; then, there were songs, some learned some popular or traditional, in every one of the languages of the peninsula; then a small pamphlet was read through of which I had had printed a million copies, that were sent to all the schools of Spain, and which contained a selection of six of the finest pieces of Spanish verse or prose from the Middle Ages to our day; finally, the last movement of Beethoven's Ninth Symphony was played by the Madrid orchestra and choir.

I do not think I err in saying that it was the first time in our history when at an official gathering, songs in all our languages were heard. I insisted on that very note in another of my initiatives for that day. On the beautiful esplanade by the Royal Palace, we celebrated in the open air a festival of folklore dances of Spain to which we invited dancing groups from every province. It lasted between two and three hours in the early afternoon and it really was splendid. I have not forgotten a group from Zamora that looked like a cathedral stained-glass window moving to the strains of an organ, and a set of four young men from Ibiza dancing while holding a kind of billiard cue in one hand (spear) and a hoop in the other (shield) with a beautiful effect of rhythm and sense, for one could see and enjoy the gestures of war raised to the level of beauty.

Another of my endeavours in the same sense aimed at presenting the Spanish classical theatre in a popular form. I hoped at some later date to set up a few roaming companies that would tour the country, carrying light, cheap material easily transportable, so as to be able to turn into a theatre any odd bullring they might come across. As a preliminary I got some trusted and able producers to organise a show of Calderón's *The Mayor of Zalamea* in the bullring of Madrid. It was a huge success due entirely to the talent of my collaborators, chief of whom was Rivas Cherif, Azaña's brother-in-law. But we had first to rescue it from disaster not without a few cold shivers down our backs.

That sunny afternoon of April, I thought more than once of the pregnant dictum: 'There is but a step from the sublime to the ridiculous.' A hearty popular joviality could not but be, so to speak, waiting round the corner for us, the three members of the government of the festival, who sat together, tense and wondering, at the presidential

balcony of the bullring: Alcalá Zamora, Lerroux and I. We knew what
the atmosphere of the bullring can easily generate. And when the first
dialogues went on, seen but unheard by the huge audience, the mixture
of indignation and hilarity that trepidated in the crowd was ominous.

The loudspeakers were not working. The electricians were busy with
the wires, but that did not calm the crowd in the least, and we were
fearing that at any time the traditional rhythmical *Burro! Burro!*
(Donkey! Donkey!) meant to describe the president of the bullring
festivity would begin to be chanted by the ruthless crowd. So our imagination kept dwelling on the word when the real thing just outside,
in the *corrals* of the ring, rose in such a powerful bray that loudspeakers
were forgotten and the crowd gave itself without reserve to the utmost
joy. This gave the technicians a respite which they put to a good use;
everybody heard the actors and the play went on smoothly until the
end.

It is, of course, a wonderful play, excellent for a republican-de-
mocratic gathering; for it amounts to an exposure of personal tyranny
on the part of an army captain through an abuse of military force and
the restoration of justice by the hanging of the captain on the order of
the village mayor, whose daughter he has raped. And it contains gems
such as

> For no captains there could be
> If there had been no ploughmen

Or, when the captain, who has been unwise enough to linger behind his
troops and falls a prisoner of the peasants, demands respect for his
rank, the mayor retorts:

> On that he is right. With the utmost respect
> Take him to prison; with the utmost respect
> We shall sentence his case, and with the utmost respect
> Shall hang him;

or again when the King protests at his captain being hanged, and not beheaded, as befitted his rank:

> As there are no gentlemen here, Sir,
> We don't know how to behead.

The settings of all the scenes were created together before the eyes of
the public, the mayor's house being outlined by metal lines but lacking
both roof and walls so as to allow indoor happenings to be seen; and

when King Philip arrived in his hand-chair, escorted by four hundred men of the Madrid garrison in sixteenth-century military uniform, the enthusiasm of the crowd knew no bounds.

I still think that this was the avenue to rebuild a free, democratic Spain; but it was not to be. . . .

CHAPTER XXX

SPANIARDS, ASSYRIANS AND FINNS

M Y passing through the stage of inner Spanish politics was a brief interlude in my steadier occupation as Spain's *de facto* representative in Geneva. The first month of 1934 I was busy mostly with plans for making the Spanish delegation in Geneva less casual and personal, and more like an institution; in helping to solve the Assyrian question, and in struggling with the insoluble problem of disarmament.

On the first problem I sent to the Foreign Secretary in Madrid a circumstantial letter (January 23, 1934) repeating and developing the ideas I had already presented to his predecessors more than once – and with the same success; or lack of it. I shall not say any more on this except to emphasise that my endeavour aimed not at increasing but at restricting the power and freedom of the Spanish Delegate, which I knew were excessive. Of this letter, though, I shall pick up some points which may be worth mentioning.

I insisted on the fact that the policy I had been led to formulate and follow (or lead?) in Geneva for Spain was in accordance with the tradition of Spanish legal thought since Vitoria (Charles V's reign) and even perhaps since Palacios (Ferdinand and Isabel). But I also pointed out that this policy of intelligent pacifism based on world solidarity would enable Spain to stand on her own feet in Geneva as well as to increase her moral influence in certain sectors such as the Holy Places, the Sephardi world, the Arab world and the Far East.

I also pointed out that failure or success in what went by the name of 'Disarmament' would mean for Spain either heavy armament expenses (with no hope of improvement for the standard of living of our people) or a relatively low level of armaments all over Europe and the possibilities for the Republic of lifting our people from poverty by such means as the agrarian reform and a rejuvenation of our industry.

As examples of League problems that even indirectly did concern us I quoted the question of Austria always threatened by Nazi attempts at wrenching *Anschluss* by force, and the Saar Plebiscite, 'a problem bound to call forth deep and possibly serious repercussions, and on which as shown in the Council session just over, both parties had insistently sought the collaboration of Spain and in particular (if I may sacrifice modesty to truth) that of the Spanish Delegate in Geneva.'

I took good care to add that, since the problem was thorny and Spanish interests were not directly concerned, I had deliberately kept at a distance and avoided all claims at being nominated for the Council Committee on this issue; for I knew this always was the predisposition of Madrid, i.e. no headaches.

I was not able to remain equally aloof in the matter of the Assyrians. This was one of the one hundred and one problems the last fifty years or so created by the contraction of what once was the British Empire. In one of my less earnest books, one at any rate in which whatever earnestness there is lies hidden under more light-hearted tales, there is a yarn in which I revealed to the world the secret for making serpents: you take a hippopotamus and warm it until it is nice and soft and then you pass it through thinner and thinner holes in a steel plate until it becomes a serpent. If, while at it, you do not carry on the process to the (for the hippopotamus) bitter end, you are apt to get a crocodile.

The number of crocodiles Britain has left in the world just because she got bored while turning her river-horses (or gun-boats) into serpents is terrific. India-Pakistan, Burma, Singapore, Borneo, Israel, Cyprus, Malta, Gibraltar, Ulster, Quebec, Belize, Guiana, Jamaica, Trinidad, the Falkland Islands, quite an impressive fleet of indigestible crocodiles – one of which, and by no means the smallest, was Iraq, which in its turn concealed two other minor crocodiles, the Kurd and the Assyrian.

The Kurd has just closed its terrific mouth (at least for the time being) while I write these lines. The Assyrians gave me and Oliván a number of headaches in 1933, 1934 and even later. It all began in 1925 when Britain made up her mind to give up her mandate over Iraq and set up an independent monarchy under King Faisal. It was not easy, for both Turkey and Iraq claimed the province of Mosul, not because of its folklore or its fidelity to Mohammed but because of its oil. Furthermore, the readiness of Iraq to run an independent State did not seem very convincing to most members of the League. Britain, on the other hand, was convinced that Mosul should go to Iraq, where future independence would in those days remain wholly dependent on London at both ends of the bus route that goes from Whitehall to Mansion House. Sweden, represented by Undén, opposed this on matters of principle, on which it should be said in Sweden's honour, his country could speak with authority since the days of the Aland Islands dispute. It was after one of the long and hard meetings the Council had for weeks been devoting to the Mosul issue that I came across Cecil (who had borne the brunt of it and, I am sure, must have gone through moments of terrible mental strain, for he himself was an Undén made to play the rôle of a Pitt) and in despair he said to me: 'This man [Undén] reminds me of the Irishman who left a meeting crying out: "I have never seen fifteen more stubborn men in my life!"' In the end, mostly through the skill of Quiñones de León, Britain got what she wanted. The Council, however, had insisted on the mandate remaining in force for another twenty-five years, yet Britain succeeded in getting this wish considerably watered down by adding 'or until Iraq should be qualified for admission to the League'; in the hope, of course, that in a few years' time Undén might be somewhere else, for he was a busy man.

This kind of proviso quietly tucked away in a League resolution was meant to work like seeds that matured just when expected, wanted or made to by the expert gardener. By 1929, Britain found that her ward, Iraq, had made such wonderful progress in the art of self-government that she declared herself ready to recommend the League to declare her mandate ended and to admit Iraq to the League as a sovereign, independent State. Here was a noble sight indeed: a big Power ready to give up her mandate twenty years before she was expected to, indeed required to do so by the Council. The League Mandates Commission and the religious and racial minorities of Iraq did not, however, share this enthusiasm and there were not a few observers who thought that Britain's haste to get rid of the mandate was due to her desire to deal with Iraq direct without the presence of the Mandates Commission of the League as a chaperon. This indeed was the case.*

Iraq was not fit to govern herself. Iraq is not a nation. 'The child of the League', Frank Walters calls her. She was, like Jordania, like most of the 'nations' that were to swarm later in Africa, an artificial creation invented by the colonial powers. No comparison whatever with the nations that emerged out of the emancipation of Spanish America; for in this case, what happened was that every university gave birth to a nation, through the fostering of an *élite* conscious of a personality of its own. Iraq and Jordan were born of agreements between Britain and local chieftains with royal ambitions, no doubt based on some real factors, loyalties, traditions, but by no means on a national consciousness, while the peoples concerned were pestered with internal stresses due to dissident races and religions.

The Assyrians were one of these dissident groups. They claimed to descend from the Assyrians of antiquity and, for all I know, they did represent what remained of the Old Assyrian (Christian) Church. They were themselves an ill-adjusted mixture of tribes who from time im-

---

* And I regret to say that the treatment of this aspect of the story is one of the weakest spots in the otherwise excellent *History of the League of Nations* by Frank Walters (p. 524).

memorial had lived in the mountains of Iraq, with other tribes running away from persecution in Turkey or Persia. I was apprised of those facts by the Assyrian hereditary Patriarch, the Mar Shimun, who began to pay me frequent visits. He was young and handsome and his very white face and chiselled features were enhanced by large black eyes that seemed now and then to become even brighter when he smiled because he then uncovered a dazzling double row of very white teeth that shone between his thick lips. His hair and beard were very black. He spoke quietly and without gestures, with the poise of a man whose authority was beyond challenge. 'Of course,' he would add after a long statement of 'facts', 'Your Excellency need not believe everything I say.' And we smiled at each other with our eyes in complete agreement.

This man conceived his patriarchate as a pharaoh would have done, as a king-pope, and he quietly and courteously put it to the Government of Iraq to which he would, of course, remain loyal both as a person and as the head of his people; a proposal that naturally enough did not find favour in Iraqi official quarters. But, since the Iraqi Government promised to be co-operative in such matters as housing, all seemed well to the League Council – until all went wrong. The homeless Assyrians got impatient and invaded Syria (July 1933). The French authorities who ruled Syria then, forced them to recross the Tigris into Iraq whereupon a skirmish, almost a battle, was fought between the eight hundred Assyrians and an Iraqi detachment sent to intercept them. The Assyrians recrossed the Tigris again and the French interned them.

There was no reason why the story should not have ended there, at any rate for a few years, but for the fact that Iraq was not yet ripe for independence. The inconclusive battle on the Tigris acted on the Iraqi army as an irritant and within two weeks the shooting of prisoners began, followed, on August 10, 1933, by a massacre of Assyrians during which hundreds of men were killed and hundreds of homes pillaged and destroyed. As the news reached Geneva (August 31st) the seventy-sixth session of the League Council was about to begin, and on the initiative of Ireland, Mexico and Norway, the matter was considered, or, rather, should have been considered. But King Faisal died and the discussion, though urgent, was adjourned to October.

So October came and the Iraqi government insisted on the 'fact' that the responsibility for the massacre lay in fact on the shoulders of the massacred – a principle as time-honoured as anything in human history. Iraq, however, promised that it would not happen again. The Council nevertheless thought it would be best to find a safer place for the Assyrians. This was the task that was entrusted to a committee presided over by me, a job that was gradually taken over by my assistant, Oliván, since it implied more travelling than I had time for. The first suggestion, some land in southern Brazil, would have been suitable, but at the cost of £600,000; and when the Council expected Britain to foot that bill, Britain declared her liability to be limited to a share of that sum proportional to that of her share in the League budget. No member of the Council – or of the League – could agree to that, considering that the coming of age of Iraq had been forced down an unwilling League's throat precisely by Britain. After months and years of endeavours, rooted in a curious mixture of goodwill, cleverness, an astute combination of charity and national development and what not, the Assyrian question was lost in the desert, partly of Iraq, partly of Syria, partly of League paper, and all was left in readiness for another crocodile to turn up in the Middle East some day.

Both Oliván and I had to deal in those days with another of Britain's crocodiles, this time, strangely enough, navigating in the far North. It was an old story, dating from the First World War, when Britain, perilously short of cargo ships to sustain her food supplies, had secured a number of Finnish bottoms *manu militari* which, considering that Finland had got her independence from Russia on December 6, 1917 shortly after the abdication of the Tsar, and immediately entered into an alliance with Germany, can hardly be considered as abusive; nor was the history of Finland until she entered the League clear cut enough to serve as guidance for the issue when it was submitted to us.

What Finland wanted was a money settlement to pay for the services of her ships. Britain agreed to a conciliation procedure, which the Council entrusted to me, and which as soon as I realised how entangled it all was from the legal point of view, I handed on to Oliván. As it all happened in Geneva, though, I kept control of the negotiation. The Finnish representative was a distinguished politician named Holsti, who had been Foreign Secretary, and was amiable and cordial even when not stimulated by whatever it was he took to combat the icy winds of his country. The British representative was Eden; and I must record that this was the only case in which I found fault with his manner. I was, of course, an arbitrator, what we in Spain quaintly call '*un amigable componedor*', and I stuck to this part in the play; the moves, if any, were made after hearing the advice of Oliván; and nearly always in agreement with him. At one stage, on his extremely well-argued proposition, I decided something which did not please Eden's advisors; I don't think he gave much personal thought or attention to the whole thing and he just lent his name and authority to what his man told him. He happened to see me standing somewhere before or after a meeting of something or other and came to me to put his case against, consisting mostly of a repeated statement: 'I am very angry, I am very angry,' which it was plain he wasn't.

It was a pure matter of procedure; some paper or some face being turned in this or that direction; but the move happened to suit the Finns or help their case for the time being. It did not touch or prejudge the final report which, when presented, was unanimously passed by the Council with the unreserved approval of both parties. Then, something happened which took both Oliván and me aback. Finland decorated us both with the Grand Cross of the White Rose. I wasted an hour explaining to Holsti that it put us in an awkward position. It was no good. The papers had been signed and sealed by the great men, and so Knights of the White Rose we remained.

CHAPTER XXXI

LOUIS BARTHOU

THAT grain of sand in Cromwell's ureter that Bossuet made famous, that half-an-inch on Cleopatra's nose that Pascal brought to light in one way and Shakespeare in another, remind us of the power such trifles possess to alter the fate of the world. There was a woman in Paris in those days . . . did she matter at all? Her name was Madame Stavisky. She was a well-known hostess, which means that her table was well provided with good fare on top and with important guests around. One of them, keener than most, observed that the flowers skilfully strewn over her table were so arranged as to cover the holes in her tablecloth.

No one knew where Stavisky got that lot of money she spent (or seemed to). Not even he, as it turned out. When the affairs of the Bayonne official pawnshop, *alias Crédit Municipal*, were examined too closely for Stavisky (who had been its financial adviser) though too late for the state, a secret came out: Stavisky had succeeded in dragging for six years the procedure of a prosecution for a forged cheque for three million francs. Even Madame Stavisky proved unable to cover up that hole with her skilfully strewn flowers, and the Chautemps ministry fell.

I was sorry, for I liked Chautemps. He was friendly and easy-going, human and modest, and his husky voice seemed to be tuned to a key of common sense. 'Well, you know, *Monsieur l'Ambassadeur*,' he would whisper to me at some banquet or other, 'if we delay war by three, two, one year, that is so much gained for every man and woman to go on living and procreating. . . .' But the country was too deeply shaken for such simple sense, and an ex-President of the Republic had to be brought in to lead a new government. Monsieur Doumergue chose as his Foreign Minister Louis Barthou.

Now, Louis Barthou was no ordinary politician. True, he was an old hand at the game, well into his seventies, and so seasoned that he was already Minister of Public Works when in 1909 a decree dispensing me from passing an examination to enter the Paris school of Mines was printed in the official *Journal* over his signature. This was the first link between us. But there were other links less fortuitous. We were both deeply involved in letters. He was a member of the French Academy, tantamount to being a Field Marshal of Literature; and he was said to be the possessor of a fine collection of manuscripts, many of them invaluable pieces in the handwriting of Victor Hugo.

This devotion to Hugo was also a strong link between us, though I was apt to pull at it somewhat viciously now and then. 'But, *Monsieur le Président*, the fact is Hugo was the greatest comic poet France ever had, only he was not aware of it.' This made him flare up with indignation.

These talks on poets and poetry used to bubble up between us while we walked from the Bergues to the League or vice versa. I told him I had myself written poetry by Victor Hugo, no worse than some of the great master's, and recited one or two to him, which he was generous enough to appreciate.

> *Ame, énigme éternelle et sublime, mot sombre.*
> *Haut sommet de lumière et précipice d'ombre,*
> *impénétrable Tout issu du clair Néant,*
> *est-ce que tu serais le Dieu que l'homme admire*
> *ou le profond miroir où Jehovah se mire*
> *comme l'immense ciel dans l'immense océan.*

and so on for yards. This was the kind of sport he liked best. But in certain quarters of the Paris political world, his reputation was not beyond reproach. He was considered as an unreliable politician, particularly since the famous '*Coup de Cannes*' when, as a Cabinet Minister in Briand's government, an intrigue within the cabinet had ousted Briand while he was negotiating with Lloyd George at Cannes, and the move was attributed to Barthou's initiative and leadership (January 1922). A few months later, a sharp-witted journalist, describing a somewhat moving ceremony at the French Academy, wrote: 'As no politics were involved, Monsieur Barthou could betray nothing but his emotion.'

He may have had it in him to behave that way in politics, but nothing of it came through in his day-to-day commerce with us in Geneva. He was friendly and sensible, and he could smile and even laugh. Indeed, and this was a third link between us, he often risked losing a friend through his inability to withhold a good joke, a foible in which I may have been just a wee bit less unwise than he was. This side of Barthou gave rise to a few incidents presently to be told. He was a good deal my senior, yet, or perhaps owing to it, he gave many a sign of a definite salacious trend in his mind and imagination.

The conjuncture of Barthou and Eden should have worked as a boon to the League and world affairs, for both were capable and reasonable men and as such got on well with each other. But the general horoscope of the period was bad, and Europe had to contend with two dictators who were neither capable nor reasonable, nor did they really get on well together. It says a good deal for the capacity of human beings even as realistic as statesmen or at any rate politicians are supposed to be, that the League, led by them, persisted in the hopeless task described as 'Disarmament' while Hitler was openly and almost cynically preparing the Second World War. Hitler's military budget for 1934–5 increased expenses by 90 per cent and included over two hundred million dollars for the air force, in the teeth of the prohibition of such a thing prescribed by the Treaty of Versailles. Despite Eden's honest and enlightened endeavours to darn up the tattered cloth of peace by travelling between capital and capital, the negotiation between the four powers had led to nothing but a sheer waste of time; and Tardieu, then Prime Minister, who was not a man to feed on words, hopes or promises, said so crudely in a note to Britain (April 17, 1934). Henderson called the conference for May 29th (1934).

He had been rather left out of it all and was entitled to feel some resentment; but he turned out to be too insular, too closely shut in within his island and language, to utter that resentment in an idiom that would have called forth the hearty acquiescence of many of us, who were, if not resentful, at least sharply critical of the big powers' talks. He chose to single out the French for his bitterest reproaches, when it was obvious that the trouble originated elsewhere, and with a hard glare at Barthou, he shot at him: 'Monsieur Barthou is the fourth French Minister of Foreign Affairs I have known since the Conference began.' Barthou was not a man to whom one could shoot arrows of any kind, without exposing oneself to a volley of wit. He rose to the occasion, didn't trouble about Henderson, who was not in power anyhow, and, staring hard at Simon, let fall: 'There are countries that change their Minister without changing their policy, and countries that change their policy without changing their Minister.'

For reasons that will become clearer anon, I know that his barbed arrow was deeply resented in London and that the fact was duly reported to Paris. But who could stop the ebullience of Louis Barthou? I once told him what I was later to apply to a bigger man, Winston Churchill, before I applied it to a more modest man, i.e. myself: 'You are too young for your years.' One of the most difficult characters in Geneva was Colonel Beck. There have been Foreign Secretaries (Eden or Barthou, most of all Briand) who have had (as we say in Spain) the 'gift of people', *el don de gentes*; others who did not try hard enough or tried too much to please but didn't, as was the case with Simon; but Beck seemed to enjoy being unpleasant and probably thought this manner an essential weapon in the armour of a strong man. He was – in fact like most of us – thoroughly fed up with the big powers for having arrogated to themselves the give-and-take of the whole Conference only to waste our time, but his displeasure, far from being like ours a kind of move to defend the Covenant, was in Beck an irritation felt by him as a Pole who thought that Poland was as much a great power as Italy. So he took his first opportunity to suggest this delicate aspect of things with a special bitterness towards France; whereupon Barthou assured him in a speech, in which the music by no means fitted the words, that France was aware of the fact that 'Poland was a great power, indeed a very great Power.' Beck's face became as red as a tomato and again Warsaw was incensed and Paris was fully informed of it.

Then Henderson presented a draft resolution on which Barthou delivered a speech; and in the course of the debate I rose to argue something or other which I have forgotten; whereupon Barthou argued back in terms that seemed to me out of place. I gave no immediate sign of displeasure but back in my office I instructed my delegation that every one was to cut every French colleague and cease altogether dealing with them. When Massigli noticed that I would neither talk to nor even look at him, he evidently rang up Paris on his own. At any rate the next morning François Pietri, Minister of the Navy, turned up at the Bergues and entered my room.

To my surprise – and it was genuine – he answered with his usual, friendly, clever smile: 'Well, you know, when we were told Simon was angry, well, there you are, these things do happen; when the news came that Beck was angry, we all said: "Well, that is part of the shape of things." But when we heard that you were angry . . . then . . . I was sent to Geneva.' I told him my story, including my grief at having to quarrel with a man I liked so much; he left me with an 'I'll soon be back.'

He was back within ten minutes. All was clear. Barthou would publish a letter of apology in *Le Temps* and would bring me the text himself. 'When?' – 'At once.' – 'No', I retorted, 'He is the Foreign Minister of France, I shall go up to him.' Pietri smiled. 'Let him come down. Let him come down.' Barthou came, again his charming self, and put in my hands a hand-written letter the text of which he read to me. It was published in *Le Temps* on June 10, 1934. It was a frank and noble apology cast in most generous terms towards me and my work, and in praise of Spain.

The very next day the Conference came to an end. There were futile attempts at keeping it going on a few vegetables for lack of meat. The most voluminous of which was a kind of pumpkin presented to the League by President Roosevelt on the manufacture of and traffic in arms, as empty a calabash as could be fancied since we had already scooped it out in 1925 and found it uneatable. The trouble was, and still is, that nothing to do with disarmament ever makes sense, since either the general state of the world adds up to dissent or to consensus, and in the first case disarmament is impossible and in the second disarmament would be spontaneous.

CHAPTER XXXII

BARTHOU AND STALIN

S HORTLY after Hitler left the League, when we were still hearing so to speak the bang of the door shut behind him, we began to perceive rumours and mutterings that suggested a change of heart in Moscow towards Geneva and the Covenant. The trouble was that we all knew that 'Russia' meant 'Stalin' and that Stalin had no heart, so how could it change? The answer was by no means discovered but aptly put to the world by General de Gaulle about a third of a century later: *les nations sont des monstres froids*. Whatever other statesmen may think about this dictum, the description fits Stalin like a glove; and, as the cold monster that he was, the Russian tyrant thought of no one else but his true opposite number, Hitler, another cold monster who, oddly enough, could now and then boil over like a pot of tigress's milk.

This undoubtedly was the reason why Stalin, for whom the 'spirit of Geneva' was just drivel and the Covenant just a piece of paper, had agreed to talk to the League for years and even to send Litvinov to the Disarmament Conference. Litvinov was by no means as cynical about the League as Stalin. While Stalin was a russified Georgian, and so, in a way, both a shut-in and a provincial mind, Litvinov, like most intelligent Jews, had a universal mind and was able to portray in it a world of sixty-odd nations, granting to each a fairly adequate colour, shape and location. Though, of course, on sufferance, and so to speak, on a trial-and-error basis, Litvinov was thus at the time allowed to carry on a foreign policy more and more based on the League.

For a *Realpolitiker* such as Stalin, there could be no doubt that Hitler's departure from the League did not merely mean the tearing up of the treaty of Versailles but his liberation from the bonds of the Covenant; and that this loosening of both his tethers foreboded danger all round but more especially for Russia. On this point, the writings of Nazi pundits left him in no doubt, if such proofs had been needed. Russia had every reason to fear the onslaught of the German nation. Litvinov was therefore allowed to play the card of the Covenant in this dangerous game of poker.

We should be doing Stalin an injustice if we singled him out for blame for this. True, his policy amounted to using the League as a mere shield for the defence of his own nation; but that sin was general in those days, and events both past and then still future fully illustrate the fact: every nation was still (are they not still to-day?) too confined within her patriotism to consider the Covenant as anything higher or better than a stick to beat her enemies with when in danger, and in the case of big powers, as an instrument for ensuring that their particular policy prevailed.

Furthermore, in true big-power style, Russia viewed her move towards 'the League' mostly as one towards the big powers in the League. 'The League is you and us,' Laval said once to Eden. And to me, one evening at the Bergues, angry at something: 'If not, I shall soon kick their League log cabin to smithereens.' Laval was no diplomat and feared no verbal excesses; but we may still have to tell of other persons' actions and words which for all their refinement and apparent loftiness actually concealed no higher feelings towards the League.

Russia was then between two formidable powers both openly berserk. If Hitler let loose boded no good for Europe, Japan, let loose, boded no good for Asia. Russia was in both continents, threatened on the main street and in her back yard. Where can I find friends? That is what her policy now meant: friends, that is, people ready to fight for her, for a nation, be it remembered, who barely sixteen years earlier had outraged the whole liberal-socialist world by breaking every rule of behaviour, towards men and peoples. The British City and the legendary French stocking where the family gold is kept had been the most deeply offended. Britain was still unripe for a change: but France was readier to listen if only because Hitler was for her a more immediate danger.

This was the canvas on which Barthou had to embroider. For France, Hitler's rise was far more fraught with danger than for Britain. Hitler was ready to compromise with Britain, Why? Simply because he was in his core imitating Britain, or so he thought. Britain (as well as France) was now reaping the harvest of her inability fully to enter into the new era of the Covenant; a fact which she had revealed by refusing to translate '*Societé des Nations*' into anything more respectable than 'League of Nations'. A British Empire there had been before Woodrow Wilson, and a British Empire there was to be after him. Very good. But then, why not a German Empire? Are we not both blonde beasts of prey? This was a question Hitler put to Britain in all honesty; and, it seems to me, on a solid ground – indeed, perhaps the only honest question that ever rose in his mind. Hence his no doubt genuine readiness to share the world with Britain.

But not with France. The French were not blonde beasts and they spoke a low Latin dialect not worth reading or speaking for a *Herrenvolk*. The French knew that the danger for them was earnest and immediate; and (though they liked Eden) their experience of Simon had made them suspicious of British help if and when it came to blows. How about Russia?

After decades of running after Russia, the West must find it hard to replace itself in the ambiance of those days. Let me recall that when we invited Russia to attend the preliminaries of Disarmament in the middle twenties, no one would take a meal with Litvinov or Lunacharsky until I took the initiative; and when at the Disarmament Conference (1932) I pointed out in a speech to Litvinov that his hurry to disarm tomorrow was just hot air and that Russia had better stop that nonsense and join the League, he was still so inhibited by the state of political leprosy his country was living in that he argued 'Why doesn't the Spanish Republic recognise us?', whereas it was obviously for Soviet Russia to recognise the Spanish Republic.

The fact was the West was less terrified than horrified of Russia, and not without reason either. So it took Barthou the best part of a year to shepherd the League in the direction he wanted it to go. Most nations weren't even represented in Moscow; and Switzerland, in particular, was still at daggers drawn with Russia over the murder of a Soviet diplomat in Lausanne, whose murderer, Russia thought, had been let off too easily by the Swiss.

There were a number of hurdles. First of all, Russia had hinted at a special invitation, following the precedent of Mexico, confirmed in 1932 in the case of Turkey. Russia's insistence on this was almost certainly less a matter of prestige than one of prudence. She knew she was not loved, rather the reverse, and wished to shield herself against a rebuff. But an invitation to join the League was not an idea to be found in the Covenant, and therefore it had to be adopted by unanimity. This was simply out of the question. So it was quietly agreed that the invitation would not come from the League but from as many nations as Barthou could muster; it being understood that the recalcitrant ones would abstain or even vote against, for Russia could be admitted on a two third majority.

Poor Barthou had to fight another battle on the question of submitting the election to the Sixth Commission of the Assembly. Here again, Russia may have been over-cautious rather than struggling for prestige, for precisely because their debates used to be less formal than those in the plenary Assembly, Commissions might give an opportunity to adverse delegates for saying things that would be better left unsaid. Barthou and Beneš, who acted throughout as his visible emanation in this episode, did their best to wrench an implicit approval for their plan to skip the Commission stage altogether. They were unable to conquer the opposition of the small powers led by de Valera, and in the end, to the Commission it had to go. Possibly to guard against the danger inherent in the procedure, which they sensed from the very first day of the Assembly, they had seen to it that I was elected chairman of that

Commission. The matter went through smoothly enough without any exertion on my part.

Soviet Russia was then and has remained since an inveterate con-temner of small nations. Respecting nothing but power, she is apt to think of them as children who should be seen but not heard. And yet, this Assembly of 1934, during which she was admitted, was to show how reasonable small nations can be. The most important of the privileges she claimed for herself as a big power was that of holding a permanent seat in the Council. Every one of the small nations, even those who abstained or voted against her admission, proved willing to grant her that privilege. Russia was thus admitted to the League with the full honours due to her power and rank. She was not long in proving that she did not deserve it.

That Assembly had also to elect a number of non-permanent mem-bers of the Council, Spain among them. The 1926 Assembly had agreed that the three so-called 'semi-permanent' members (Brazil, Poland and Spain) could be indefinitely re-elected if they obtained a two-thirds vote to that effect. Spain had re-entered the League on this under-standing. In 1934, we got our seat easily. While I was being congra-tulated by many friends, I saw Barthou rise and come to my place in the hall. (I should say in passing that this sight – delegates of the big powers coming to talk to the Spanish Delegate – had never been seen until I took over the delegation.) Barthou smiled and said: 'We have elected the country, of course, but we also have elected the man.' I made some modest noises; but I liked it, being no less vain than others, indeed, vain enough to think that Barthou was right.

The Association of Journalists accredited to the League gave a luncheon in honour of Barthou and Litvinov to which all the Council members were invited. The menu was decorated with a scene depicting a rather enterprising courtship, the Don Juan being Barthou and the lady an imaginary 'Russia' fortunately more beautiful than our friend Litivinov who was no Apollo. This cartoon provided Barthou with an easy basis for a brilliant improvisation (more or less prepared) in which jest and earnestness were skilfully interlaced and spiced with his usual light but peppery salacity. When he sat down I handed on to him a menu on the back of which, while he spoke, I had jotted:

> *Pour que l'Europe désarme*
> *En pleine sécurité*

Il faut une parité
Entre le danger et l'arme.
Mais lorsque la France s'arme
De l'enthousiasme éloquent
Du successeur de Briand,
Qui ne se sent pas à l'aise
Devant la grâce française
Qui désarme en souriant?

All this happened towards the end of September 1934. On October 9th Barthou was dead. That morning, King Alexander of Yugoslavia had landed at Marseilles on a state visit, and Barthou had received him on behalf of the French Government. But in his country, the King was looked upon by most Croats as a Serbian tyrant; and this split in a nation of fierce and hot-blooded men was and still is one of the most dangerous sores Europe suffers from. Marseilles would in no case have been an adequate place to receive so threatened a guest, when protocol and naval pageantry might have made it plausible to receive him in Toulon; but on top of it, security precautions seem to have been more casual and careless than is usually the case in France. An *oustashi* was able to approach the open carriage in which the King and Barthou were driving through the crowd and to shoot the King dead. Barthou was allowed to bleed until, nearly dead, he was conveyed to a hospital where a young doctor in charge of the casualty ward would not accept responsibility for dealing with such an important person. When a more qualified doctor arrived, Barthou was dead.

In less than a year, he had succeeded in raising his office to that level of competent dignity it had reached with Briand and lost with Laval. When in my light-hearted improvisation I described him as 'Briand's successor' I was not flattering him, I was uttering what we all thought at the time. True, he had begun on an intransigent note, and I even remembered once having shown to a friend a somewhat unorthodox spelling of his name – *Barre-tout* – which eventually came back to me as such a good joke, you know, you would never guess! But Barthou was perhaps the best case I have seen of a man transfigured by Geneva. Though he sounded like an intellectual, he was an intuitive soul, and he was able at once to understand and appreciate Eden, and to sense the fundamental change implicit in Geneva, the new perspective, the new feeling for things, a truth few men who went there from the big powers seem to have understood, namely, that Geneva did not mean at all that the great powers had to abdicate to the crowd of small ones, but that their pre-eminence, while remaining intact, while possibly increasing, had to adopt a different style.

All that wisdom was now dead, and on its ashes a quarrel had to be fought between the little Entente, led by Beneš, intent on punishing Hungary and (if possible) Fascist Italy for their share – indirect but definite – in the crime and the guilty nations themselves. Eden had to deal with it as *rapporteur* of the Council. He did it wisely and firmly, and I was able to give him as much support as I could.

CHAPTER XXXIII

EUROPEAN TRAVELS

S OON after my release from the embassy, I went to Venice in my capacity as member of the Committee of Arts and Letters of the Institute of Intellectual Cooperation of the League (25–28 July). Italy being the host state, the Italian Commission took upon themselves to swamp the Committee with all kinds of guests, chosen for their fascist proclivities. Many of them were Italians, but the Institute was too weak to put its foot down when the Italian Commission invited foreign fascists also. One of them was a Spanish admirer of Mussolini known as Giménez Caballero.

He had a ready pen and a ready tongue, but I suspect his watch did not work well, for on the day he should have spoken he was not available. The next day, when our agenda called quite a different subject, he asked to speak and produced a typed 'speech' out of his pocket. It was in Italian, not an official language at League meetings, but known or understood and heard with pleasure by all in that gathering in spite of the obvious political intent of the choice of language. It turned out to be a forcible plea in favour of discipline as the supreme virtue of a modern man. He insisted so much on this theme, not merely with arguments but with a certain amount of energy which at times seemed to me unnecessary, that I suddenly realised that he was really out of order, for his speech obviously bore on the item of the agenda for the day before.

I whispered the fact to Focillon who happened to be my neighbour. Focillon, one of the cleverest, acutest, most penetrating minds I have known, beamed with joy, for he had been pining under the fascist twaddle of the orator; so he raised his finger on a question of order: and put it to the meeting that Giménez Caballero was talking twenty-four hours too late. The Chairman ruled that it was so, and begged our fascist colleague to keep to the subject of the day; whereupon, Giménez Caballero went on hammering *discipline* on to our rebellious minds, wholly indifferent to the chairman's rule and to the respect he owed to our society.

For everything that was not work, our host was Count Volpi, Mussolini's Finance Minister, a Venetian potentate who took his duties in earnest and received us not merely in a lavish but in a refined and sophisticated style.

I shall not endeavour to recollect and record how many banquets he offered us, but I must mention his luncheon at the Lido. I happened to be sitting next to a red-haired or red-wigged Countess in her fifth or sixth youth, keen as nails, clever as the Devil, talkative as a cockatoo and, despite her years, attractive, indeed fascinating. She was a scion of one of the great Venetian families and had met everybody who was anybody in Europe. It was rumoured in my ear that in her first or second youth she had contributed to lead astray no less a Don Juan than Wilhelm II.

The meal had hardly begun when the Countess opened the conversation with a tale of woe – told with fire, sparks and spirit – on the evil eye which afflicted King Alfonso of Spain. This reputation, possibly based on his being XIIIth of that name, was, I knew, general in Italy, though I had never come across signs of it in Spain. But the Countess was overwhelmingly informed. 'He arrived at my cousin's, Prince Somethinghini, for a week-end ... you know the Somethinghinis of Genoa who were admirals of your Philip II and one of them was a cardinal and another one was executed by the order of Pope Pius the ... well I don't remember, but it doesn't matter, because he had committed incest, my cousin, I mean, not the Pope, you know, don't you, well, there he was in Genoa for a week-end at their Palace on the coast, and that very evening, a fishing boat was lost with all her crew right under the window of Alfonso's bedroom. He then went to a shooting party at the Aldobr ... no, it was at the ... doesn't matter either, it was at the Abruzzi anyhow, and on the very first morning, while retrieving a partridge, one of the servants, his gun went off and he killed another man. All that in one week. The next week, he was at my sister-in-law's, and the very day Alfonso arrived, her maid died suddenly, never ill before, not a headache ....'

This went on and on with marvellous precision and volubility so that I was relieved when our host gave the signal for coffee which was to be served in the patio of the hotel. I had been standing alone for a while in the patio, sipping my coffee, enjoying silence and watching the other guests, when Volpi beckoned me and took me aside. 'Just got a ring from Rome. Dollfuss has been murdered.' We were shocked and for a while commented on the deed and its possible consequences. Hitler seemed to be operating on an underground front as well as in the limelight.

The meeting over, I took the night express for Paris. When the next morning I came out to stand in the corridor while my bedroom was being tidied, a young couple, after some hesitation, drew near me and greeted me explaining that they had recognised me although they had seen me only once, at a lecture I had delivered in New York. They were Peruvians. Then he said: 'Your King Alfonso is an odd man!' – 'We are all odd,' I retorted. 'Ah but he ... Imagine that we, my wife and I, were walking out of the Hotel Imperial in Vienna, where we were staying, and he came out and passed before me ... well, all right, he is a King ... but before my wife as well, and not a word of apology or a polite gesture ...' – 'But,' I asked, 'was King Alfonso in Vienna?' And he answered: 'Didn't you know? He was the last visitor Dollfuss received.'

That autumn was pretty busy in Geneva, mostly with the after-effects of the deed of Marseilles, evoking as it did, sinister remembrances of the deed in Sarajevo. I had, however, an interlude in Vienna, where I had been invited by the *Kulturbund*. This League of Culture was mostly Jolan Jacobi, a Hungarian live-wire, and I am not sure that in this case any mention of her nationality is required for, in those days at any rate, in Vienna, a live-wire was sure to be a Hungarian. My assignment was a lecture on some aspect or other of world affairs, and my visit to Vienna signified my return to a sufficient political freedom to enable me to begin again my activities as a lecturer.

Vienna was then no longer the capital of the Double Monarchy, a European institution wide and complex enough to suggest a carry-forward of the Habsburg Empire; but even though shrunk from her rank as the political capital of an Empire to that of the head-city of little Austria, Vienna remained in fact to a remarkable degree the cultural and social capital of southern central Europe. This eminence she had managed to retain was due for a good part to her clever, keen, cultured Jews.

They added the yeast and the salt. The dough was not bad either. A stern indictment went about in those days to the effect that the Austrian was *dumm, faul und gefrässig*, dumb, lazy and gluttonous; but this seems rather a caricature than a portrait, for the Viennese are too southern to vie with their German cousins in productivity (as we horribly say now-a-days), yet not negligent; while if they are too northern to compete with the Italians at the games of wit, they are by no means dull; and, of course, why should they abstain at table when their cookery is so good (which, by the way, suggests neither dumbness nor laziness). On top of this solid foundation, Vienna has grown a tradition of culture and refinement as the centre of the German Empire, a great Court with all that a great Court means in courtesy and manners, and a truly European perspective.

Paris is French and London English; Berlin is German and Rome, despite the Vatican, is Italian, for (we must bow to the fact) Italy has made the Vatican more Italian than the Vatican has made Italy or even Rome universal. But Vienna is European. In Vienna one is definitely in Western Europe, but certain churches and other buildings, certain ways, such as the omnipresent tipping (even to reward the dubious service of the liftman of a leisurable lift), an echo of those Turkish marches Mozart suddenly springs in most unexpected places, the omnipresence of Hungarians the stark profiles of whose powerful features obviously hails from Asia, something leisurely and strange in the air, made one think of the East German of course, but very Italian as well, and Slav and even Spanish after nearly two centuries of close relations between the two dynasties; so that the sense and the conviction grows that this city is the natural capital of Europe, and Austria her District of Columbia.

Meanwhile, von Papen, who was Hitler's Ambassador in Vienna, was besieging me with invitations for anything — lunch, dinner, breakfast, tea. The fact was I had nothing to offer. All my time was booked. In the end, I was able to come to tea. He had no one but me. I wondered whether it was due to skill or to necessity. A few days earlier the *Kulturbund* had given a dinner for me. While we were waiting, von Papen arrived and came straight to me (we had never met before) and introduced himself, the person who happened to be talking to me having vanished, as I thought, rather abruptly; and so we were free to sit down on a sofa and talk until we all flocked to the dining-room, which von Papen and I entered together. We then parted towards our seats and, soon after we all had sat down, I noticed that von Papen was sitting between two empty chairs.

I was sitting between Jolan Jacobi and the dinner chairman who was Princess Rohan, the daughter of that impressive Count Apponyi who had carved for himself such a prominent figure in the Hungary of the nineteenth century. So, once again in Vienna, when I was in a place that mattered, I was sitting between two Hungarian women. I asked them what had happened to von Papen's neighbours. They told me it was the usual thing. Those two guests had paid for their tickets, and finding they had been seated next to von Papen, had left, It must have taken all the coolness of the man who had brought in Hitler to destroy his country to carry on calmly as if eating in isolation was the normal thing for a servant of the Nazis; on the other hand, perhaps he was enjoying it with the thought; you wait and see!

So, when I entered a few days later the drawing-room of the German Embassy and found myself face to face with von Papen, and tea was served for just two, I knew what was happening. And that face, too.

Its dominant feature was a pair of eyes incredibly blue. Well, at forty-eight as I was then, more than half of which had been spent north of the Pyrenees, I had come across many pairs of blue eyes; but I remembered none that insisted on their colour as blatantly as those before me. They were aggressively blue, as if asserting the purity of their Aryan blood (though I understand the eye is the one place in the body the blood, even when Aryan, is not allowed to enter).

What they did not know, those eyes, was that I was carrying on an experiment in Vienna, and that they were to be submitted to it there and then. Ever since I had arrived in Austria, I had taken care not to part from anyone whose opinion was worth having, without asking a question: 'If there were a plebiscite here today on whether Austria wants the *Anschluss* or not, how many Austrians would vote for it?' In no case had I got a figure below fifty per cent. Austrians or foreigners, diplomats and playboys, taxi-drivers or ladies in costly furs, they all answered 95 per cent, 75 per cent, 60 per cent, 80 per cent – never below 50 per cent. So I put my question to von Papen, and with a straight, earnest face, he pushed through his blue Aryan eyes: 'We shouldn't get a single vote.'

What an asinine answer, I thought. And how insulting for his guest to utter such an obvious lie assuming I was going to believe it. Had my host put the figure at anything below 50 per cent he would have made me feel that he was perhaps better informed or shrewder than the high number of people who thought otherwise; but by pretending the figure was nought, all he proved was that he was dumb enough to think I was dumb enough to believe him. Furthermore, the way he put it amounted to an admission that he saw the *Anschluss* as *his* cause, for which he was working; and while this fact was, of course, no secret, it seemed to me odd that he, in his official capacity, should admit it. I told the story to Schuschnigg when I went to take leave of him. His smile was bitter.

Schuschnigg had come to my *Kulturbund* lecture and sat through it, in the first row of the audience, wrapped in scholarly attention. He struck me as an academic mind, who had strayed into politics; yet, one feature kept intruding into my observation of him as I sat in his office: his fingers. They were thick with earthy vigour, reddish and rough, and they made one think of carrots and turnips rather than pianos and violins such as one would have expected of a Viennese intellectual. He was correct, prim, modest, simple and courteous – all under a leaden cloud which he seemed unable to shake off no matter the subject of the talk or the person of the talker.

This trip to Vienna afforded me the pleasure of meeting a first-rate Viennese who, of course, was a first-rate European. Shaw said of a countryman: 'He is a typical Irishman – born in Manchester.' Coudenhove-Kalergi could have said: 'I am a typical European. My mother was Japanese.' His father was half-Belgian half-Greek. The flower of all these disparate roots was a perfect European and a perfect Japanese. Talking once in his house with him and two other Viennese, one of whom was Mataja, who had been Minister of Foreign Affairs, the three Viennese pointed out how extra-Austrian they all three were for none of the three was of German extraction; a natural result of the multinational, indeed pre-European character of the Austro-Hungarian Empire.

Count Coudenhove-Kalergi was the first active European, who conceived and proposed a European federation. This idea was his brainchild and he is entitled to be considered as the father of Europe. His charm was so exceptional, his skill as a writer – one of the few who can lend spring, speed and sprightliness to the heavy German language – his gift for exposition and his ability to handle human beings – not by the thousand, but in small groups – were so remarkable that his ideas made considerable progress and in the end he was able to persuade Briand to do something.

Briand had that artistic side to his nature without which no politician rises to statesmanship. Churchill possessed the same gift. Briand saw the point (remember how Churchill also saw the point of offering a political union to France when it was put to him by Monnet). Thanks to Briand's imagination and energy a European Commission was created in 1931, but the idea was premature and it all but lapsed on Briand's death.

That Hungarian hold over Vienna, nothing daunted by diplomatic immunity, had invaded the Spanish legation. One of the first persons the Spanish Minister Comin introduced to me was his Trade Expert, 'Doña Emilia Rauman.' With the sceptical approach of the average Spaniard of those days, I was instinctively disposed to believe that the ability of a woman is sure to be in inverse proportion to her looks. I must have taken a fairly poor view of her ability, for she was very handsome. I suspect that Comin observed my scepticism, for not only did he seize the first opportunity to sing her praises to the point of describing her as the key mind in the legation, but he soon organised an evening in which Frau Rauman read to us an essay she had written on new, as yet unpublished documents, being the Diary of an Austrian Ambassador in the days of Charles II of Spain. I was impressed by the quality of the research as well as by that of the Spanish in which the translation was written – and spoken. But, of course, Mrs Rauman was a Hungarian.

Who would have guessed that day that such an excursion into the past was but the pre-history of – but I must not anticipate.

CHAPTER XXXIV

ETHIOPIA AND ITALY

I N 1925 I published in London my fantasy *The Sacred Giraffe*. Towards the end of this book, the reader will find a treaty the text of which must be reproduced here, for it provides the key to the Italo-Ethiopian dispute.

> HAVE AGREED on the following text:
> The two contracting parties solemnly declare that the independence of the queendom of Lybia is indispensable to the peace of the world, more so even than the Lybians themselves are aware of, and do hereby pledge themselves to maintain the aforesaid independence by all the means in their power.
> They moreover declare that the above applies with particular stress to one particular half of the Lybian queendom for each of the two contracting parties, to wit:
> The independence of that part of the queendom of Lybia which lies east of the river Glo is more especially indispensable to the peace of the world from the point of view of Ebony, and Her Splendour the Queen of Ebony declares that she pledges herself more especially to maintain the said independence of the said part of the said queendom.
> And
> The independence of that part of the queendom of Lybia which lies west of the river Glo is more especially indispensable to the peace of the world from the point of view of Assinia and Her Splendour the Queen of Assinia pledges herself more especially to maintain the said independence of the said part of the said queendom.
> The two contracting parties agree to consider the above text as the common frontier between their respective meanings, each of which lies on opposite sides of it, and declare that they will faithfully stand by what they mean, each on its side of the said text.
> The which to affirm before the world they sign below.

Before I enter into the narrative of the actual events, I may be allowed to quote again, this time from a dispatch sent to the Spanish Foreign

Minister, on September 16, 1935. I had just told the Minister that Eden
had recently assured me that in his opinion he and I were the only members of the Committee of Five* who thought of the Covenant at all.
And I went on to say:

> Nevertheless, if one is to understand with some insight
> the present British policy, one must not lose sight of the fact
> that all British policy turns on two totally different poles that
> should be kept clearly separate: there is an Albion conscious
> of her power and impelled by an urge for power, who (en-
> dowed with a wonderful traditional spirit rooted as far back
> as Henry VIII and the great Elizabeth, through Cromwell)
> keeps intact and maintains, indeed tries even in our less propi-
> cious days to expand, that British Empire the beginnings of
> which were erected at the expense of the Spanish Empire
> from 1588 on. For this Albion incarnated in the permanent
> staff of the Foreign Office [and in the Services and the City],
> Spain is and remains an enemy. For this Albion, the League
> of Nations is a powerful element for the expansion of her
> power, which she handles with her usual skill and persever-
> ance. And there is an England, governed by this Albion, gene-
> rous, humanitarian, puritan, sincerely desirous of bringing
> about a better world, charitable and always ready to help the
> weak against the strong out of a movement of her heart. This
> England it is to whom we owe the Covenant and from whom
> we may hope the successful establishment of an international
> just system.
>
> There is no opposition between these two British forms
> which, for the sake of clarity I describe as Albion and Eng-
> land. There is no opposition between them because England
> has but an obscure awareness of the existence of Albion, while
> Albion feels a deep respect for England, which she knows how
> to make use of for her own purposes. Rather than two strains
> of opinion that might come to affront each other, they are
> two states of mind that might even occur together within the
> same Englishman, in whom the one of the other will emerge
> as the play of circumstances will have it.**

---

*Eden, Laval, Rustu Aras and Beck, with me as chairman. They were all Foreign
Secretaries. I was nothing.

** I believe this dichotomy came to me from an article in the *New Age* by that genius
A. R. Orage.

Now Ethiopia entered the twentieth century as a state governing about six million Africans of several extractions, religions and cultures, in a space of 35,000 sq. miles surrounded by territories more or less protected by Britain, Italy and France; and these three nations, notably the two first ones, were eager to show the world, but more especially the Ethiopians, that they considered the integrity of Ethiopia as an indispensable condition of their own national felicity; so much so that they were even able to define to which part of the Ethiopian territory the deep concern of each of them would apply in case of threat to the said precious integrity.

So on December 16, 1906, they had concluded a treaty by which Britain, France and Italy declared that they would 'co-operate in maintaining the political and territorial *status quo* in Ethiopia', and that, were it to be threatened or altered they would 'make every effort to preserve the integrity of Ethiopia'. The only reason I can find for doubting that the High Contracting Parties were plagiarising my *Sacred Giraffe* is that the treaty had been signed in December 1906 and my book was published in 1925; but lest I am thought to be too touchy about it, I shall copy a few more items from the treaty of 1906, to show how close it kept to my fancy of 1925.

The High Contracting Parties agreed 'to act together in order to safeguard' their special interests in Ethiopia, most of which they expected to wrench from the Ethiopian Government by concerted action, and then, they defined such interests as follows:

(a) The interests of Great Britain and Egypt* in the Nile basin, more especially the waters of that river and its tributaries (due consideration being paid to local interests) without prejudice to Italian interests mentioned in (b);

(b) The interests of Italy in Ethiopia as regards Eritrea and Somaliland (including the Benadir) more especially with reference to the *hinterland* of her possessions and the territorial connection between them to the west of Addis Ababa;

(c) The interests of France in Ethiopia as regards the French Protectorate of the Somali Coast, the *hinterland* of their Protectorate, and the zone necessary for the construction and working of the railway from Jibuti to Addis Ababa.

*This of course means: the interests of Great Britain both direct and through her protectorate, the Egyptian State.

I refrain from further details though they would add much concrete material to heighten the colour and design of the picture of the pre-history of the Italo-Ethiopian conflict; for no adequate vision of such conflicts can be formed without realising that the two main props of the Covenant, namely the British and the French peoples, were tethered in their movements by these 'pre-historic' commitments that their govern-ments had entered into. Nor would it be fair to condemn their bygone governments for having entered into such commitments, since they conformed to the style and custom of those days. There was then no Covenant and little thought or even dream of it. Thus the ill-fate of the nations who had to live in 1935 was to have become something not un-like historical sirens, whose tails of power-political sharks conflicted with their upper bodies of rational beings. No wonder that even the best of their statesmen were at times unable to make head or tail of it all.

Of the three powers, the most ambitious in Ethiopia was Italy. She was also the least fortunate; for on a difference of interpretation of an older treaty (Uccialli, May 2, 1889) and relying on the backing of Britain who on April 15, 1891 had recognised not only Eritrea and Italian Somaliland but Ethiopia as being 'within the sphere of influence re-served for Italy', Italy invaded the territory of her *protégée* who resisted by force of arms and won the battle of Adowa (1896) by sheer power of numbers and a certain aid in armaments from France. By the treaty of peace (October 26, 1896) the treaty of Uccialli was abro-gated and Italy recognised Ethiopia as 'a sovereign and independent State'.

Since Ethiopia was not a party to the treaty of 1906 and her emperor Menelik II had expressly washed his hands of it, Italy had to tread care-fully and always with an eye on Britain and another on France; and so, in 1919 she had sought Britain's support to build a railway connecting Eritrea with Italian Somaliland, offering in exchange support for Britain's plan to build a dam at Lake Tsana and a motor road from the Sudan to the dam. This proposal was turned down by Britain in 1919 but accepted in 1925, in an exchange of notes whereby the two heads of mission in Addis Ababa were 'to concert together for common action' so as to get both concessions at the same time. Britain, more-over, declared that if her concession went through, she would 're-cognise an exclusive Italian economic influence in the west of Abyssinia.'

It is hard to see how such a concession could be squared with the Covenant; and when Ethiopia protested on that account, many were the delegates of small powers who thought she was right. But it is worth noticing that France objected to the Italo-British deal of 1925, not on the strength of the breach of the Covenant but on that of the treaty of 1906; and this attitude of Britain, France and Italy in 1925 was in everybody's mind when towards the end of 1934 the first clouds of the coming storm darkened the blue waters of the Lake of Geneva.

This threat seemed at first to abate. Italy and Ethiopia had struck a treaty of 'constant peace and perpetual friendship' (August 2, 1928) which bound them both 'not to engage, under any pretext, in action calculated to injure or prejudice the independence of the other' and 'to submit all their disputes to conciliation or arbitration'. Evidently, that 'constant peace' was not to be so constant and that 'perpetual friendship' was not to be so perpetual as not to admit of a dispute now and then. The Italians might have suspected that should such a dispute turn up, it would come from Paris, where troubles for Italy used to come from in those days; but the first dispute bore all the signs of being made in London.

On December 5, 1934 shots were exchanged in Wal-Wal (Ogaden) between an Italian and an Ethiopian force which cost the lives of about one hundred Ethiopian soldiers and thirty natives in the service of Italy. The spot had been garrisoned by Italy since 1930 but lay about fifty miles beyond the border between Ethiopian and Italian Somaliland, therefore fifty miles inside Abyssinia; on the other hand, it was also one hundred miles beyond the British Somaliland border supposed to be surveyed by the British-Ethiopian commission, whose escort had fought the Italians; so that it is not clear why such a Commission should have been there at all, nor why it should have to go about protected by an escort out of all proportion with its needs.

But that is about all that can be said for the Italian case. It was well known, indeed a matter of public knowledge, that for over a year, Mussolini had been preparing his army for the conquest of Ethiopia, and that by December 1934, everything being ready, there could be no more preparations, so the shooting had to begin. Mussolini had unrolled before his people an imperial plan 'that stretches until the nearby millenium, the year 2000' and this plan pointed 'South and East', 'Africa and Asia'. It was therefore plain that either this plan was incompatible with the Covenant, and therefore Mussolini was heading for a collision with the League, or it was still valid in a world ruled by the survival of the fittest for imperialism, and then Mussolini was heading for a collision with Britain and with France. As it turned out, the world was both ruled by the Covenant and by Darwin, so that Mussolini had to collide with both the League and the powers, and the outcome was that he became Hitler's slave and died like a slave, his head down.

Ethiopia began by offering to arbitrate the dispute under article 5 of the Italo-Ethiopian Treaty of 1928; but Italy rejected the offer in plain violation of the treaty, and demanded reparations which were to include an apology from the governor of Harrar, a salute to the Italian flag at Wal-Wal, and adequate punishment of the Ethiopian officers concerned; whereupon Ethiopia submitted the incident to the League (December 14, 1934) and on January 3, 1935 requested that 'every measure effectually to safeguard peace be taken' in accordance with article 11 of the Covenant. As usual in these cases, Mussolini insisted (just as Japan had done in the Manchurian crisis) on dealing direct with his victim, an attitude which, by itself, was a clear violation of the spirit and the letter of the Covenant.

But the appeal to the League, if agreeable to the people of England, was less welcome to the gentlemen of Albion; and as for France, it raised the spectre of a real problem. Hitler was re-arming and destroying the Treaty of Versailles not by words – though he uttered also plenty to that effect – but by deeds; and Laval knew that Mussolini was at daggers drawn with Hitler. There were two motives for this: one, that Hitler did not trouble to conceal his plans for annexing Austria, a country which the Duce considered as his special preserve; and the other was that Hitler had stolen some of the Duce's stage properties, such as frowns, shrieks, parades, flags, slogans and even his very shirt and his title: Führer-Duce. The outcome of it all was that Laval went to Rome (January 1935).

The very date (though it had been pre-arranged in Barthou's days) put Laval in the advantageous position of having something to offer, namely: how far and how loud would France bark with the League wolves if and when the Ethiopian crisis came before the League. It so happened that when, a few days later, I arrived in Geneva (where I used to stay at the Bergues, as did the French), as I entered the dining-room for my evening meal, I saw a strange sight (due no doubt to the late hour) the dining-room was empty but for a solitary figure at the left hand corner on the entrance-door side: Laval. He beckoned to me and I sat at his table.

He was in Geneva straight from Rome. From my first glance at him, I gathered that he was pleased with himself. Laval was not a man who could – or if he could, who would – hide his feelings. If he was in a good mood, he let it be seen; if in a bad mood, also; for he had little or no feeling for the other fellow. Obviously, his trip to Rome had been worthwhile, at any rate in his eyes. He saw I was curious and there and then produced a paper out of his pocket. 'There. You can read it while we sit here.' It was not a method favourable to concentrating, let alone memorising a paper; so, beyond what seemed to me a bargain between

Italy forsaking any claims in Tunis and France ceding to Italy a packet of shares (2000) of the Jibuti – Addis Ababa railway, there was little I retained save a few territorial concessions to Italy, mostly made up of sand surrounded by sand.

I returned the paper and said: '*Si c'est tout, vous l'avez roulé*'.* That pleased him and his horse-dealer's eyes shone with pride. I insisted that there must be something unsaid, or rather unwritten, and he swore there wasn't. I concluded that there was: and thinking it over in my bed, I missed one but I guessed another one of these secret agreements. It did not occur to me that there would be military stipulations for mutual co-operation in case of an aggression from Hitler; possibly because of my own scepticism about Mussolini actually coming out against his most brilliant pupil; but I guessed that there had been a tacit agreement on this very simple proposition: 'provided you are on my side in Europe, you can do what you wish in Ethiopia.' This agreement may have been conveyed by no more than a wink. But you should have seen what Laval could say with a wink.

The man best placed to form an opinion on this point – i.e.: how many devils could fly about in one of Laval's winks – was Eden, who often had to deal with him and with the winks' chief recipient, Mussolini. He did his best and was nonplussed. Eden refers to the subject in at least three passages of his *Memoirs*. In the first (p. 123) he concludes that 'Laval was sufficiently equivocal to give Mussolini the chance to exploit his attitude. Certainly the Duce got the worst of the bargain, on paper, and the best in licence.' In the second (p. 209) he gives his own version of a short talk with Laval in which Laval told him how he had warned Mussolini 'to be careful that his efforts in Abyssinia were confined to economic objectives.' But in his third (p. 224) he relates with lively details how, on reminding Mussolini of this very scene, the Duce 'flung himself back in his chair with a gesture of incredulous astonishment.'

---

* If that is the lot, you've taken him in.

CHAPTER XXXV

THE POWERS AND MORAL POWER

I T will simplify my task in relating how this dismal story unrolled its fate-laden episodes if I copy here a few lines from the *History of the League of Nations* by my friend and one-time colleague Frank Walters, who was Under-Secretary General of the League.

> If now Italy was unwilling to allow the Council to discuss her relations with Ethiopia, if she felt it as an affront to have to deal in public, on equal terms, with the representative of Haile Selassie, this attitude was only too well understood in the Foreign and Colonial Offices of London and Paris. In common with Italy, Britain and France had for fifty years formed an effective zone of separation between Ethiopia and the rest of the world. It seemed to them only natural that the new trouble should also be dealt with among themselves [. . .] Accordingly, the proceedings of the Council were made to alternate with conversations between Britain, France and Italy, in which the Covenant was often forgotten and the interests of the League were treated as of small account.

How about Russia? Was she not the power representing a new society, a new world? Was she not 'peace-loving'? Well, no. The Soviet Union was just another big power – and, at times, really concerned with, indeed frightened by, the Nazi and Japanese threat. Far away, hidden behind his secret police and his absolute rule over press and radio, Stalin kept an anxious watch on events that were becoming more and more threatening for Communist Russia; and in Geneva, Litvinov, no less anxiously, was playing the Geneva game fully aware of the fact that if things went awry he would be the first to fall.

The Saar plebiscite had been for Litvinov almost a nightmare. Seen at this distance, one wonders why he or any other intelligent and sensible observer such as he was, should have felt the slightest doubt on the issue of that plebiscite. True, the Saar basin cut off from Germany by the Treaty of Versailles simply, to say it in French, because *la raison du plus fort est toujours la meilleure**, was governed by a League

---

*The reason of the stronger man is always the best.

344

Commission with such wisdom that no complaint had been received by the League; but that did not make the Saar less German, and peoples are so made that they prefer their own rule even when bad to foreign rule even when good. The plebiscite was due in 1935. In due time, the Council had to prepare a kind of 'electoral law' for the plebiscite; and as Saar affairs had always been at the Council the preserve of the Italian Delegate, we found ourselves in the ironical situation of having to designate as our draftsman for an electoral law, i.e. the rules for the expression of the public opinion of a land, no less a 'democrat' than Aloisi, Mussolini's mouthpiece in Geneva. The Council flanked him with Cantilo of Argentina and my assistant, López Oliván, an excellent jurist and a genuine liberal.

Though their plan and timetable were exacting down to every detail, this Committee worked punctually and all was ready for the chosen date: January 13, 1935. Trouble came from Hitler, under threats of disorders. The coolness of the Governing Commission and the wise decision to set up an international force to keep order turned the scales in favour of common sense. We had been convoked to Geneva, so as to be at hand for events. There were no events. The vote was quiet. But I remember Litvinov, walking to and fro in the *Salle des Pas Perdus* of the League, putting his desperate question to every one of his acquaintances: who is going to win? When he did so to me, my answer was: over ninety per cent for going back to Germany. He saw the point but was very much concerned. The vote was 477,000 for Germany; 46,000 for remaining under the League; 2,000 for France.

It was under the impression of this vote that Litvinov sat at the Council to discuss Ethiopia. Given the circumstances, the political philosophy of Soviet Russia, the general pattern of forces before us, it was not realistic to expect of Litvinov that he should give the slightest thought to the Covenant; and as for Ethiopia, how many 'Ethiopias' hidden away in the Euro-Asian immensity of Stalin's empire were going through worse treatment than that now threatened by Mussolini.

This attitude favoured Italy rather than Ethiopia, at any rate, on procedure; so that when (soon after my talk at dinner with Laval) we sat at the Council table, we did have on our agenda the Italo-Ethiopian dispute, but France and Britain managed to keep the issue in the narrow channel chosen by Italy and we had to be content with a promise of a direct settlement under the 1928 treaty and advice about avoiding such incidents (as that of Wal-Wal) in the future. This said, the debate was adjourned (January 19, 1935) until the May session. Italy, therefore, had won the first round.

Ten days later, on January 29th, the news that five more victims, all Somalis in the service of Italy, had succumbed, opened wide the tap of military 'preparations'. Two divisions were mobilised in Italy and the government let it be known that it was ready to spend eight hundred and fifty million dollars to obtain satisfaction in Ethiopia. General De Bono was sent to Ethiopia as commander-in-chief and general Graziani as civil and military governor of Somaliland. All pretence was useless. Mussolini was openly and blatantly on the war path.

Yet, pretence there was. Haile Selassie sent a telegram to the League (March 16, 1935) showing how the hopes expressed by the Council in January had been belied by events, and asking that the conflict be dealt with under Article 15 of the Covenant, that it should be effectively submitted to arbitration and that the Italian military preparations in Eritrea and Somaliland come to an end. The Emperor of Ethiopia was squarely within his rights as a member of the League. On March 22nd, Italy rejected the Emperor's plea. 'There were no such military preparations, just mere precautions in view of the aggressive policy of Ethiopia. Italy had never intended nor did she intend to evade the application of Article 5 of the 1928 Treaty and therefore Article 15 of the Covenant did not apply.'

No one but the Aloisi Government could have uttered such blatant untruths without either smiling or blushing; and no one round that Council table, including the Italian delegate, was unaware of what they meant. They meant that Mussolini did not intend either to arbitrate the conflict with Ethiopia or to submit it to the procedures laid down by the Covenant. But Italy, after all, even loaded with steel as she was at the time, was not a match for the League, nor did other problems, such as the mere fact of distance, reduce the League potential as it could be argued they had done in the case of Japan. The real reason why the League Council allowed itself to be sidetracked by its three other permanent members was brought out by this fateful coincidence: on the very day Haile Selassie cabled his appeal to the League (March 16, 1935), Hitler announced to Germany and to the world that the peace-time strength of the German Army would be thirty-six divisions, and to that effect he promulgated a law introducing conscription.

The situation was absurd, yet natural. Every nation was rearming because every nation was afraid of Hitler; and Hitler rearmed because the other nations were rearming, while the Treaty of Versailles had 'justified' the disarmament of Germany on the ground that it would enable the others to disarm. All these 'ifs' and 'buts' were but the trimmings of a situation which in its bare bones was grim enough. The outcome of it all was that neither Britain, France nor Russia could demand anything from Mussolini. Indeed, the Duce took his chance and invited France and Britain to discuss the situation – i.e. that created not by him but by Hitler – at Stresa. Now Laval had requested the

League Council to meet on Hitler's military proclamation; and the Council meeting had been arranged for the beginning of April. Then the true power-relation between the League and her Council's permanent members (France, Britain and Italy) was revealed: these three governments 'told' the League that they were meeting at Stresa on April 11th and that they expected the Council to meet afterwards.

Eden, who had been travelling all over Europe and visited Berlin with Simon, and Moscow, Warsaw and Prague without him, had met with such a severe storm while flying over Germany that he had strained his heart and had to miss the Stresa Conference. This was a pity, for had he been there, the outcome of that Conference might have been different. As it was, and despite his efforts to see that the Ethiopian dispute was discussed there, the Conference led to nothing but negative 'results' even on the matter of rearmament; and the most negative of all was that Ethiopia was not even mentioned at Stresa at all – which amounted to a tacit permission to Mussolini to do his worst.

We owe it to Vansittart's honesty that Drummond can be exonerated from this major failure to understand what was going on, and to his vanity that he sets down his responsibility in the deed with a proud sense of what was due to his intellect (p. 520). Drummond wanted the British 'to *begin* by warning the Duce of our wrath'; but Vansittart 'thought better tactics might be to land Mussolini first and lecture him after' – the tactics which in the end prevailed; and against the view not only of Drummond but of Robert Cecil as well, of whom Vansittart typically writes that he 'was clamouring that "this vital question [the Nazi breaches of the Treaty of Versailles] should be transferred to the wider atmosphere of Geneva" and the collective loquacity of fifty-eight other nations.' (pp. 518–19)

The manner was worthy of the matter. The big-power ministers drafted their own decisions (or lack of them) in the form of a report which they expected the League to swallow whole and no qualms allowed; and Ramsay MacDonald hinted to the press while still at Stresa that I was to be the *rapporteur* to the League Council, oblivious of the fact that such a thing could not happen without the acquiescence of the Council, of my Government and of myself. The European situation was growing more and more fragile and the Ethiopian affair made it even more difficult. Simon, MacDonald and Laval, on arriving in Geneva, begged me to take on the report. My first condition was that I should be free to draft it as I thought fit. They assured me their draft was the very thing and would need no changes. I stood my ground. They accepted though shaking their heads; but my Government would have nothing to do with it. I suggested to Madrid that I be flanked by two colleagues, and then my Government relented. When the Council gave me

Denmark and Chile, the two Council members most hesitant in any condemnation of Hitler, I knew our part in the play was over.

We set to work all the same, taking the Stresa report as a basis; but we altered it in a way that Vansittart and Laval were (I thought) sure to reject. When the time came to put it to them, Vansittart was almost contemptuous: 'The French won't look at it.' Laval was contemptuous and angry. '*Je donnerai un coup de pied à leur baraque de Genève.*' I was at peace with myself. I had not asked to have the job. They wanted to cover their poor goods with my pavilion. That is why they had given me the job. It was up to them to take it back. They did and we all were, if not happy, at least content.

The meeting of the Council was all that could be expected of Laval, Simon and Aloisi; a stiff, discourteous, take-it-or-leave-it presentation of a resolution as long-winded as ineffective, and a series of objections, reservations and even rejections on the part of all of us, followed by a second wave of stiff, short and altogether arrogant remarks from the three 'Stresans' when they heard the Turkish Delegate announce that his country would no longer be bound by the limitations imposed by the Treaty of Lausanne for her use of the Straits. As for the resolution itself, Laval, Simon and Aloisi refused to reply to several requests made by some of us for explanations.

This scene was exceptional in the history of the League and due to the conjunction of Laval and Simon, two men as incapable of understanding the League as any that went to Geneva. For the Covenant they felt little but contempt, frank and open in Laval, stiff-shirted and clean-shaven by hypocrisy and good manners in Simon. They confronted us with a fearful dilemma: to submit to an intolerable dictation or to suggest to Hitler that we were divided and did not back a resolution which on the whole condemned him. We voted yes, all but Denmark*, who abstained. I still wonder whether we should not have insisted on another form of words.

---

*In her case the matter of principle was reinforced by the fact that she was then pursuing a pacifist doctrine and was practically disarmed.

CHAPTER XXXVI

MORE ROPE TO MUSSOLINI

A S the coastline stands clearer to the eye at a distance than to the eye close to it, so seen at our historical distance are we now able to appreciate how and why the League was then declining. In its essence, the League of Nations was something more than the nations of the League. It was an institution that professed to do its best to protect peace, and therefore, to stand for Justice when attacked by Force. Now, having on its agenda at the same time Hitler's rearmament and Mussolini's aggression against Ethiopia, the League, under pressure from three powers (one of them the aggressor), was passing a resolution condemning Hitler-Germany for rearming (most of its members being unaware that Britain was preparing to conclude with Hitler-Germany a treaty of naval rearmament no less contrary to the Covenant); while in the case of Ethiopia, the League Council, under pressure from the four powers, kept postponing the procedure of arbitration and allowing Mussolini to arm and attack his victim.

Thus then was the civilised world undermining the foundations of its own peace and order. That 'something more' the League was, *its moral power based on the Covenant*, was bound to suffer when the peoples of the world saw it applied in such a way that it became a tool for big nations to rearm and to appeal to the lesser powers to be ready to repel the aggressor – in the European case – yet to allow the aggressor to do its worst in the African case. The reason for this was that Simon (with Vansittart), Laval, Aloisi and Litvinov had no faith whatsoever in the League as such, but only as a more or less efficient instrument to recruit other nations in their service; and that they remained attached to the obsolete ideas of powder and steel inherited from the previous century. It is a grim comment on the failure of the League in these two cases (Manchuria and Ethiopia) that a number of studies on these events published in the 1960s hardly mention moral power in their analyses.

How about the United States? The conflict was complex enough to make her policy even more confused than usual. In so far as it was an attack against world 'law and order', it could interest and even arouse the public opinion of the United States, if not to the rescue of the League, at least to that of the Kellogg Pact, which was a kind of American version of the same gospel: but in so far as it meant yet another scramble for territories and concessions between three European powers afflicted by imperialism, it was bound to cool whatever ardour was generated by the first aspect. Cordell Hull was an attractive, gentle southerner, yet not an original or powerful statesman, and he tried to navigate the narrow waters left to him by the hard rocks of the facts to the best of his limited ability, hampered by his desire for as limited a liability as the isolationist sector of his countrymen demanded. He was, moreover, handicapped by the chief circumstance which had impaired the effectiveness of American foreign policy ever since the death of Woodrow Wilson: her absence from the institutions of the League.

For good or ill, the League was the forum where the public affairs of the world were debated, the public opinion of the world was informed and orientated, and whenever possible, decisions were taken and, in some cases, problems actually solved. The U.S., a prominent member of the world, chose to remain away from this forum; and, with the best will in the world, even men as ready to do their best as Cordell Hull was, as able and forceful as Roosevelt was, were bound often to sound the wrong note at the wrong time and to be altogether out of tune and even of hearing. The outcome of it all was that the 'co-operation' of the U.S. in keeping Mussolini at bay under two men as willing and able as Roosevelt and Cordell Hull was no more efficient than had been that of the unsympathetic Hoover and Stimson in keeping Japan out of mischief.

Mussolini meanwhile carried on his policy of delaying tactics in Geneva, and military preparations in Rome. Conciliation and arbitration were painted on a horizon that kept receding before our eyes. Laval and Eden – who was taking a growing share in League affairs – were very much concerned about the breaking up of the Stresa front against Hitler, if Mussolini in his warlike mood pulled too hard at the Covenant. The attitude of Aloisi in Geneva grew stiffer and stiffer, though he tried his best to avoid a break; and in the end, towards the May meeting of the Council, in which Mussolini again was determined to delay and postpone the conciliation procedure, Laval and Eden agreed to draft a resolution to be submitted in their joint names to the Council. The chief aim of this resolution was to prevent a threat of military intervention which Mussolini had made public.

The text had been submitted to the Duce, who had objected to precisely what mattered most: military intentions. Haile Selassie had again appealed to the League on this score. The draft resolution prepared by Eden and Laval did not say much, but even that stuck in Mussolini's throat. In the end, he swallowed, it. Its wording could not be more modest considering it was the League Council that passed it: it reminded 'both parties', meaning, of course, Italy, of the obligations they had incurred – oh, no, not under the Covenant, but under the 1928 Treaty between the two. The resolution was less soft on arbitration and conciliation: this procedure had to be completed by August 25th or else the Council would meet again. It had to.

I took a trip to London in May, and (I find in his *Memoirs*) I had tea with Tom Jones at his flat on the Friday before May 12th, when he writes to Lady Grigg about it. I shall let him speak:

> Madariaga came to the flat to tea on Friday and was more alarmist about the European situation than almost anyone I've met lately. *Very* severe on Simon, very appreciative of Eden and would be willing to see Eden Foreign Secretary. I said that was impossible and suggested L.G., but Madariaga says L.G. is too insular, not a real friend of the League. M. very nervous of Germany's sudden use of its air force against England and France in some mad moment, and wants to push the abolition of military aircraft and the internationalisation of civil aircraft as the only hope. I am trying to arrange for him to see S.B. and L.G.

Tom reports our conversation somewhat cooler than it actually was, on my side, at any rate. He spoke of L.G. for the Foreign Office before I spoke of Eden. Whereupon I retorted: 'Never. Never on your life.' He was rather taken aback and I now suspect that the idea of putting the F. O. under the great Welshman was his – which would appear to be confirmed by their later trip together to Hitler Germany. Naturally enough, he asked: 'Then, who?' and I firmly answered: 'Eden.' He was no less taken aback, and said 'That's impossible.' But I gave him my reasons and he seemed to be impressed.

I was, of course, unaware of the fact, revealed by Eden in his *Memoirs*, that he, Eden, was about the same time urging upon Stanley Baldwin the need to speak in Geneva with but one voice: if he was not to be Foreign Secretary (at 38) he preferred to go somewhere else – the Admiralty, for instance, rather than serve under another Foreign Secretary. He was, of course, quite right, and timely too, for S.B. was at the time preparing a change of government, over which he would preside as Prime Minister, and it had been agreed that the change-over would take place in July.

Though Eden was always correct and discreet, indeed loyal to his cabinet colleagues and in particular to his chief, Simon, we all were able to perceive clearly the difference between a man who understood the League and the men who didn't. As it turned out, the obvious fact that Eden was for Britain an asset abroad came through despite his youth; and Baldwin would have appointed him but for Neville Chamberlain, another definitely anti-League man, who wrenched from Baldwin the appointment of Samuel Hoare, as if Providence had preferred to bring out in the most dramatic form how right we were who advocated Eden. The solution was Hoare Foreign Secretary and Eden Minister for League Affairs. Eden accepted it reluctantly on Hoare assuring him that it would not last very long. He did not know how right he was!

Now Eden was too able and too well-informed to be unaware of the fact that there is no such thing as League Affairs, since all foreign affairs were or should be League affairs. Indeed, that very idea was the core of all he had been saying to Baldwin and to Hoare. The decision had therefore its bad side, in that it kept Eden under the authority of a politician who was in fact an outsider; and in that it institutionalised the false idea that League foreign affairs were just a special section of general foreign affairs; yet it had a good side too, for Eden was now a Minister in his own right with more gold braid and a seat in the Cabinet.

The Italo-Ethiopian dispute meanwhile went, of course, from bad to worse. The time allowed to Italy was crammed by the military with further ship-loads of troops, food and ammunition, which kept the Suez Canal busy; and the Italian soldiers standing on deck, passing between two rows of British soldiers who calmly watched it all, now and then gave vent to their disdain for Britain by emptying their bladders as they went by; whereupon the saucier of the tommies sitting on the edge of the Canal would shout: 'Show it while you still have it', or words to that effect, which, given the stern ways of the Ethiopians towards their prisoners of war, was in too many cases prophetic . . . with a vengeance.

We, in Spain, are all familiar with the situation we describe as 'two bulls in the ring'. The matador does not like it. No one does. That was the situation we, of the Council, were facing; and while it is idle to speculate as to whether Britain and France (or for that matter Spain or Sweden in their places) would have acted more firmly towards Mussolini if Hitler had not been by then let loose in the European ring, the fact is that we all were conscious of there being two bulls ready to gore us. Eden went to Rome (June 30, 1935).

Important territorial concessions were proposed to Mussolini on June 23rd in Ogaden as well as a railway link between her two colonies, while a port ceded by Britain in British Somaliland would be ceded to Ethiopia as compensation. Disliked by the French, this proposal was rejected by Mussolini. The Committee of Conciliation and Arbitration was in the doldrums when the Council met (with Litvinov as chairman) on July 31, 1935; the usual pressure and fear of the worst held its hand from bold measures espousing the Covenant point of view, and kept it close to the shore of Italian policy in every way. It was decided to meet again on September 4th with a statement that, this time, we would deal with the actual conflict and not merely with how to postpone our decision.

This was by no means good for the League; but, worse still, Britain, France and Italy informed us that they would open negotiations towards a settlement of the Italo-Ethiopian Conflict, and this, it must be owned, was disastrous. It again assumed that the conflict was one between Italy and Ethiopia, while it was really one between Italy and the League; it removed the issue from the League jurisdiction to one of sheer pre-Covenant relations; and it removed from our procedure the very victim of it all – Ethiopia.

And yet, it might have been worse. Mussolini wanted the three power talks altogether outside the League. Eden and Laval insisted that they had to take place under the aegis of the Council; Hoare, as Eden relates, thoroughly agreed but would have accepted Mussolini's condition; so that, in the end, Eden was saved from a position that might have been irretrievable for him by the unexpected climbing down of Mussolini himself on this specific point. Eden was already labouring under another trying situation. After a visit to Rome in which he had put to the Duce (June 23, 1935) the serious consequences which his actions might have in Europe, Eden had expected a written confirmation of his warnings to be sent to Rome on the part of his colleagues. Nothing was done. Then he repeatedly put to his Cabinet colleagues a point whose importance cannot be denied: 'If the worst comes to the worst and one of the parties resorts to war in disregard of its obligations under the Covenant, what should be the attitude of H.M.'s Government?' Eden insisted time and again – as we now know from his *Memoirs* – on the obvious fact that he should be empowered to meet this question, which he foresaw could be put to him in public but more likely in private and in the course of negotiations: '... the Cabinet will appreciate that I shall be placed in an almost impossible position in Geneva. I shall certainly be asked this question by Monsieur Laval and by others, e.g. Monsieur Litvinov as President of the Council, and perhaps by the Spanish Delegate as representing the neutral group and by the representatives of one or two of the smaller powers.'

He was right to mention the Spanish Delegate, because all my friends in the neutral group, as well as my own Government, kept asking that question; and Eden's answer would have been adequate and correct: 'If such a situation should arise, and if the case were clear beyond dispute, H.M.'s Government would be prepared to fulfil their obligations under the Covenant, if others would do the same.' Had Eden been the Foreign Secretary, this clarity of thought and will would have forced Laval to brake Mussolini if only for fear of public opinion; but the Foreign Secretary was Hoare.

Some American radio news agency invaded my garden in Madrid with cameras and cables to get my views on events and in particular on Hitler's dangerous plans. They took a very long time to settle down mostly because of the traffic noise, for the day was lovely and sunny, and I was to speak in my garden. Every time they at last got their 'silence', i.e. a level of tolerable noise, a window would bang or be violently shut by a neighbour or a car accelerate or a street vendor extol his tomatoes or radishes taking Heaven for his witness. At long last there it was. I began to speak. After a sentence and a half, a donkey endowed with a powerful baritone voice produced a magnificent bray from nowhere anyone could see. We all (including many spectators at nearby windows) doubled up with laughter. All over again! 'No' cried out C.H.M.A. from our own window above. 'No. Just carry on and apologise: "We are sorry that Hitler cut in before his turn."'

Ever since my resignation from the embassy and a few weeks later from the Cabinet, I had been able to enjoy a certain amount of leisure, though all too frequently broken by a call to Geneva. I held no post whatever: but from May 1934 until the very eve of the civil war (July 1936) the successive governments expected me to be ready to go to Geneva whenever the Council, the Assembly or an important Committee would be sitting. This state of affairs made it obviously very hard for me to earn my living as a man of letters, since it deprived me of both my time to think out opinions and events and my liberty to judge them publicly. After much patient advocacy I at last succeeded in having a bill presented to Parliament, setting up a post as Permanent Delegate, with a modest salary and an even more modest establishment. The bill was lost, because the Foreign Affairs Committee of the Cortes, on the proposal of one of its members, by profession a diplomat, argued that everybody knew I was to be given that post, which carried ambassadorial rank, while I had not stood for the examination required to enter the diplomatic service.

Obviously it was not just such an asinine argument that had carried the commission. It was something worse and graver. When the Lerroux-Gil Robles combination had returned to power, a virulent campaign had been unleashed in the centre-right press against Azaña. I have always been what the British describe as a crossbench mind. It seemed to me that such a campaign was unutterably stupid, not only because it was unfair to the man who, with all his faults, was far and away the most capable of our statemen, indeed our one and only statesman, but because it was not in the interest of any republican party, still less of the Republic, so to undermine a political asset. I thought so and said so clearly and squarely in an article printed in a Madrid newspaper; much to the displeasure of a number of centre-right Members of Parliament and Cabinet ministers, who gave me to understand that, in view of my attitude, the bill to set up the post of Permanent Delegate would be lost.

CHAPTER XXXVII

IN URUGUAY AND ARGENTINA

T HAT summer (1935) Saavedra Lamas asked me to visit Argentina as a guest of his Government. My own Government took the opportunity to officialise my private trip giving me Spanish collars of the Order of Charles III to hang on the necks of four Spanish American Presidents: Terra of Uruguay, Justo of Argentina, Alessandri of Chile and Benavides of Peru. I left Spain on a German ship which did me the courtesy of flying the Spanish flag all the way.

I remember that crossing because of two characters who had become the most prominent members of the family the passengers are apt to weave together after the first two or three days. Those two seemed to have all the ideas, and the initiative to organise everything with *gusto*, glee and energy. They were the most successfully disguised when we held a fancy dress ball; the most liberal with the champagne. One was a Frenchman, the other an Englishman. The day before we landed, I discovered that they were visiting the South American continent on behalf respectively of the British and of the French armament industry.

Terra, my first host*, was then governing Uruguay in an unusual way, for a man who had been elected on a liberal democratic platform, which was in those days indispensable if one was to appeal to the population. Uruguay was then the Switzerland of Spanish America, enlightened, liberal, peaceful, public-spirited, well-educated, knowing no excess either of private wealth or of private poverty; so that for such a community to be ruled by such a man, on the whole rather mediocre, in such a dictatorial manner, did not seem justified at all.

Then came the time for Justo of Argentina. The highest praise he merited was that he carried his name well. True, he was a general, but an intellectual one and one who had been elected in the way prescribed by his country's constitution, i.e. by the free vote of his countrymen. He was a real general, though, and had been Minister of War and commander-in-chief. He told me himself that he had had to bale out of military planes no less than three times, one of them unintentionally, for he just fell overboard during manoeuvres. His pilot's name hap-

---

* This is meant in a geographical order, for in fact I went first to Buenos Aires. I arrived in Montevideo on July 12th and returned to Buenos Aires on July 16th; on July 24th I flew over to Santiago; and on July 31st to Peru.

pened to be Alegría ('joy' or 'mirth'); and his fall was known at headquarters by a signal this pilot sent: 'Minister of War fallen overboard –
Joy.' The general told me the story with great glee, adding: 'Within an
hour or so, I turned up at the H.Q. after a solitary walk through the
forest, and I was soon up in the air again.'

For a Spaniard, this direct plunging into 'Spanish' life so far from
Spain could not be more stimulating. Uruguay and Argentina happen
to be the most 'White' nations in South America, the most important
non-Spanish contingent in their population being Italian. In those days
my predominant impression not merely of these two countries but of
the whole continent was the excellent level of intellectual development
in the men and women I met. But in those days, the wealth of Buenos
Aires had not succeeded in creating a beauty of its own. That immense
conurbation on the edge of that vast plain of water spread at its feet
was but an ill-assorted museum of imitations of European architecture,
mostly French, some Italian, some English, and even some Spanish, so
that when the genuine little Spanish cabildo or Town Hall of vice regal
days suddenly appeared before one's eyes one could hardly believe that
so much 'real imitation' could have grown out of such a little grain of
inimitable reality.

Architecture is the most communal of all the arts. This imitative
quality of most of that big capital betrayed the period of imitation the
Argentine soul had gone through since their wars of emancipation
had severed it from mother Spain. The mood of independence did not
admit Spanishness even as a spontaneous and natural utterance of the
blood and spirit in the nation; and this forced the Argentines to a mood
of imitation. The only European people the Argentines need not imitate
is the Spanish; for they are Spanish; possibly also, the Italian, insofar
as they are Italian; furthermore, if they are just themselves, they will
spontaneously be *Spaniards who have moved to the other side of the street*,
and while they will, of course, bear their Spanishness with a difference,
they will be once-removed Spaniards for all that.

Diverging Spaniards we all are, like the branches of a tree, for whom
growth and divergence are one and the same thing. But the sap, the colour, the shape of the leaf and the taste of the fruit will keep a oneness
for all that – unless we all re-converge again with every other branch of
every other tree in the world and finally become Chicagoans.

CHAPTER XXXVIII

CHILE

'THAT little hill on the left is the Aconcagua' said the pilot, who had invited me to his technological *sancta sanctorum*. Blue and white were the two colours that filled the eye: an immaculate sky and virgin snow. And the several thousand feet of one of the proudest peaks in the planet seemed but a 'little hill' as it rose above a white landscape itself thousands of feet above the sea.

That sea was the Pacific (by the way one of the most patent misnomers in history as Magellan soon learnt in the tough way that sailors learn); and on the edge, Santiago. Born within a few miles of the old Santiago (de Compostela), I kept wondering at the vagaries of man's adventures on our Earth, that had brought the name of the Apostle from the corner we in Galicia know as 'Finisterre' to this shore that deserves the name in a way the Spanish cape never did. For Chile does impress the visitor as the Ultima Thule of our Christian civilisation; and our imagination boggles at the idea of 'seeing' New Zealand and Australia, Indonesia and China, across the immense sea the sight of which brought Balboa to his knees in Darien.

These Chileans who walk about the city are mostly the descendants of those *conquistadors* who dared invade a bastion made so fiercely impregnable by nature and defended by one of the most valiant and heroic of all the Indian peoples. When Almagro made ready to cross the Andes into Chile through passes no man had ever dared cross in winter, his Inca friends warned him that such a thing was impossible. But Almagro argued that the discoverers and conquerors of Peru were men 'whom the earth and other elements were bound to obey and Heaven to favour.'

The nation that was to be Chile was helped, though, in what mattered most, the acquiring of social discipline and solidarity, precisely because the Chilean community had to grow under the constant threat of the valiant Araucanians, sung by the poet-conquistador Ercilla with the honesty, indeed the generosity, of a clean adversary. Ercilla was a Basque; and since his days, this nation of strong men has contributed more than its share to the Chilean blood and spirit.

Chile was a place of exile for the hot-heads and all those who felt at odds with authority whose seat was Lima. The brilliant Court of the Viceroy was the earthly paradise of the aristocracy and of the rich merchants and landowners of the continent; so the more adventurous, vigorous, unruly had to face the danger of exile; which nearly always meant Chile. Now, Chile was of course 'the end of the world', boredom for the gay-dogs of the brilliant vice-regal Court; but it was also a virgin country, open to men endowed with vigour and initiative. A couple of centuries of this regime must have enabled Chile to recruit by natural selection the most enterprising and go-ahead of the human material available.

Spain allowed no foreigners to contaminate her subjects with heresies. Blood was not in the picture. But a few Irishmen did get there through Spain, where Irish names constellate the political and the military history of the mother country. Ambrose O'Higgins was one of them who, sent as a child to Spain from his native Ireland, and trained for the Church by his Jesuit uncle in Cádiz, preferred a more adventurous life in South America, where in time he became Captain General and 'President' of Chile, and later Viceroy of Peru. By a Chilean woman of good family, this Irish-Spaniard had an illegitimate son, Bernardo, who was sent to Britain, France and Spain for his education, and returned a Chilean 'patriot' and a freemason. He was one of the heroes of the emancipation of Chile.

With the emancipation, the floodgates of immigration were burst open, and here again, Chile benefited by her remote situation which put a premium on enterprise, persistence and courage. One comes across non-Spanish names in every country of South America but in none are there more of them than in Chile.

The sea and the Andes possess so inexhaustible a store of beauty that Chile, running all the way between the one and the other, can be compared to a long serpent of splendour. What fails is the earth on which the serpent crawls. While its beauty lasts, it is unforgettable; but if you leave the country northwards towards Peru, there comes a moment when the rocky, sandy land made alive with seeds, grass, wiry growth rich with flowers and leaves, all forms of vegetation, vanishes: and in its stead, the space that separates the sea from the mountain is covered with a dead grey.

The weather was fine but as we were coming close to Lima, it got hazy. When Pizarro chose the spot on which his capital, Lima, was to be built, he did not know that for nearly half the year it is protected from the sun by a permanent haze; otherwise he would have chosen another spot, if only to make it less hard for aircraft to land. As it is, planes have to fly out to the sea and descend to a level under the blanket of haze when they are on a level with the city, when they venture inland.

CHAPTER XXXIX

PERU

LIMA can still suggest the grandeur and the splendour of its life as the vice-regal capital of the south Spanish American empire, only comparable to that of Mexico, the vice-regal capital of the northern part; but only 'suggest.' Not even recall it or bring it to mind; for two cruel earthquakes have destroyed much of its fabric, and a steady flow of immigration – a good deal of it Asian – has altered its population. Furthermore, the population of Peru has always comprised a higher proportion of natives than those of the three southern countries I had just visited. The motive and circumstances of my visit defined the layers of society in which I should be moving – and these were predominantly, though by no means exclusively, white; indeed, the presence of the other two bloods in the élite was perhaps the chief difference I found in Peru; but a stroll in the streets around the hotel was enough to show that, numerically, Lima is mostly Indian and when not Indian (with some black), Chinese or Japanese.

The political and literary circles in which I moved struck me as just as keen and well-educated as those whose company I had enjoyed in Montevideo, Buenos Aires or Santiago. If there was a shade of difference it was, I felt, in a more definite polarisation between pro-Spanish and anti-Spanish ideological attitudes – a split that had not struck me as vocal at all in the other three capitals; and I soon perceived that the 'pros' were nearly always Catholic and conservative, and the 'antis' free-thinkers, marxists and generally left, unless they were just militant pro-Indian (often half-caste). But whether anti- or pro-Spanish, they struck me as keen and clear, no matter the purity or otherwise of their white blood. Now and then, an attractive, elegant, wealthy businessman, looking like a general, Ambassador or inquisitor, straight out of a classic Spanish picture, would reveal himself both a free-thinker and an ardent pro-Spaniard. This kind of man would almost always be a Sephardi.

I should not have been surprised if the President whom I decorated with the collar of Charles III had himself also been a Sephardi. For all I know, the idea of being mistaken for a member of the Chosen People might have horrified him; yet a man whose name is 'Benavides' and who rises to the top of both the military and the civil ladder in a country in which there are so many clever men does suggest a Jewish ancestry.

360

His ceremony, by the way, was the grandest of the four. And I wonder where the film may be of all of them, which I had taken with a private 16 mm camera by me or others of the staff attached to me; for it vanished with all my belongings in 1939.

For a Spaniard, a first visit to the University of San Marcos is bound to be a moving experience. In no field did Spain endeavour to apply her political philosophy, her explicit recognition of the duties of the Spaniards towards the natives, than in that of education. The religious orders founded colleges in many cities both for 'Spaniards' and for the sons of the native élite, and universities were set up in every city suitable for them as soon as possible. The University of San Marcos was founded in Lima in 1551, barely thirteen years after the conquest had been achieved; and yet it was not the oldest but the third, after those of Santo Domingo and Mexico. San Marcos is a delightful building, whose patios are alive with greenery and whose corridors conceal classrooms one or two of which are show pieces for tourists. It is difficult to imagine it without Luis Alberto Sánchez as its rector, but at that time he was still in exile, being an *Aprista*. I had met him in Santiago.

The leader of *Aprismo*, Victor Raul Haya de la Torre, was not in his country either. I had met him in Switzerland. Still a very young man he had incurred the suspicion of the Federal Government because he had been in the Soviet Union and talked to Lenin. He founded his party *Alianza Popular Revolucionaria Americana*, shortened to APRA, in Mexico and had the sense always to realise that Marxism was a doctrine that did not correspond to any of the real features of Spanish America.

Lima resembles almost every other city in Spanish America in that, as a city, its interest lies with the Spanish vice-regal days. (I do not say 'colonial' days because the Spanish American countries never were colonies, in the French or British sense of this word. They were 'Kingdoms' just as Castille, Aragon, or even Naples; and this distinction is not merely verbal, but constitutional as well.) The chess board of streets between the Plaza San Martín and the Palace is a delightful district. It reminds the visitor of similar districts in other capitals such as Caracas; though in Lima it rises to a level of beauty unrivalled anywhere in Spanish America with the exception of that jewel which is Bucaramanga, in Colombia.

Lima must have been one of the first cities not merely of Spanish America but of the Western world to possess a regular canalisation of fresh water, 'much to the annoyance of the medical profession' the chronicler says, for fevers and digestion troubles all but vanished in the city and the leading doctor in the city declared that 'the water had cut his income by about 3,000 pesos a year' (about 1575). This boon gave an added impetus to the cultivation of gardens and patios that were as green and coloured by flowers as the gardens themselves, as one may still observe while walking through the narrow, straight streets, by casting an indiscreet glance at the patio beyond the entrance halls. Some of the façades are beautiful with a charm less regular but more lively than classical models.

The city still carries the air of greatness, elegance and wealth that made of it such a centre of gracious living throughout the three centuries of Spanish rule. Visitors in the eighteenth century speak of as many as five to six thousand *calesas*, carriages for four persons as well as the coachman (who rode a mule), gilded all over and richly decorated, not to speak of nearly as many coaches more luxurious. And the beauty, wealth and style of living of the Limeñas was proverbial all over the world for originality and style. All this can still be felt in Lima as one walks about, for one feels the splendour of the past in certain homes that have seen better days, where poverty reigns but has not, so to speak, taken root.

CHAPTER XL

PERU: LIMA, CUZCO

THE past in Peru is Spanish. Is Spanish in Peru the past? Yes in some sense. No in another sense. There are two aspects in which Peru has not merely ceased to be Spanish because she has grown out of it all, but because she has taken a position antagonistic to Spain in religion and inter-racial relations. The identification of the Peruvian pro-Spanish sector with traditional Spanish middle class ways, such as going to mass every Sunday and to confession every year at Easter, would range any free-thinking, non-practising Catholic, or Protestant Peruvian (few as they are) in a sector of opinion prejudiced against Spain.

Most of them would, moreover, adopt an anti-Spanish attitude when they come to consider the condition of the Indian natives under the Spanish empire. And this sector is apt to appeal to those who descend from both Indians and Whites. 'Facts should tell,' one is apt to conclude; but they really don't. And the reason why facts do not tell is because 'facts' carry a good deal of subjective elements in their apparently objective constitutions; so that when we say 'facts should tell' what we are really saying is: 'facts should tell who are those who define facts one way and those who define facts in another.'

There is yet another aspect to it, which I observed from my very first trip to Peru. The pro-native (*indigenista*) intellectual was apt to be a marxist. The overlapping of the two ideologies was inevitable, since in Peru the working class.is mostly native, the white class comprises all the employers, and the foremen and blue-collar men are half-caste. But this is by no means a rigid correspondence. One meets with many professors who evidently are partly Indian, and they may be anti- or pro-Spanish. The fact is that the issue is complex and requires a good deal of discipline and a genuine sense of justice in those who would study it with no axe to grind.

A number of episodes from my stay in Lima come to mind as I write all this. I had, of course, the benefit and pleasure of an acquaintance with the Spanish Consul General in Lima. He happened to be married to a handsome Limeña, looking very white, but you never can tell. The very first day we met, this keen, intelligent and hospitable woman let herself go to say to me: 'You Spaniards were too much in a hurry to destroy everything Inca you found here.' I took an air of offended innocence: 'We, Spaniards? I assure you, Madam, I never destroyed anything Inca here. This is my first visit. When Pizarro came, God only knows where I was. And if you mean my ancestors, none came here. Yours did. It was your ancestors, not mine, who did it, both the good and the bad.'

Incredible as it may sound, this is a perspective that no Spanish American seems ever to have tumbled to. They all praise us for the conquest or damn us for it and what followed it. But it is well known that most of the *conquistadores* turned *pobladores*; and therefore, most of the merit and the blame of that episode of mankind lies at the door of the Spanish American Whites; while the three centuries of Spanish domination, no matter how judged, were the outcome of a give-and-take collaboration between European and American 'Spaniards' (i.e. Whites) in which most of the time most of the actual power was in the hands of the American Whites. Good or bad, let anyone judge as he feels about it. But that good and that bad was due at least as much to the ancestors of the present Mexicans, Peruvians etc. as to those of the present Spaniards.

That Spanish past was of course far richer in human content than the present mind of the world can even imagine. It is only since the industrial revolution and the growing invasion of our life by technological progress that the economic prejudice has begun to dessicate our thought and sensibility to the point that we see everything in terms of exploiters or exploited. There was plenty of both then in the New World, though possibly less than in the Old; but there was plenty of human life around them as well, which people lived far more fully than statistics can express.

An Indian has entered the Viceroy's room in Lima (sixteenth century). He brings a complaint against a 'Spaniard' (i.e. a Peruvian White) who happens moreover to be a rich landlord decorated with some title or other. As the Indian is putting his case, and the Viceroy's secretary is writing it all down, the rich Spaniard is announced and the Viceroy has him asked in. The Spaniard enters the room, goes to the Indian and slaps his face. The Viceroy summons two or three of his '*oidores*', magistrates who, with him as President, form the *Audiencia* or Supreme Court of Peru, there and then has the Spaniard sentenced to have his hand cut off, calls the executioner, and has that hand cut off within minutes of its crime.

I don't say this story is exemplary, typical, normal. I say it happened, and that is saying a lot. And many more such things were happening, good, bad, indifferent, that made those three centuries worth living – all due to the fact that there was a common belief running through the lifeblood of the whole nation, for Peru was a nation different from

Spain, one of 'those Kingdoms' on a par with Castille, Aragon, Naples or Sicily, whose unity consisted in that they all lived under a King who was rich in moral authority – indeed far richer in it than he deserved at any rate in the seventeenth century.

All these complexities and many more fermenting in folds within folds hidden away within a situation far richer in feelings than any observer can ever adumbrate, stood there, so to speak alive, before my eyes in the half-caste city *par excellence*, Cuzco. The old imperial capital of the Incas, though shorn of much of its splendour and the poorer for the loss of some of its most imposing buildings at the greedy hands of the conquistadors, could still be felt alive in the air of the place, and struck one's eyes with awe at the mere sight of the stone walls that bore the mark of their builders. The Spaniards, by the merely empirical, utilitarian decision to build their Castillian cities right on top of these brown Inca walls, had created a living symbol of Peru: a graft of the Spanish stem, branches, flowers and fruit on to the stem and roots of the Incas, the most directly half-caste city that could be imagined.

The mould of the Indian capital was still there and it could be felt as one deambulated about the city; emptied though from its Indian content, it had been hispanised by time; and, in many ways, Cuzco lived then and still does like most provincial cities of Spanish America, according to Spanish, mostly Andalusian, standards and habits. The Cathedral, the University, the official buildings, constant features that I had found in Uruguay, Argentina, Chile, seemed to take on a new colour, for the Indian blood in their human element came through more clearly and oftener.

The professor of history who guided my steps looked almost a pure Indian, though he probably was a half-and-half. He was one of the most attractive persons I met during my whole trip. Cleanliness seemed to me his most pronounced feature: cleanliness of body and mind, free from that brooding mood that affects many Peruvian (though seldom the Mexican) *mestizos*, a man evidently at peace with himself. His erudition both on the Spanish and on the Inca side of the history of his country was prodigious; his even-mindedness and fairness exemplary. 'Here,' I thought more than once, 'is a free man.' I owe to him an unexpected and profitable episode.

We were standing on broken ground near the fortress of Sacsahuana, just outside the city, when an Indian of mature but by no means old age passed within earshot. He was walking-running, with that curious hopping step so typical of Peruvian Indians; and I was struck by his dress: breeches and hose, long frock, a hat like a halo, every garment black.

My friend saw I was interested, hailed the Indian and spoke to him a few words in Quechua. 'Who are you?' – 'I am Bernardino González and I belong to Don So-and-So.' The professor let him go and turned to me with a smile.

'That is Peru,' he said. 'The Indian has a Spanish name, and he still belongs to a "Spaniard", owner of Indians, although legally this link does not exist and has been abolished over a century ago. And on top of it, see what he is wearing: a typically "Inca" costume, which is, of course, the Spanish dress and hat of the days of Charles III.' And it was then that I realised why I had been so fascinated by that Indian's clothes. They reminded me of a style, but which? The professor had revealed it to me. . . . Later I was daily to pick up bits of knowledge, revelations of this kind. While on top of one of the hills around Cuzco, we were able to admire its general aspect, the orderly quadriculation of its streets, the evenness of the old Spanish houses, and the beauty of their roofs–all but one. And that one hurt the eye. One could almost hear the discordance it made, as if someone were hammering aloud on a tin plate in the quiet of the afternoon. The roofs were all tiles. That noisy one was made of corrugated iron.

The problem of so many cities! They must grow. They cannot be locked up within a kind of museum. Yet, to erect a modern building in the middle of Cuzco, Siena, Oxford, Salamanca. . . . There were two such houses in Cuzco. Good in themselves, they struck one as monstrous. Why not let the city grow another modern twin and leave the old her style immaculate? That would not prevent it from growing. In Cuzco as well as in Arequipa, the Peruvian Towns Planning Office had entrusted the building of hotels to an outstanding and sensitive architect: the result is superb. Modern. Yet in old Spanish style, these hotels provided the ideal solution for the problem of the old and beautiful city that must grow.

One clear, moonlit night, we drove to San Sebastián. Nowadays almost a suburb of Cuzco, it was in the vice-regal era a Spanish-built Indian settlement far enough from the capital to live a life of its own. It bore all the marks of its founders. A chessboard of modest but clean and well-conceived one-storey houses, each with its back yard and space enough for a back garden, and in the centre a big square, very big indeed, for what, after all, was meant to be a village. In the centre of the square, a big fountain, the circular basin of which is made of searchingly sculpted bronze. One whole side of the square is ennobled by a big church, again, one thought, far too big for the village.

None of your economics, please, for this kind of life had nothing to do with ours. Those friars who thought out, planned and built the village, the church and the bronze fountain were not worrying about the balance of payments, nor did the silver mines of Potosí enter at all into the picture. They were thinking in human terms; they wanted a self-contained community, well-housed, well watered and well inspired by a faith. Hence the oversized fountain and the oversized church; so as to impress the Indians with the importance of what is important.

We were not long before luck or chance presented us with a live picture of it all. We had been visiting a house, just any house in any street, which our guide had led us to, simply because it happened to be vacant. We had walked into the back yard and, finding that they all opened on to each other, had ventured into the back yard of the neighbouring house. I glanced through the window into the room of that inhabited house. It was very modestly furnished, indeed one wondered whether there was any furniture at all save a low chair on which a young Indian woman was sitting feeding a child with some pap. The 'bed' was made up of brown blankets upon blankets laid on the tiled floor, and here and there, a skin of some sheep, alpaca or llama. Modesty on the edge of poverty. On the wall, above the bed, a coloured lithograph of Murillo's *Inmaculada*.

CHAPTER XLI

CÓRDOBA

CÓRDOBA. What name could evoke more Spanish echoes and more varied! Old Roman, Visigothic, Moorish, uppermost of course, for Córdoba was the Baghdad of the West, and then all that goes with the art of bull-running inaccurately known in English as bull-fighting which it is not. So, when a Spaniard goes to Córdoba at the foot of the Andes, his heart is bound to be full of expectations. The Córdoba I saw then did not disappoint my hopes. It was fortunately still 'undeveloped'; a truly Spanish city, full of simple but deep-rooted charm, gentle leisure and quiet beauty. A university, of course, and an eager curiosity for the things of the mind, and common sense.

All these cities I had visited in the vast continent impressed me in similar ways: intellectual ability; a certain detachment and generosity in the thinking and attitude of the persons one met; and yet, human differences which, despite the unity of the language and the customs, were perhaps as wide and possibly as deep as those one would observe in Europe. And on top of it all, the question sometimes put, sometimes tacit, but always present in everybody's mind: why can't we run our countries?

For it will not do to attribute that failure to intellectual incapacity. I have often tried to solve this conundrum. A quarter of an hour spent with a good bunch of Spanish American educated men will suffice to satisfy the most fastidious critic that they are as capable as any similar group of Europeans. What prevents them from making good as countries?

In those days, the world was more severe towards them than it can afford to be today. For today, our poor European world has given so many proofs of its own incapacity that we all appear to be tarnished by the same brush. Yet, 'Spanish America is different', and it may well be that she is so because her nations have all inherited the Spanish curse-blessing: theology.

Three centuries of theology have made of the Hispanic peoples incurable sceptics as to the possibility of turning our world down here into anything reasonable. To Albert Camus, who lamented that the world is absurd, I used to answer: 'What would you expect it to be:

reasonable? *That*, indeed would be absurd.' That is the normal Spanish position. And when all is said and done, that may be the reason why the Hispanic world never seems to be able to settle down to a normal life. For them, the normal is the abnormality of absurdity.

CHAPTER XLII

BRAZIL

O N the 13th of August, the hotel buttons in Buenos Aires brought me a cable from Río de Janeiro. Macedo Soares, the Brazilian Foreign Minister, invited me to come as a guest of the Government to lecture in São Paolo and Río, a fortnight in all. I thanked but declined because I had to be at my seat in Geneva as a member of the League Council on September 4th in the morning, and the business was no other than the Italo-Ethiopian dispute. Macedo Soares cabled that he guaranteed that I should be in Geneva on September 4th. There were no air lines in those days; but I knew Macedo Soares, and concluded that he had something up his sleeve; so I accepted.

I sailed to São Paulo and so had a glimpse of Santos. These cities of southern Brazil are generous of their space, and of their time as well. Life in them must flow at a gracious pace. Not so, however, São Paulo, which even then was already sick with the fever of economic progress. This city is the true economic and financial capital of Brazil. It pulsates as do New York, London or Zurich; yet in spite of it all, the Brazilian tempo seems to influence it, not to slow it down, but perhaps to put some Creole grace in its speed.

A night in a train, and I was in Río. It was then still more in the style of Santos than in that of São Paulo; a leisurely city in which it was a pleasure to loaf about along those lovely streets nearly all protected from the heat by superb rows of trees. The guide books say that Río has twenty-three bathing beaches, some of them miles long; and all lovely. Río, though the capital of the whole country, impressed me as less cosmopolitan than São Paulo, so that it let through its Portuguese origin better than her busy rival. This Portuguese character of Brazil suggests a curious symmetry.

Barring Cuba and Santo Domingo, I know of no country in which the colour of the skin counts less either way. Insofar as it ever did in Spanish America, it stained its man less in itself as the sign of a different seed, than as that of 'illegitimacy' which it often was. This 'context' became less marked with time; so that today in Brazil which is probably the American country comprising the highest proportion of black blood, the fact of being black means next to nothing.

There is one side to this question which is sometimes neglected. It was vividly brought home to me, years later, as I was driving towards Río from the high hills west of it. At a turn of the road, we were struck by one of the most wonderful sights it has been my fortune to behold, the most powerful, yet harmonious picture one could imagine: a market of fresh vegetables and fruit gathered from the lands of a nearby village. The pumpkins and the melons and the beetroots and the egg-fruit and the oranges and the lemons and the cabbages and the carrots and many more creations of mother earth I had never seen before, all flooding one's eyes with the light of the sun turned into all the colours one could dream of or had never dreamt – and the whole of it lifted, offered, let roll again, put away, produced, tossed about by men and women the colour of charcoal, ebony, coal, bronze. That, thought I, was the key to its beauty. The same vegetable colours handled by whites would have lost half their beauty. It was the 'black' colours of those men and women that turned the scene from a banal picture into an unforgettable experience.

The features of the white variety of man are, I believe handsomer than those of any other; but its colour is not good. This can be shown by watching any fashionable beach. A crowd of naked whites is a sorry sight, on the whole rather repulsive. A crowd of negroes or of East Indians is handsome, for the colour of these peoples is handsomer than the whites'. It is perhaps the combination of these two 'conclusions', that explains the outstanding success of the mulatta, if as it often happens, she combines the features of the white and the swarthy colour of the black.

Spanish and Portuguese are so closely related that in São Paulo and in Río I lectured in Spanish as a matter of course, and conversation is easy in both languages simultaneously. It was a pleasure to address audiences so wide awake, so able to catch the slightest hint or intention, so liberal and free-minded. Itamaraty, as they call their Foreign Office, treated me royally. Entertaining in Brazil is most enjoyable for the guest, of course, but also for everybody else as well, including the host; for the climate is gorgeously warm and allows a good deal of open-air gatherings.

In smaller, more intimate circles, the same near perfection of entertainment was time and again offered to me; and it happened now and then that the evening was ennobled by good music. There never was a pretence of 'culture' about this. If and when there was music offered, it was of the best, and one could feel that it was enjoyed without self-consciousness, indeed with the knowledge of the genuine music lover.

What Macedo Soares had up his sleeve was a seat in the zeppelin. We left Río in the morning of August 31st and, after a whole day in the air in view of the coast, we landed at Pernambuco where we stayed the night. I dare hardly say a word about Pernambuco, which I saw for less than a day, save that it left on my mind the impression of a city of long, wide, well-paved and well-lit avenues and that the population seemed to me definitely to comprise a higher proportion of blacks than Río. We left at night on September 1st.

The actual living-quarters in a zeppelin were but a small proportion of the total bulk of the craft; and this in itself, apart from the slow speed, must have been one of the chief causes why this mode of transport did not prevail. Much as they differed in construction from anything railways have developed, since the cabin was just a kind of basket under the balloon, the living-quarters were very much like a second class sleeping-car. There was a corridor, and berths in pairs one above the other, and at one end, a room that did as a lounge and as a dining room. One navigated at about four hundred metres above the sea.

It was a bit boring. Nothing happened and there was little to do for a non-smoker, non-drinker. The only relief I had from my monotonous *far niente* was a radiogram. We saw a ship just sailing under us. This must have been on September 2nd. During the evening of September 3rd we cut the western coast of Morocco; and by sunrise we were sailing out of Morocco into the Mediterranean. Following the eastern coast of Spain, we flew over Provence and Switzerland, and landed at Friedrichshafen in the early morning of September 4th. Bath and breakfast, and by eight we were in an aeroplane on our way to Stuttgart, where I changed over to another plane for Geneva. Macedo Soares had not quite, but nearly, fulfilled his promise. I should have been in Geneva at my League Council seat at 10 a.m. I arrived for the afternoon meeting at three o'clock. I found no lack of black clouds.

CHAPTER XLIII

WITH ITALY BUT AGAINST FASCISM

WHEN I entered the Hotel des Bergues, I found the hall pretty full – fuller than usual, I thought. In the crowd, a small yet corpulent chap seemed to be smiling at me somewhat diffidently through thick eyeglasses. I stepped towards him, put my arm round his shoulders and cried out: 'Cassuto!' I thought his eyelids trembled a bit and his eyes shone with tears. 'You must come for a talk'; and we parted while my mind went back to those days when we had met in London and often dined together in some tavern or other around Fleet Street. Once we had been invited to lunch by a Japanese colleague; and as we went out we stood there on the pavement looking at each other for half a minute, then I took his arm and said: 'Let's go and have lunch somewhere.' He rocked with laughter and delight, and we had a square meal at Simpson's.

Still, I mused, nothing to bring out so much emotion! And though I saw him once or twice during that session, it was not until we met again in London many years later, exiles both, that he revealed to me the key to the episode. Cassuto was a journalist, a good linguist and a shrewd mind. Very decent, though endowed with the required amount of light-hearted scepticism to pass muster in Italy. He was a Jew. And when Mussolini betrayed that Italian tradition among others – for Italy always was the most liberal and human society in Europe towards the Jews – and became anti-semite, Cassuto got naturally worried. He then began to drop hints about knowing me very well, and one or other of the walls of the Palazzo Venezia, all of which had then excellent ears, thought it worth while to try what this line could yield.

That meeting at the entrance hall of the Bergues – he told me – was then going to be crucial for him. Had I passed by cutting him as a fellow whose face said nothing to me, he was finished. Were he recognised, he might be kept as a good link and a possible influence on my views. Cassuto told me all this in London years later, and was still moved when he added: 'When you put your arm round my shoulders, I knew I was saved.'

Indirectly, this episode, even before it was fully revealed to me, did suggest the weight which the Italian Government attached to my attitude on Ethiopia. Mussolini could, up to a point, work on the other three big powers, but little or nothing on Spain or on Spain's chief delegate in Geneva; and he was aware of the power of public opinion, which was the only weapon I could brandish and knew how to wield. It so happened that at least two of the three powers he more or less could wire-pull in secret were precisely those whose public opinion I was then abler to influence, and perhaps even more so, that of the United States.

Italy had then in Geneva a very friendly, reasonable and able permanent second delegate, Bova Scoppa by name; and I noticed that this excellent man was always ready to seek my opinion and advice, which I gave with a mixture of sympathy for the other view and a forthright definition of what I thought right or wrong. I am afraid that one day I put him in an awkward corner. We were walking along the lake, all the day's work behind us, at the hour of sunset propitious for sitting back and reflecting. And he kept talking to me of Mussolini's greatness. I seized his arm, made him stand still facing the lake and asked: 'Do you really think he is so great?' And he: 'Oh but, *Monsieur l'Ambassadeur*, I assure you that he. . . .' 'Then tell me, why doesn't he set out to rule Europe instead of limiting his ambition to that little Italy?'

A Fascist Italy and a Republican Spain could not be expected to feel in any sort of harmony, and (as we now know) by the autumn of 1935 Mussolini was already actively conspiring to bring down the Republic. Nevertheless (or possibly because of it), the Government in Madrid were most cautious about relations between the two countries, and at every step I had to justify my actions not to prove my staunch anti-fascism but to assure the Spanish Government that the Italians were not getting too angry with me and therefore with them. This was made in some ways easier and in other ways harder by the utter incompetence of the Minister of Foreign Affairs at the time in office. I shall quote now from my September 16, 1935 dispatch, from which I extracted earlier a page on England-Albion.

> Until now, paradoxical though it may seem, we have succeeded in having the Spanish Delegation in the Council considered as the strictest guardian of the Covenant and yet as the special confident of the Italian Government, who is specially grateful to us. What follows may contribute to explain the paradox.

Here I developed the idea of the double soul of Britain, Albion-England, and went on:

> The present situation is very similar. Albion is thinking of Lake Tsana and the Nile; perhaps also of Italy's new general

preponderance in the Mediterranean, in Egypt, in India and in the Muslim world, of her pan-Asiatic and pan-Islamic dreams and generally of this Napoleonic surge that Mussolini means to Rome; while England is thinking of the Covenant. Had Mussolini not blundered by attacking so shamelessly he would have got whatever he wanted in Abyssinia, while England would have stood by totally indifferent.

From the day of my arrival here [September 4th] I had the intuition, confirmed by events every day, that Albion wants war with Italy making use of the Covenant as a recruiting flag for England; and my policy (being sure that it was the best way of interpreting my Government's intention) has been to uphold the Covenant through and through in this conflict, yet not to allow that the Covenant should be made use of in order to solve an imperial problem between Britain and Italy by means of war and at our cost. This task is not hard nor can it at any time lead us to any sort of unpleasantness with the British delegation, since the very situation demands that the British delegation be bound to walk in step with its own public opinion, and therefore to hold that its first concern is peace, and that peace and the Covenant must be defended together. The tendency to war is visible only in moments of absent-mindedness or of passion, and in attitudes taken subconsciously and when the mind is not watching.

From the day before yesterday I am optimistic. I no longer believe it impossible that we should reach a reasonable agreement thus avoiding that Albion works so as to have it fail and put the Covenant to some use.

Thus you and the Government may understand that, sincere and loyal upholders of the Covenant as we are, determined never to tolerate any scandalous infraction of it, we should nevertheless be flexible towards Italian proposals so as to prevent any break; that is why the British delegation has to acknowledge that they find in us their main support, while Italy is grateful to us for trying with our best will to find a solution that does not humiliate her.

It is not easy, at this distance from events, to define how far the picture thus painted was at least subconsciously overdone owing to the fears of Madrid. I can supply two or three memories to suggest that it may have painted my relations with Rome somewhat brighter than they actually were. One is the unpleasant flow of letters I received from Italian people at the time, all, I am sure, inspired by the worst possible xenophobia such as fascism was cultivating at the time. I shall spare the shame of divulging any details on this unsavoury subject; but I shall record that these letters came all from very modest levels of education or lack thereof, and that it was a striking feature of the episode that while I got no praise from Italy at all (nor was I expecting any) I got no blame whatever from the well-educated layers and professions.

The one exception, and a very prominent one, did come from Italy, but it was not Italian. I got a number of letters of truly inept and rude criticism from my old Hampstead friend Ezra Pound. My powers as a critical mountaineer have never allowed me to discover in Ezra Pound the peaks of poetic genius that some of his friends have described. His *Cantos* seem to me fully to deserve their author's own award – a failure as a work of art. But he was and remains an excellent minor poet. The sad side to his venture into politics at this time was that he lost his poetry while remaining a minor. The general level of his letters was that of a naughty and not very clean boy of twelve. Clean, indeed! All I'll say about this is that I refrained from asking him why he didn't type them on toilet paper.

Then, the press. Unable to bite my real self, they made up a Salvador de Madariaga for home consumption; a picturesque rag-and-tow doll every Italian scribbler of the fascist tribe was encouraged to shoot at. I recollect one of their masterpieces: '*Un Madariaga, uscito dal Secretariato per incapacità*'. All this made me suspect that while Italian official men in Geneva from Aloisi downwards remained friendly and even sought my opinion and advice, the drums of a no less official propaganda in Rome were beating hard against my '*incapacità*' to appreciate fascism.

CHAPTER XLIV

SIR SAMUEL HOARE AS DON QUIXOTE

WHEN the Council met on September 4th, the powers had been negotiating in Paris, it was said, with no success whatever. But that depended on a concrete question. Success – for whom? France and Britain had to report failure; Italy, however, could have reported success – though she of course didn't. From the very beginning, Italy had been riding an old horse of Italian wisdom: *il tempo è gallantuomo*. The more time the League lost, the more time Italy won. And one of the best and safest ways for the League to lose time was to hand on a problem to the powers.

When Eden had reported and Laval had backed him with a fair amount of good hopes, Aloisi proceeded to demonstrate that Abyssinia was such a monster that Italy would perform a good service by overpowering her. Meanwhile, he would no longer sit at the Council table with Ethiopian delegates. The Council could not officially work without the two parties being present. This, and other considerations, led to the creation of the Committee of Five composed of the Foreign Secretaries of France, Great Britain, Poland and Turkey plus the representative of Spain. I was elected chairman and asked to get in touch with both parties.

Easily said. Ethiopia was of course willing; but Italy was not. And our proposals, conciliatory as they would have to be, had to navigate between the danger of not being acceptable to Mussolini and that of scratching too hard the fair face of the Covenant in whose defence strong statements had been made by the Scandinavians and the Little Entente.

While we, of the Committee of Five, worked hard to explore the road to conciliation, a fierce, rigid – I was going to write warlike – speech was made at the Assembly on behalf of the Covenant, the whole Covenant and nothing but the Covenant. Who was this new knight of the Stern Countenance? None else but Sir Samuel Hoare, oh my prophetic soul! That intuition that Albion was ready to go to war against Mussolini behind the Covenant as a white shield, there it was before my eyes. Walters, in his *History of the League*, reviewing the attitude of the delegates to Hoare's speech, writes: 'Among the few European voices which were silent in this debate were Switzerland and Spain, both reluctant to admit the possibility of having to oppose the

Italy they admired . . .' (II. 649) Republican Spain admiring Italy? The President of the Committee of Five, entrusted by the Council with the work of conciliation, backing a bellicose Sir Samuel? All this happened on September 11th. On September 16th I wrote to the Foreign Secretary in Madrid that I had felt that such a situation was brewing: i.e. a war between Italy and Great Britain, under cover of the Covenant, which would have put the whole of liberal, idealistic, honest, sincere 'England' behind a power-thirsty Albion.

Fancy? Let us see. A glance at Eden's *Memoirs* will show that in point of stiffness, Hoare's speech went beyond what Eden had ever said or would have said, even in what concerned the duties of Britain as a League member. Hoare's text was then 'more royalist than the King, and more papist than the Pope'. When, however, Eden tried to moderate its tone (an odd situation indeed) he was met with the argument that senior ministers had gone through it, and notably Neville Chamberlain who 'had been through the text with him [Hoare] paragraph by paragraph'. This was the same Neville Chamberlain who was to cry STOP to sanctions 'that midsummer madness'.

Who could believe that Chamberlain and Hoare were out to defend the Covenant against all aggression? 'In conformity with its precise and explicit obligations, the League stands, and my country stands with it, for the collective maintenance of the Covenant in its entirety and particularly for steady and collective resistance to all acts of unprovoked aggression.' This was interpreted by Eden to mean that his country had decided to stop Mussolini even if it meant using force (p. 262). The Home Fleet arrived in Gibraltar on September 12th.

Strange. Very strange. Eden not allowed to say what Britain would do if – and Hoare a few weeks later, sent to Geneva to swear allegiance to the Covenant in its entirety. The Fleet out. And last but not least, Vansittart. As soon as he was back in London, Hoare wrote to Eden that 'his firm speech was going to be backed by action. He and Vansittart agreed that we must now show strength and not allow the Committee of Five or the Council to delay or make some futile proposal.' Isn't that true Vansittart vintage? So that the idea of trying to negotiate a conciliation was futile and 'strength' was to be applied to Italy. Who would believe that Vansittart would fight for the Covenant, when he was plainly assuming that the Council could do nothing but what Britain allowed it to do? Who but a Vansittart, who would not dream of Britain fighting to defend yellow men against yellow men, would dream of Britain fighting to defend black Ethiopians against white Italians?

Bluff? Eden denies it firmly (p. 261). Electioneering? Possibly. The Government was warned by the chiefs of staff that Britain was not ready to fight Italy. In particular, it is argued, there was no air cover for British warships; and it is pointed out that two British warships were sunk by the Japanese for this very reason six years later. That seems to me rather a proof of the very reverse, namely that the lack of air cover had not yet been adequately estimated in London. Whether for electoral or imperial purposes, the speech aimed at using the Covenant, not at serving it. Add to it Laval's too-clever manoeuvring in order to protect Mussolini in private and the standing of France in public. Our work in Geneva – including Eden's – was by no means easy. Thus, after all I have written on that naval show in Gibraltar, I find in a report of mine to the Spanish Foreign Minister (November 2, 1935) that, according to Eden 'this concentration was due to the Italian press campaign directly aiming at the occupation of Malta.'

Essentially, however, what was happening was that those who would couldn't, and those who could wouldn't, defend the Covenant for the sake of the Covenant. Britain was for the Covenant if and when it suited her to put a stop to Italy's expansion; France insofar as it would stop Hitler from rearming and marching on in every direction at once. The British had concluded a naval treaty with Hitler Germany which, they naïvely thought, covered their sea-flank against Hitler's advance westward, and dropped threats of getting out of Europe altogether if Laval didn't play his rôle as Britain's brilliant second in the Mediterranean against Mussolini. How could the League succeed?

So now, while my Government was afraid lest I should become as Quixotic on Ethiopia as I had been on Manchuria, Vansittart was afraid lest I would be too easy-going in favour of Mussolini and less passionate a defender of the Covenant than he or Hoare or possibly Simon or Neville Chamberlain were. Nor was Vansittart alone in fearing this, as will later appear. While Hoare broke a lance for the Covenant, we of the Committee of Five tried to find some conciliatory solution. Obviously this kind of work has often to be carried out at an irrational level, and therefore in a conventional or even *sous-entendu* sense. We suggested that the League should give assistance to Haile Selassie for the reform of Ethiopia, and that, to that effect, the Council would appoint experts to be agreed by the Emperor. We did not hide from His Majesty, lest he had not guessed already, that 'some' of these experts would be Italian. Furthermore, there was a hint of territorial adjustments in favour of Italy.

What if Italy refused? War? Sanctions? France said she would align herself with Britain; but Britain would only act if it meant aligning herself with France; and while every one of the chief actors talked to everyone else, the Committee of Five recorded its own failure to please both sides (September 25, 1935). Meanwhile, all warlike spirit had gone out of the London Cabinet, and Laval kept side-stepping when he could not step backwards. The Council took note of the failure of its Committee of Five, and led by the British and the French it turned down a request from Haile Selassie for impartial observers to establish the facts with regard to any aggression. This, of course, took the form of appointing a sub-committee to study the idea.

That did not prevent Titulesco from criticising the proposals of the Committee of Five on the ground that they were contrary to the sovereign rights of Abyssinia; an elegant move, for it invoked the right of the victim in order to reject the proposals, which was what the aggressor wanted. These contortions were part of the game and revealed the general fear of applying sanctions, a point on which I shall have to return for it is crucial.

By then (October 3, 1935) the actual physical aggression had begun – an air-raid on Adowa. The Council met on October 5th; well led by Eden, it acted with speed and common sense, indeed with courage. A Committee of Six was appointed to report within twenty-four hours. It was presided over by Armindo Monteiro, of Portugal, an excellent mind and a man of integrity. This Committee reported that 'The adoption by a state of measures of security on its own territory, and within the limits of its international agreements, does not authorise another state to consider itself free from its obligations under the Covenant.'

When French magnifying glasses were pointed at that paragraph, it was discovered that it looked uncommonly like the Rhine. So the Council had to abandon the general and embrace the particular: 'The Committee has come to the conclusion that the Italian Government has resorted to war in disregard of its obligations under Article 12 of the Covenant.' That meant sanctions.

Now sanctions are all very well in theory but whether they can really work in practice is another matter. The fat was in the fire. The Council would have to work without the parties. It had done so before and would do so after; but this time it decided to call itself 'Committee of Thirteen' and chose me for its chairman, somewhat to the relief of its President at the time.

The Committee of Thirteen issued its report. It plainly condemned Italy as the transgressor not only of the Covenant but of the Kellogg Pact, the 1928 Italo-Ethiopian Treaty of Friendship and the Optional Clause of the Statute of the Permanent Clause. On October 7th it was voted by the whole Council, including Ethiopia but excluding Italy.

The Assembly had dealt with all its agenda and should normally have dispersed, but hadn't because the Ethiopian dispute was sure to come back to it, and urgently; for the Council's report was before it and sanctions had to be decided upon – a grave and delicate affair for every member state. The procedure was carried out under the guidance of Beneŝ, its President. No easy task. We were now under Article 16 which was too clear for diplomacy and too exacting for caution.

> Should any member of the League resort to war in disregard of its covenants under Articles 12, 13, or 15, it shall *ipso facto* be deemed to have committed an act of war against all other members of the League, which hereby undertake immediately to subject it to the severance of all trade or financial relations, the prohibition of all intercourse between their nationals and the nationals of the covenant-breaking State, and the prevention of all financial, commercial or personal intercourse between the nationals of the covenant-breaking State and the nationals of any other State, whether a Member of the League or not.

One single adverse vote would have paralysed the Assembly; but the Article does not speak of the Assembly. It speaks of its members; and so despite contrary opinions from Albania, Austria and Hungary, the members of the Assembly set up a Committee of Co-ordination composed of representations of all the member-states which delegated its power to an executive of Eighteen members presided by Dr Vasconcellos, once a Foreign Secretary of Portugal. On Eden's proposal, all exports of arms were stopped; while all but Luxembourg and Switzerland agreed to continue to send arms to Ethiopia.

CHAPTER XLV

SANCTIONS

A detailed account of the game of sanctions that started then in Geneva would be a sheer waste of time. Every nation had carefully to consider two broadly antagonistic interests – both 'selfish' though, for nations are collective human beings that have not yet risen to conceiving selflessness. On the one hand, their trade, business, human relations of all kinds with the outlawed nation; on the other, that perspective put to them in a truly first-rate speech by the Haitian delegate Alfred Nemours: 'Great or small, strong or weak, near or far, white or coloured, let us never forget that one day we may be somebody's Ethiopia.'

That sanctions campaign was an eye-opener for many of us. The model case was Switzerland. The quality and intensity of her 'Spirit of Geneva', no one could doubt; and yet, was she in a position actually to apply Article 16? Closely knit together in matters of trade, finance, culture and human relations with that Italy whose people differ from those of her own Ticino in almost nothing but their passports, Switzerland was a model case; for what nation could say that she was not interested at all in the risks and difficulties and ready to apply sanctions one hundred per cent? I was thus gradually led to elaborate a kind of sketch of a theory of sanctions leading to the conclusion that, as a practical means for coercing a nation, sanctions will never work.

Here it is briefly put. Sanctions imply an appeal to solidarity between nations. But between nations as between individuals there are two kinds of solidarity: one is physical, undergone, passive; the other is moral, creative, active. The patients in an epidemic typify the first kind; an orchestra playing music typify the second. A thousand cars on a packed road are submitted to a physical passive solidarity which they undergo, but cursed with a total lack of active, moral solidarity.

Nations have been knit by technological progress into one thick tissue of physical solidarity; but despite the League and U.N.O. they remain recalcitrant to moral solidarity. The endeavours of Britain to use the Covenant against Italy; or of France to use it as a recruiting poster against Germany, fairly well illustrate the second point; the awkward position of Switzerland and the less than enthusiastic attitude of many a second rank nation, particularly the Mediterranean and Central European ones, in the case of Italy-Ethiopia, illustrate the first.

Furthermore, this analysis suggests that sanctions fail – indeed, are bound to fail – because, as an idea, they stand within the gap between material solidarity, run ahead, and moral solidarity, lagging behind the actual state of world relationships. In other words, sanctions are too advanced an idea from the point of view of the progress of moral solidarity, but also an obsolete idea from that of the material solidarity of nations.

This, to my mind, is the important point. For even if nations felt the call of moral solidarity and accepted its risks, the putting into practice of any 'sanction' as envisaged by Article 16 would have gone counter to the growing weaving of interests of all kinds among nations, so that there is no guarantee that a punishing nation would not be more gravely injured than the 'punished' one. The image of the organism comes naturally to mind. Some of the sanctions of Article 16 would amount to a man tying a wire hard around his wrist so as to punish his hand; but the rest of the body would suffer as much as the hand. The English put it forcibly; it amounts to 'cutting off your nose to spite your face'.

On February 12, 1936 a report prepared by the oil experts Committee of the League was published in Geneva. It showed that an oil embargo would force Italy to surrender to the League on condition the U.S.A. limited its exports to the pre-1935 level. In 1938, Mussolini told Hitler that an effective oil embargo would have forced him to go back home in a week. These facts must have been known to the governments concerned long in advance. And yet, the oil embargo failed. It failed because it was not applied.

The League Sanctions Committee adopted some brave words: arms embargo; no loans or credits; no imports from Italy. They raised numerous problems for nearly every European nation, a fact which contributed to provide an air of reality to the exercise, but it is doubtful whether it had any effect; for on the one hand the objectively recalcitrant states would not hurry to put those 'brave words' into practice and on the other no machinery was proposed or set up for an actual working of such concrete ideas. Furthermore the one effective sanction, oil, remained untouched.

On October 8th I wrote to Lerroux, then Prime Minister, on that talk with Eden that morning, in which my British colleague partly read and partly commented on a document on the outlook for sanctions. For Britain the easiest and most efficient of them would be to prohibit all imports of Italian goods. According to British figures, the total proportion of Italian exports absorbed by member states was 70 per cent.

Eden thought also of forbidding credits and loans and sales to Italy of coal and oil. In his view, Britain was bound to favour the no-coal sanction precisely because it would hit her; but he attached much importance to the drying up of the supply of oil, which would, of course, hit Rumania, the Soviet Union and Persia. 'Persia', however, meant the Anglo-Persian Oil Company which again meant Britain. He did not seem to worry about American counter supplies.

I reported to Lerroux that, though firm, Eden struck me as most reluctant in all this; that in his view the conflict did not seem soluble unless Mussolini fell first and that, in any case, it would be less difficult by means of territorial shuffling than through mandates and other ideas not easily reconcilable with the Covenant – which was Laval's way.

I made the letter wait overnight so as to add to it a note on a talk I was to hold with Laval on the evening of the same day. I suggested to the French P.M. that sanctions should be so timed as to adapt them to our own public opinions, not yet used to the notion of an international solidarity, only to find that he went a good deal further than I on the same road. He complained of the priority granted by Britain to the prohibition of Italian imports, which he thought was too harsh a measure, since it tended to set up new trade currents and habits. He saw three phases: stopping credits and loans; no mineral raw materials (which meant fuel and oils) and in general things useful for an army; and only then, the boycott of Italian goods, to act as a threat in case Mussolini refused to accept a reasonable compromise.

This eventuality was in his view most unlikely; and I put to Lerroux that, in my view, Laval was bound to fail because Mussolini would demand a settlement incompatible with the requirements of both Ethiopia and the League; therefore with British public opinion. I therefore rallied myself to Eden's opinion, that it was unlikely that a satisfactory solution could be found unless Mussolini fell.

Laval, though, who told me that Beck had spoken to him in the same sense, begged me to help him to moderate the press in this sense; and I concluded my letter to Lerroux that we should remain equally far from both extremes, taking account of our international interests and of our own public opinion, unfortunately not yet very much aware of what such interests really were.

A secret agreement between Hoare and Laval had limited the League action to the bourne beyond which there might be a war against Italy. The Secretary of State of the U.S.A. wrote to the League Sanctions Committee with best wishes and no help. At a meeting of the Commission my friend Massigli lent over me from behind, bowing very low, for he is a very tall man, to whisper in my ear that Laval would be pleased if I proposed an oil sanction. I therefore declined to do so, for I knew he was carrying on a double-faced policy, but the Canadian Dr Riddell (half Hoare half Laval) did so not very much later; for he suggested oil, steel and coal to be added to the materials already subject to sanctions (in theory). Oil, however, is very much of a sovereign, so the Commission decided to consult the governments, i.e. to do nothing.

This was during the November meeting of the Sanctions Committee, which even Hoare and Laval honoured with their presence. To be sure they both added the weight of their vote and opinion to the resolution fixing the date for the sanctions to begin and enjoining on every nation to see that they were applied within the bounds of their respective sovereignties. But Hoare and Laval had another message up their sleeve; they reported that they were discussing with Italy the possibility of coming to an agreement.

Count van Zeeland, the Belgian Prime Minister, whose presence had surprised many of us, then rose to propose that Hoare and Laval should be formally asked to find a solution to the conflict. By whom? The Committee was not the League. Which conflict? That between Italy and Ethiopia, when Italy was already fighting well within Ethiopian territory, or that between Italy and the League, when Italy had already been declared as the aggressor? Count van Zeeland was not the Belgian public man the League liked best. In a cluster of first-rate League figures – Hymans, de Brouckère, Theunis, Carton de Wiart, Rollin – all members who were thorough members of the team, so to speak, he seemed to remain rather aloof, above the Assembly, away from the Council, a confabulator rather than a negotiator. He evidently knew more about the Hoare-Laval plans than he would say. And the feeling was general that he was speaking on a brief prepared by his two partners. That uneasy and possibly unfair suspicion that sanctions were being hindered less by the big nations than by big business did but increase (again possibly unfairly) when Count van Zeeland undersigned the off-the-stage activities of Messrs Hoare and Laval.

CHAPTER XLVI

MORE TALKS

ON November 2nd I had a long interview with Sir Samuel Hoare. He had most courteously offered to call on me at my hotel, which I declined as the younger man that I was. I went to the *Beau Rivage* and he asked to know my opinion on the dispute. He volunteered his own: every solution to be arrived at without forcing the Negus and so as to obtain the official approval of the League. Possibly some cession of territory as suggested by the Committee of Five. Upon his renewed request for more of my views, I told him that one of our chief troubles was that neither Laval nor Mussolini realised the strength of collective opinion in Geneva, which made them imagine that an agreement between France and England was enough. I did not tell him but I remembered that Laval had said to Eden, 'The League means you and us'; and with that phrase in mind, I drew Hoare's attention to the danger of overlooking the opinion of nations that are later expected to assume delicate or even dangerous rôles while reducing them to the status of an opera chorus. He assured me that his Government were dead against such a way of doing things and that their determination to work through the League was sincere.

I urged him to send back the 'talks' to the Committee of Five (to which they were to return in any case) as soon as they had reached enough body to pass muster as a negotiation; and advised that the Negus should be kept in touch with what was being discussed so as not to stray too far from what he could accept; and even that, at some opportune stage, the two adversaries should be encouraged to talk to each other direct, now that Mussolini, though more threatening in the field, had been morally weakened by being declared the aggressor. I also recommended that the British Government should call Mussolini's attention to the fact that his press campaign against Geneva was contrary to his best interests.

I then changed the subject. Spain, I complained, is not kept informed in general, though often, as in this case, no country had a bigger stake in what was happening. Hoare promised to put that right and to keep Ayala (our Ambassador in London) informed. I went on to emphasise the similarities between Britain and Spain in what we would now call geopolitics and therefore our receptive attitude to co-operate. Tangiers, for instance, where we had been excessively sacrificed to France, a subject Hoare promised to study.

You never saw such a speed in the blossoming of promises into facts. Ayala informed by cable, Laval talked to on Tangiers the same day. Wonderful. How did I know it? Before the evening meeting of the Committee of Eighteen I came across Hoare and Eden in the street, and they both begged me to speak in the public debate of the Co-ordinating Committee, which, they told me, was to meet at their request 'to make Laval affirm in public his fidelity to the procedure of the League of Nations in his negotiation with Italy.' They insisted that after Laval and Hoare, as well as van Zeeland who wished to speak, I should speak also. I accepted (I wrote to my Government) in view of the circumstances.

It was a heavy day. In the morning, my call to Hoare. In the afternoon, meeting in the street with Hoare and Eden; then, the sitting of the Committee of Eighteen; then the Committee of Co-ordination with speech by request; then the Committee of Eighteen again, and before it I had a talk with Aloisi. He was pleased with my speech and reported to me his morning talk with Hoare by whom he knew of my talk with him. All this weaving of talks! The best one can say about it is what I once answered to a man who at question time during one of my lecture tours in the U.S. countered my praises of the League by contemptuously arguing that there was that League unable to solve the Polono-Lithuanian dispute, allowing the two delegates to come every year before the Council just to slang each other lustily. 'How wonderful,' I retorted. 'Suppose we still had the Kaiser and Lloyd George coming every year before the Council to call each other names, instead of Paschendaele soaked in British blood and France covered with American and Canadian cemeteries – as well as her own!'

And yet, deep down, (why? it would be worth exploring) talks and talks are trying to the spirit. To return to mine with Aloisi: it was mostly reduced to explaining his stand on what was being offered to Italy by Britain (for that is how he saw it), listening to my sermon on 'don't you believe that the League equals France and England, and do not go on calling us all names that don't fit, and try not to think so much of Britain's evil intentions (which he wildly exaggerated) and a little more on the moral forces that bear on the issue.'

Titulesco was very worried. He was linked with Italy by a kind of cultural sympathy, Rumania having always prided herself on her Latin ancestry; and he feared for his country the economic consequences of an oil embargo that would very concretely hit Rumania's oil exports.

At the Committee of Eighteen he had ably led a move to secure collective compensation for those countries whose interests would be more directly hit by sanctions – a proposal bristling with practical difficulties and bound to fail. He gave a dinner at the Bergues (where both he and I lived) to which he invited Eden and his financial advisers and, for some reason or other, me. Eden came late; and Titulesco disappeared, only to return with three magnificent bottles of Cognac Napoleon, one he generously shared with his guests, one he gave Eden and another he gave me.

No amount of alcohol, even of such choice quality, could convince British Treasury officials of anything they rejected *an sich*, so I shall witness to the fact that neither the advisers nor their chief showed any signs of fear before the precious flood, which they were able to swim over victoriously. I never drink anything stronger than sherry, and so I kept my bottle and put it away. It may appear that bottles of brandy may also have their destinies. This happened on November 13, 1935; by July 18, 1936 our civil war had begun. Titulesco's Napoleon brandy was still in my cellar in Madrid, intact. When the siege of Madrid began, my sisters handed the precious bottle to a hospital for the wounded republicans. It was consumed and enjoyed by the hospital's 'Responsible', who happened to be communists.

I shall not put a full stop to this melancholy tale without making it clear that much as I dissent from the theory, and still more so the practice, of communism, I am by no means suggesting that drinking the brandy that was meant for the wounded was one of the established communist principles. In fact, God knows how many of the deprived wounded were communists who, like so many of them, fought and died for their faith in Spain. All I say is that, as fate would have it, that bottle went that unexpected way.

CHAPTER XLVII

THE HOARE-LAVAL BOMBSHELL

I was in my house in Madrid when Guariglia, Mussolini's Ambassador, rang up asking whether he could bring me an oral message from the Duce. I received him in the living-room downstairs, where we had a grand piano and a big sofa, the rest of the room being more especially fitted as a dining-room. The receiving and the dining sections could be, and at that late morning hour, were, separated by a curtain that ran just behind the sofa on which Guariglia and I were talking. The maid was setting the table for lunch; and the Fascist Ambassador was too uneasy to conceal his anxiety, and now and then cast a glance at the thick, opaque curtain. I kept half fearing half wishing that the maid would drop a dozen knives or a pile of dishes. But all went smoothly and quietly, at any rate in our dining-room.

The Duce wanted me to go to Rome and find a solution with him. Had he been a less absurd man, less hollow, less of a mere façade, this proposal would have appealed to me. I had by then assimilated enough vital elements from both sides to have been perhaps able to strike a verbal bridge on which – given some time – a more permanent half-way house might have been erected. But Mussolini being the wax-works he was, the yield of my trip to Rome would have been exactly nil. I asked Guariglia some questions, and told him that all I could say was that I should report the position to the Council and stand by its decision.

When I put the matter to the Committee of Thirteen (over which I presided) some of my colleagues were for, some against, and the motives were by no means of the same kind. One of the most positive was Titulesco, who made no bones about declaring that the proposal had the advantage that, if I succeeded, the success would be put down to the credit of the League, while if I failed it would be put down to my debit and nothing would be lost. I retorted with a verse from Racine

> . . .je n'ai mérité
> Ni cet excès d'honneur ni cette indignité*

Meanwhile I could perceive in certain sections of the Council some concern at my going to Rome unchaperoned. With the sixth sense one

*I have deserved neither that excess of honour nor that indignity.

develops in such matters, I thought this breeze blew from France, even though in somewhat devious ways; and I am not sure that Titulesco's remark might not have concealed a subtle manoeuvre towards the same aim – which was soon revealed: it would be better, someone suggested, if I were to go to Rome accompanied by the Secretary General. As the Secretary General was a Frenchman Laval would feel safer than if a League hot-head, as I was supposed to be, were sent alone. The decision was taken, yet the trip was lost in the maze of events.

I was again in Madrid when the telephone rang and I recognised the voice of Laval. 'Do you have power to call a meeting of the Council?' I answered that it would no doubt meet if I asked it to, but that it was safer to convene the Committee of Thirteen, about which, as chairman, my powers were not in doubt. 'Comes to the same, doesn't it?' he asked. I agreed. I cabled all round and left for Geneva via Paris that very night.

The next evening, as I was walking along the P.L.M. Paris station platform to catch my Geneva train, I saw Laval talking to Norman Davis. I joined them: they were talking Spanish. Davis knew no French, Laval no English; but both could get along in my own language. Laval asked me to give up my sleeping-car accommodation and move to one of the bedrooms in his coach.

As soon as the train had run out of the din of the outer station, he produced a paper from his pocket and said: 'There. That is what we have agreed with the *Anglais*.' And so I became acquainted with the famous Hoare-Laval plan. We studied it together for a while, then talked it over for a good hour. I made it quite clear to him that it would not do. And when asked why, I answered: 'British public opinion won't look at it.' He looked at me with cold, sceptical eyes. For him, public opinion meant the press, and no government was a government who could not manipulate its press. That was what his eyes were saying.

I glanced at my watch and moved to the door. 'Where are you going?' And I answered: 'Back to my sleeping-car.' He stared at me in silence. I left his coach.

When the next morning we clattered into Geneva, two of my countrymen were at the station to greet me: José Plá, of the League Press section; and Pedro Rosselló, the Secretary General of the International Bureau of Education. They were all agog with the now famous plan. 'What is going to happen?' they asked. 'Britain won't have it.' 'But then, Hoare?' – 'Well, he will have to resign.'

What had happened? A setback which might have led to a catastrophe for Italy, a rescue operation on the part of Laval and a moment of aberration on the part of an exhausted Hoare. By late October, Italy was financially so weak that the lira had to be devalued by nearly a quarter. The military conquests of De Bono were nowhere to be seen, and Badoglio, who had succeeded him, did not seem to be doing much better. Discontent was widespread. Had the oil sanctions been applied, Mussolini might have had to surrender or fall. He staged a number of ostentatiously threatening moves against France, which Laval took as hints; and the operation was prepared so as to spring the plan on Hoare as he passed through Paris on his way to do a bit of skating in Switzerland. (December 7, 1935.)

The stories do not quite tally. Eden gives chapter and verse to show that Hoare had no instructions and no intention of reopening a negotiation with Laval; but Vansittart's version implies that Hoare had kept Laval from coming to London by promising to see him in Paris on the way to his skating-pool; furthermore, Patterson, the British Abyssinian expert, was carrying on a kind of permanent negotiation with his Quai d'Orsay opposite number, St. Quentin; and to crown it all, the one and only Vansittart was at the time in Paris, and Eden himself tells how he warned Hoare (as he left for Paris) of Vansittart's tendency to be more French than the French.

Laval's attitude to the oil embargo was that the Americans had no power to enforce it ('They told us so') and that the Germans would violate it ('that was also true!'). This is of course pure Vansittart; for, granted that Hitler would betray, he was not very well placed to play that game in oil embargoes; and as for the U.S.A., it is surely fantastic to claim that her Government could not enforce an oil embargo if it really wished. But, of course, Vansittart is pleading for a scheme which next to Laval owed most to him and to his pro-French and racialist foibles. How irrational it all was is shown by the fact that this ineffective and inapplicable oil embargo becomes a cause of possible war in his arguing with Eden.

The plan was presented as the least bad possible. This was not so. It was much worse than it need have been. An 'exchange of territories' by which Ethiopia ceded 60,000 square miles to Italy and Italy 3,000 to Ethiopia (or, if she refused, a similar gift of land to be made by Britain and France); and about half of the country (160,000 square miles) reserved for economic expansion under Italy; and, on top of it, a form of words that hardly masked sheer annexation. Laval claimed that this plan was in accordance with the proposal of the Committee of Five, which was plainly untrue.

Hoare had committed an incredible blunder: before leaving Paris for Switzerland he had consented to the issue of a joint Communiqué in which the existence of an agreed plan was announced though its actual terms were reserved until they had been approved by the British Cabinet and by the League; whereupon leaks began to appear in the French press. The British Cabinet, caught in the dilemma of either disowning their Foreign Secretary, still skating, or covering his action, took the more honourable and less honest course, and Eden had to come to Geneva to face the music. To crown it all, on December 10th, Hoare fainted while skating, fell and broke his nose (I mean his physical one). The British Delegate withdrew the plan on the ground that the League rejected it. Hoare resigned on December 18th. On December 19th during the debate in the House of Commons, the Prime Minister admitted that a mistake had been committed. On the same day, the Committee of Thirteen met and duly buried the body of that mistake with no regrets. The Governments of France and Britain were the losers in moral authority; Eden was sensitive enough to feel it. Within a few days he became Foreign Secretary (December 22, 1935) – half a year too late.

His stand would be clearer and more forthright than that of his predecessors, but his task would be incomparably harder precisely because Eden, *rara avis*, realised the weight of moral forces in world affairs; while the general handling of the Italo-Ethiopian dispute by the League, particularly the Hoare-Laval episode, had played havoc with the moral authority of the League, as well as with that of the British and French Governments. Laval had fallen and the French Foreign Office was now in the hands of Flandin, a much taller but hardly a loftier man.

Eden laid down his definite lines of action: oil sanctions and a return to the report of the Committee of Five as a basis for negotiations. But it was plain that the U.S. would not give up the oil profits of its big business; while Flandin was even more determined than Laval to shield Mussolini from the consequences of an oil embargo by arguing both that the embargo would not work and that it would infuriate Mussolini and so endanger peace. As for the Committee of Five, Flandin had even less use for it than Laval, and was no less than Laval determined to carry on private negotiations. At the turn of the year, the Italo-Ethiopian dispute was at its highest, France, Britain and the League, at their lowest; while Hitler was sharpening his *baionets* and keeping his powder dry.

The means were there; but the League had lost heart. The sanctions that were being applied did work, but those that had just been adopted in principle (coal, iron) were given up for lack of statistical support or, as in the case of oil, sent back to the governments for consultation, which meant doing nothing about it.

The actual war was taking daily a more and more savage turn on both sides, though Italy, as the more civilised of the two adversaries, was incurring the heavier responsibility. The Council appealed to the parties (March 3, 1936) to be ready to seek peace terms 'in the framework of the League and in the spirit of the Covenant.' This appeal had been proposed by France. It really meant the opening gambit in another game of chess between the two powers and Mussolini. The same rules of the game operated on us, and we endorsed Flandin's appeal. Ethiopia accepted the next day. Mussolini after a few days. Four days after the Council's appeal, Hitler invaded the Rhineland in violation of the Treaty of Locarno.

CHAPTER XLVIII

FREELANCE ACTIVITIES: MEETING WITH FRANCO: THE WORLD FOUNDATION

AFTER I felt the Lerroux Government in the spring of 1934, I had gone back to my vocation as a freelance author, if now and then also a freelance politician. The former event was but a return to normal; the latter took place in the nature of things, whether I sought it or not. I felt attracted by European and world politics but repelled by national politics. This contrast was due to a bunch of reasons, chief of which, perhaps because I felt competent in the wider, but incompetent in the restricted political sphere. The brief passage through a ministry had blown away whatever illusions or delusions I may have harboured on how to reach the outer or European sphere through the inner or national one. If such delusions there were, they really sprang from plain common sense, unless I were to return to some form of international civil service, a prospect abhorrent to my anarchistic understructure.

With the hindsight now available, I incline to think that there were sectors and men in Spanish politics that were perhaps keener to push me into Spanish politics than I was myself to enter that path so that, at that time, two antagonistic forces must have been operating on my destiny: one working to keep me out of Spanish politics and the other one to sweep me into it. The first came from my political friends, the liberal and the socialist left, whose protagonists were less keen than they should have been to foster a recruit in whom they saw another competitor; the second came from the right, especially the Lerroux quarters, when it was felt that the party was in need of new men with a clean slate.

Among those 'radicals' (as they styled themselves) in search of new virginities some were more active than others, and one at least I had to consider as a direct emissary of Lerroux himself; for not only was he generally considered to be a 'His Master's Voice' sort of person but he put it to me in so many words that if I only became a freemason, Lerroux would hand me over the leadership of the party. To which I answered that such a prospect was yet one more reason why I should never become a freemason.

At that time or soon after, I had to face a far more concrete offer which, had I been susceptible to its charms, would have been deadly. A minister of the navy kept extolling to me the glory of leading such a patriotic work as the building up of the much neglected Spanish Navy.

The more he sang the less I heard; for by an elementary form of reasoning I became convinced that there was a trap in the works, and I kept thinking of our proverb: 'When the wine-keeper sells his wine-butt it either leaks or tastes of pitch.' A few months later, an unsavoury affair about a submarine and the funds to pay for it burst into the open, and I knew what I had been spared.

This was the general atmosphere in which I was living when I received strong advice to meet the head of our Army General Staff, one Francisco Franco. The advice came from one of the men whom I trusted most: my one-time under-secretary at the Ministry of Education, Ramón Prieto Bances. He was an Asturian and, as such, knew Franco well, for though a Gallego by birth, Franco had become more or less an Asturian by his marriage into a well-known Oviedo family. I do not think that Prieto's idea went further than that it would be a good thing if two prominent Spaniards met; nor do I to this day believe that the meeting was due at all to Franco's instigation. I asked them both to lunch.

We met at the Hotel Nacional in October and remained together for two or three hours. Franco spoke rather less than the usual Spaniard would have done in similar circumstances, though by no means evincing either secretive or supercilious tendencies. I was struck by his accurate and precise rather than striking or original mind; and by his obviously sincere though never self-vaunted public spirit. I was not able to observe then either the cruel streak in his character or that *petit-bourgeois* fondness for property which he was later either to manifest or to develop.

I was myself at the time going through a fermentation of my own ideas on liberal democracy, and setting down my new views in a book published in Madrid in 1935, in Paris and London in 1936 and in New York in 1937. Its very title *Anarchy or Hierarchy*, suggested the chief lesson we liberal-democrats had to draw from our adversaries on the right and on the left: how to save that hierarchy which is the very architecture of the state. My chief ideas were two: the first was that while liberty is the very air of our spirit, without which our spirit wilts, democracy is but a set of practices and can be revised and adjusted; the second, that, particularly for the nations born of Rome, direct universal suffrage was dangerous and should be replaced by a system whereby direct suffrage should lapse at the level of municipal elections, and all the other collegiate bodies of the state should be elected by the bodies immediately below. We talked a good deal about this and I eventually sent Franco a copy of my book.

In that book I painted the contrast between the one-man-one-vote democracy, in which I do not believe, and my own way of having of-

ficial representative bodies elected; and I described the first as 'statistical' and the second as 'organic' democracy. Insofar as Franco's
propagandists have tried to represent his system – or lack thereof – as
'organic democracy', I must own that my book must have been used
at least as a raw material to prop with ideas what is at bottom a hardly-
disguised form of praetorianism.

One detail lingers in my mind from that day. We took a taxi, the three
of us, in which Franco and I, both short men, were easily accommodated, while our 'bridge' Prieto, a very tall man, had to perform feats
of acrobacy to fit his legs into the scanty space left for him, and we drove
to the War Office, to drop my guest there. On the way, Franco criticised
my plans for army organisation with a sigh: 'Where is the money to
come from'; and I, incorrigible innocent that I am, pointed out that
the military and naval attachés in our embassies abroad cost us tons
of money and were no earthly use. He seemed surprised. I told him
that once at my Paris embassy I told Legorburu, my air attaché (whom
I shared with the London embassy), that I assumed he would be going
to London for some air manoeuvres. It was the first Legorburu had
heard about them. He wondered whether they were still a secret. I
answered I didn't think so, because I had read the whole thing in my
copy of *The Times* two or three days earlier. Franco seemed worried
but not much.

The main sediment left in me by my experience of world affairs and
my meditations upon them was that the chief obstacle to peace and
common sense lay in the states, by which I mean the machinery for
carrying out national life. I should not have been ready to accept mere
'nationalism' as the villain of the piece. Indeed, nationalism as the mere
awareness of the collective self seemed to me a fact of life, and one to
be respected; it was, furthermore, a 'neutral' fact so to speak, in that
if it can, and generally does, get led astray towards aggression, in-
transigeance, power-lust and war, it could, in other circumstances,
harness its formidable strength in the service of peace and common
sense. The problem was who led it.

I then came to feel that an entity was wanted to lead and guide the
public opinion of the world. My experience of the clouds of journalists
that used to fly around chief delegates was deplorable. Though some
were only bad while others were worse, they incarnated the most detes-
table form of nationalism; and the governments they served – or
thought they served – were too harried, worried, hurried, to raise their
heads and hearts from the next-day task; nor would most of them, if
less harried, have kept their sights any higher any longer for lack of a

world perspective or too much thinking of their constituencies or both.

Something else was wanted. First a group of truly free men, then a sum of money to allow them to act on public opinion without any state, party or class fetters. An American Foundation was not the answer, for, admirable though they are, they remain thoroughly American, as they have a perfect right to do. What was needed was a World Foundation, whose motto was to be *Patria Patriarum.*

Two American women brought me then their invaluable co-operation. One was a wealthy widow of Chicago, whose very name was well-known in the world of public affairs: Mrs Anita Emmons Blaine. She held a number of gatherings in her Chicago home, which were useful to launch the idea. Mrs Blaine seemed to have inherited the international urge of President Harrison's Secretary of State, her relative, though in a more universal form than Blaine's perspective which was just continental. She allowed us to keep a secretariat for the time we struggled to set up the real thing. The other American woman was Ruth Cranston, a freelance journalist who had worked for the *Christian Science Monitor* and knew both Europe and Asia well. She was a thoroughly convinced advocate of the idea and worked with efficient fervour as secretary of the organising Committee.

I had been putting together this Committee as well as I could in the intervals of representing Spain in Geneva and shielding myself against shooters and stabbers in the back. The work involved a good deal of travelling, and in this endeavour I had visited the U.S. during February of 1936.

I find an echo of it all in a letter I sent to Augusto Barcía, then Foreign Secretary of Azaña in the Cabinet that had just taken office after the general election that had resulted in the victory of the popular front. My trip was private and, at the time, I held no official post; yet, the Italo-Ethiopian dispute was on, and the idea that I was the Spanish permanent delegate in Geneva was rooted everywhere outside Spain, even in official quarters, so before my departure for the U.S.A. I went to call on Bowers, the American Ambassador in Madrid, and told him that while over there I wanted to be neither discourteous nor indiscreet, so I should leave the matter of meeting official persons to the American Government. Bowers wrote to Roosevelt, I understand, recommending that I should be heard and as soon as I arrived in New York our embassy in Washington suggested that, as the prorogation of the neutrality law was being discussed it might be best if I avoided Washington until that issue was out of the way.

Later my presence in Washington was requested by Cordell Hull who wished to see me. Well, he didn't. He was ill. Diplomacy or virus? Who knows? The fact is that my talk with Phillips, his Under-Secretary, was a sheer waste of time, and my visit to Wallace, then Minister of Agriculture, though very much worth while, had nothing to do with Geneva. As for Roosevelt, he seems to have rated me too low or too high. Most of my friends explained his dodging me as fear of the anti-Geneva lobby in his country.

This lobby was very strong. My impression, gathered from talks with a number of worth-while persons in Washington, including Colonel House and Governor Harrison of the Federal Reserve Bank, was that the country had been impressed by the vigour of the League of Nations up to the moment when the Hoare-Laval proposals became known, and would have been ready even to back a petrol boycott; but that those unfortunate proposals had brought back the anti-League wind stronger than ever. A curious situation, for American opinion seemed to hang on how 'Geneva' acted or reacted, instead of holding to its own objective view of the event, and leading instead of being led. The fall of Hoare and, soon after, of Laval, did not detract from the victory of the anti-League lobby, and this makes one wonder whether the previous pro-League fashion had been as strong as some of our friends saw it or said it was. The combination of the Hearst press, the isolationist-imperialists led by Senator Hiram Johnson and the evangelical pacifists of Senator Nye, was at any rate most unconvincing.

I was struck by the utter mistrust of the sincerity of British policy that I found in Washington; and I actually reported to my Foreign Minister that 'there exists but one possibility (not one certainty) of restoring some trust in British policy and that is that during the coming meeting in Geneva Eden assume the leadership of the petrol sanction, no matter what goes on here.' Otherwise, I saw nothing but a complete neglect of Geneva on the part of the U.S.A. And my conclusion was: 'This case confirms the law that seems to rule the relations between the League and the U.S.A., that at every moment the best course for Geneva will be to go straight ahead as if the U.S. did not exist' ('straight' meant of course 'in obedience to the Covenant').

In my letter I devoted a paragraph to the Inter-American Conference the U.S. were then preparing – what, I asked, was its aim? To consolidate what has been achieved, to build up an American League of Nations or (more likely) to launch an electoral plank with much show of the former and much hope of the latter? I discussed the matter with the Mexican ambassador, Dr Castillo Nájera, who assured me that the whole Spanish American contingent were ready to 'carry on singing in a chorus a new version of the Monroe Doctrine', but the Mexican President, who rang up and spoke to the Ambassador while I was with him, gave him instructions to insist that 'Mexico's acceptance [to attend the Conference] was subordinated to fidelity to the League of

Nations': And I added: 'Castillo saw Sumner Wells yesterday afternoon and was able to tell me in the evening that this Mexican reservation had not pleased Washington.'

Those were the days when Henry Wallace's reputation was at its
highest. He was admired as the leader of American liberals. There is
perhaps no word in the dictionary of politics that more closely apes
the qualities of rubber than that word 'liberal'. From almost red-revolu-
tionary that it can mean in the U.S.A. to dyed-in-the-wool reactionary
that it can mean in France, it lends itself to all kinds of interpretation.
Henry Wallace, who began left of centre, ended as close to communism
as it was possible in those days in his country.

He was an amiable man who had made a fortune by skilfully com-
mercialising the properties of hybrid maize plants, endowed with a
transparent honesty and an idealistic turn of mind; and I assumed,
perhaps too readily, that he would be willing to listen to my song. This
was, as usual with me, more directly concerned with long-view situations than with short-term problems. I had in mind the future of
Spanish America. I told him I believed the policy of the U.S.A. towards
their southern neighbours was hopeless, and could be summed up in
goody-goody words and thoroughly bad deeds. Then I stated my con-
structive proposals.

The main point about Spanish America (including Brazil) was that it
was almost unpopulated. A South America inhabited by 250 million
people would find most of its problems solved and offer the U.S.A. a
huge market. But these millions would have to be predominantly
European. If we want them to go there not just to make money quickly
and return to Europe, but to take root there, they must be Spanish (and
Portuguese), with some Italians.

The chief error of the U.S.A. in this field is to fail to discriminate the
true, long-term interests of the country from those of private individuals
or firms intent on exploiting the South Americans, which, of course,
estranges them from the U.S.A.* One other error of the U.S.A. is to
pursue in the New World a stubborn anti-Spanish policy. For instance,
the U.S. is always invited to all Spanish American gatherings organised
by Spain; Spain is never invited to Spanish American gatherings organised by the U.S. And yet their interests could easily be harmonised.
Spain seeks the safe development of Spanish culture in the continent in
which she implanted it, and the absorption of a good part of the quarter

---

* This is by no means a monopoly of the U.S.A. If the three big tin-mine owners of
Bolivia, two natives and a German Jew, had ploughed at least a part of their huge
profits into national education and development, that unfortunate country would be
happier and quieter than it has been for a century.

of a million over-population she produces yearly, two aims neither of which is in any way contrary to *the true legitimate* interests of the U.S. My plan aimed at a set of tripartite agreements between any given Spanish American country (land and legislation), the U.S. (capital and technology) and Spain (emigration and technology) to raise emigration above the low, commercial, human cattle-transportation level it then had attained to a modern sociological feature of the relations between civilised peoples.

Wallace was interested and tried to get me an interview with Morgenthau, the Secretary of the Treasury, who had just returned from a holiday in Spain and, I was told, turned by his experience into a Spanish fan; but the Secretary of the Navy (a cousin of the President) died and all interviews went by the board. Wallace promised to put my views to Morgenthau and to Roosevelt. 'By and by' is easily said.

I did not talk to Wallace in Puerto Rico; but I did in a number of other worth-while places. Americans are prone to deplore the load of poverty with its sequel of disease and crime brought to New York by the Puerto Rican colony. They imagine it is the fault of the Puerto Ricans. But if they only read their Poinsett*, they would soon discover that the misery of Puerto Rico is made in the U.S.A. Under Spain the island was a paradise. I put it to my friends that complete independence was the best solution. In those days, a federation with Cuba and Santo Domingo might have saved the three islands from their present misery, for it is true that Puerto Rico itself is peaceful and prosperous, but at the price of that dreadful sociological cancer which is the colony of exiles in New York.

---

* *Notes on Mexico made in the Autumn of 1822* by J. R. Poinsett, London, 1825.

CHAPTER XLIX

TWO BULLS IN THE RING

B Y the end of March, many observers were getting impatient with our inactivity (as they saw it) in the Italo-Ethiopian dispute. The bold, frankly aggressive actions of Hitler on the Rhine did not seem to them a sufficient reason for our circumspection on the equally bold but even more aggressive actions of Mussolini in Ethiopia. The widespread use of poison gas even for operations against civilian populations was being reported all over the world, and critics of the League were turning bitter.

On March 31st the *Journal des Nations*, a French language newspaper published in Geneva, chose me as the butt of its reproaches. 'On March 23, 1936,' it wrote, 'the Committee of Thirteen – having, thirteen days too late, taken note of the answers of both parties to the appeal that had been sent them on March 3rd – entrusted Mr de Madariaga, President of the Committee, with the task of informing himself with the parties, and of taking all measures tending to obtaining within the framework of the League of Nations and in the spirit of the Covenant the cessation of hostilities and the final settlement of peace.'

That was simple enough, indeed, as simple as playing billiards, which requires nothing but knocking at one ball and then at the other. Yet I was chided because all I had done was to see Grandi and Martin in London and to go back to Madrid, which plainly showed that my mission had failed (what else could it do?). But Oliván who sent me the cutting from Bern was alarmed at the state of public opinion in London and Geneva owing to the nefarious activities of Mussolini's aviation in Ethiopia. What worried him was that we (Spain) should bear the brunt of any odium our apparent inactivity might generate.

I called the Committee of Thirteen to meet and report progress (or lack thereof); and the Italian press was not slow in hinting that there had been official British pressure to induce me to take that decision. But Britain (in the French picturesque saying) had then 'other cats to whip'. The hot plate on the table was now Hitler's invasion of the Rhineland, and not far-away Ethiopia. The Council met in London (end of March) to deal with Hitler; and on March 29, 1936, Eden (behind whose more attractive figure the other three were sheltering) presented a statement in which he, Flandin, van Zeeland and Grandi assured the world that 'scrupulous respect for all treaty obligations is a fundamental principle of international life and an essential condition of the maintenance of peace.'

The best authority of the four was Grandi, for his chief had beaten the record of infringement of treaties in one single stroke and was leading a war in Ethiopia; so the proposition was not only true but exemplified by one of the four men who vouched for it.

Needless to say, this document hung in the sun on a line held at one end by hypocrisy and at the other by cynicism, could act as nothing short of a red rag for Hitler. If Mussolini, why not he? Furthermore, he knew full well that the Council could be considered as composed of two totally different parts or parties: the power-party, composed of the permanent members, and the moral-authority party, composed of the smaller nations, and that, in what concerned him, the power-party was worried and divided, while the moral-authority party was by no means disposed to grant its help to a Flandin who in point of moral authority was no better than Laval.

London being more attractive than Geneva for a freemason, radical Republican (for there was a monarch in it), Augusto Barcía, my Foreign Secretary, came to the Council and so I was reduced to second fiddle and advisory rôles. I met Ribbentrop, who struck me as a mediocrity, and I followed the official work though devoting a certain not unimportant amount of my attention to the work of the World Foundation.

France wanted a League official statement to the effect that Germany had violated the Locarno Treaty. This was at its best a very odd request; for the Locarno Treaty had been put forward by Austen Chamberlain as a line of policy deliberately outside the League, or, in other words, as a balance-of-power contrivance instead of a moral-power forum. And now, when it failed, the balance-of-power people (although they were carrying on a similar policy in the Ethiopian dispute) came hurrying back to the Covenant for an injection of moral power.

We all (but two) declared that Germany had violated the Treaty of Locarno, but Ecuador was absent, for fear of offending Germany, and Chile abstained behind a legalistic barrier. The episode did not increase the authority of the Spanish American countries in Geneva. The Council could do nothing but fail – which by now, it was fairly used to doing.

Such was the true background on which I, as President of the Committee of Thirteen, was supposed to be working for an agreement between the parties to the Ethiopian dispute. The human situation had deteriorated because Flandin was far worse in substance even than Laval (though a good deal better in manner) and he often got on

Eden's nerves. He twisted the March resolution of the Committee of Thirteen to mean that Italy and Ethiopia were to negotiate directly, my presence and that of the Secretary General being purely 'moral' (in *his* sense, which meant just formal, say, like two portraits on a wall). Strangely enough, his aim seems to have been to keep the League out and Avenol and me in under the roof of responsibility, in case the negotiation failed. Eden was just short of indignant. The Australian, Bruce, capable enough but blunt, not very much endowed with insight, as well as handicapped by his linguistic incapacity, was bamboozled enough to side with Flandin, as did Titulesco for more than one reason, the one reason being the general French line taken by the Petite Entente, and the 'more than' to be described at a more opportune moment.

I had to explain, and did it in unmistakable terms, that there was no such agreement within the Committee about direct negotiations but only about talks in our presence (Avenol's and mine) which would certainly not be passive; then, I stated that no one thought any longer that it was possible to uphold the Covenant in its integrity, and that, therefore, principles must suffer. But we do not as yet (I added) hold a mandate from the Committee of Thirteen to negotiate on that basis, i.e. to salvage all we can of the Ethiopian interests yet being aware that the result will not be four-square with the Covenant. If such a situation is fully and explicitly recognised, I am willing to negotiate; if the Committee is unwilling to recognise it openly, even then, I would do so, but on condition that the Committee of Thirteen would sit permanently so as to register and endorse any sacrifices that would have to be made; otherwise I was not prepared to stage a play on 'The whole Covenant' just to spare the responsibility of all but one of the Thirteen members of the Committee.

Aloisi came to see me the next day. He was displeased with the way things were going and 'feared' that Italy would not be represented at the next meeting of the Committee which, he complained, I had convened for the following Thursday as a form of pressure. I denied the pressure and told him he had better be present at the next meeting, for his proposal might be rejected by the Negus even as a basis for discussion, in which case, I should have to declare the phase of conciliation ended. What then? he asked. And I advised him to bring me some substantial proposal, and not just procedure matters. I know this struck home, for soon after he left, I received the visit of Pilotti, the (Italian) Deputy Secretary General, who told me so. Which induced me to repeat the mixture as before. Pilotti, by his own attitude rather than by his words, confirmed me in my belief that the League had still enough strength in Rome for us to get some results.

Eden was determined to get on with sanctions, for which the preliminary step was officially to declare the failure of reconciliation. This suited neither Italy nor France, and sure enough, Aloisi presented to me a plan I found unacceptable as utterly incompatible with the Covenant, so I proposed to adjourn for one day. During that interval, Avenol prepared a précis of our interview with Aloisi which he read to Oliván and me just before Aloisi's arrival for the second interview. It struck us both as far too one-sided and tendentious for a Secretary General, but we accepted it with some slight amendments, just so as to get on, and keep safe our bridge between France and Britain. When Aloisi arrived we told him of the summary prepared by Avenol; he (somewhat naïvely, I thought) declared he would put all his trust in us and would not ask to see it. After he left us, Avenol saw in our eyes that we had guessed the trick: he had prepared the text with Aloisi's collaboration and behind our backs.

There and then, I improvised a working luncheon with Eden, Paul-Boncour, Avenol and Oliván, in the course of which, brushing aside the far too clever paper, I gave the true version of the interview. By then, we knew Aloisi's plan had been rejected by the Ethiopians. Pressure on Aloisi brought a slight improvement of what was meant by 'direct negotiation' and I made a good deal of effort to have this accepted by the Ethiopians. However, they didn't.

I decided to declare conciliation at an end. It seemed to me healthier for the moral authority of the Council. But I had to get Paul-Boncour's acquiescence, which I did thanks to another step I took: to ask Eden to postpone his plan to call the Sanctions Committee and call the Council instead. Eden agreed though he exacted from Paul-Boncour a promise that, after the French general election, they would take on a firmer line.

This is perhaps the place to set down that on May 8, 1936, Paul-Boncour wrote me a letter to the effect that he and I had been getting letters threatening us both, and that those letters had been sent from Paris. He enclosed a note from the police to the effect that their 'minutieuses recherches' had led to nothing and that the writers of the letters were certainly using false names – which was, I thought, a very shrewd remark to be made by the police. 'What comforts me,' Paul-Boncour added, 'is that [I] am no better treated than our Spanish friend in this truly too vague a note, which puts a final stop to something I should have liked to see carried further more actively.'

The conquest went on. Badoglio, who had succeeded De Bono as commander in chief, defeated the Ethiopians at the battle of Lake

Ashangi (March-April 1936). The Emperor had to exile himself. The Council met on April 20th. Aloisi spoke with assurance of Italy's loyalty to the spirit of the Covenant, and was generous enough not to keep the Council out of the negotiations, which now would be *direct* with no interpretations, but insisted that they were to be away from Geneva. In case a doubt remained as to the worst fears of the fact in everybody's mind, that there were two bulls in the ring, Aloisi concluded that Italy's action in Europe was subordinated to the settlement of the conflict with Ethiopia.

It was a gloomy Council which, while accepting the inevitable, maintained sanctions – at any rate on paper – and, much to the indignation of Aloisi, recorded a protest against the use of poison gas.

But the sitting of the Council on May 11th was gloomier still. The decree of annexation of Ethiopia had been officially sent to the League by Mussolini, and Aloisi argued that since there was no longer such a state, there could be no representative of it at the Council table, nor such a thing as an Italo-Ethiopian conflict on the agenda. On our refusal to admit either of these two claims, Aloisi left the hall. The Council decided (May 12, 1936) to adjourn for a month but to let sanctions continue. Meanwhile, Argentina asked that the Assembly be summoned, which was done for June 30th.

That month brought a good deal of change. On June 4, 1935 the popular front had won the French elections, Léon Blum was President and Yvon Delbos Foreign Secretary. This was perhaps the most antifascist Government France could possibly produce. It is not for us, mere actors, to criticise the author of the play: but we sometimes wonder.... A year or two, indeed a couple of months earlier for the arrival of Léon Blum on the stage, might have spared the world, Ethiopia and even Italy much suffering and shame. Here was a keen intellect, a diaphanous honesty and that touch of artistic sensibility failing which no politician can ever rise to statesmanship. Yvon Delbos was a competent, honest man, possibly somewhat lacking in imagination, but straight and sincere.

On June 10, 1936 Neville Chamberlain, generally considered as second man in Baldwin's Government, made his famous speech describing sanctions as 'the very midsummer of madness', a direct and open attack on Eden whom everybody knew in England to be the chief advocate of such a course. By then, not unnaturally, he had lost confidence in their efficiency but he thought – and rightly – that they should be lifted as they had been imposed, by collective action. Yet this incident, along with Hoare's re-entering of the Baldwin Cabinet as First Lord of the Admiralty, did somewhat dim the image of the best Foreign Secretary, by far, that Britain had sent to Geneva.

The Assembly met in an atmosphere of defeat and self-shame. Sanctions were shelved with the vote of all but New Zealand and – a remarkable feature – South Africa. The recognition of the annexation of Ethiopia was a bitter pill to swallow. The Emperor himself had just spoken to the Assembly in true, dignified, indeed noble terms, interrupted by a volley of insults from the Italian journalists in the press gallery, among whom I was sorry to detect my friend Cassuto. The issue was in keeping with that tension Don Quixote-Sancho with which all of us were only too familiar. Even Eden, even Blum, had to keep an ear on what Sancho Panza had to say, and an anxious eye on Hitler. A text meaning nothing was put to the vote on the tacit understanding that it meant that we would all look away while Italy did her worst. Finally, there was a lot of talk on a reform of the League. Few knew, though some may have felt, that death would come sooner than reform.

Who wants to speak? Who could desire to speak on so funereal an occasion? Eden came to my desk to ask me to speak. I said 'No'. A little later I left on his desk a piece of paper. Later, months later, already an exile, I dined at a big hotel in Whitehall with Lloyd George and Tom Jones. We talked about the Spanish Civil War. I was surprised to find in my pocket a paper I did not expect there, fished it out and found a copy of what I had put on Eden's desk. I read it to my host and my friend. Lloyd George grabbed it and I never saw it again. I believe it ran somehow as follows:

> To speak or not to speak that is the question
> Whether t'is nobler silently to suffer
> The shame and blast of an outrageous fortune
> Or by raising one's voice, seem to condone
> A deed that cries to Heaven.

CHAPTER L

A SECOND TRIP TO CENTRAL EUROPE

I T was a welcome change to have to go to Budapest (June 6–10, 1936) for a meeting of the Committee of Arts and Letters. I am not quite sure what it was we actually talked about under that loose label 'Towards a New Humanism', none of whose three terms was tight enough to hold in check our imagination. Furthermore, the meeting, as recorded by my memory, afforded an opportunity for other than official events, which were in themselves perhaps more to the point than our actual talks. Budapest is in itself, like Venice and Frankfurt, a city so rich in history, character and beauty, that one was sorry to have to *do* something or anything in it instead of just live and do nothing. I remember one day going to the opera in the same taxi with Duhamel. We were the guests of the city for a show in our honour; and Duhamel lamented that he did not know a word about the play they were giving – *Un Ballo in Maschera*. 'Never mind,' I comforted him. 'I have been told in Buenos Aires, where they have seen them all, that all operas run on the same plot: the tenor wants to lie down with the soprano, and the bass objects.' Later in the evening, as we were listening to the third act, Duhamel whispered in my ear: 'I am afraid the affairs of your bass are going from bad to worse!'

Hungary was by then no longer the brilliant second of Austria in the Dual Monarchy; but had nevertheless kept much of her old splendour, at least in Budapest, and one was impressed by the elegance and swagger of her men and the beauty of her women. Hungarian men had – it struck me – looks of so vigorous a character that one could, indeed should, call it a handsome ugliness. They were all handsomely ugly men; and one could detect in them features, gestures and postures that hailed from beyond the frontiers of Europe.

One evening, during a stately dinner at one of the finest houses in Buda, my neighbour, a Budapest woman, said to me: 'You remember the other day I told you about that Count E. who had erected a big poster at the gate of his estate: NO DOGS. NO JEWS.' – 'Indeed, I do. And you added that, as a well-known rabbi entered the park while the Count was riding out, the noble lord whipped the rabbi's face right and left with his horse-whip.' – 'Good. Look then opposite. Third from the lady of the house is the Count's son. Fifth, the son of the rabbi.'

She turned on me her lovely blue eyes and asked: 'Wouldn't you call that progress?'

Our minister or rather chargé d'affaires was Carlos Arcos. He had some title or other; Count, I believe (though whipless). I dubbed him *chargé de rien à faire*, which he enjoyed because he loved fun, and did not mind because he knew I knew it was not true. He was the ideal diplomat, active, *ma non troppo*, one whose sphere or activity is never surrounded by a stratosphere of fuss. In his leisurely way, he did all that was needed to make my stay both pleasurable and useful. He gave a dinner for me to which he invited enough but not too many people of quality yet not mainly of outward and social quality; and he had it presided over by the Archduke and Archduchess. The Imperial House had always kept in Budapest a Habsburg couple to act as a kind of Vice-Royalty for social occasions. They were, of course, bourgeois, as everybody had become by then in Europe, thought they accepted such royal trappings as being seated at the head of the table in a house that was not their own. He looked like a retired colonel, and she, red-wigged, like – well, she reminded me of the famous passage in Balzac about a cook (I quote from memory): 'This woman had a magnificent face though not adequate to her trade for it was the face of a grenadier!'

I had enjoyed her imperial conversation at table, so when we left the table and moved about I discreetly melted away as she sat down on a short sofa just wide enough for two. I soon realised that Arcos had organised his evening with Napoleonic precision. His male guests had to go and serve one quarter of an hour each at that sofa, to keep her Imperial conversation going; and so they all did quite happily, for she could talk and to some purpose; furthermore, she had produced a huge Havana cigar at which she pulled masterfully, so that the conversation was not only substantial but aromatic.

Logically enough, Arcos thought that, since I had been exempted from sofa-service because I had sat at table to the right of the Archduchess, I should be recruited for service to the Imperial conversation with the Archduke. He was far quieter and less versatile than his royal spouse, talked little and with good sense; but he had his north-north west, and that was Beneŝ, Masaryk (junior) and 'all that crowd'. In his aversion for the leaders of independent Czechoslovakia there was perhaps less a political or a dynastical than a personal, almost domestic grudge. At one or two turns in the conversation, it seemed to me that what His Imperial Highness found most heinous in the behaviour of Beneŝ was not so much that he had disjointed Prague from Vienna as that he had slept in H.I. Highness's bed in such and such a Castle, 'Indeed, Sir, in my own sheets!'

I thought it best to abstain from raising the subject of Admiral

Horthy. This admiral without a navy or indeed a coast, this Regent of
a monarchy without a King, was good enough to invite me to lunch at
the Palace in Buda, where he lived in a royal style. He must have been
the model for Franco, who was thus led to declare Spain a monarchy so
as to live like a King, with no intention whatsoever of allowing anyone
to sit on that empty throne. Horthy, though, had more façade than
Franco (if perhaps less inner power). He was tall, handsome, dignified,
every inch a Regent and, last but not least, he had a wife who would
have been a majestical queen had the wind of history blown that way. We
had a quiet luncheon, the three of us, and talked generalities about the
perilous state of Europe. I asked Horthy what he thought about the
Anschluss; and his answer seemed to me interesting: 'If we, Hungarians,
had a northern neighbour as big as Germany is in proportion to Austria,
and speaking Hungarian as we do, I believe we would all vote for an
Anschluss.'

Prague was quite a different experience. To begin with, I knew the
top men, Beneŝ in particular. I am painfully aware of his mistakes, but
on this score, I think of Beneŝ as I think of the Poles: it was very hard
not to make mistakes when one lived in those days in such a dangerous
part of the world. Indeed, in our days, also, as the case of Dubček has
shown. Beneŝ was at times pathetically dependent on French opinion,
and I remember one day how at the Council he evidently changed the
course of what he was saying at a mere crossing of glances with Avenol.
But Beneŝ had a cruelly difficult task and he faced it with integrity
and courage. If once or twice his courage fell short of the level required
by the situation he was facing, it was because what his critics expected
of him was inhumanly courageous. Munich may have been one of such
cases. He might have chosen to fight Hitler, even when left in the lurch
by France and Britain; but it was hard to fight for what might have
resulted in turning his country into a Soviet satellite – as she is today.
He was a sincere republican liberal-socialist. I found an alliance with
him at Geneva a fruitful concern and I believe a force that strengthened
the League and its institutions. In Prague, he lived with all the dignity
expected of a head of state, but in a style of the uttermost simplicity.
The Spanish reminiscences are in Prague even more telling than in
Vienna, and the Castle had been redecorated by the Republic with
elegance and good taste.
I finished my trip in Vienna. It was of course a private tour, though
my position in Geneva opened many a door for me; and I had no special
official reason to go to Vienna, but I had made there a number of friends,
and I wanted to go to the opera. The city was far more agitated than the
previous year, indeed, at times quite stormy; and I heard that the local

Nazis were daily increasing their pressure. I went to the opera to hear the *Rheingold* played at one stretch, without intervals, the conductor comfortably sitting in a huge armchair. I soon noticed that the first soprano had a bad cold, but that she managed to sing through it with an admirable pluck; and I was thus admiring her both for her voice and for her courage when she seemed to go through a far stronger emotion, I thought, than the text warranted. Then an abominable stench filled the air we were breathing, and I saw three or four spectators leave in some haste. I remembered that I had been told about stinking bombs being one of the favourite weapons of the Nazis. The air grew more and more repulsive to breathe, but no one budged, the conductor went on with his gestures, the soprano had recovered, the opera unfolded its drama and its harmonies, the air began to be respirable again – we had won.

Next day I went to call on Schuschnigg. He told me he had concrete proof of the connivance of the German Nazis in these miserable tricks; and though I avoided putting him in a position to have to give me his opinion on what he saw coming, I could see that he was even more pessimistic than the year before. But I cannot say that I felt prophetic at all. Indeed, so deeply-rooted was I in the liberal tradition of Europe that I do not think I saw, even then, that Hitler would just steal the freedom and sovereignty of Austria. It is now hard for me to place myself in the state of mind I must have been in then, when so many devastating experiences have debauched our sensibility and our imagination; but the fact is that, while I saw Hitler as a threat to France, to Russia, even to Britain, in the old style, I did not imagine him as a robber of small nations. I thought he was after an empire, colonies and all that; after Austria also, but in a less infamous way. To leave that unsaid would have detracted from the truth.

It is hard to disentangle within the image of a memory what was there when the event happened and what the memory of it has become by mental fermentation and growth; but in this case I am kept within the bounds of fact because I remember another event that infringes on it: namely my shock and its very shape on receiving the news of Hitler's rape of Austria. I was in Scott Mowrer's room at the *Chicago Daily News* when the news of Hitler's invasion of Austria was trotted in by the telegraph tape; and I still feel now the emotional waves of the shock I felt then, which strike me today as singularly naïve; for what overwhelmed me was that such a thing could happen at all. 'But one does not behave like that!' I cried out to Scott Mowrer. Had I known of Belsen and the other ante-rooms to hell . . . .

I was by then growing sceptical as to our method on the intellectual side of the League, though by no means as to the importance of an intellectual approach. It seemed to me that if we wished to establish peace among men and nations, the ordinary political approach was bound to fail while it remained merely anti-war, for what was wanted was a conversion, a change of heart, particularly among the more evolved powers. But I felt that this conversion could not take place unless it was intellectually prepared.

To that end, I thought that our work was not well conceived. To be sure, there had been a huge progress since Henri Bonnet had taken over from Luchaire, and our exchanges had been stimulating and fertile; but I found them a little haphazard, somewhat too much like the work of a bee gathering pollen. I felt the need of something more systematic.

Furthermore, I felt the need of some sort of a faith, a common faith that would hold together the world commonwealth. In the World Council of Religions there were some minds who then solicited my cooperation, guessing some sort of affinity; but in my view the several religious confessions, or as the English so wisely call them, *denominations*, seemed to me the equivalent of nations in the field of belief, so that they develop their own frontiers, definition and nationalism, even when they are not actually and openly nationalistic as is the case with some forms of Hinduism or Anglicanism.

The religious slant in the search for an organic solution to the problem of peace seemed to me irrelevant. What was wanted was a permanent state of consensus or at least of debate on what is going on in the minds of men, with a stress on synthesis. We needed a two-fold endeavour towards synthesis: one aiming at unity in the fundamental ideas on science, knowledge and the mutual illumination to be obtained from the confrontation of the several disciplines and specialisations of our search for truth; and another aiming at a unity or at least a harmony between the essential attitudes of the many peoples of the earth towards their past, present and future, so that, after a while, we should be able to write on our history books what Victor Hugo wrote on a copybook of his early poems: *Bêtises que je faisais avant ma naissance*.

I was then of the opinion that the League Institute of Intellectual Co-operation could be the kernel or seed of such a development; and my idea was to alter its method of work so as to give it for a basis an assembly of men known for their contributions to all the forms of intellectual activity – religion, philosophy, sciences and the arts – to meet, say, every five years, and a council of at most fifty members to act as the administrator of the findings and wishes of each assembly and as the preparatory committee of the next. I saw those quinquennial assemblies as, in a way, lay councils of a lay church.

There was an obvious link, indeed almost an identity between these ideas and those that were then driving me to create the World Foundation. A booklet defining this foundation and its aims was then printed at the Oxford University Press; on the first page of it was said:

> Undeterred by the growing virulence of war-like tendencies, and stimulated by the yearning for peace equally intense throughout the world, a group of men have been working for some time on the following proposals. They now put them forward as one of the means whereby in their opinion constructive peace endeavours should be raised above mere pacifism and presented with a concrete aim—the intelligent organisation of life on this planet.

The group, composed of nineteen persons, included Norman Angell, Arnold Foster, Guglielmo Ferrero, Stephen King-Hall, Lord Lytton, Thomas Mann, Phelan, Jules Romains, Arthur Salter (now Lord Salter) and Arnold Toynbee.

CHAPTER LI

ON THE WAY TO THE CIVIL WAR

MEANWHILE the Spanish Republic was going from bad to worse. I was unable to rest on the comfortable attitude that it was all due to those beastly reactionaries, for, in my view and experience, the left were no less – if no more – responsible than the right for what was going on. My chief objection to the right was their stupid adherence to their position of pre-eminence in the state, and their refusal to accept what the middle and upper classes in other countries had long before understood as reasonable reforms; but I found the left chaotic, messianic, too slow to reform and too quick to rebel. It was unpardonable that after five years in office the Republic had proved unable to carry out a thorough agrarian and a no less thorough tax reform.

Under its second parliament, controlled by the right, the Government had become more and more reactionary in appearance, because the President, who would not entrust Gil Robles with the leadership of a Cabinet though he was constitutionally entitled to it, had to rely on men who, but yesterday, had served under the King. Thus we were soon (September 1935) confronted with a Cabinet presided over by Chapaprieta, a downright monarchist. Nevertheless, the new Prime Minister was a man of clear ideas firmly held and applied, and he tried to restore the balance of the budget by measures which happened to hurt the interests of the lower middle classes and were applauded by the big moneybags; but the second batch of reforms, which Chapaprieta with statesman-like impartiality aimed at the moneybags themselves, caused his downfall. The President then took yet another leaf from the book of Alfonso XIII; he called on Portela, another monarchist, and granted him that plum so dearly coveted by monarchist Prime Ministers in bygone days: the decree dissolving Parliament (January 7, 1936).

The general election took place on February 16th and was a victory for the left. I have carefully and objectively analysed this victory in my *Spain*; and my conclusions were as follows:

LEFT	Thousands of votes
Socialists and Communists:	1,793
Left Centre (Azaña)	2,413
Total Left	4,206

Right Centre (Lerroux)	681
Right	3,784
Total Right	4,465

Since the left considered Lerroux as right, in their view, counting votes and not seats, the election was a triumph (if slight) for the right; but these names are shallow. I went on to analyse the results by actual positive meanings, and these were my results:

	Thousands
Marxist, anti-clerical, anti-militarist	1,793
Non-Marxist, anti-clerical, anti-militarist	3,193
Anti-Marxist, clerical, non-militarist	3,783
Anti-Marxist, non-clerical, anti-parliamentarian	a few

It follows that, with the interpretation of the figures *most benevolent for* the left, in the last election, Spain voted

    – by two to one against marxism
    – by two to one against clericalism and militarism
    – by eight to one against a socialist revolution
    – almost unanimously against a military rising.

Such were the results when studied in depth. On the usual criterion of seats, it was a victory for the left, but most of all for Azaña. What the majority of the country evidently wanted was to be governed by Azaña. This would have been the least bad, possibly the best way of securing the survival of the republic. But it was not to be.

Meanwhile, on my return from my visit to the U.S. I sought Azaña and Barcía and put it to them that I was really on a world mission on my own, but would carry on in Geneva if wanted. Both urged me to remain available, and with both I discussed the reform of the League in the light of my experience of it and of the opinion of the nations associated with us. I had kept throughout an attitude favourable to sanctions, yet fully aware of its dangers and of the consequences it might have for Spain. When Chapaprieta was Prime Minister, I had rung him up from Geneva and put it to him that it might come to blows, so I wished to know where we stood. He retorted: 'Well, we have signed the Covenant, haven't we? Then, let us go ahead.' This was the 'reactionary' man, whom many, in the loose vocabulary of the day, would not hesitate to call 'fascist'.

But what was the view of Azaña, the leader of the left? As soon as I broached the matter, he reacted with vivacity. 'The first thing you must do is to get me rid of Article 16. I will have nothing to do with it.' And he added: 'What do I care for the Negus?' What could the many Europeans and Americans I knew do with these statements from a liberal monarchist and from a near-socialist republican? They did not tally with the stereotype of Spain, of right and left, and other ready-made labels. And yet, despite a certain flippancy that went with his shy, inhibited manner, Azaña's attitude was perhaps the more responsible of the two. Was Spain ready for such adventures even if well meant? The upshot of it all was that it clinched my determination to try to reform the League.

I put my ideas to both Azaña and Barcía. I believe Azaña followed what I had to say and I am sure he liked it, though he did not get actually inside the subject; I do not believe Barcía understood at all. He was not only much less intelligent, but one of those men who live on the surface of things, and do not even try to enter into the subject in discussion. He did, however, give me a general sort of blessing.

On May 9th and 10th I sent cables from Geneva reporting on the meetings we, 'neutrals', had had on a number of subjects including Abyssinia and the proposed reform of the League, on which I informed my Government that I had verbally proposed something on the lines of my talks in Madrid. The Dutch Foreign Secretary, who was present, requested me to put my ideas on paper. I informed my Government that I had accepted. The memorandum was of course preceded by a note explaining that it embodied my own ideas, that it did not involve my Government but that my Government would be ready to exchange views on the subject on the basis of the memorandum as on any other similar basis. At their request, I distributed confidential notes to Argentina, France and Britain.

The substance of my proposals was:

1. The Covenant must be revised to make it more practical.
2. No textual amendment is either needed or desirable.
3. Nations to reserve their rights to limit their general obligations under Article 16 as long as (a) the League was not universal, (b) Article 8 (disarmament) had not been applied.
4. Express acceptance of the obligations of Article 16 for concrete political and geographical zones defined by the states concerned.
5. Simplified Covenant reduced to Article 11 for such states as wished to remain outside the League.
6. Abolition of the unanimity rule in the application of Articles 10 and 11.

7. Stress to be put on preventive rather than punitive procedure.
8. No collective security without collective policy.

On the 20th of May, Eden wrote to me, 'If I may say so, I think it is a most interesting paper which we are submitting here to very careful study.' Massigli sent me a long, well worked out, unfavourable criticism. But other forces were at work, far less interested in peace and in the Covenant than in attacking the Government and getting rid of me. A devious way, passing, I do believe though I am not in a position to prove it, through a couple of left wing members of the Secretariat, leaked my paper to the press and a vicious campaign against me was launched in Spain, mostly in the socialist press, accusing me of acting on my own without government authority – which was utterly false – and of having published the paper – which indeed looked very much like a not very clever trick for diverting the responsibility of the leak from its true authors.

This enabled the socialist press to raise the tone of their campaign. Articles, notes, cartoons. I was diluting the Covenant to please fascism. I was acting on my own and with no knowledge of the Government. Barcía was besieged by eager journalists, all trembling lest the Covenant (which they had never read) were imperilled by my manoeuvres. Barcía lost, if not his head, his memory; and declared that if I had 'presented a memorandum' which he did not know, it would be on my own account and risk and without counting on the Government, and 'I have requested the Under-secretary of State to inform foreign chanceries at once.' One of the newspapers appended to the Foreign Secretary's words these even more memorable ones: 'The attitude of the Government is logical, since at the latest ordinary sitting of the Council of Ministers, it was decided to declare the ratification of our fidelity to the Pact and to the Covenant.'

Barcía's memory could play him very bad tricks. The Socialist Party issued a statement damning my memorandum for all they were worth and concluding that it was high time the Spanish Government recognised the Soviet Union. Barcía assured me we had not yet done so; and I assured him that I had initialled the terms of such a recognition with Litvinov two years earlier. He was not convinced until I found the paper in his file.

He had also forgotten my talks with him and with Azaña; my telegram telling him I had spoken to the neutrals along the terms we had discussed in Madrid; his written approval. But when he was reminded, he acted as what he was, an honest man. There was a meeting in Geneva, to which he went, but he took me with him and as I then held no office at all in the State I had to be reappointed every time I had to go. Everybody was puzzled. Azaña, the man who wanted me 'to rid him of Article 16', had become President of the Republic. He did not say a word.

At the meeting of the neutrals in Geneva, Barcía went out of his way to praise me and my work in almost fulsome terms, partly, I thought, to undo the harm done by his friends' press campaign, partly to ease his own conscience. The Committee decided to meet again in Geneva, but actually did in London. And the campaign then had risen to such terms of acerbity that C.H.M.A. rang me up in despair. I gave her some ammunition, mainly written proof of the fact that the Government knew and approved all I had done, which she passed on to Fernando de los Ríos, one of the most indignant of my critics. Nevertheless, the Executive Committee of the Socialist Party, of which he was a member, carried on the campaign.

There were so many forces working on the evolution of that episode that there may even have been some not yet apparent at the time. As I look back on it all, I believe the left in Spain had made up their minds that I must go. It seems obvious to me now that if the left were so intent on this change, the purpose must have been as international as the change aimed at. I incline to think that behind it all, the group Largo-Araquistain-Vayo was already preparing a sudden bold sort of action to carry the Republic over to a near-communist socialism, and that they wanted their own man in Geneva. And I think that Fernando de los Ríos was taken on board having first been taken in, which explains that he forgot not merely his subjective link of friendship with me, but his objective link with truth and the facts.

I had another meeting with the neutrals in London to which I must return presently; then I returned to Madrid where I called on Casares Quiroga and Barcía, and told them I was giving up my work for the Government. I published a note, telling the whole story, and I continued thus:

> The reaction of the press and of the Socialist Party rests therefore, so far as procedure is concerned, on no basis whatsoever, and therefore it does not affect me. As for the essence of the policy which the note implies, it is not for me to discuss it, but for the Government. Nevertheless, I hold myself at the disposal of the parties if they should think my opinion useful to them.
>
> It is not my wish either, to express an opinion on the attacks which on this occasion have been leveled against me in the press of all shades of opinion. All I intend to do is to declare that in these circumstances I am not prepared to continue in the service of the State.

I had never served the State till the Republic was set up. I cease therefore after five years of service which I did not ask to render. In April 1931, I was professor of Spanish Studies in the University of Oxford and happened to be on leave holding a course of lectures in the University of Mexico. I asked no post either directly or indirectly of the Provisional Government. Without consulting me, they appointed me Ambassador in Washington. On May 13, from New York, when the Republic was one month old but for one day, I accepted the Embassy and resigned the Chair. From April 1934 I have served continually as *de facto* permanent delegate in Geneva. I have no appointment, no post, no salary, no office, no secretary, no files. I have nothing but my good will. I cannot even resign, for I have nothing to resign from. I therefore renounce the only thing I possess, the honour to serve the State of a nation which was great and will be great again if all Spaniards are at one to wish it.

I should only like to add that my faith is firmer than ever in the League of Nations as the only form of international give-and-take capable of saving the world from a catastrophe without precedent, and also to express my gratitude to my collaborators of these five years among whom I wish to single out the admirable López Oliván.

The press of the Left forgot the most elementary principles of the profession, and the Note was only published in bits, the most important items being omitted. *El Socialista* silenced it altogether.

On the advice of my doctor, I took a month's rest in a country house I had in Toledo. It embodied the earnings of an American lecture tour. A bungalow but for my small study that made up the whole of its first floor, it was just big enough for a man and wife and two girls, and stood in the midst of about a couple of hundred olive trees. It had been discussed in a debate in parliament where Eduardo Ortega y Gasset, the older but smaller brother of the philosopher, had accused me of being a *latifundist* on the strength of it. When I had tried to divert to my olive trees a thread of water that hit the top-right corner of my wall on its way to the Tagus, the municipal Council of Toledo (a socialist majority) voted against because I had been a minister in Lerroux's Cabinet; so I had to raise the water again from the Tagus by pump and pipe after it had wasted its time falling down all the way.

Melancholy thoughts on what touched not my interests, but my political faith. This faith had already born the brunt of a big frustration. For some reason or other, though I had worked with Lerroux because he insisted on it, my objective hopes as a Spaniard were with Azaña and Prieto, and as it happened, these two men had committed what I thought was the worst aggression against the Republic. The matter is too important not to be told at some length.

The Constitution prescribed (Article 81) that the President can only dissolve Parliament twice under his mandate; but that should he do so, the third Parliament must begin its work with a debate on whether the second dissolution had been justified, and if it finds that it had not, the President is *ipso facto* dismissed. There is nothing to be said for this rule. It was down-right stupid. Yet, such is the privilege of human liberty, it was made far stupider by every one of the men who had to do with it.

First of all, by the President, who, by then, had ruled in such a tortuous, subjective, almost capricious way that he was no longer thought of as a possible Head of State at all by either Azaña or Gil Robles or indeed anyone that mattered in the country but for a couple of exceptions. Then by Azaña and Prieto, who had come to some sort of an understanding, whether explicit or not, whereby Azaña would be raised to the Presidency and Prieto would govern as Prime Minister.

Now this in itself could have been an excellent way out of the difficulties the Republic was struggling with; but the way chosen by the two conspirators was disastrous.

They chose to apply Article 81, or rather to misapply it in more ways than one; for as objective republicans (and if a republican is not objective, he is not a republican, since object =*res*) Article 81 should not have been applied, because it was the Constituent Cortes that had voted the Constitution and therefore could not declare the Constitution to have a retroactive effect. Still, the argument though wrong was debatable. What was not debatable was that the Assembly voted that the dissolution that had created it had not been justified. Now, this vote was a cynical lie. The Cortes that had been dissolved were ruled by a majority of the right; the new Cortes by a majority of the left. A dissolution of the first had therefore been justified by a formidable vote of the electorate; and the winners cynically declared it hadn't because they wanted to expel Alcalá Zamora. It was again the dreadful cause of all the political ills of Spain: power is preferred to justice; subject to object; individuals to institutions. The Constitution was degraded to the rank of a mere crowbar to force open the door of the Presidency for another man.

Such were the thoughts I was brewing while walking alone under my olive trees, listening now and then to Mozart's *D minor Piano Concerto* or writing my speech for my reception into the Spanish Academy. Every day I felt more and more convinced of my inadaptability to Spanish home politics; and, therefore, more and more pessimistic about the possibility of my rendering both Spain and Europe the services I thought I was capable of performing in the international world.

Then, tragedy began. I had noticed that when I had called on Casares and Barcía, they seemed to me endeavouring to repress some deep worry, as if my own farewell were but a drop on an already fairly full glass. One of Marañón's girls rang me up to tell me, with tears in her voice, that Dr Polo Benito had been murdered in Toledo. I knew him slightly. He was a liberal-minded, pleasant enough canon of the Cathedral of Toledo. The civil war had begun. News from Madrid was nil. Communications non-existent. There was shooting now and then down below my house on both banks of the Tagus.

One morning, a military plane flew in, dropped a bomb on Toledo and flew on, drew a wide half circle, flew over our grounds, and flew over Toledo to drop a second bomb. This dismal sight of a nation committing suicide went on almost every morning.

It was very hot, and I never went out between 10 a.m. and 6 p.m. At about six, I used to walk here and there. I felt more helpless and useless than I had ever felt in my life. I knew no one in Toledo; and there was nothing I could do. In Madrid, even assuming that I could get there at all, I could do just about as much. I was trying to imagine some way of getting myself in the current of things again when, one evening, at dusk, I saw my own car stop at the small plaza below the parapet. Four men came out of it, three armed with rifles, the fourth, I guessed, with less visible weapons.

They were a fair representation of the left side of our civil war: one (the driver) belonged to the party of Azaña, the other three were an anarchist, a socialist and a second socialist of a slightly different obedience. They explained that my sisters had 'put my car at the disposal of the revolution', a statement to be interpreted anon; that they (the four) kept it in my garage; that they had an assignment in Toledo (this I gathered later consisting in having lunch with a brother-in-law of one of them); and that when my sisters knew that they were coming to Toledo, they had asked them to come and fetch me and take me to Madrid.

I hurriedly packed my things and joined them. 'Where do you want to sit?' they asked. And I answered: 'by the driver'. They wouldn't have it. 'You see, that is the most dangerous place and we feel responsible for your safety.' I sat in the middle of the back seat, with one man on each side, his rifle standing between his knees. All the way we could see cars of all makes, from the humblest to the most luxurious, lying 'dead' on the roadside, in ditches sometimes, the harvest of the first onrush of the mob of the car-less to get hold of somebody else's envied possession. The human bones showing through the flesh of revolutionary rhetoric.

We were soon to see the reaction to that bee-line for booty. At every village or township we were stopped by an armed guard. They wore no uniform, but those faces did express earnest business; and the car was thoroughly searched for booty, for, as one of these village revolutionists said: 'We are not thieves.' We got used to it, and we knew that a man with a gun barring the road meant a search for booty.

Then we arrived in Villaverde, the last small township or suburb before Madrid. There, the 'guard' was very suspicious and in every way what one would have expected of a well-indoctrinated communist. I remembered that a few weeks earlier, I had had a talk with one of the local fellows, just a chance meeting, in Getafe, the Air Force centre and airfield close to Madrid, and from what he said I inferred that the new mayor of that important place was a man who came from no one knew where and whom every one called *El Ruso*; and for the first time, I saw the meaning of the password our driver had given all the way from Toledo: 'Rusia 1'.

The guard growled, 'Who's that man?' My companions did not like his authoritarian tone. 'None of your business.' The guard would have no jurisdiction qualms. He just would not let me pass on. One of my fellow travellers gave my name. As soon as the guard heard it he shouted. 'Out with him. We'll do what is wanted.' The driver intervened, 'He is not don Dimas' (a homonym who was M.P. for Toledo and belonged to the right) 'He is Don Salvador, the Ambassador.' To which the guard retorted: 'Well, just as good for us. Out with him.' This time my companions were angry. 'Don't be an ass. Don't you see we are driving him to gaol.' That did the trick, and I was free. We started off, and by one of those feats of stupidity nature seems so freely to supply, on leaving I raised my hand in a gesture of farewell I've made all my life, which any reddish observer might have taken for a fascist salute. It was too dark or he didn't care. We drove on.

My sisters explained to me that the run for other people's cars had been the first sign to show that authority had collapsed. In a whiff, everybody's car had vanished. She thought it best to give ours to the party of Azaña, and from that day, the car was fetched in the morning and brought back in the evening. The weather was good and the countryside fresher than hot Madrid. But the news of what was going on was dismal; and the Casa de Campo, the royal pavilions by the river, was the stage for a systematic machine-gunning of anybody who displeased or might displease any of the leaders of the extremist left or any man on the spot who had a weapon.

The Government were more or less blockaded in the Ministry of Marine. I rang them up, and explained that if they thought there was anything I could do, I should be ready to do it; that otherwise, I'd better be given an official paper to enable me to go to Geneva where I had an office of the World Foundation waiting, for which I was responsible;

and that I'd better have an escort of two detectives (for I thought that detectives went about always in pairs like our *Guardia Civil*).

I left for Valencia one evening, the last of July. My escort was a police officer in mufti who told me, coolly, that he did not expect to survive the trouble, for the revolutionists considered him as a fiend. I had with me a diplomatic secretary of our Geneva consulate. In Valencia we caught a train for Barcelona and there I found chaos. No one knew anything about anything, particularly as to who was in command. Power. Power was the thing. The official authorities (two of them: the central and the Catalan or home rule authority) and the 'popular' (a Committee of Workers dominated then by the Anarchists) were treading then on each others' toes. So did, physically, the thousands who crowded their offices in the hope of being able to travel.

My official titles and papers prevailed and I was able to get the attention of a Counsellor, a minister of the Catalan Government, whose name was by no means separatist: España. He put me on the rails, so to speak, for I caught a train to Port Bou. There, the station services, customs and passport offices were all under the authority of a few local anarchists. My papers were in order, but a cable from the Ministry of Finance (?), a man I knew well and whose name was also Franco, forbade all Spaniards to leave Spain. I showed my papers to the senior gunman and said: 'You make up your mind, but try to do so before the train for Perpignan leaves.' He did. I left. That night I slept well though in one of the most dreadful and miserable hotels I have had to endure in my life.

I must now come back to that meeting of neutrals, which was to be my last, in the spring of 1936 in London. We met in my room in a West End hotel. When we had wound up our activities, I noticed that Dr Münch, the Danish Foreign Secretary, lingered behind with his assistant. They at last left, and I saw them to the lift. Before we parted, in the corridor facing the lift, Münch shot at me: 'I have written officially to Oslo to ask for the Nobel Peace Prize for you.' As the matter had never been either mentioned or hinted at before, I was rather surprised, the more so as I differed from Dr Münch in a matter of principle: he was a pacifist and I never was. However, I thanked him and we parted.

During the spring and the autumn I had not one but several hints to the effect that Münch's request was being acted upon: yet the time came when Nobel Prizes ripen and the Peace Award was granted to Dr Saavedra Lamas. This kind of thing has never cut short my sleep by as much as five minutes. But more time went by and I happened to call on Dr Lebreton, the Argentine Ambassador in London. We were on very good terms, and we talked of everything in the world and its sub-urbs. . . . So, no wonder, we landed on Saavedra Lamas. He smiled with his eyes, enjoying his coming story by anticipation.

'I bet you don't know how he got his Peace Prize. Throughout that year, Hull had been preparing his own treaty – you know, everybody does; why don't you draft one, by the way? – and he was going to present it to the Inter-American Conference that was to meet in Buenos Aires, in December. He thought of nothing else. The treaty was to be a success. To make sure it would, he drafted it with nothing inside the words, you know how it is done, of course, and there it was. Still, he worried. So, one of his aids had a brain-wave. "There is but one safe way. The Conference is in Buenos Aires; therefore its President will be Saavedra Lamas. He must have the Nobel Peace Prize and he must know you gave it to him". Cordell Hull acted on this advice, Saavedra Lamas got his prize, and proceded to sabotage the Conference. And Hull said to his friends: "I have never seen a more perfidious man in my life."'

Se non è vero è ben trovato. But I still think that Cordell Hull had a modest idea of perfidy.

EPILOGUE

THERE is perhaps nothing more provident in Providence than the decree that denies to man any foreknowledge of his future. If when I left Spain at the beginning of August 1936 I had seen myself writing these lines in the middle of August 1972, still in exile, I dare not say what would have happened in my life, but I do say that it would have robbed me of most of my courage. It is only natural that I begin this survey of the events covered by this book (1921–1936) from the viewpoint of my own life, since after all it will define the perspective and attitude with which I shall afterwards endeavour to outline the period itself.

Everything in my life appeared as preordained to prepare me for precisely what I was to do between 1921 and 1936. A new type of person was required to enter the ranks of some kind of supra-national service. The world was gradually absorbing the nations into a wider framework. We were moving towards a world structure the bricks for which were no longer to be the nations but the Continents. Since nothing is either good or bad but thinking makes it so, what was required was a change of heart, a rise above nationalism and even above patriotism.

Shall I dare say that we, Spaniards, might perhaps provide one of the best quarries for such a material! I am not saying that we are the best material for the new man; but merely that we might be one of the best quarries for it; or in other words, that good material might be expected from Spain. As an empire-builder retired from business, Spain had known it all and was ready for a change. Furthermore, our very psychological set-up, our defects not less than our qualities, made of us people inclined to neglect the middle stretches of the heart, where civic virtues flourish, and to cultivate either the self or the universe, at the two extremes, so that we were and are fairly good recruits for world affairs rather than for the now obsolete international affairs, whose fundamental basis is still the nation.

On this general background, destiny singled me out for a life as a European and world citizen, by, curiously enough, an early intervention of what now bids fair to become our tyrant – technique. In 1898, my father was convinced of one fact: 'We lost that war [i.e., against the U.S.], indeed our Empire, for lack of technique.' A masterly flash of intuition. Hence, two decisions: I am to become an engineer; I am to be educated in France. This begins an expatriation that will keep me abroad for most of my life; and widens my education over a sector of the mind that I, born a poet, would never have spontaneously imagined or understood.

It so happened that my literary vocation revealed itself as no obstacle to the absorption of mathematics or physics. This enabled me to follow a technical path in my higher education. Furthermore from my removal to the Latin Quarter, I became thoroughly immersed in an English-speaking group of Britons and Americans. One of this group became my wife in Scotland (1912). My Europeisation went on at a quicker pace. In 1916 I settled in London, leaving my railway-career for my literary vocation. In 1920 I published my first book *Shelley and Calderón*, Oxford University Press. In 1924, *The Genius of Spain*, also published by the Oxford University Press. When I joined the Secretariat (1921) I had made a name in English and Spanish letters and was soon to make one in French; while my command of the three languages for both public writing and speaking was a good deal better than the average.

The rest is told in this book. I may therefore be justified in saying that I had become a fair, if premature specimen of a European parliamentarian. Had the world evolved more in conformity with the hopes of some of us, I should have been swallowed by European politics and thus my literary vocation would have been starved. At least as a possibility this seems likely. But the world took another direction, and by 1936, I was a liberal European parliamentarian in a world that seemed to have very little time for parliaments, for Europe and for liberty. This was the chief cause of my exile.

Obviously the failure of the Spanish Republic was one of the causes of my own failure. She had been born so neatly that she fully deserved the affectionate name that she had been given while she was a hope: the Pretty Girl. I cannot, of course, go here into any detail as to why the 'Pretty Girl' lost first her charm and later her life. On some aspects of this tragedy this book sheds already enough light for the reader to have formed his own opinion. I am inclined to apply to our short-lived Republic a well-known Spanish dictum: *they all, between them, killed her, but she it was who alone died*.

'They all'. That is part of my trouble. Am I to waive the responsibility of the Spaniards themselves in the event? Of course not. They bear the heaviest load. A people endowed with outstanding gifts, they have not been granted one of the most precious: political sense. For political success they lack objectivity. Their nature is too rich, their personalities too volcanic and strong, for objectivity. Hence the constant invasion of their public life by subjective values, irrelevant to progress and prosperity, relevant to character and drama.

All this should be acknowledged. But are the European nations aware of their own responsibilities in the tragedies of Spain? The two disasters of Spanish history are the discovery of America and the death of Prince John, heir to Ferdinand and Isabel, which linked Spain with the house of Burgundy. Deflected from her natural course, which should have been the Europeisation of Northern Africa from Morocco to Egypt, thus securing the southern frontier of Europe, Spain bled to create Spanish America and to struggle for the salvation of the Dutch and the Germans, a rather remote banner for her long-suffering people.

And when the *ancien régime* falls and the issue becomes the adaptation of Spain to the post-French Revolution days, what help does Spain get from France and England? The perfidy, selfishness and stupidity of Napoleon and the indifference, arrogance and coldness of Wellington. As for what went on during the Spanish American war, during the Spanish Republic and during the Spanish Civil War, it is best to be discreet.

The net result was that the Spanish Republic was unable to insert herself into the Europe of the early thirties so as to contribute to save Europe from Hitler and from Stalin, and to make it possible for the League to survive. This meant that the national basis that I needed for my activity in a liberal-democratic Europe vanished.

Europe herself, that liberal-democratic Europe on whose existence my very *raison d'être* as a public man rested, was not long in sinking also into a sea of chaos. And this was the worst disaster of all; for Europe had led the world for many centuries and as the most enlightened of her sons had seen – de Tocqueville, for instance – she was approaching an era when she had either to emerge as a Continent of Nations fully conscious of her unity, or to perish as the colonial empire of Russia, of America or of both. And the true meaning of the failure of the League of Nations was that the toughness of nationalism stood in the way of the blossoming-out of Europe and left her carved on the plate of the Soviet Bear.

The disaster may well have been due to a change in the speed of history. Spain was given at least a century to recover from the loss of her Empire; Britain and France had but a few years if any, for the liquidation of their empires coincided with the rise of the two super powers that lowered them to the status of satellites, though of the first magnitude.

Consider Germany, Italy and Japan. These three nations defied the Atlantic world and were much maligned for doing so; but if one tries to look at the event in a historical perspective, the issue becomes clear: while Spain, France and Britain were the big powers of the sixteenth, seventeenth and eighteenth centuries, Germany, Italy and Japan did not attain their coming of age until 1870. Germany was retarded by the Holy Roman Empire, Italy by the Vatican. It was therefore not till the twentieth century that they were able to cast a roving eye in search of their empires. I am talking neither politics nor economics. I am talking psychology.

So, the tragedy of the Europe I have endeavoured to depict in these pages was that just when nationalism should have been put under lock and key (as in the very wise flag of the Republic of Geneva), in order to raise a Continent of Nations and save the spirit of Europe, the nationalism of all the big powers was being heightened by the coming of age of two of her most creative nations, Italy and Germany, in search of an empire, which in its turn, stimulated the old nationalism of France and Britain, as their own empires crumbled down.

I hesitate to bring back my puny self in among all this greatness; but I do so because I believe that my own annihilation in the midst of this political earthquake, in which we are still living and dying, is in a sense symbolical. I was by nature and training a citizen of that Continent of Nations that was not to be. Not yet. One of my activities, at the very time I began my exile, aimed at setting up a 'World Foundation' whose motto would have been *Patria Patriarum.* I was not merely thinking it, I was feeling it. The forces that destroyed Europe, the Spanish Republic and me were far too vast, strong, rooted in history and psychology for me, Spain, or Europe, to resist their onslaught. The future is in the eyes of God. But one thing is certain. If peace and the spirit of Europe are to remain alive, we shall need more world citizens and more Europeans such as I tried to be.

Just as one cannot write without drawing strokes on the paper, up and down, right and left and diagonal, so we cannot relate events without colouring them with our own palette of good, bad and grey, clever, stupid and mediocre. But it would be senseless to fancy oneself as a kind of magistrate sitting in judgement for a thorough-going appraisal, eulogy or condemnation endowed with a lasting value. The forces at work in that ocean of energy which is mankind were overwhelming for even the strongest individual spirit. We, poor men, even the biggest of us, did our best. We were not able to do better. When we endeavour to go through it again in our battered souls, the feeling that comes to the surface is best cast in that poignant utterance of Othello: 'Oh Iago, the pity of it.'

INDEX

In this index the League of Nations is denoted by LN.

This index has been prepared for Messrs, D. C. Heath, Limited of Farnborough, Hants, by R. Haig-Brown, "Lambrook House," Wootton Grove, Sherborne, Dorset, England, DT9 4DL

Salvador de Madariaga (in Peru in 1934).

2a. *Joseph Avenol in 1934. (above)*
2b. *Albert Thomas. (right)*
2c. *Quiñones de León. (below)*

3a. *Madariaga with Louis Barthou,
French Foreign Minister, in September
1934 while Madariaga was Ambassador
to Paris. (right)*
3b. *Jean Monnet (1921) in his office at
the League. (below).*

4a. Harold Butler in about 1921. (above)
4b. Lord Robert Cecil in 1923. (right above)
4c. Allen Dulles after the War in 1945. (right below)

5a. Madariaga in Paris with the Rumanian Titulesco (left) and Anthony Eden (right) setting out in 1935, for a session of the Committee of Thirteen. (left)

5b. Sir Eric Drummond in 1926. A Dutch member of the Secretariat, Pelt, is opening the door of the taxi. (right)

6. *The 87th Session of the Council of the League (May 1935) presided by Maxim Litvinov. Madariaga is fifth from the left at the Council table.*

7. *The 91st Session of the Council of the League (March 19, 1936) at St. James's Palace. Madariaga is at the far left.*

8. A session of the Committee of Thirteen. The Rumanian delegate Petrescu-Commène is seated at Madariaga's right. At the far end of the table are Paul Brown and the Spanish delegate Palacios (with beard). On the left is the Japanese delegate Sato, behind him (white-haired) Lange. In front, facing the camera is the American Burton. Carton de Wiant is on Madariaga's left.